CHOICE CENTERED ASTROLOGY

The Basics

BY
GAIL FAIRFIELD

RAMP
CREEK
PUBLISHING INC.

Cover concept by Jon Wessel
Cover design by Dennis Kaill
Cover art by Sheila Mohn
Internal graphics by Dennis Kaill
Author photograph by Jeff Gering
Typesetting and book design by Annie Graham & Co.

Printed and bound in the United States of America

Published in the United States of America by:

Ramp Creek Publishing, Inc.
P.O. Box 3
Smithville, IN 47458-0003

International Sta͞   : 0-9625088-1-0

Library of Congre͞   ͟0-61168

For "Grace" and "Janie"

AUTHOR'S ACKNOWLEDGMENTS

I extend my heart and my appreciation to:

Joanne Wickenburg whose solid teaching inspired me as I moved into this career in Astrology,

my clients and students who have helped me learn how to teach and write,

those in my Advanced Class who reviewed the infant manuscript: Barbara Bruch, Ken Collins, Marie Eken, Maureen Jones, Linda Newell, and Deborah Taylor,

Betty Fairfield, Mary Larson, Swain Rowley, and Marcia Smith who read the developing manuscript,

Debra Clark, Donna Cunningham, Joanne Wickenburg, and Louise Wisechild who were especially generous with their insight and wisdom regarding this book,

Mary Ellen Carew, who was wonderfully honest and clear in her editing,

Dennis Kaill for his expert and thorough graphic design work,

Dawn Lewis for her patient photocopying,

Judith Pendleton of Annie Graham Publishing Services who "held my hand" during production,

and my family, who have loved and supported me during the writing and revising process.

THANK YOU ALL!

CONTENTS

xv

FOREWORD

Some Thoughts on the Nature of Choice

When you picked up this book, no doubt you were drawn, as I was, to the idea of a *choice centered* Astrology. You may even have wondered if this was a contradiction in terms. Traditionally, the stars were thought to reveal our fate. Happily, however, Astrological thinking and insight has been evolving away from the fatalism of earlier times. With Gail Fairfield's choice centered approach, the awareness that Astrology is not based on fate but on possibilities and potentials has come to full maturity.

As one who has been involved in both Social Work and Astrology for more than twenty years, I found Gail's approach a natural, much needed advance. After fifteen years in both fields, it finally dawned on me that I approach a Chart reading the way a social worker would, with the following questions in mind:

1. What is the problem?
2. What is this individual's contribution to the problem?
3. What are the options?
4. What resources are available?

Psychologically oriented Astrology has become a wonderful tool for answering questions one and two. To answer question four, Astrologers still have to seek out specific resources in their own communities.

Question three, about available options, is given a most articulate treatment in this book. In particular, Gail's delineation of the different ways of using a Planet's energy – by owning it, denouncing it, glorifying it, projecting it, blaming it on others, or denying it – is an exceptional contribution. It encourages readers to think through the ways they're using the Planets in their own lives. The step-by-step delineations of the Planets, Houses, and Signs in this book help readers become conscious of the choices they've already made, discover whether those choices are working for them or against them, and explore the other options that are available.

From earliest childhood, we are programmed to act, feel, and think in particular ways by our parents, relatives, teachers, peers, ethnic or religious groups, television producers and advertisers, and society as a whole. This programming extends to nearly every part of life. We're taught what it means to be a woman or a man, what roles we should take in various arenas, and what possessions and personal qualities are desirable. We learn what values to have, what styles of communication and emotional expression are appropriate, who is acceptable and important and who is not. We're also taught to judge or value ourselves and other people on the basis of these learned standards.

Is anything wrong with that? Isn't that simply what education and child rearing are designed to do? Not all of our programming is negative, after all; large parts of it may work in our favor. The problem arises in areas where we're different from the values and standards of our group and where we find the expected behavior uncomfortable or even oppressive. For instance, women who aren't suited to mothering may still be programmed to feel something is wrong with them, that they're failures if they don't have children. Men who are highly sensitive and emotional are judged against the macho stereotypes. Fortunately, we live in an era that supports choice in these areas to some degree, although we still live with mixed messages.

Another problem arises when our families are dysfunctional and our programming is negative or destructive. Adult children of alcoholics (ACA), for instance, are programmed not to communicate about family problems, not to feel or not to bother others about their feelings, and to take care of others even at the expense of their own basic needs. Many are programmed to be victims and to continue the family pattern of addiction as a way of coping with unmanageable emotions and isolation. The work done by twelve-step programs and other groups for ACAs and people from dysfunctional backgrounds is essentially deprogramming.

Even if the programming is done by wise, insightful, whole parents who are supported by similarly whole adults, it's still programming. It does not necessarily take into account the child's personal temperament. Programming, by nature, is anti-choice. Any Astrological reading is useful in identifying who you are, apart from who your family, peers, and culture say you ought to be. Choice centered Astrology GIVES you a choice, rather than reinforcing the social pressure to remain in the mold, in lockstep with family, friends, neighbors, and society.

I would caution you, however, not to turn the profound principles of the choice centered approach into an opportunity for a New Age put-down. Superficial and arrogant students of metaphysics – Wonderbread Metaphysicians I call them – take the idea that we create our own reality and turn it into a hostile form of one-upmanship. They feel vastly superior to others whose reality isn't as successful in worldly terms as their own. I can hear them out there, now, saying "Why did you CHOOSE to get into one betrayal after another in job situations? Where does it get you to choose that?" The victim – I mean the client – then gets to feel guilty for having a problem, because it obviously means they're incapable of choosing properly, even though they've now been informed that they have a choice. I was even told recently by a smug metaphysical sophomore that she doesn't feel bad when a gay man with AIDS dies because, after all, it was his choice. That's not spiritual wisdom, that's sugar-coated, New Age homophobia.

The thing is, there are choices and choices. The level at which we make some extremely difficult choices is not always accessible to the conscious mind. As long as motivation and past programming are repressed and operating without the individual's awareness, you can point out all the choices you like, but the individual may still be powerless to take the positive option. For instance, some people make crucial decisions in childhood such as "I'll never get married" or "I'll fix them, I'll fail at everything I try," and then forget having made them. Uncovering such decisions and canceling them may be necessary before the person can have the freedom to choose something else.

Astrology is a superior tool for conscious insight into motivation, programming, and past decisions. I've found that even without therapy or healing work, some clients have used the jolt of consciousness a reading can provide to make major shifts in direction. When they come back a year later, I'm amazed at their use of the information and their progress. For many people, though, insight alone is not enough. Therapy, healing work, and perhaps the support of a self-help group may be needed to release past programming, especially negative programming by a dysfunctional family.

Other choices are made at the level of the super-conscious. There are people who resist therapy or who don't seem to benefit, and I suspect that many of them have made choices on that level. For example, it may not help to tell people who are addicted to alcohol, drugs, food, or debt that they have a choice about how to use Neptune: to continue in the addiction, or to seek a spiritual path. The heavy drinker or drug user may still have some degree of choice, but those who are truly addicted have lost the power to choose whether to use the substance or not. It's only when they've reached the point of total powerlessness, only when they're so beaten that they surrender on a soul level, that they finally get free.

And it's at the soul level that some extremely important choices like addiction are made. That level is involved in the period before birth when life tasks, associates, and even parents are selected. The Birth Chart itself may be chosen, since there is evidence that a chemical in the baby's brain sets off labor. Thus, the Chart of the moment of emergence from the womb is both a choice and a map of pre-birth choices. Furthermore, it sets up the timing for all periods of challenge and choice for that lifetime.

Pre-birth choices are generally not conscious, yet they can override decisions of the conscious mind and even appear contrary to the best interests of the individual. They are the experiences the soul selects for growth in that lifetime. Addiction is one such choice. Disability is another. Such experiences are not punishment for past life misdeeds. In order to be complete, each soul chooses to have each possible experience in the course of hundreds of incarnations.

It's important to know that even tough pre-birth choices like addictions or abusive mates need not be life-long sentences. By becoming conscious, learning the associated lessons, and healing yourself of the residual effects, you can finish up in less than a lifetime. Then, you can go on to more pleasurable forums for growth and development. Choice centered Astrology can be an excellent means of achieving consciousness and an important guide to healing.

Finally, there are collective choices to be taken into account. It is a mistake of the Me Generation (the Pluto in Leo folks) to think they are the center of the Universe and have unlimited freedom of choice. Humanity as a whole makes certain choices at various times in history. People born within that era must live within the matrix created by those choices. To some extent, their individual choice is delimited by them. The Signs through which the outer Planets – Uranus, Neptune, and Pluto – travel are indications of the current challenges and choices. The extent to which we participate in the collective unfolding of choices is shown by the strength of the outer Planets in our Charts. The area of life in which we are both most responsive and most responsible to the collective is shown by the House positions of Uranus, Neptune, and Pluto. (Gail explains how to interpret these Planets in their Signs and Houses in this book.)

For instance, we in our era are experiencing great difficulty with relationships. People by the millions are visualizing and affirming their ideal mates, and yet millions are single or in unfulfilling relationships. Taken on the individual level, this may feel like failure or neurotic choice. The book *Smart Women, Foolish Choices* has sold hundreds of thousands of copies, indicating that many of us feel we are making choices that are not in our best interests.

The key here, I feel, is a collective choice to change the nature of relating itself, away from a traditional model of dependence and rigidity of roles, into a new model of independent, equal, and fully developed human beings who are together by choice and not by bio-determined necessity. Our era, in which the old model of relating no longer suits us and the new model is not yet fully realized, is difficult. Yet it serves the evolution of the collective. On the individual level, this period of the evolution of commitment may be painful; on the collective level, it is a period of hope.

And, yes, the individual apparently chooses whether or not to be born in a given era and thus whether to be part of that collective experience. Furthermore, individual choice in each moment can influence the collective outcome. By choosing to "clean house" emotionally and by acting as an example to others, you can help the collective through the tough choices it has to make, now, about life on Mother Earth. By choosing to extend a hand or a kind word to a homeless person, you uplift some of the fear and despair that is polluting our emotional atmosphere. On the other hand, by denying that social injustices like apartheid exist, you contribute to the collective denial of the oneness of all beings. So, individual choice does count for something, even at the collective level.

How do you know whether the troublesome patterns in your life are a result of false programming, neurosis, pre-birth agreements, or collective choice? If they cause you or those around you pain and suffering, then it's time to take another look at the choices you've made. You are always free to choose again. Each time we, as individuals, choose not to go into negative behavior, we strengthen ourselves. We also become examples to others, some of whom will be empowered to make more positive choices. And, as more and more of us exercise the exquisitely human gift of choice, and as the consciousness of choice extends to the collective, we'll all grow and evolve more rapidly.

My compliments to Gail Fairfield for extending to Astrology the liberating and enlightening approach she developed for Tarot in her fine book, *Choice Centered Tarot*. The student who learns Astrology from this book will learn to think in choice centered terms from the very start. As more and more of us learn to approach a Chart that way, Astrology will evolve into an ever more useful tool for thinking about our lives and deepest dilemmas.

Donna Cunningham
July 1989

DONNA CUNNINGHAM became a licensed therapist (MSW) in 1967 and an Astrologer in 1970. She is certified as a professional Astrologer and speaks at national and international conferences. In 1986, Professional Astrologers Incorporated gave her their annual award for contributions to the field. Donna is the author of *An Astrological Guide to Self-Awareness, Being a Lunar Type in a Solar World,* and *Healing Pluto Problems,* as well as many additional books. Her perspective on Astrology combines the psychological and the spiritual.

ONE

The Foundations of Astrology

CHOICE CENTERED ASTROLOGY is more than just a book title; it's a philosophical approach to Astrology based on my choice centered orientation to life. The phrase "choice centered" came to me early one morning in 1980 when I was searching for a title for my Tarot book. At first, I thought it *was* just a book title until I realized that I had been developing the concepts of choice centered living since the early 1970s. In that book, I applied my world view to the Tarot. In this book, I'll interweave choice centered theory with Astrological principles.

I believe that our lives are determined by our unconscious and conscious choices, not by the vague force known as "fate." I feel that, if we live by fate, we have little power in our lives. Fate gives us only two choices: waiting around to see what will be dished out OR getting psychic predictions about what will be dished out and then waiting to see if they come true. In either case, fateful living happens *at* us. Choice centered living, on the other hand, happens *because* of us. I feel certain that we create our life experiences out of a combination of the choices we made before birth and those we make every day. This doesn't mean that our experiences are always easy and wonderful. It does mean that, at any time, we have the option of changing or improving them. Minute by minute, and year by year, we make decisions that allow us to act, and to react to the adventures we create in the context of our lives.

Astrology can enable us to analyze our past, present, and future choices. It can trigger insights that allow us to examine our unconscious decisions. It also can present us with a conceptual framework to support us when we want to enhance and improve our conscious choices. Astrology can help us have compassion for ourselves, for our past "mistakes," and for our current struggles. Occasionally, we may even be tempted to lay the blame for our propensities and predilections at Astrology's door. Since I really do believe in choice centeredness, this book will not support the "blame your Astrological Sign" point of view. Instead, it will remind you that you always have a choice about how to create and respond to your life experiences.

By opening this book, you've already made a decision to explore Astrology from a choice centered perspective. This means you have a desire to understand basic Astrological principles and a willingness to entertain the notion that your life might be choice centered.

HOW ASTROLOGY WORKS

Astrology, in its many uses and applications, includes everything from the daily blurbs in the newspaper to financial advisories and weather forecasts. It interests people from all cultures and all walks of life, attracting everyone from world leaders, philosophers, psychologists, and psychics to entertainers, factory workers, bookkeepers, and researchers. It's a broad field, encompassing as many facets as there are individuals who pursue it. The commonality of our experience as students of Astrology lies in our willingness to believe that the movements of the Planets have some relationship to the living of our lives. Whoever you are, now that you've decided to study Astrology, you'll want to understand how it functions. In the rest of this Chapter, I'll discuss how it works and present several theories about why it works. I'll also describe your basic Astrological tool.

The study of Astrology, from any perspective, begins with calculating the exact positions of the Planets and other galactic bodies at specifically chosen times. Up until the 1970s, these positions had to be figured, carefully, by hand. Fortunately, we now have a choice. By using computers, we can arrive quickly at accurate calculations. Whether you choose to work by hand or by computer, you'll organize the resulting data into a map of the sky at a given moment: an ASTROLOGY CHART.

Charts, in and of themselves, are mathematically interesting, but they are only the doorway to the more meaningful world of Astrology: CHART INTERPRETATION. Over the centuries, through careful and deliberate observation, people have found correlations between the patterns in the sky and the events occurring in their lives. Gradually, a basic body of knowledge has been compiled, adapted, and reinterpreted, era by era. Even now, as evidenced by the emergence of a choice centered Astrology, the concepts and theories continue to evolve. As a result, while we might find the interpretations of 200 AD amusing, the people who come after us will undoubtedly find our language and concepts dated. I'm convinced, however, that despite these changes in application, the core concepts of Astrology will consistently hold true. It is a system that works.

Why does it work? Before I present some answers to that question, let me briefly explain how Astrology *doesn't* work. In itself, Astrology is not magical, religious, or psychic even though people who study Astrology may exhibit those qualities. So, your study of Astrology won't take you into magical rituals, devil worship, or mystical understandings about the Universe. In fact, as you study Astrology from the choice centered approach, you'll choose the changes, if any, that will occur in your perceptions and your life. Choice centered Astrology will help you understand how the measurable phenomena of the planetary movements correlate with the seemingly non-measurable phenomena of our subjective experiences. That correlation can be explained through several theories.

One of these theories suggests that the gravitational and magnetic forces that affect the Earth also have an effect on us. Scientists have discovered that the Moon affects the tides and that sunspots and eclipses correspond with political and geological tension. Expanding on these theories, it makes sense to hypothesize that animals and humans might also feel the influences of the "heavenly" bodies: the Sun, Moon, and Planets. From this point of view, depending on where and when you're living, you'd experience different "cosmic" influences which would trigger biological and emotional responses in you. The Planets might actually compel you to act and react.

Another point of view is that the Planets describe us rather than influencing us. This perspective is expressed in the phrase "as above, so below," which means that whatever occurs in the "heavens" is reflected on the Earth. At the heart of this hypothesis is the belief that the whole Universe operates in an orderly and predictable fashion. As a result, any one portion of the Universe exhibits the same logic, cycles, and patterns that will be found in any other portion. One of these forces of change doesn't *cause* the others. They are all a part of the same rhythm, and they all reflect each other. According to this theory, the planetary cycles would match biological, emotional, geological, and political moments and movements on Earth. Therefore, your birth would reflect the Universal themes of its time and place. And, by interpreting the planetary patterns at that time, you can discover how you fit into the greater scheme of things.

At a spiritual level, an Astrological Chart could be a description of a soul's expression on Earth. This theory presumes that each soul is born into a specific body, personality, family, class, race, culture, and historical period and it also assumes that, within this setting, the soul is attempting to express itself as creatively as possible. If this is true, then your Chart would describe the nature of the body and personality that your soul has chosen for this life. In addition, your Chart would show something about the kind of emotional and practical environment it has selected.

From a choice centered outlook, any of these theories could be true. Even if the Planets compel us to act, we can still make choices about how we react to their influences. If our Charts reflect predictable Universal patterns, we face choices about how we utilize the forces represented in those patterns. And, if our Charts are truly descriptions of the bodies and personalities chosen by our souls, we certainly make choices about how to best express those souls within this reality. Each of these theories, in its own way, makes sense. So, choose the ones that fit into your own system of beliefs. And, remember that whatever the underlying reason for its effectiveness, Astrology can be useful to you by providing you with a theoretical framework for self-understanding. This framework is based on your Astrological Chart.

THE NATAL CHART:
YOUR BASIC ASTROLOGICAL TOOL

Astrological Charts can be constructed for the "births" of everything from people, relationships, and pets to businesses, organizations, and countries. Anything that has a starting point has a BIRTH TIME and PLACE. And, anything with a Birth Time and Place can have a BIRTH, or NATAL, Chart.

A Natal Chart shows the positions of the Planets, at the exact time of someone's birth, relative to the location of that birth. This time should be noted at the first breath. Usually, this is the baby's birth cry or coo. Even if life-support systems or Caesarean Sections are involved, the baby's impulse toward independence from her mother, which is represented by separate breathing, is the Astrological moment of birth.

Natal Charts are incredibly unique in that exact planetary patterns only repeat themselves every 26,000 years or so. It's true that if two people are born at the same moment in time, in the same town, they will have matching Charts. If their family, economic, and ethnic situations are similar, their lives could mirror each other. On the other hand, twins born close together in time, with only small differences in their Charts, may choose dissimilar ways of using their energies in order to individually express themselves. Your own options will be reflected in your Natal Chart just as mine are represented through the symbols in my Chart (Fig. 1-1).

As you read this book, you'll be exposed to concepts and techniques that will help you decipher the potential symbolized in your Natal Chart. Through reading it, you'll discover some of what I know about the essentials of Natal Astrology from a practical, yet choice centered, perspective. You'll find psychological and concrete meanings for each Astrological symbol and you'll be encouraged to choose among multiple interpretations and applications for the ones that suit you best. I've gathered and refined this material over fifteen years of study and professional work. It's been tested in my life and in the lives of my clients and students. And, even though I'm always discovering new angles on old theories, this book does contain the basics.

CHOICE CENTERED ASTROLOGY: THE BASICS is organized in the ways I've found most useful when teaching classes. In Chapters 2 and 3, I'll explain the system of Astrology. Specifically, Chapter 2 will deal with the technical features of an Astrology Chart, while Chapter 3 will cover the

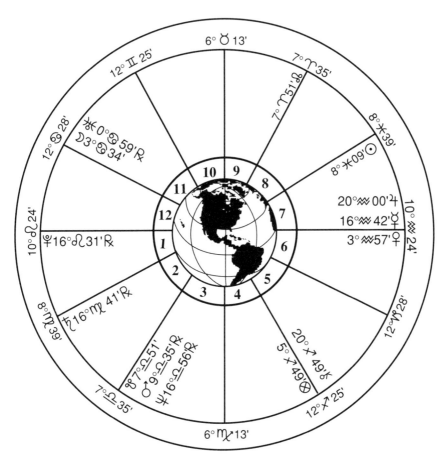

Figure 1-1: Gail Fairfield's Natal Chart
2-27-1950   3:52 pm Standard Time
Foochow, China
Longitude 119E19   Latitude 26N05

dynamics of choice centered Chart interpretation. In each of these Chapters, I've made it a point to distinguish between the FUNDAMEN-TALS and the DETAILS. By mastering the fundamentals, you can inter-pret your own Chart and those of your friends and family. If you want to go further, you'll probably want to understand the details as well.

Once you've come to understand the fundamentals of the system described in these two Chapters, you can utilize the in-depth interpreta-tions of Chapters 4, 5, 6, and 7 to expand your knowledge. In the last Chapter you'll find information and processes you can use to begin doing

Astrological "readings" for yourself and others. All in all, there's quite a bit of information in this book, but my intention has been to structure it in an accessible manner. Your use of the book is up to you; you can choose to read it all at once, dip into it whenever you're in the mood, or study it in a sequenced, disciplined manner. Use the approach that feels right to you. After all, it's a choice centered book. Take what you want and leave the rest. You can always come back to it later.

Welcome to the world of Choice Centered Astrology!

SUMMARY

In this Chapter, I discussed my choice centered orientation to living, described how Astrology works, and presented several theories about why it works. I also explained that the Natal Chart, the Chart based on your Birth Time, Date, and Place will be your basic Astrological tool.

EXERCISES

1-1   Think about why you're interested in Astrology. Do you already know or believe that it works? Why do you think it works?

1-2   Take a moment to think about why you've decided to read CHOICE CENTERED ASTROLOGY: THE BASICS. Make a list of the things you hope to discover through reading this book.

1-3   Imagine what you'd like to do, in the future, with your Astrological knowledge. Ask yourself whether you're interested in finding out more about yourself and your friends or in eventually becoming a professional.

TWO
Astrology as a Technical System

It's easiest to learn to read Astrology Charts if you have one or more of them in front of you. Therefore, throughout the book, I'll utilize two specific Charts as references: one is that of a young girl that I'll call Janie (Fig. 2-1); the other is that of a grown woman I'll name Grace (Fig. 2-2). In this Chapter, I'll use their Charts as examples while I discuss the TECHNICAL FEATURES of Astrology. In accordance with my choice centered philosophy, I'll present the Astrological features that are consistent in most Charts as well as describing some of the optional ones. As you read, you'll find out how to get a copy of your Chart. You'll also find out just how the Houses, Signs, and Planets and other important factors are represented in a Chart. You still won't know what any of this means, but by the time you go on to Chapter 3, you'll have a sense of the mechanics. The rest of the book will be devoted to the interpretation of the symbols that you'll learn to recognize in Chapter 2.

In addition to using these Charts, you'll probably want to apply the ideas and concepts to your own Chart. You may even want to look at the Charts of family members and friends. If you want to work with your personal collection of Charts, it would be a good idea for you to get them before reading any further. You can hand-calculate them but, as I explained in Chapter 1, it's not really necessary in this day and age. For that reason, I'm not going to discuss Chart calculation in this book. Instead, I'll assume that you'll be getting your Charts from a computer.

In order to have a computer calculate your Charts, you will need to give it some information. For each Chart that you want, you'll have to give the computer the following data:

BIRTH TIME (as close to the MINUTE as possible)

BIRTH DATE (day, month, year)

BIRTH PLACE (City, State, Country)

Of these three pieces of data, the one that can be tricky to find is the Birth Time. The first place to look for it is on your birth certificate. If you don't have yours, you can usually get a copy from the appropriate hospital, County, or State Records Department. If your Birth Time is not recorded

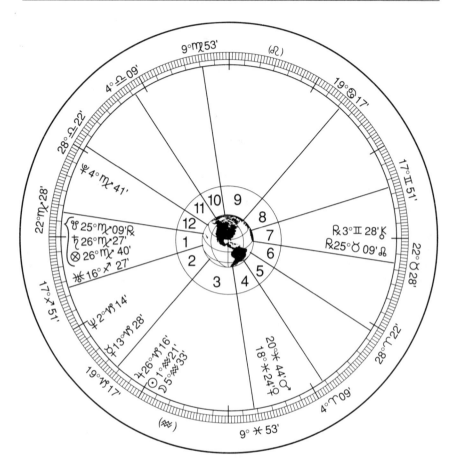

Figure 2-1: Janie's Chart
1-21-1985   2:52 am PST
Seattle, Washington, U.S.A.
Longitude 122W20   Latitude 47N36

on your birth certificate, it's possible that your baby book or birth announcement (if you have either of these) might contain it. Barring these options, a parent or relative might remember the time. At least, they might remember if you were born in the middle of the night, before lunch, after work, or "around 10 AM."

If you absolutely cannot find a Birth Time, you can work with a SOLAR CHART until the time reveals itself to you. This is a Chart calculated for a specific day and location, using the Sun's position as a starting point. Most computers can calculate this kind of Chart for you. You could also make a GENERIC Chart, calculated for a basic time of 6:00 AM or Noon.

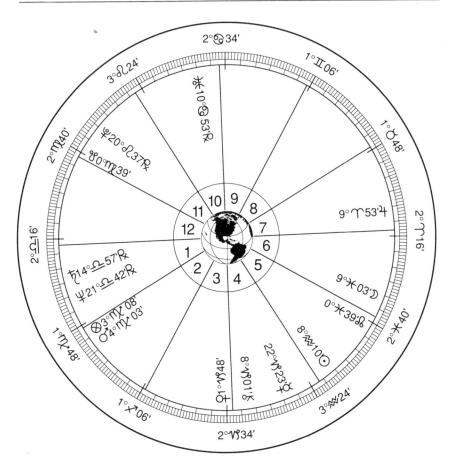

Figure 2-2: Grace's Chart
1-28-1952   9:28 PM CST
Bloomington, Indiana, U.S.A.
Longitude 86W32   Latitude 39N10

If you cannot find a recorded or remembered time and you don't want to use a Solar or Generic Chart, you can PSYCHICALLY DETERMINE THE TIME or ASTROLOGICALLY RECTIFY YOUR CHART. In order to get the Birth Time psychically, you could ask for the time in a dream or meditation, put various Birth Times on small pieces of paper and "randomly" choose one, or use a pendulum (see Appendix A for how). If you want to pursue Chart rectification, you'll need to have a fairly sophisticated knowledge of Astrology. It involves working backwards from the events of your life to find the Chart that must have symbolized the events. To do this, you would begin with a Generic Chart and adapt it as you analyze the timing and nature of the changes in your life.

After you've decided on your Birth Time, Date, and Place, however you confirm them, you're ready to have a computer calculate your Chart. If you order from a COMPUTER SERVICE (see Appendix B for options), that's usually all you'll need to send in: Time, Date, and Place. If you order from Ramp Creek Publishing, you can get a Chart in which all the symbols are abbreviated in English letters. With some other computer services, you may also be able to request that the Chart be printed in words, not symbols.

If you have an Astrology program for your own computer (see Appendix B for possibilities), you'll be choosing to do a little more work. You'll have to use an Astrological atlas such as *The American Atlas* or *The International Atlas* (both by Astro-Computing Services) to look up:

TIME CHANGES, such as Daylight Savings Time, War Time, Summer Time, and Double Summer Time, that were in effect at the Birth Time

LATITUDE AND LONGITUDE of the Birth Place

With this data in hand, you can proceed by following the directions in your Astrology software manual. With Charts in hand, you can begin to familiarize yourself with the basic elements of Astrology. As you look at your Charts, you may find that they don't seem to match the diagrams in this book. Have faith. Keep reading, using Grace's and Janie's Charts as examples, until you find the information that explains how your Chart was erected. Somewhere in this Chapter, it should become clear. If you reach the end of the Chapter and still can't make sense of your Chart, you might consider ordering one from Ramp Creek Publishing. Ramp Creek Charts will reflect the formats presented in this book.

In the following sections, I'll describe the technical features of a Natal Chart. First, I'll discuss the fundamentals. They, alone, will prepare you for using the interpretations in the rest of the book. If you're interested in more depth, you can go on to read about the technical details.

THE TECHNICAL FUNDAMENTALS

There are really only nine basic technical features that you absolutely need to understand in order to make sense of an Astrology Chart. These fundamentals are outlined and diagrammed below.

1. The Chart is a MAP OF THE SKY at the Birth Time, relative to the Birth Place.

2. The EARTH IS IN THE CENTER of the Chart.

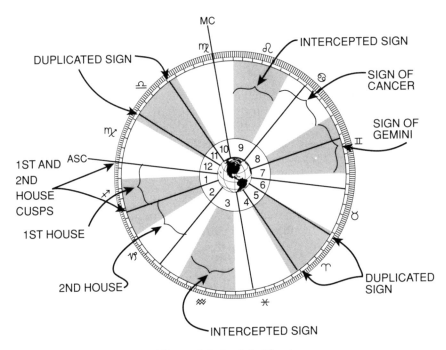

Figure 2-3: Janie's Chart
The Grid of the Houses and Signs

3. The Chart is divided into twelve sections, usually unequal in size, called HOUSES, which correlate to Earth-related times and locations. The Houses are denoted by the numbers 1–12 in the center of the Chart. They go counterclockwise around the circle (Fig. 2-3).

4. The Chart also contains twelve sections, always equal in size, called SIGNS which correlate to sections of the sky surrounding the Earth. Each Sign is named, abbreviated, and symbolized by a GLYPH (symbol) (Fig. 2-4). The Signs also always go counterclockwise in a Chart, in order from Aries through Pisces (Fig. 2-3). But, depending on the Birth Time, Aries could begin anywhere in the circle of the Chart. Each Sign is divided into thirty sections called DEGREES. Each Degree is divided into sixty MINUTES.

5. The TWELVE SIGNS AND THE TWELVE HOUSES OVERLAP each other to form a grid (Fig. 2-3). How they overlap will change from Chart to Chart. The lines that show where they overlap are the HOUSE CUSPS, the beginnings of each of the Houses. The House Cusps are labeled with the Degrees and Minutes of the Signs at their point of overlap with the

Houses. Some Signs are totally contained within Houses. They are called INTERCEPTED SIGNS. If a Chart contains Interceptions, some other Signs will overlap two House Cusps. These are called DUPLICATED SIGNS.

6. The PLANETS are objects in the sky whose positions change from minute to minute and, therefore, from Chart to Chart. They also have names, abbreviations, and symbols (Fig. 2-4). They are placed in the Chart according to their positions by Sign and House (Fig. 2-7). If they have an R after them in the Chart, they were seen to be RETROGRADE at the Birth Time. This means that, seen from the Earth at that time, it appeared that these Planets were moving backwards.

7. The POINTS are mathematically calculated positions that vary from Chart to Chart. Like the Planets, they are named, symbolized by glyph or abbreviation (Fig. 2-4), and placed in the Chart according to their positions by House and Sign (Fig. 2-7).

MIDHEAVEN: at the top of the Chart, the 10th House Cusp

ASCENDANT: at the left of the Chart, the 1st House Cusp

NORTH NODE and SOUTH NODE: always exactly opposite each other

PART OF FORTUNE: calculated combination of the positions of the Sun, Moon, and Ascendant

SIGNS			PLANETS			POINTS		
NAME	AB.	SYMBOL	NAME	AB.	SYMBOL	NAME	AB.	SYMBOL
ARIES	AR	♈	The SUN	SU	☉	NORTH NODE	NN	☊
TAURUS	TA	♉	THE MOON	MO	☽	SOUTH NODE	SN	☋
GEMINI	GE	♊	MERCURY	ME	☿	PART OF FORTUNE	PF	⊗
CANCER	CA	♋	VENUS	VE	♀	MIDHEAVEN	MC	M
LEO	LE	♌	MARS	MA	♂	ASCENDANT	ASC	A
VIRGO	VI	♍	JUPITER	JU	♃			
LIBRA	LI	♎	SATURN	SA	♄			
SCORPIO	SC	♏	CHIRON	CH	⚷			
SAGITTARIUS	SG	♐	URANUS	UR	♅			
CAPRICORN	CP	♑	NEPTUNE	NE	♆			
AQUARIUS	AQ	♒	PLUTO	PL	♇			
PISCES	PI	♓						

Figure 2-4
Names, Abbreviations, Symbols
Signs, Planets, and Points

8. Certain correlations among the Planets, Signs, and Houses, have come to be interpretationally significant. These NATURAL associations (Fig. 2-5) assign one Planet to each Sign and House except in the case of Venus, which has two. Through these connections, planetary RULERSHIPS of the Signs and Houses are established. A Planet, wherever it's located in the Chart, is said to Rule any House that has its Sign on the Cusp (Fig. 2-7). It would also be a Ruler of the House containing its Sign through Interception. The Points *do not* have Rulership associations.

9. The ASPECTS, with names and symbols of their own, are specific distances (Fig. 2-6) that can be measured between any pair of Planets or Points. Any two Planets or Points that are approximately these designated distances apart are said to be in Aspect to one another (Fig. 2-7). Aspects are not denoted on a basic Chart. Usually they are found through a visual scan or a computer analysis. For an initial, fundamental interpretation of your Chart, you do not have to understand the Aspects. Later, you'll probably want to explore them.

HOUSE	SIGNS	PLANETS
1	♈ ARIES	♂ MARS
2	♉ TAURUS	♀ VENUS
3	♊ GEMINI	☿ MERCURY
4	♋ CANCER	☽ THE MOON
5	♌ LEO	☉ THE SUN
6	♍ VIRGO	⚷ CHIRON
7	♎ LIBRA	♀ VENUS
8	♏ SCORPIO	♇ PLUTO
9	♐ SAGITTARIUS	♃ JUPITER
10	♑ CAPRICORN	♄ SATURN
11	♒ AQUARIUS	♅ URANUS
12	♓ PISCES	♆ NEPTUNE

Figure 2-5
Rulerships

NAME/DEGREES		AB.	SYMBOL
CONJUNCTION	0°	CO	☌
SEMI-SEXTILE	30°	SS	⊻
SEXTILE	60°	SX	✶
SQUARE	90°	SQ	□
TRINE	120°	TR	△
QUINCUNX	150°	QU	⚻
OPPOSITION	180°	OP	☍

Figure 2-6
Aspects

Figure 2-7 shows Janie's completed Chart with the Planets, Points, Rulerships, and Aspects highlighted.

Using these nine fundamentals of Chart mechanics, you can familiarize yourself with the significant technical features of your own Chart. To solidify the concepts in your mind, you might also choose to go through a few of the Exercises at the end of this Chapter. Then, it will be up to you to decide whether to go on reading Chapter 2 or to skip to Chapter 3. In the rest of this one, I've explained the technical features and options in more detail. In Chapter 3, you'll find the interpretational system.

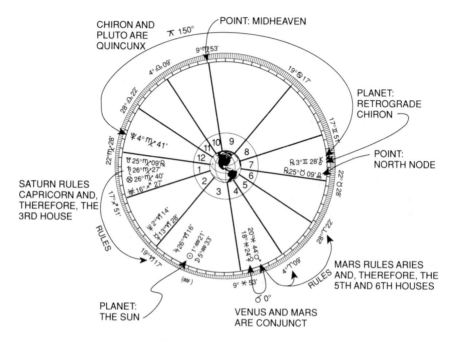

Figure 2-7: Janie's Chart
Planets, Points, Rulerships, and Aspects

THE TECHNICAL DETAILS

An ASTROLOGY CHART IS A MAP OF THE SKY, at a given moment in time, seen from the perspective of the Earth. Therefore, the Earth can be imagined in the center of each Chart. We know that the Sun, not the Earth, is actually at the center of our solar system. HELIOCENTRIC Astrologers take this into consideration by calculating Sun-centered Charts, which they interpret at the level of broad Universal patterns. You might choose, at some time, to explore Heliocentric Astrology yourself. However, I feel that since we were born on Earth and are dealing with Earth-oriented lives, it's most useful, at the beginning level, for us to erect and use GEO-CENTRIC, Earth-centered, Charts. I'll be doing that in this book.

So, for now, envision the Earth (and your Birth Place) at the center of the Chart circle and notice the lines, numbers, and Astrological glyphs that are scattered around it. Initially, they may all look like hieroglyphics, but these squiggles are the keys to unlocking the seemingly mysterious world of Astrology. The three most important sets of symbols in every Chart are those representing the HOUSES, SIGNS, and PLANETS. Familiarity with these building blocks, with a few other important POINTS, and with the RULERSHIP and ASPECT relationships among all of them will provide you with a practical foundation for interpreting any Chart.

The Houses

The first set of Astrological building blocks is THE HOUSES. In order to understand them, pretend that you're actually standing in the center of the Chart, at the Birth Place, looking out in all directions. Then, imagine that the sky above and the Earth below have been flattened so that they can be represented on this piece of paper. And, finally, visualize yourself drawing six intersecting lines on the now-flat Earth, dividing it into twelve pie-shaped sections.

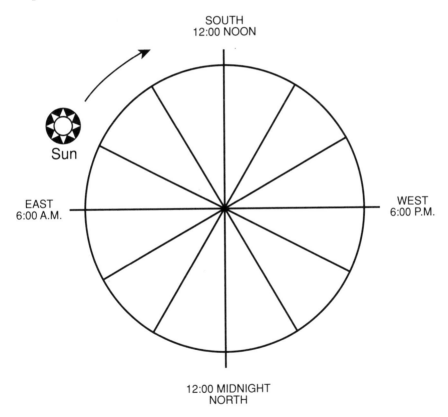

Figure 2-8
The Houses: Compass Directions and Time Divisions

These twelve sections, or HOUSES, reflect compass directions and times of day (Fig. 2-8). Specifically, the East symbolizes 6:00 AM, a generic sunrise time; the South is 12:00 Noon, when the Sun is overhead; the West is 6:00 PM, or sunset; and the North is Midnight. The South is to the top of the Chart because, in the Earth's Northern Hemisphere, the Sun when overhead at Noon, is actually South of us. Since Astrology was formalized in this hemisphere, our somewhat skewed perspective has become integrated into the system.

Two of the intersecting lines that create the Houses are especially significant in terms of Chart construction and interpretation. One of them, the HORIZON line (Fig. 2-9) goes from the left (East) to the right (West), of the Chart. It's called the ASCENDANT (ASC) at the left of the Chart and the DESCENDANT (DES) at the right. In most House systems, the 1st House begins with the Ascendant, and the 7th House, exactly opposite it, begins with the Descendant. The Ascendant, loosely speaking, represents

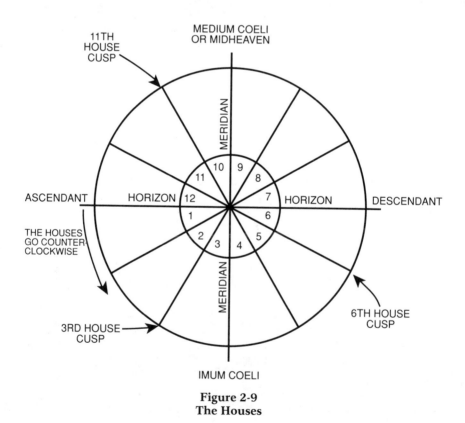

Figure 2-9
The Houses

the point of sky that would be on the horizon if you would look East from the Birth Place, at the Birth Time; the Descendant would be the Western horizon.

The other important line is called the MERIDIAN (Fig. 2-9). It runs from the top (South) to the bottom (North) of the Chart. Its Southern tip, The MEDIUM COELI (MC), is usually called the MIDHEAVEN. Theoretically, the Midheaven is the point above you as you look up from the Birth Place. In most Charts, it begins the 10th House and its opposite point, called the IMUM COELI (IC) begins the 4th House.

The four other lines that intersect the Horizon and Meridian lines combine with them to form the boundaries of the twelve Houses. Each of the twelve boundary lines begins a House and each is called the CUSP (Fig. 2-9) of the House it begins, going counterclockwise.

The Houses provide an Earth-oriented graph, defining the Chart in terms of time (the 24 hours of our day) and space (360 Degree circle of territory surrounding every point on the Earth). Generally speaking, the distance the Sun travels in the sky from Sunrise to Noon is symbolized by the portion of the circle that is included from the 1st House to the 10th (going clockwise). The distance it travels from Noon to Sunset is represented by the distance from the 10th to the 7th House Cusps, and so forth. As a result, people born at higher latitudes (North or South), where the Sun spends shorter or longer amounts of time in the sky, depending on the time of year, will have some very small and very large Houses. People born near the Equator, where day and night are always nearly equal in length, will have Houses that are nearly equal in size.

Figures 2-10 and 2-11 show the changes that would occur in the House sizes if a birth occurred on the Equator or at 55 degrees of Latitude North,

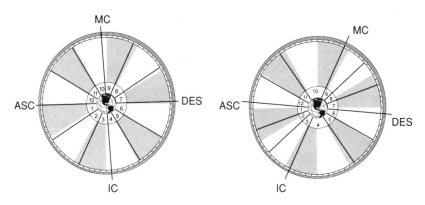

Figure 2-10
Equatorial Birth Place

Figure 2-11
Higher Latitude Birth Place

at the same Time, Date, and Longitude. As you can see, the Meridian Line stays the same, no matter how far North or South the birth occurs. The Horizon Line changes to accommodate the Earth's orientation to the Sun at varying Latitudes. And, the sizes of the Houses change accordingly.

Since a specific birth occurs at only one time and place, it would seem that only one Chart could be drawn for every Birth Time. Although it's true that the Horizon and Meridian lines which set up the basis for the Houses never change, it is possible to find some differences among several Charts cast for the same time and place. These variations lie in the INTER-MEDIATE HOUSE CUSPS: the Cusps formed by the lines that are not the Horizon and Meridian lines. These Intermediate Cusps are based on the mathematical HOUSE SYSTEM that is used for the calculations. In terms of the technical details, choosing your House System will be one decision that you'll make. Over time, you'll probably experiment with several systems.

The House Systems, are, fortunately, internally consistent. Within each one, the Intermediate Cusps are always calculated in opposite pairs. This means that, whatever the system, any accurately drawn Chart can be folded in half – in any direction – and be found to mirror itself. Every House in a Chart is the same size as the one opposite it. And, in all the systems, the House sizes will add up to make a full 360-Degree circle.

Although there are more than 100 different House Systems, they can be divided into two primary groups: EQUAL and UNEQUAL HOUSES. After you understand the distinctions between these two types, you can more easily choose a system within one of the groups. These distinctions are suggested by their titles and described in the following sections.

EQUAL HOUSE SYSTEMS

These systems divide the 360 Degrees of the Chart into twelve 30-Degree sections. Ordinarily, they are calculated by beginning at the Ascendant and proceeding counterclockwise in a regular fashion, marking off the House Cusps every 30 Degrees. If the Equal Houses are based on the Ascendant, the Midheaven will probably not fall at the beginning of a House, although it will usually be noted on the Chart. An Equal House Chart can also be constructed by using the Midheaven as the beginning point. In this case, the Ascendant will fall within a House, not at the beginning of the 1st House. Occasionally, an Equal House Chart will begin at the position of some other point that seems significant to the Astrologer. Figures 2-12 and 2-13 show the Houses of Janie's Chart in Ascendant and Midheaven Equal House form.

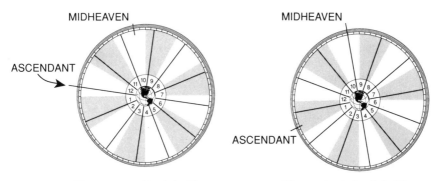

Figure 2-12: Janie's Chart
Ascendant-based
Equal House Chart

Figure 2-13: Janie's Chart
Midheaven-based
Equal House Chart

UNEQUAL HOUSE SYSTEMS

In these more commonly used systems, the Horizon and Meridian lines always mark out the beginnings of the 1st, 7th, 4th, and 10th Houses. But, they vary in the ways they divide up the Intermediate Houses. There are 100 or more Unequal House systems, usually named for the people who discovered them. Some of the most commonly used ones are Koch, Placidus, Porphyry, Regiomontanus, and Campanus. Figure 2-14 shows Janie's Chart done in the Koch system.

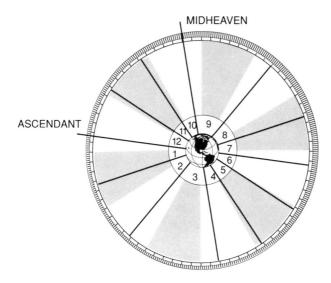

Figure 2-14: Janie's Chart
Unequal Houses: Koch System

CHOOSING YOUR HOUSE SYSTEM

Unfortunately, none of these systems is truly the "right" one. After all, the Houses represent our Earth-centered (or limited) point of view, not cosmic intelligence. Each of them can be interpreted with value and accuracy but it's up to each of us to choose the ones we prefer. When I first began studying Astrology, I used Ascendant-based Equal House Charts. From there, I went on to Placidian Charts; now, I tend to use Koch. As a result, I've used Koch Houses throughout this book, except in the cases where I've indicated otherwise. You might want to spend some time researching the subtle interpretational changes that occur when switching your own Chart from one House System to another. Through this process, you can find the one that most closely matches your own experience and values. Of course, when you're ordering your first Charts from a computer, you won't have done your research yet. In that case, you can let the computer operator choose a House System for you. (You'll probably get Koch or Placidus if you do this.) Or, you can get several at the start so that you can begin comparing systems.

NAME	AB.	SYMBOL
ARIES	AR	♈
TAURUS	TA	♉
GEMINI	GE	♊
CANCER	CA	♋
LEO	LE	♌
VIRGO	VI	♍
LIBRA	LI	♎
SCORPIO	SC	♏
SAGITTARIUS	SG	♐
CAPRICORN	CP	♑
AQUARIUS	AQ	♒
PISCES	PI	♓

Figure 2-15
The Signs

The Signs

The SIGNS, Astrology's second set of building blocks, are equal segments of the sky around the Earth. If the Earth were the center of an orange, the orange wedges would be the slices of sky, surrounding the Earth, representing the Signs. The whole orange, or the whole group of Signs, is called the TROPICAL ZODIAC. Originally, the Signs of the Tropical Zodiac were named for the constellations that appeared in sections of the Universal sky (hence, Astrology as the study of the stars). Centuries have passed since then, and the constellations are no longer exactly in those portions of the sky. SIDEREAL Astrologers have chosen to create systems that take these Universal changes into account. As you progress in your Astrological studies, you might choose to explore Sidereal principles. However, in this book, I've chosen to use the Tropical system; I've presented the twelve Signs as designated sections of the sky around the Earth, symbolic sections that reflect our Earthly reality.

On all Astrological Charts, the Signs will be represented by GLYPHS (symbols) or by abbreviations that are fairly standard, with some variations due to handwriting and creative design styles. These names, abbreviations, and symbols for the Signs are reviewed in Figure 2-15.

The Signs begin somewhere in the Chart, with Aries, and proceed in a specific, consistent order (Fig. 2-15) counterclockwise around the Chart. Since they are equal in size, they each take up 30-Degree sections of the 360-Degree spherical space around the Earth. Each of those 30 Degrees (°) is named, from 0° through 29°, as a location within a Sign. The 30° point of each Sign is actually 0° of the next Sign (Fig. 2-16).

Because each Sign has its own group of 30 Degrees, 23° of Taurus is quite different in location from 23° of Libra. And 23° of Taurus is even distinguished from 12° of Taurus. To make things more precise, we divide each Degree into smaller sections, called Minutes ('). There are 60 Minutes in one Degree analogous to the 60 Minutes within one hour. By using the Degrees and Minutes, we can pinpoint locations such as 15° and 29' of Cancer, 5° and 17' of Scorpio, or 27° and 2' of Capricorn. These specific positions in the Signs are usually designated as follows:

DEGREES   SIGN   MINUTES

They are written out using either the glyphs, the abbreviations, or the words for the Signs. Some examples for 23° and 15' of Taurus follow:

23° TAURUS 15'   **23°♉ 15'**   **23°**   **23°**
                                        TA   **♉**
                                        15'   **15'**

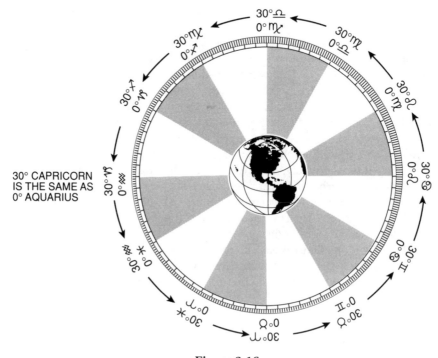

30° CAPRICORN
IS THE SAME AS
0° AQUARIUS

Figure 2-16
Signs: Beginnings and Endings

Figure 2-17 shows several examples of how various positions in a Chart could be noted, by Degree and Minute of Sign.

SIGNS ON HOUSE CUSPS

Since the Houses are Earth-based segments and the Signs are sections of the sky, they rarely begin and end at the same point. Instead, they overlap each other. The Degrees and Minutes of the Signs, at their intersections with the Houses, will be shown on the Chart. Technically speaking, a HOUSE CUSP is actually a point defined by a specific Degree and Minute of a Sign. One special Sign, called THE RISING SIGN, is the one which falls on the 1st House Cusp. But, all the Signs on all the House Cusps are important. For effective Chart interpretation, it's critical to know which Degrees of which Signs fall on the Cusps of the Houses.

In Equal House Charts, the House Cusps will all have the same Degrees and Minutes on them. This is because the Degrees and Minutes of the Ascendant (or Midheaven) are used to set the boundaries of every House

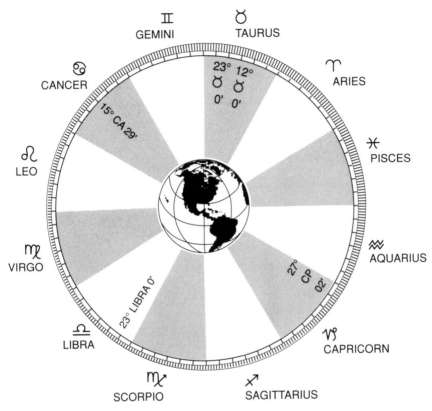

Figure 2-17
The Signs, Their Degrees and Minutes

Cusp. In other words, starting from the 1st House, the Signs go, in order, clockwise around the Chart, with the Houses intersecting them at perfect 30-Degree intervals. Therefore, although the Signs change, the Degrees and Minutes of every House Cusp are the same. Figure 2-18 shows Janie's Ascendant-based Equal House Chart, with the Degrees and Minutes of each Sign written on the House Cusps.

In Unequal House Charts, the Degrees and Minutes on the House Cusps will vary. The Signs begin and end at their regular 30-Degree intervals, but the Houses will contain varying amounts of those Signs. In fact, the sizes of the Houses are actually determined by the total number of Degrees and Minutes (of one or more Signs) included in the House. Figure 2-19 shows the Degrees and Minutes of the Signs that fall on Janie's House Cusps according to the Koch system.

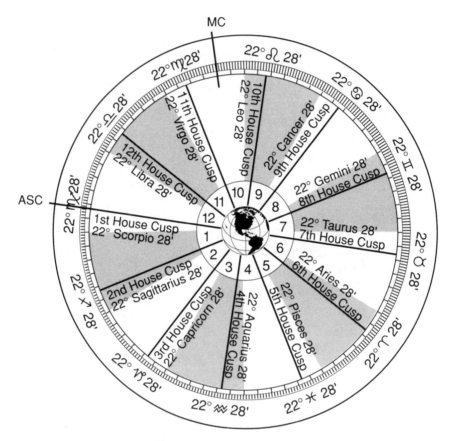

Figure 2-18: Janie's Chart
Degrees and Minutes of Sign on the House Cusps
Ascendant-based Equal House Chart

INTERCEPTED AND DUPLICATED SIGNS

In Unequal House Charts, because the House sizes vary, entire Signs actually can be contained within a large House. This containment is called an INTERCEPTION (Figs. 2-20 and 2-21) and is usually noted by the appearance of the Sign in the outer circle of the Chart between the House Cusps. Sometimes, two small Houses will be almost contained within one Sign. As a result, there will be a DUPLICATION of that Sign on two Cusps (Figs. 2-20 and 2-21). Because the Chart halves mirror each other, if one Sign is Intercepted, the opposite Sign will also be Intercepted. If a Sign is

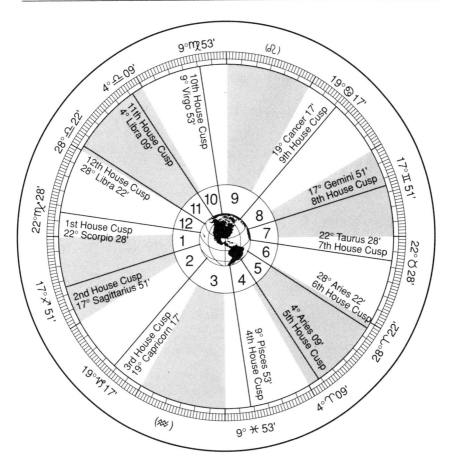

Figure 2-19: Janie's Chart
Unequal Houses: Koch System
Degrees and Minutes of Sign on the House Cusps

Duplicated on two House Cusps, the opposite Sign will also be Duplicated. In Charts that have been calculated for extreme Northern or Southern Latitudes, more than one pair of Interceptions and Duplications may occur. In Equal House Charts, none will occur. Depending on the Unequal House system used, the locations of the Interceptions and Duplicated Signs may change. This is demonstrated in Figures 2-20 and 2-21 since they are both diagrams of Janie's Chart, calculated by two different Unequal House Systems: Koch and Placidus.

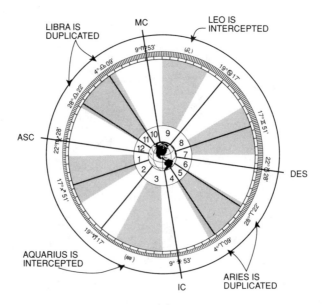

Figure 2-20: Janie's Chart
Koch System: Intercepted and Duplicated Signs

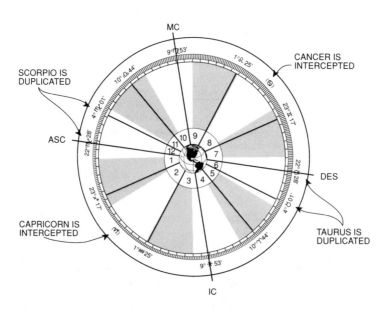

Figure 2-21: Janie's Chart
Placidian System: Intercepted and Duplicated Signs

The Planets

The PLANETS of our solar system comprise the third set of building blocks found in Astrological Charts. The SUN and MOON are technically called the LUMINARIES and are not actually Planets. But, for the sake of simplicity, I'll be including them in this group and be referring to them all as the Planets. Aside from the question of the Luminaries, it would seem that the remaining Planets, as named by elementary school textbooks, would be pretty easy to identify. In actuality, this is the area of Astrology that is most changeable because new Planets and other galactic bodies are constantly being found by astronomers. As each one is discovered, we're faced with the choice of deciding whether to include it in our Charts and, upon including it, how to interpret it.

Currently, there is much discussion about whether to include Chiron* and the Asteroids (see Appendix C) in Astrological Charts. And, there are always theories about new, soon-to-be-discovered Planets and old, no-longer-existing Planets. At some point, you may want to do some personal research so that you can decide what to include in your Charts. In this book, the traditional Planets, the Sun and Moon, and Chiron will be included in every Chart. Their names, glyphs and abbreviations are reviewed in Figure 2-22.

PLANETS IN ORBIT

We need precise planetary positions for our Charts, but given the complexity of the planetary pathways, calculating the positions by hand is impossible for most of us. All the Planets, including the Sun and Moon, do appear to pass through all the Signs, in order from Aries to Pisces, but they do not move through the Signs in the same way. They differ in how long they take to complete their cycles because their speeds and orbit lengths vary. Some Planets spend quite a bit of time in each Sign, moving only gradually from Degree to Degree. For example, Pluto may spend a whole month at 10° of Scorpio, going slowly through the Minutes, while the Moon whips through an entire Sign in two and a half days. The Planets also have vary-

---

* Chiron (Kī‘rŏn) was discovered in 1977. It was first called an Asteroid, but since it's not in the Asteroid belt (between Mars and Jupiter) and is, on occasion, brighter than an Asteroid should be, there's speculation that it's a comet. It may have come from a group of comets that are normally beyond Pluto. While its orbit is irregular, it does seem to be predictable – at least for the next thousand years or so. Astrological research has shown that it does have significance, so I'm including it as a galactic "body" and calling it a Planet.

NAME	ABBREVIATION	GLYPH	ALTERNATE GLYPH
THE SUN	SU	☉	
THE MOON	MO	☽	
MERCURY	ME	☿	
VENUS	VE	♀	
MARS	MA	♂	
JUPITER	JU	♃	
SATURN	SA	♄	
CHIRON	CH	⚷	⚷
URANUS	UR	♅	
NEPTUNE	NE	♆	
PLUTO	PL	♇	♇

Figure 2-22
The Planets

ing orbital shapes and patterns. The Moon orbits the Earth as it goes around the Sun; the Sun's Astrological path is really determined by the Earth's orbit around the Sun; Pluto's orbit is sometimes outside and sometimes inside Neptune's; and Chiron weaves in and out of Saturn's and Uranus's orbits. Figure 2-23 shows rough orbit patterns for the Planets.

Fortunately, we don't have to know the physics and math for figuring out where the Planets are located when we want to erect Charts. We can get the exact planetary positions from tables in a computer or a computer-generated book. These tables are called EPHEMERIDES. An EPHEMERIS, in book form, shows the Degrees and Minutes of Sign for each Planet at Midnight (or Noon), Greenwich (England) Mean Time. The daily Sign locations are shown under the columns headed LONG or LONGITUDE. These book positions do need to be adjusted for the time and location of each birth in order to get accurate Charts, but computers can perform these calculations for us. Astrology software programs include the information that can give us detailed data on Planet locations. An Ephemeris is useful to have, however, since it gives a general picture of the daily sky. Figure 2-24 shows a mock-up of part of an Ephemeris page. It doesn't include Chiron because that Planet is normally found in its own Ephemeris, not in a general one.

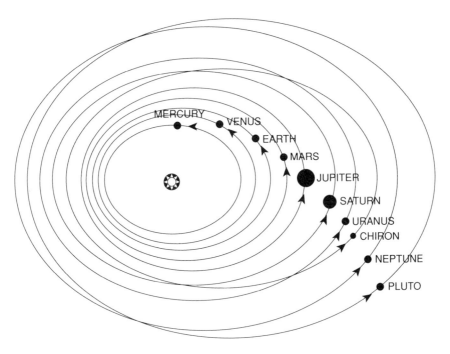

Figure 2-23
Planetary Orbits

LONGITUDE						FEBRUARY, 1989				
DAY	SU	MO	NN	ME	VE	MA	JU	SA	UR	NE	PL
1 W	12 AQ 07	3 SG 58	5 PI 07 R	27 CP 34 R	26 CP 36	7 TA 10	26 TA 19	9 CP 06	3 CP 29	11 CP 03	15 SC 07
2 TH	13 AQ 07	16 SG 55	5 PI 05	26 CP 58	27 CP 51	7 TA 45	26 TA 22	9 CP 13	3 CP 32	11 CP 05	15 SC 07
3 F	14 AQ 09	0 CP 17	4 PI 59	26 CP 12	29 CP 06	8 TA 19	26 TA 25	9 CP 19	3 CP 35	11 CP 07	15 SC 08
4 SA	15 AQ 09	14 CP 05	4 PI 59	26 CP 12	0 AQ 21	8 TA 54	26 TA 27	9 CP 25	3 CP 38	11 CP 09	15 SC 08
5 SU	16 AQ 10	28 CP 17	4 PI 56	26 CP 02 D	1 AQ 36	9 TA 29	26 TA 31	9 CP 31	3 CP 41	11 CP 11	15 SC 09
6 M	17 AQ 10	12 AQ 50	4 PI 56	25 CP 59	2 AQ 51	10 TA 04	26 TA 34	9 CP 37	3 CP 44	11 CP 13	15 SC 09
7 TU	18 AQ 11	27 AQ 36	4 PI 53 D	26 CP 15	4 AQ 06	10 TA 39	26 TA 37	9 CP 44	3 CP 47	11 CP 15	15 SC 10

Figure 2-24
Ephemeris Mock-up for February, 1989

PLANETS THAT ARE DIRECT AND RETROGRADE

An Ephemeris or computer will also indicate each Planet's DIRECTION of motion. If a Planet is moving in the ordinary way, it is said to be DI-RECT (forward). The Sun and Moon are always Direct. The rest of the Planets go RETROGRADE periodically. This means that, seen from the Earth, they appear to be moving backwards. It is an optical illusion; the Planets never actually move backwards. But, Retrograde Planets do have interpretational significance, so we carefully note them in our Charts. Ret-rograde Planets are indicated in an Ephemeris or in a Chart by the ℞ (R, r) notation. The ℞ is placed toward the inside of the circle, after the Degrees and Minutes of Sign.

In Janie's Chart, Chiron is Retro-grade (Fig. 2-25). In the Ephemeris (Fig. 2-24), Mercury is Retrograde at the beginning of the month, but it goes Direct (D) on February 5.

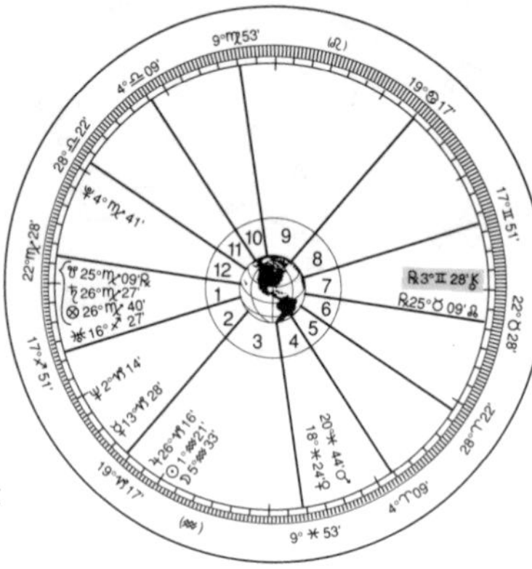

Figure 2-25: Janie's Chart

Although the cycles of Retrogradation are predictable, they do vary from Planet to Planet according to how each Planet's orbit relates to that of the Earth. For example, Mercury's Retrograde motion on the sample Ephemeris page is the end of one of several three- or four-week periods that occur every year. Venus and Mars Retrograde for around six weeks every other year, not necessarily at the same time. And, the rest of the Planets, from Jupiter through Pluto, Retrograde every year for four to six months. Their Retrograde periods are all unique, although they often overlap each other. As a result, it's not uncommon to have one or more Retrogrades in any given Birth Chart.

PLANETS IN SIGNS AND HOUSES

It's as though, seen from the Earth at the center of the Chart, we view the Planets through the slices of the sky representing the Signs. If each Sign were a different color, we could say that the Planets reflect those colors as they move through the Signs. If each Degree of a Sign changed shades, the reflection would be even more specific. In fact, for Chart interpretation, we need that specificity. It's important to know the exact position of each

Planet by Sign and by Degree and Minute within that Sign. So, we place the Planets in our Charts according to their precise Sign positions. Since those Sign positions fall within specific Houses, by locating the Planets according to the Degrees and Minutes of their Signs, we automatically position them in the appropriate Houses.

One standard way of denoting the Planets in Charts is to place the symbol for each Planet in its correct location in the Chart, and to define its position by using the following formula:

PLANET   DEGREES   SIGN   MINUTES

Depending on your visual preference, you could write the Planets horizontally or vertically. For example, Saturn at 9° and 2′ of Gemini could be written:

♄ 9° ♊ 02'   ♄
9°
♊
02'

Janie's Mars is located at 20° and 44′ of Pisces. If it fell at the left of the Chart, it would normally be written as follows:

MA 20° PI 44'

However, since it's on the right of the Chart and we want the symbols for the Planets to be placed next to the rim, Mars is written, in this Chart, like this:

20° PI 44' MA

Figure 2-26 shows Janie's Chart with the Planets added. Note how the Planets are written next to the rim and the Degrees and Minutes of Sign are shown toward the center.

PLANETARY RULERSHIPS

An important factor to consider in interpreting Astrological Charts is the powerful association between the Planets and their NATURAL Signs and Houses. These relationships are not specific to particular Charts. They are based on the correspondences that exist among the three basic building blocks. Because of similar interpretational features, each of the twelve Houses is associated with one of the Signs and one of the Planets. A special name is given to the Planet–Sign associations: RULERSHIP. Additionally, both Planets and Signs can be called the Natural Rulers of their associated Houses.

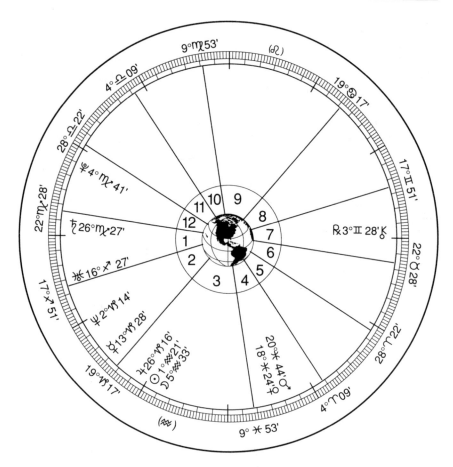

Figure 2-26: Janie's Chart
Planetary Positions by Degrees and Minutes of Sign

As you can see in Figure 2-27, since we have twelve Houses and twelve Signs, these two elements match up quite nicely. If everything were neat and tidy, we'd also have twelve Planets. Maybe, after we've discovered all of our Sun's Planets, we will. However, since we have only eleven galactic bodies at this point, Venus still has two Signs (and Houses). Actually, the Planet-to-Sign correlations have evolved considerably in the last few centuries as new Planets have been discovered. Currently, there is still some discussion over Chiron's Sign, so I've included my preference and the alternative in Figure 2-27. This Figure also shows the old Rulerships that were in effect before Uranus, Neptune, and Pluto were discovered.

HOUSE	SIGN	PLANET	OLD OR ALTERNATE PLANET
1ST	ARIES	MARS	
2ND	TAURUS	VENUS	
3RD	GEMINI	MERCURY	
4TH	CANCER	THE MOON	
5TH	LEO	THE SUN	
6TH	VIRGO	CHIRON	MERCURY
7TH	LIBRA	VENUS	
8TH	SCORPIO	PLUTO	MARS
9TH	SAGITTARIUS	JUPITER	CHIRON
10TH	CAPRICORN	SATURN	
11TH	AQUARIUS	URANUS	SATURN
12TH	PISCES	NEPTUNE	JUPITER

Figure 2-27
Rulerships

On occasion, the Signs will match their Houses all around a Chart – with Aries on the 1st House Cusp, Taurus on the 2nd, and so forth. In that case, the Chart is called a NATURAL CHART. In most instances, however, the Signs do not fall on their Natural Houses and the Planets do not necessarily land in their home Signs.

The Points

In addition to the Planets, there are a number of other POINTS that you can choose to include in your Charts. They are mathematically calculated positions, not symbols of actual objects in the sky. Most of them are interesting, but a Chart containing *all* of them can become unwieldy to analyze and interpret. For that reason, I've included only the five Points that I consider most important in this book. Earlier in this Chapter, you were introduced to two of them: the MIDHEAVEN and the ASCENDANT. Here are descriptions of the remaining three: the NORTH and SOUTH NODES OF THE MOON, and THE PART OF FORTUNE.

THE NODES OF THE MOON

The NORTH AND SOUTH NODES OF THE MOON are also called the Dragon's Head (North) and Dragon's Tail (South). The Nodes symbolize the places where the Moon's orbit around the Earth intersects with the flat plane of the Earth's orbit around the Sun. Figure 2-28 shows roughly how they are derived.

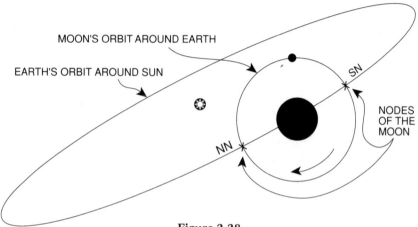

Figure 2-28
The Nodes of the Moon

Like the Planets, the Nodal Points move through the Signs, but unlike the Planets, their general path moves backwards through the Signs, from Pisces to Aquarius to Capricorn, and so on, to Aries. As you can see from the sample Ephemeris page (Fig. 2-24), the Nodes change direction quite often, going Direct and Retrograde several times a Month. The North Node is usually included in an Ephemeris or a computer Chart, and the South Node is always exactly opposite it, by Degrees and Minutes of Sign. In other words, if the North Node is at 5° and 7' of Pisces (Feb. 1, 1989), the South Node will be at 5° and 7' of Virgo. So, given the North Node, you can draw in the South Node for yourself. The mock-up Ephemeris, like many Ephemerides, shows the path of the TRUE NORTH NODE, its actual position at Midnight each day at Greenwich, England. Some Ephemerides also include the MEAN NORTH NODE, a position figured by averaging the True Node positions over a period of time. The Mean Node is always Retrograde. When given a choice in an Ephemeris or computer software program, I use the True Node. Therefore, I'll use it throughout this book. The symbols and abbreviations for the Nodes are shown in Figures 2-29 and 2-30.

Figure 2-29
The North Node (NN)

Figure 2-30
The South Node (SN)

THE PART OF FORTUNE

The PART OF FORTUNE (Pars Fortuna), is one of a number of Points that come from ancient Arabian Astrology. As a group, they are called the ARABIAN PARTS. Each one is calculated by adding and subtracting specific Planets or other Astrological positions from each other, according to predetermined formulae (see Appendix D for an explanation of the math). The Part of Fortune is the most important of these Parts and is routinely included in most Astrological Charts. It is found by combining the Degrees and Minutes of the Sun, Moon, and Ascendant, as follows:

ASCENDANT + MOON − SUN = PART OF FORTUNE

The Part of Fortune will not appear in an Ephemeris since it is not a point in the Universal sky. It will appear on most computer-generated Charts. The symbol and abbreviation for the Part of Fortune, the one Arabian Part that I'll include in this book, is shown in Figure 2-31.

Figure 2-31
The Part of Fortune (PF)

The Completed Chart

In a well-designed Chart, the Planets and other significant Points will be legibly symbolized at specific Degrees and Minutes of their Signs and located within the appropriate Houses. Because the Houses and Signs overlap irregularly, several Planets or Points within one House may not be within the same Sign. And, those within the same Sign won't necessarily be in the same House. So, accurate, legible positioning of the symbols is quite critical.

A quick check of the accuracy of your Chart consists of locating the Sun, Mercury, and Venus. The Sun should be placed in the part of the Chart associated with the time of day you were born. For example, if you were born around Midnight, the Sun should be close to the IC. If you were born at 3 PM, it should be somewhere in the 8th or 9th Houses. Wherever the

NAME_____

DATE_____TIME_____

PLACE_____TIME   ZONE_____

LATITUDE_____LONGITUDE_____

HOUSE SYSTEM_____

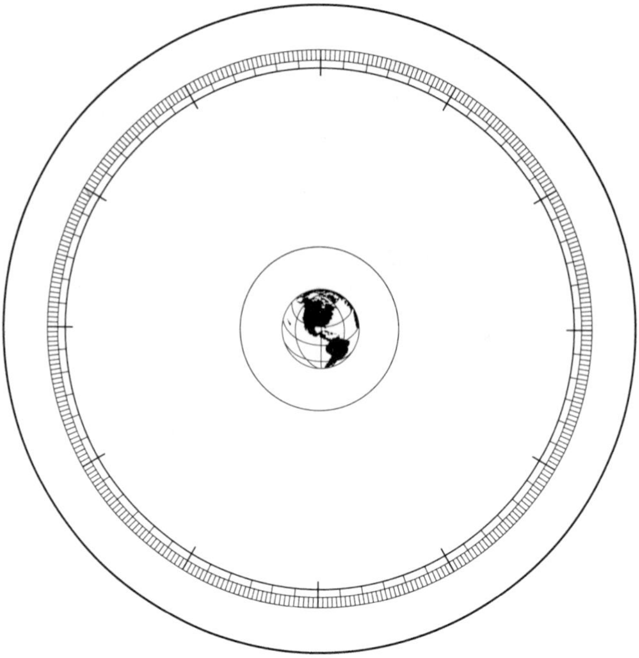

♈ ARIES	♎ LIBRA	☽ MOON		
♉ TAURUS	♏ SCORPIO	☿ MERCURY	♄ SATURN	
♊ GEMINI	♐ SAGITTARIUS	♀ VENUS	⚷ CHIRON	
♋ CANCER	♑ CAPRICORN	☉ SUN	♅ URANUS	☊ MOON'S NORTH NODE
♌ LEO	♒ AQUARIUS	♂ MARS	♆ NEPTUNE	☋ MOON'S SOUTH NODE
♍ VIRGO	♓ PISCES	♃ JUPITER	♇ PLUTO	⊗ PART OF FORTUNE

Figure 2-32
A No-Cusp Preprinted Chart Blank

Sun is located, Mercury and Venus should be within one or two Signs of it. These rules of thumb don't, of course, really check for detailed accuracy. But, they do help to make up for some human error!

Computer-generated Charts are usually quite legible, and many Astrologers work directly from them. You may feel comfortable doing this. In that case, once you've received your Chart from the computer, you're ready to go on.

If you want to copy your Charts onto personalized Chart blanks, you'll have two major options with regard to the format: blanks *with* House Cusps and blanks *without* House Cusps.

CHART BLANKS WITH *NO* HOUSE CUSPS

The most basic Chart format is a circle on a page. It may or may not have the Sign divisions or the 360 Degrees of the Zodiac marked out on it. Figure 2-32 shows a pre-printed Chart blank of this type. This one does show the 360 Degrees of the Zodiac.

Beginning with a blank circle such as this, you create the whole Chart, Sign by Sign, House Cusp by House Cusp, Planet by Planet, and so forth. You'll need to remember to place the Sign on the 1st House Cusp toward the LEFT of the Chart. Then, draw in the House boundaries according to their locations in each Sign and label the House Cusps with the appropriate Degrees and Minutes. After that, place the Planets and other Points in their positions, also by Degrees and Minutes of Sign. The advantage of this kind of Chart format is that the resulting Chart is visually quite accurate. The disadvantage is that it's time-consuming to draw up these Charts. Janie's Chart is shown in Figure 2-33, on a No-Cusp Chart blank.

CHART BLANKS *WITH* HOUSE CUSPS

The second type of Chart format is easier to use but less visually accurate. Its basic design contains generic, equal-sized Houses. Figure 2-34 shows one of these. The House Cusps are already drawn in, leaving you to write in the Degrees and Minutes of Sign on each one. After that, you can draw in the Planets and Points. In Figure 2-35, Janie's Chart is shown again, on this kind of Chart blank.

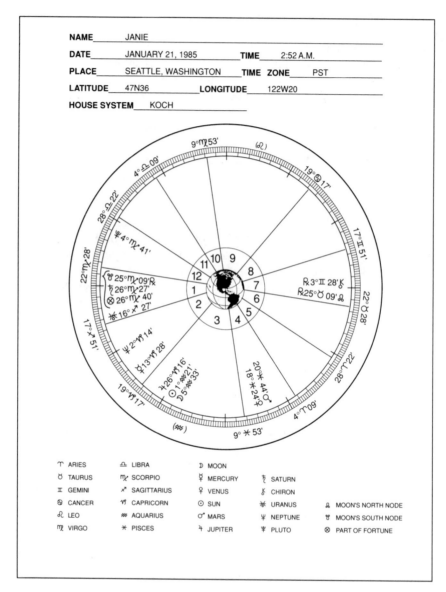

**Figure 2-33: Janie's Chart
On a Preprinted No-Cusp Chart Blank**

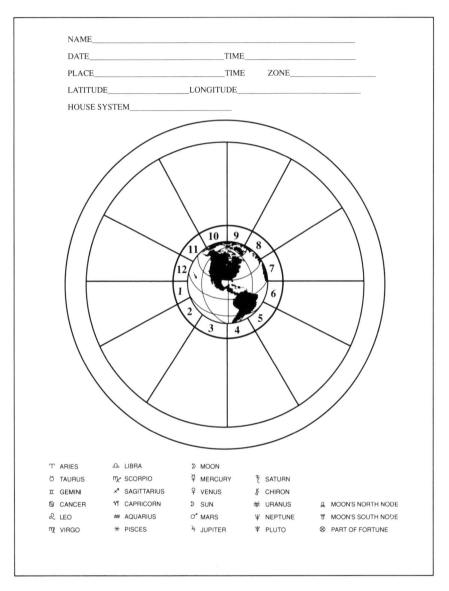

♈ ARIES	♎ LIBRA	☽ MOON	
♉ TAURUS	♏ SCORPIO	☿ MERCURY	♄ SATURN
♊ GEMINI	♐ SAGITTARIUS	♀ VENUS	⚷ CHIRON
♋ CANCER	♑ CAPRICORN	☽ SUN	♅ URANUS
♌ LEO	♒ AQUARIUS	♂ MARS	♆ NEPTUNE
♍ VIRGO	♓ PISCES	♃ JUPITER	♇ PLUTO

☊	MOON'S NORTH NODE
☋	MOON'S SOUTH NODE
⊗	PART OF FORTUNE

Figure 2-34
A Preprinted Chart Blank with House Cusps

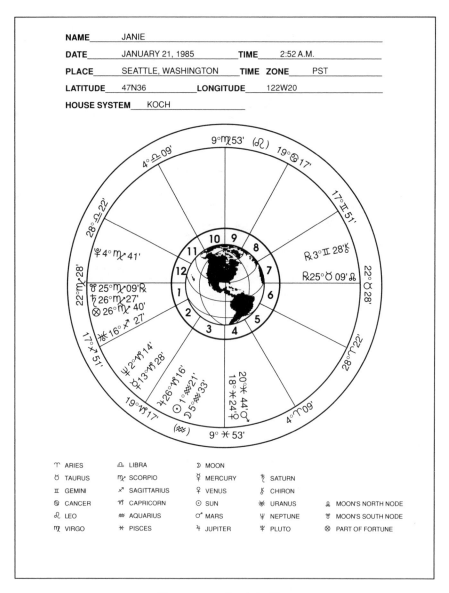

NAME_____ JANIE

DATE_____ JANUARY 21, 1985   TIME____ 2:52 A.M.

PLACE_____ SEATTLE, WASHINGTON   TIME ZONE____ PST

LATITUDE___ 47N36   LONGITUDE____ 122W20

HOUSE SYSTEM___ KOCH

♈ ARIES	♎ LIBRA	☽ MOON		
♉ TAURUS	♏ SCORPIO	☿ MERCURY	♄ SATURN	
♊ GEMINI	♐ SAGITTARIUS	♀ VENUS	⚷ CHIRON	
♋ CANCER	♑ CAPRICORN	☉ SUN	♅ URANUS	☊ MOON'S NORTH NODE
♌ LEO	♒ AQUARIUS	♂ MARS	♆ NEPTUNE	☋ MOON'S SOUTH NODE
♍ VIRGO	♓ PISCES	♃ JUPITER	♇ PLUTO	⊗ PART OF FORTUNE

**Figure 2-35: Janie's Chart
On a Preprinted Chart Blank with House Cusps**

Figures 2-36 and 2-37 show Ascendant-based and Midheaven-based Equal House Charts for Janie, using preprinted Chart blanks with House Cusps. Notice how the Planets and Points can change their Houses but never their Sign locations when the House Systems are changed.

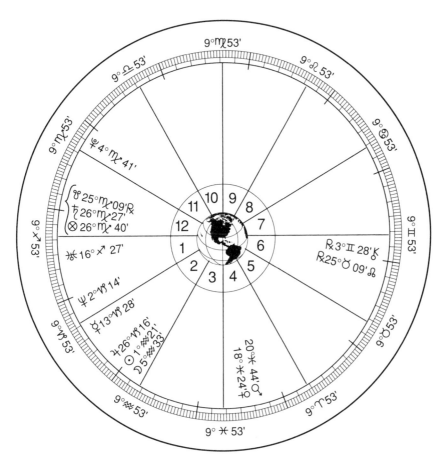

Figure 2-36: Janie's Chart
Midheaven-based Equal House Chart

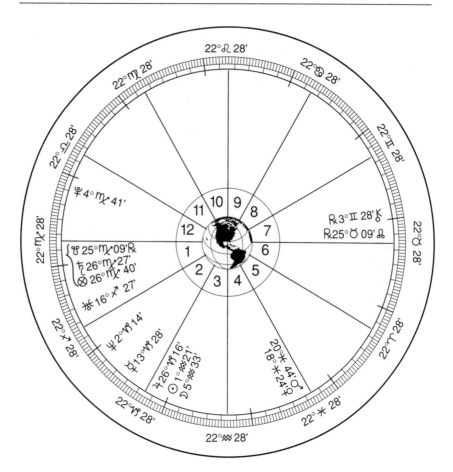

Figure 2-37: Janie's Chart
Ascendant-based Equal House Chart

The Aspects

As soon as you have your Chart calculated and printed or copied onto a Chart blank, the ASPECTS between the Planets and Points can be figured out. They are derived from measuring the angular distances between any two positions in the Zodiac. Essentially, they are the result of figuring out how far it is, by total Degrees and Minutes, from one place to another. It's possible to find the distances between any and all of the Planets and Points, but some of the distances, those that correspond to the SEVEN MAJOR ASPECTS, are more significant than others in terms of interpretation. (Eight other Aspects are discussed briefly in Appendix G.)

The Major Aspects are the angular distances that begin with 0° and continue at 30-Degree intervals up to 180°:

0, 30, 60, 90, 150, AND 180

These Aspects, their names, abbreviations, and symbols, are shown in Figure 2-38. Since the Planets are rarely *exactly* the Aspect distance apart, there is a margin, called the allowable ORB which describes the acceptable variation. Aspects that are close to exact are called TIGHT Aspects, while those that are within the farther range of the Orb are called WIDE. I think that, in most cases, the 6°–8° of Orb that are shown in Figure 2-38 are workable. But, if the Sun or Moon are involved, I do allow an Orb up to

ASPECT NAME	SYMBOL	ABBREV.	# OF DEGREES BETWEEN TWO PLANETS OR POINTS	ALLOWABLE VARIATION (DEGREES OF ORB)
CONJUNCTION	☌	CO	0 DEGREES APART	-8 TO 8 DEGREES (8) (10 FOR SUN OR MOON)
SEMI-SEXTILE	⊻	SS	30 DEGREES APART	24-36 DEGREES (6) (8 FOR SUN OR MOON)
SEXTILE	✶	SX	60 DEGREES APART	52-68 DEGREES (8) (8 FOR SUN OR MOON)
SQUARE	□	SQ	90 DEGREES APART	82-98 DEGREES (8) (10 FOR SUN OR MOON)
TRINE	△	TR	120 DEGREES APART	112-128 DEGREES (8) (10 FOR SUN OR MOON)
QUINCUNX	⊼	QU	150 DEGREES APART	144-156 DEGREES (6) (8 FOR SUN OR MOON)
OPPOSITION	☍	OP	180 DEGREES APART	172-188 DEGREES (8) (10 FOR SUN OR MOON)

Figure 2-38
The Aspects

2° wider. As you become more sophisticated in your understanding of Astrology, you'll probably experiment with various Orbs until you find the ones that work the best for you.

Most Astrology computer programs can be used to calculate the Aspects, and an easy, paper-and-pencil system for finding all the Aspects is described in Appendix G. But, it's practical to be able to recognize the important Major Aspects at a glance when interpreting a Chart. This is possible through a technique of visually sorting the Planets according to Sign placement (the House locations make no difference in terms of Aspects). In a visually accurate Chart, one in which you've drawn in the House Cusps yourself, the relationships between the Planets and Points, by Sign, are fairly easy to see. Once you get used to watching for the different distances you can measure them by eye, or even by ruler.

In a Chart with preprinted House Cusps, the angles between the Chart features will be less obvious. In that case, a wheel of the Signs (Fig. 2-39) is a useful mental image to hold, when searching for Aspects.

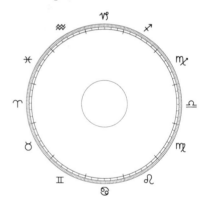

Figure 2-39
Wheel of the Signs

The easiest strategy for finding Aspects is to begin at the Ascendant and go around the Chart, counterclockwise through the Houses, figuring the Aspects to each Planet and Point. This "figuring" actually just means noticing any other Planets or Points that are at close to the same Degree of the same Sign or of another Sign. For example, if the Ascendant is at approximately 2° of Cancer, Planets at 3° of Gemini (Semi-Sextile), 1° of Scorpio (Trine), and 4° of Capricorn (Opposition) would all form Aspects to it. A Planet at 29° of Pisces would also form an Aspect (Square) to this Ascendant, even though it may not be immediately obvious. By distance, it's close to 90 Degrees away.

HINTS FOR FINDING THE ASPECTS IN A CHART

THE CONJUNCTION ☌ (0°) : Planets that are very close together are considered to be Conjunct. Even if they cross House or Sign boundaries, as long as they are within 8 Degrees of each other, they're still in Conjunction.

THE SEMI-SEXTILE ⊻ (30°) : Planets that are about a Sign apart are Semi-Sextile. Most of the time, they'll be at about the same Degree of Signs that are next to each other. They may also cross Sign boundaries and still be considered Semi-Sextile if they're about 30 Degrees apart.

THE SEXTILE ✶ (60°) : Planets that are two Signs apart are Sextile. The easily recognized ones will be at the same Degrees of Signs that have one extra Sign between them. The others may cross Sign boundaries but will still be approximately 60 Degrees apart.

THE SQUARE ☐ (90°) : Squared Planets are three Signs, or a fourth of the Zodiac, apart. If they're not at similar Degrees of their Signs, they can still be considered Square if they have 90 Degrees between them.

THE TRINE △ (120°): Planets that Trine one another are four Signs, or about a third of the Zodiac, apart. Although they're often at similar Degrees of their Signs, they are still Trine, whatever their Sign positions, if they're 120 Degrees apart.

THE QUINCUNX ⊼ (150°) : Quincunx Planets are in Signs that are one away from being opposite each other. Although they're often at similar Degrees in their respective Signs, they're considered Quincunx solely on the basis of the 150 Degrees between them.

THE OPPOSITION ☍ (180°): Planets that are Opposed to each other are visually opposite each other. Whether or not they fall at similar Degrees of their Signs, they're in Opposition if they're approximately 180 Degrees apart.

A few of the Aspects in Janie's Chart are shown in Figure 2-40; a few of Grace's are in Figure 2-41.

DIAGRAMMING THE ASPECTS

When you're ready to keep track of the Aspects you've found, you have several options. Your choice will depend primarily on your visual preference. If you get your Aspects from a computer, it will print out the actual Degrees, the abbreviations, or the symbols for them. Most computers are selective, printing out only the Aspects that are within Orb. This can be

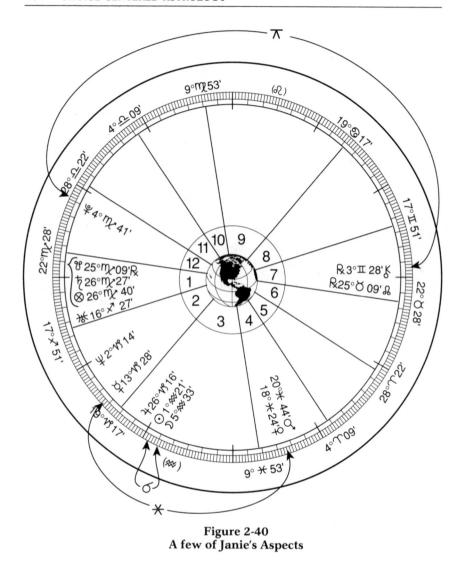

Figure 2-40
A few of Janie's Aspects

great because it saves you from having to figure out all the distances between the Planets and Points. It also can be a problem if you disagree with the computer programmer's choices for Orbs. If you have your own Astrology software, you can probably adjust the Orbs for yourself. Otherwise, when ordering from a computer service, you'll want to double-check

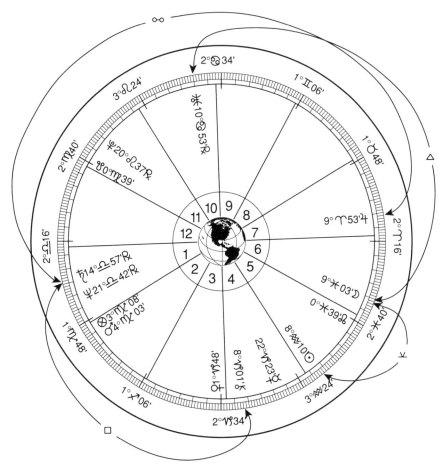

Figure 2-41
A few of Grace's Aspects

the Aspects on the basis of your preferences regarding Orbs. Figures 2-42, 2-43, and 2-44 show three different mock-ups of computer printouts for the Aspects. The first two sets of Aspects are shown in ASPECTARIANS, box-grids in which the Aspects can be noted. The third one indicates the Aspects by drawing lines between the pairs of Planets or Points.

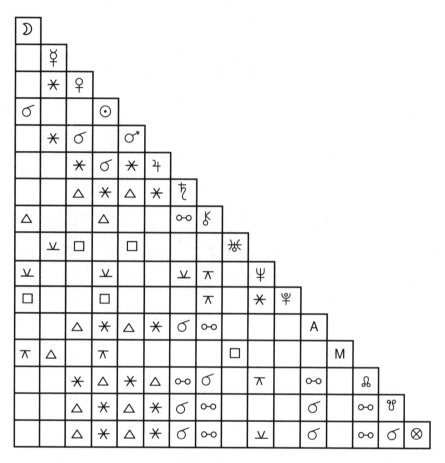

Figure 2-42
Janie's Aspectarian

	SU	MO	ME	VE	MA	JU	SA	CH	UR	NE	PL	NN	SN	PF	A	M
SU		SS		SS	SQ	SX	TR	SS	QU			SS	QU	SQ	TR	QU
MO	SS			SX	TR		QU	SX	TR			CO	OP	TR	QU	TR
ME										SQ	QU	SX	TR			
VE	SS	SX			SX			CO				SX	TR	SX	SQ	OP
MA	SQ	TR		SX		QU		SX	TR			TR	SX	CO	SS	TR
JU	SX				QU		OP	SQ	SQ						OP	SQ
SA	TR	QU			OP			SQ	SQ	CO	SX					
CH	SS	SX		CO	SX	SQ	SQ		OP			SX	TR	SX		TR
UR	QU	TR		TR	SQ	SQ	OP						TR			
NE			SQ				CO				SX					
PL			QU				SX			SX						
NN	SS	CO	SX	SX	TR		SX							TR	QU	TR
SN	QU	OP	TR	TR	SX		TR							SX	SS	SX
PF	SQ	TR		SX	CO			SX				TR	SX		SS	TR
A	TR	QU		SQ	SS	OP						QU	SS	SS		SQ
M	QU	TR		OP	TR	SQ		TR				TR	SX	TR	SQ	

Figure 2-43
Grace's Aspectarian

**Figure 2-44: Janie's Chart
Some Aspect Lines**

If you don't choose to get your Aspects from a computer, you can fill in Aspectarians or draw colored or patterned lines directly onto your Charts to keep track of them. You also can list the Aspects at the bottom of the Chart by hand.

In that case, you may want to use the Astrological convention of denoting the Aspects according to the SPEEDS of the Planets or Points in-

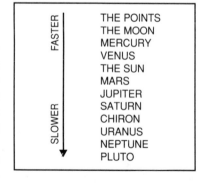

**Figure 2-45: Relative Speeds of
Planets and Points**

volved. Their speeds are determined by their orbits (Fig. 2-45). Note that all the Points are considered to be equal to each other and "faster" than the Planets.

Once you've determined which Planet or Point of each Aspect pair is the "faster" one, you can write out the Aspect according to the following formula:

FASTER PLANET/POINT   ASPECT SYMBOL   SLOWER PLANET

Some Aspects from Janie's Chart are shown in Figure 2-46.

CHIRON	QUINCUNX	NEPTUNE
⚷	⚻	♆
MOON	CONJUNCT	SUN
☽	☌	☉
MARS	TRINE	SATURN
♂	△	♄

Figure 2-46
How to Write Out the Aspects

SUMMARY

In this Chapter, I've discussed the technical factors involved in constructing or deciphering Astrology Charts. Remember that the fundamentals were outlined at the beginning of the Chapter. They're also summarized very briefly below. If you understand these terms, you can easily go on to the rest of the book, which focuses on Chart interpretation.

A BIRTH CHART: calculated from the BIRTH TIME, DATE, and PLACE

THE TWELVE HOUSES: usually unequal in size; correlate to Earth time and to location of birth

THE TWELVE SIGNS: always equal in size; correlate to sections of sky around the Earth; each Sign contains 30 Degrees; each Degree contains 60 Minutes

HOUSE CUSPS: where the Signs and Houses overlap; form the basic grid of an Astrological Chart

INTERCEPTED SIGNS: Signs wholly contained within their Houses

DUPLICATED SIGNS: Signs falling on more than one House Cusp

PLANETS: galactic bodies in the sky; placed in the Chart according to their positions in Signs and Houses

RETROGRADE PLANETS: Planets that appear to be moving backwards

PLANETARY RULERSHIPS OF SIGNS: special association between each Planet and Sign

THE FIVE POINTS: mathematically calculated; *not* objects in the sky

MIDHEAVEN: at the top of the Chart; the 10th House Cusp
ASCENDANT: at the left of the Chart; the 1st House Cusp
NORTH NODE and SOUTH NODE: always opposite each other
PART OF FORTUNE: combination of Sun, Moon, Ascendant

ASPECT: distance between any pair of Planets or Points

EXERCISES

For Understanding the Fundamentals

2-1   Find out when and where you were born: Time, Date, and Place.

2-2   Order your Chart from a computer service. You may get ONE FREE COPY of your Natal Chart if you mention this book and send your Birth Data with a self-addressed, stamped envelope to:

RAMP CREEK PUBLISHING, INC.
P.O. Box 3
Smithville, IN 47458-0003

2-3   Make or buy flash cards or quick-reference guides which will help you learn the symbols for the Signs, Planets, and Points.

2-4   Locate the following in your Chart:

THE HOUSES
THE SIGNS
HOUSE CUSPS
   (BY DEGREES/MINUTES)
INTERCEPTED SIGNS
DUPLICATED SIGNS
THE PLANETS
   (BY DEGREES / MINUTES)
RETROGRADE PLANETS
THE NODES OF THE MOON
   (DRAW IN THE SOUTH NODE)
THE PART OF FORTUNE

For Understanding the Details

2-5   Order several different Charts from a computer service and decipher them. Locate all the Chart features listed in Exercise 2-4.

2-6   Order one Chart from a computer service in several different House Systems. Notice the changes in:

INTERMEDIATE HOUSE CUSPS
INTERCEPTED AND DUPLICATED SIGNS
POSITIONS, BY HOUSE, OF THE PLANETS
   AND OTHER POINTS

Notice how the Horizon and Meridian lines stay the same giving the same Ascendant and Midheaven in all the Charts.

2-7   Copy some Charts onto Chart blanks so you can get used to writing the glyphs and positioning the Signs and Planets on the Charts. Try using Charts with, and without, pre-drawn House Cusps.

2-8   Figure out the Aspects for some of your Charts; compare them with those from a computer.

2-9   Experiment with drawing Aspect lines on Charts; contrast them with Aspectarians. Which are easier for you to read?

THREE

Astrology as an Interpretational System

Now it's time to interpret all the features we discussed in Chapter 2. In this Chapter, I'll present basic interpretations of the Houses, Signs, Planets, and Points. I'll explain the Signs on the House Cusps, Intercepted and Duplicated Signs, and the meaning of Retrograde Planets. I'll show you how to analyze Charts according to the positions of the Planets and Points, the Rulerships of the Planets, and the Aspects formed between pairs of Planets or Points.

As you read through this Chapter, I want you to be aware that *more than one interpretation is possible for every Astrological configuration.* All, one, or none of the ideas that I present may fit. Bear in mind that the key phrases are considerably expanded in Chapters 4 through 7. Also remember that, as you become more familiar with the basic Astrological themes, you'll probably find new ways to interpret them, ways that I haven't mentioned.

When interpreting any Chart, using my ideas or your own, it's important to build in what I call a FEEDBACK LOOP. By this I mean that, whenever you analyze a Chart at the theoretical level, you also test your theories against reality. Get feedback from yourself or the other person about the applicability of the concepts. Since there are many possibilities for each configuration, it's not a "mistake" if one doesn't fit. If your first explanation doesn't make sense, keep trying related interpretations until you find one that *does* fit. Remember that the Chart is only a map of the territory; what seems to be a small hill on the map may in reality be a large mountain. Your interpretation of the numbers and squiggles in a Chart may evolve and change when you move into the territory of "real" life. So, approach the following concepts with an open mind, utilize feedback, and discover how Astrology truly relates to the living of your life.

Throughout this Chapter, I'll be using Grace's and Janie's Charts as examples and presenting several of the possible interpretations for each Astrological concept. As I discuss the meaning of specific Chart features, I'll indicate which factor I'm describing by including its abbreviation in parentheses. In some cases, my ideas don't match reality, but I wanted to give you a range of options. In the examples in the second half of the Chapter, I've included feedback from Grace in the form of her reactions to my interpretations. By comparing my theories to her comments, you can begin to understand how to use the Feedback Loop. In addition to analyzing these examples, you'll probably want to apply the concepts to the Charts of people you know. So, as you read on, keep your Chart and any other Charts you may have in front of you.

As in Chapter 2, you can read about the interpretational dynamics of the Chart on two levels. If you read carefully through the section on the FUNDAMENTALS, you'll get a basic sense of how to interpret your Chart. From there, you can go on to the following Chapters. If you're interested in a more complicated level of Chart analysis, read the section on the DETAILS as well.

THE INTERPRETATIONAL FUNDAMENTALS

There are ten fundamentals for Chart Interpretation. Using these basics you can begin to get a feeling for the meaning of the symbols in your Chart.

1. The twelve HOUSES SET THE STAGE. They represent the places and situations in your life in which actions occur. They also represent specific issues and concerns about which you have feelings. They are static areas of the Chart; they *don't do* anything. They demonstrate WHERE, in what contexts, you live your life. Briefly, the twelve Houses are associated with the subjects shown in Figure 3-1.

```
 1 -  APPEARANCE, PERSONALITY

 2 -  MONEY, SELF-WORTH

 3 -  SIBLINGS, COMMUNITY

 4 -  HOME, MOTHER

 5 -  CHILDREN, CREATIVITY

 6 -  HEALTH, JOB

 7 -  BUSINESS OR EMOTIONAL PARTNER

 8 -  SEX, INTIMACY

 9 -  TRAVEL, HIGHER EDUCATION

10 -  CAREER, REPUTATION

11 -  FRIENDS, FUTURE VISIONS

12 -  SPIRITUALITY, ADDICTIONS
```

Figure 3-1
Key Words for the Houses

2. The twelve SIGNS SET THE MOOD. They represent your needs and attitudes. They symbolize your styles of processing, ways of being, approaches toward living. In and of themselves, they *don't do* anything, but they do indicate your propensity toward behaving in specific ways. They demonstrate HOW you go about living your life. Among other things, the twelve Signs symbolize the qualities shown in Figure 3-2.

ARIES:	INDEPENDENCE, ASSERTIVENESS, PUSHINESS
TAURUS:	PERSISTENCE, RELIABILITY, STUBBORNNESS
GEMINI:	COMMUNICATION, VERSATILITY, SUPERFICIALITY
CANCER:	NURTURANCE, SENSITIVITY, NEEDINESS
LEO:	EXPRESSIVENESS, SPONTANEITY, BOASTFULNESS
VIRGO:	ANALYSIS, DISCRIMINATION, CRITICALNESS
LIBRA:	COOPERATION, BALANCE, INDECISIVENESS
SCORPIO:	TRANSFORMATION, INTENSITY, COMPULSIVITY
SAGITTARIUS:	TEACHING, EXPANSION, PREACHINESS
CAPRICORN:	STRUCTURE, ORGANIZATION, RIGIDITY
AQUARIUS:	FUTURE VISION, ECCENTRICITY, UNRELIABILITY
PISCES:	FAITH, INTUITION, VICTIMIZATION

Figure 3-2
Key Words for the Signs

3. The SIGNS ON THE HOUSE CUSPS show our attitudes and needs with regard to each of the areas of life. They show how we would prefer to approach the concerns and issues contained in the Houses. They demonstrate our orientation toward all the factors in our lives. Each Sign can be used positively and negatively.

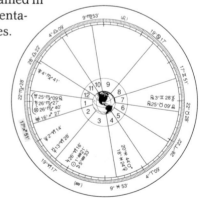

In Janie's Chart (Fig. 3-3), Sagittarius is on the 2nd House Cusp. This means that she would have an expansive (SG) attitude toward money (2). She might also teach others (SG) about self-esteem (2). She would have to be careful not to become preachy (SG) in an attempt to establish her own self-worth (2).

Figure 3-3: Janie's Chart

4. INTERCEPTED SIGNS indicate needs and attitudes that have not been appropriately supported by the family environment. If you have an Intercepted Sign, it means that the way your family utilized that Sign's energy is not the way that you want to use it. You've probably had to find other mentors that would show you how to express it. DUPLICATED SIGNS represent needs and energies that your family system has encouraged you to demonstrate in ways that feel right to you.

In Janie's Chart (Fig. 3-4), Aquarius is Intercepted in the 3rd House. This indicates that the ways that the rest of her family would have expressed eccentricity (AQ) in the local community (3) aren't the ways that she would choose.

Aries is Duplicated in Janie's Chart because it falls on both the 5th and 6th House Cusps (Fig. 3-4). This means that, by and large, the role models in her family demonstrate independence and assertiveness (AR) in ways that she finds comfortable.

Figure 3-4: Janie's Chart

5. The eleven PLANETS ARE THE ACTORS of the Chart. They actually have tasks or jobs to accomplish within your life. Each of them has a significant function or role to play. They can also operate dysfunctionally. The Planets *do act*. They demonstrate WHAT you do in your life. The functions (and dysfunctions) of the eleven Planets are briefly described in Figure 3-5.

6. RETROGRADE PLANETS act within themselves before they act in the world. Most of the time, they process their drives and apply their energies internally. Rather than using others' examples, they tend to reinvent the wheel, often coming up with creative new applications.

7. Each PLANET ACTS, IN THE MANNER OF ITS SIGN, REGARDING THE CONCERNS AND ISSUES OF ITS HOUSE. This is true for Retrograde Planets as well.

THE SUN:	TO SHINE, TO SHOW-OFF
THE MOON:	TO NURTURE, TO CLING
MERCURY:	TO COMMUNICATE, TO BABBLE
VENUS:	TO ESTABLISH VALUE, TO BE VAIN
MARS:	TO PURSUE DESIRES, TO BE INCONSIDERATE
JUPITER:	TO SEEK, TO OVERINDULGE
SATURN:	TO CONSTRUCT, TO DOMINATE
CHIRON:	TO FIX, TO CRITICIZE
URANUS:	TO INVENT, TO EXPLODE
NEPTUNE:	TO TRUST, TO CONFUSE
PLUTO:	TO USE POWER, TO DESTROY

Figure 3-5
Key Words for the Planets

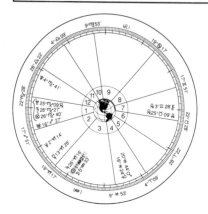

Figure 3-6: Janie's Chart

In Janie's Chart (Fig. 3-6), the Sun is in Aquarius in the 3rd House. This means that she would want to shine forth (SU) with future visions (AQ) for the community (3). She would also shine (SU) as the eccentric one (AQ) among her siblings (3). She'll need to be careful that she doesn't show off (SU) by being unreliable (AQ) in the community (3).

In Grace's Chart (Fig. 3-7), Retrograde Neptune is in Libra in the 1st House. So, she would want to be able to trust herself (R NE) to demonstrate cooperation (LI) in terms of her personality (1). She would also want to trust herself (R NE) to appear (1) balanced (LI). She would need to be careful that she didn't confuse herself (R NE) by being too indecisive (LI) in terms of her personality (1).

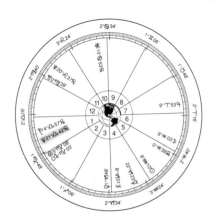

Figure 3-7: Grace's Chart

8. The FIVE POINTS represent specific resources and assets that can be activated within a person's life. They are defined according to the nature of their Signs and used in the contexts of their Houses. Figure 3-8 shows what they symbolize.

NORTH NODE:	EXPERIENCES THAT ARE NEW, CHALLENGING, OR INTIMIDATING
SOUTH NODE:	EXPERIENCES THAT ARE OLD, MASTERED, OR EXHAUSTING
PART OF FORTUNE:	EXPERIENCES THAT ARE MAGICALLY "BLESSED" OR WELL-INTEGRATED
MIDHEAVEN:	UNIVERSAL PLAN FOR THIS LIFE
ASCENDANT:	EARTHLY PLAN FOR THIS LIFE

Figure 3-8
Key Words for the Points

In Janie's Chart (Fig. 3-9), the South Node is in Scorpio in the 1st House. This means that she has already mastered (SN) the ability to express her personality (1) in an intense (SC) manner. She already knows (SN) how to be a transformative (SC) person (1). But, she'll have to be aware of her tendency to become exhausted (SN) by her compulsiveness (SC) with regard to her appearance (1).

Figure 3-9: Janie's Chart

9. The PLANETS ACT AS THE RULERS AND ACTIVATORS OF THEIR NATURAL SIGNS. They do create experiences and events in their natal Houses. But, their influence doesn't stop there. Everything a Planet does is felt in the House having that Planet's Natural Sign on the Cusp. The Planets, by their actions, also serve as keys that unlock their Natural Signs if those Signs are Intercepted.

In Grace's Chart (Fig. 3-10), Retrograde Pluto, in Leo in the 11th
House, Rules Scorpio which is on the
2nd House Cusp. So, every time she
uses her internal power (R PL) in a
spontaneous manner (LE) with her
friends (11), it has an impact on the
intensity (SC) with which she experiences her self-worth (2). On the other
hand, if she destroys herself (R PL)
by showing off (LE) with her friends
(11), she may harm her self-worth (2).
It may also cost her some money (2)!

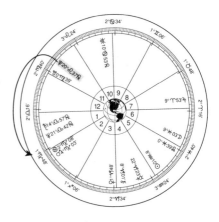

Figure 3-10: Grace's Chart

10. THE ASPECTS symbolize the style in which two Planets or Points
interact with each other. The key phrases for Aspect interpretation are included in Figure 3-11.

CONJUNCTION:	UNITE WITH EACH OTHER
SEMI-SEXTILE:	FINE-TUNE EACH OTHER
SEXTILE:	SUPPORT EACH OTHER
SQUARE:	MOTIVATE EACH OTHER
TRINE:	ENHANCE EACH OTHER
QUINCUNX:	REDIRECT EACH OTHER
OPPOSITION:	COUNTERACT EACH OTHER

Figure 3-11
The Aspects

In Janie's Chart (Fig. 3-12), Venus
and Mars are in Conjunction in
Pisces in the 4th House. Janie will
find that she can establish value (VE)
and pursue her desires (MA) simultaneously by acting on her intuition
(PI) at home (4).

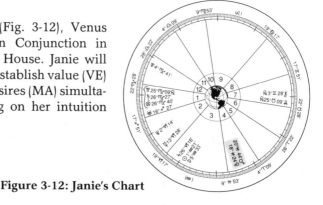

Figure 3-12: Janie's Chart

When she's using her intuitive abilities (PI) with her mother (4), she feels worthwhile (VE) and gets what she wants (MA). She could, however, become vain (VE) and inconsiderate (MA) as a result of feeling victimized (PI) at home (4).

These ten fundamental principles of interpretation may be all you need to get started in interpreting your Chart. The Fundamental Exercises at the end of the Chapter will help you evaluate your understanding of them. When you're ready, you can go on to Chapters 4 through 8. Or, if you want to understand the process of interpretation in more detail, read the rest of this Chapter.

THE INTERPRETATIONAL DETAILS

Effective Chart interpretation is based on a clear understanding of the three building blocks of Astrology: the Houses, Signs, and Planets. These key elements and the Points interact to set up the interpretational dynamics of an Astrological Chart. In this part of Chapter 3, I'll discuss the DETAILS of their individual roles, and their interpretation, by POSITION, RULERSHIP, and ASPECT.

The Houses

The HOUSES represent locations in which life activities occur. In a theater, the twelve Houses would be twelve stage sets such as the office, the home, the city street, or the mountain. In a home, they would be twelve rooms such as the kitchen, bedroom, utility room, or living room. In an Astrological Chart, the Houses represent departments or compartments of life. As such, they DON'T DO anything. They provide an environment in which events happen. They also symbolize the factors of life about which we have feelings, reactions, and attitudes. We may have negative or positive attitudes and feelings about the areas of life they represent but they, in themselves, are neutral in value.

For example, the 5th House, in representing children, provides a setting for child-related occurrences. It also names an area of life – children – about which we have attitudes and feelings. In neither case does the House dictate what the activities or reactions will be. The House just identifies that children are a department of life to be considered.

The 5th House is also associated with many other things. By expanding its meaning along with those of all the other Houses, any nameable area of life can be assigned to a House. Although these expanded interpretations are discussed in detail in Chapter 4, Figure 3-13 includes key words that describe the essential domains of each House.

FIRST HOUSE:	SELF AS IT'S PRESENTED TO THE WORLD, PERSONALITY, APPEARANCE, TITLE, ROLE, NAME
SECOND HOUSE:	MONEY, FINANCIAL AFFAIRS, POSSESSIONS, RESOURCES, SKILLS, VALUES, SELF-WORTH
THIRD HOUSE:	SIBLINGS, NEIGHBORS AND NEIGHBORHOOD, VEHICLES, LOCAL TRAVEL, COMMUNICATION, EARLY EDUCATION
FOURTH HOUSE:	HOME, ROOTS, CLAN, FOUNDATIONS, FAMILY, ETHNIC AND CULTURAL ORIGINS, MOTHER
FIFTH HOUSE:	CHILDREN, CREATIVITY, PLAY AND PLAYFULNESS, LEISURE ACTIVITIES, RECREATION, ROMANCE
SIXTH HOUSE:	DAILY ROUTINE, SCHEDULE, MAINTENANCE, TASKS, WORK, HEALTH, STRESS, PETS, CO-WORKERS
SEVENTH HOUSE:	"SIGNIFICANT OTHERS", PARTNERS, COOPERATION, ONE-TO-ONE RELATIONSHIPS, CLIENTS, NEGOTIATIONS
EIGHTH HOUSE:	INTIMACY, SEX, SHARED RESOURCES, COMMITMENT, JOINT MONEY, OTHER PEOPLE'S MONEY, INHERITANCES
NINTH HOUSE:	PHILOSOPHY, TEACHING, HIGHER EDUCATION, RELIGION, MENTORS, KNOWLEDGE, LONG-DISTANCE TRAVEL
TENTH HOUSE:	CAREER, VOCATION, PROFESSION, LIFE-WORK, REPUTATION, STATUS, FATHER
ELEVENTH HOUSE:	FRIENDS, PEOPLE OF LIKE MIND, GROUPS, ASSOCIATIONS, GOALS, FUTURE VISIONS, CAUSES
TWELFTH HOUSE:	SPIRITUALITY, ALTERED STATE EXPERIENCES, PLACES OF RETREAT, SUPPORT SYSTEMS, ADDICTIONS

Figure 3-13
Expanded Key Words for the Houses

The Signs

The SIGNS indicate the nature of our attitudes, feelings, needs, and re-actions within each area of life. In a theater, the Signs would be the lights, costuming, music, and props that support each production – the elements that set the tone or create an ambiance about a particular park or office scene. In a home, the Signs would be the furniture, colors, tidiness, sounds, and style of decor that make each room unique and reflective of the owner's personality. The Signs might even represent the owner's grooming and clothing. The Signs DON'T DO anything, but they do personalize the Houses, identifying the qualities that we want and need to experience in each area of life.

More specifically, the Sign on each of your House Cusps indicates the variety of ways, positive and negative, in which you could approach the activities of that House. For example, the Sign on your 7th House Cusp would show how you feel about partnering, what you need from a partner, and how you react to a partner. So, if you had Scorpio on that House Cusp, you would feel intense and passionate about your partners. You might also feel compulsive or violent toward them. At different times in your life, depending on your training and circumstances, you'll choose which characteristics of each Sign to express. But, most of your attitudes toward a given area of life will be related to the range of possibilities demonstrated by the Sign governing it in your Chart.

INTERCEPTED AND DUPLICATED SIGNS

If a Sign is Intercepted within a House, its needs still must be met by the activities related to that House. This can be difficult since the presence of an Interception indicates the absence of positive or appropriate role models with regard to the energy of the Intercepted Sign. In other words, if you have Capricorn Intercepted, the ways in which your family has expressed the qualities of responsibility and organization are not appropriate for you. You may simply be different from them. Or, they may have used the negative Capricorn traits by being domineering and rigid. It is often not until adulthood that we find mentors or inspirational friends who show us how to express our Interceptions in a healthy, productive, and personally comfortable manner. Until then, we tend to avoid acknowledging that we have the needs that are represented by the Interception. Or, we find ways to meet those needs in a less-than-ideal manner.

If a Sign is Duplicated on more than one House Cusp, you'll express its qualities in more than one area of life. Your family will have shown you ways of using that Sign's energy that seem to match your own values and style. You may even teach others how to use the energy of your Duplicated Sign. If you have Capricorn Duplicated, your family's way of being organized, structured, and ambitious suits you fine. You won't need to ask others how to be Capricornian; you'll be able to show them.

Figure 3-14 includes key words for all the Signs, including positive and negative interpretations for each one. These ideas are considerably expanded in Chapter 5.

ARIES:	INDEPENDENT, RISK-TAKING, PIONEERING, ASSERTIVE, ADVENTURESOME, PUSHY, AGGRESSIVE
TAURUS:	RESOURCEFUL, PRACTICAL, RESULT-ORIENTED, CAUTIOUS, LOYAL, SENSUOUS, STINGY, STUBBORN
GEMINI:	VERSATILE, ADAPTABLE, MENTALLY QUICK, CURIOUS, MULTI-DIMENSIONAL, UNDEPENDABLE, DISTRACTIBLE
CANCER:	EMOTIONAL, COMFORTING, NURTURING, "BELONGED," FEARFUL OF BEING ABANDONED, SMOTHERING, CLINGY
LEO:	SHINING, SELF-EXPRESSIVE, GENEROUS, CELEBRATORY, ENTHUSIATIC, ATTENTION-GETTING, BOASTFUL
VIRGO:	ANALYTICAL, PROBLEM-SOLVING, SERVICE-ORIENTED, PRECISE, DISCRIMINATING, CRITICAL, FUSSY
LIBRA:	COOPERATIVE, SHARING, PARTNERED, ARTISTIC, FAIR, OTHER-ORIENTED, DIPLOMATIC, INDECISIVE, VAIN
SCORPIO:	INTENSE, EMOTIONALLY POWERFUL, PASSIONATE, COMMITTED, DEEP, PROTECTIVE, PENETRATING, COMPULSIVE, VIOLENT
SAGITTARIUS:	PHILOSOPHICAL, TEACHER-LIKE, EXPANSIVE, OPTIMISTIC, SELF-INDULGENT, PREACHY
CAPRICORN:	ORGANIZED, RESPONSIBLE, STRUCTURING, AMBITIOUS, REALISTIC, AUTHORITATIVE, BOUNDARY-SETTING, DOMINEERING, RIGID
AQUARIUS:	INVENTIVE, NON-CONFORMING, VISIONARY, GROUP-CONSCIOUS, FUTURE-ORIENTED, UTOPIAN, INAPPROPRIATE, DISRUPTIVE
PISCES:	PSYCHIC, SENSITIVE, SPIRITUAL, COMPASSIONATE, HEALING, RESCUING, IMAGINATIVE, INTUITIVE, MERGING, VICTIMIZED, ADDICTIVE

Figure 3-14
Expanded Key Words for the Signs

The Planets

The PLANETS represent the active forces within the Chart; they are the symbols of conscious and unconscious purposefulness. Combined, they interact to reflect all of our drives and behavior. They are similar to sentient beings or sub-personalities within us. In the theater, they are the

THE SUN:	TO ILLUMINATE, MAXIMIZE PERSONAL POTENTIAL DISCOVER SELF, DEMONSTRATE ESSENTIAL SELF, EXPRESS LIFE FORCE, FEEL ALIVE; TO BOAST OR SHOW-OFF
THE SUN NEVER RETROGRADES	
THE MOON:	TO USE INSTINCTIVE HABIT PATTERNS, CREATE SECURITY, EXPRESS EMPATHY, SEEK AND GIVE NURTURANCE, ESTABLISH BELONGINGNESS; TO CLING OR DEMONSTRATE NEEDINESS
THE MOON NEVER RETROGRADES	
MERCURY:	TO THINK, COMMUNICATE, PURSUE STIMULATION, SEEK VARIETY, NETWORK, COMBINE IDEAS, EXCHANGE GOODS AND INFORMATION; TO SCATTER ENERGY OR COMMUNICATE MEANINGLESSLY
MERCURY RETROGRADE:	TO USE INDIVIDUALIZED THOUGHT PROCESSES, SEEK STIMULATION WITHIN OWN MIND; TO THINK UNCLEARLY OR ACT MENTALLY UNCERTAIN
VENUS:	TO FIND WORTHWHILENESS, EXPRESS VALUES, MAGNETICALLY ATTRACT, COOPERATE, SHARE, CREATE HARMONY AND BEAUTY, SYMBOLIZE "FEMALE" ENERGY OR QUALITIES; TO DEMONSTRATE VANITY ABOUT ABILITIES OR POSSESSIONS
VENUS RETROGRADE:	TO FIND AND DEMONSTRATE INNER VALUES, DISCOVER SELF-LOVE, EXPERIENCE PERSONAL HARMONY; TO ACT "STUCK-UP" OR NARCISSISTIC
MARS:	TO PURSUE PERSONAL DESIRES, ACT ON SEXUAL DRIVES, ASSERT THE SELF, INITIATE, PIONEER, SEEK NEW BEGINNINGS, TAKE RISKS, SYMBOLIZE "MALE" ENERGY OR QUALITIES; TO ACT VIOLENTLY OR DEMONSTRATE PUSHINESS
MARS RETROGRADE:	TO PURSUE INNER DESIRES, CONFRONT THE SELF, TAKE PSYCHOLOGICAL OR SPIRITUAL RISKS; TO HURT THE SELF OR EXPRESS ANGER TOWARD THE SELF
JUPITER:	TO EXPAND HORIZONS, GET "MORE", TEACH, SEEK FREEDOM, PREACH, PHILOSOPHIZE, DISSEMINATE KNOWLEDGE; TO ACT "PREACHY" OR DOGMATIC

Figure 3-15A
Expanded Key Words for the Planets

JUPITER RETROGRADE:	TO EXPAND THE INNER WORLD, TEACH THE SELF, CONTEMPLATE; TO DEMONSTRATE UNWILLINGNESS TO LEARN FROM OTHERS
SATURN:	TO ORGANIZE, DISCIPLINE, EXPRESS AUTHORITY, CONTROL OR RESTRICT, PURSUE AMBITIONS, SET LIMITS AND BOUNDARIES, TAKE RESPONSIBILITY; TO DOMINATE OR ACT "BOSSY"
SATURN RETROGRADE:	TO ORGANIZE THE SELF, DISCOVER SELF-DISCIPLINE, ESTABLISH INTERNAL BOUNDARIES, BECOME OWN AUTHORITY; TO RESTRICT OR LIMIT THE SELF
CHIRON:	TO SOLVE PROBLEMS, FIX THINGS, MANIFEST THE IDEAL VISION WITHIN REALITY, GIVE CONSTRUCTIVE FEEDBACK, ACHIEVE PERFECTION, ANALYZE; TO CRITICIZE OR NEGATE
CHIRON RETROGRADE:	TO MEND THE SELF, TO EMBODY THE IDEAL WITHIN THE SELF, LIVE OUT THE SOLUTION, EXAMINE THE SELF; TO BE SELF-CRITICAL OR SELF-NEGATING
URANUS:	TO MOVE TOWARD FUTURE VISION, BREAK SOCIAL PATTERNS, FIND INNOVATIVE NEW DIRECTIONS, CON SIDER THE HIGHEST GOOD OF THE HIGHEST NUMBER; TO REBEL OR EXPLODE
URANUS RETROGRADE:	TO EMBODY ECCENTRICITY, BREAK OWN PATTERNS, CHANGE THE SELF, EXHIBIT RADICAL URGES; TO SHAT-TER THE SELF
NEPTUNE	TO DEMONSTRATE INTUITION, EXPRESS COMPASSION, HAVE FAITH, MERGE WITH OTHERS, CREATE ALTERED STATES, DEMONSTRATE SPIRITUAL VALUES, EXPERIENCE TRUST; TO ACT ADDICTIVELY OR DECEPTIVELY
NEPTUNE RETROGRADE:	TO SEEK PERSONAL SPIRITUAL EXPERIENCE, LIVE IN AN INNER WORLD, ALTER INTERNAL EMOTIONAL STATE; TO BE CONFUSED OR FEARFUL
PLUTO:	TO TRANSFORM THROUGH DEATH AND/OR REBIRTH, REGENERATE, TRIGGER POWERFUL CYCLES OF CHANGE; TO DESTROY OR ANNIHILATE
PLUTO RETROGRADE:	TO DEMONSTRATE PERSONAL TRANSFORMATION, EXPERIENCE CYCLES OF METAMORPHOSIS, RESPOND TO A POWERFUL INNER CALLING; TO ACT COMPULSIVELY OR SELF-DESTRUCTIVELY

Figure 3-15B
Expanded Key Words for the Planets

actors, bringing the stage to life; in a home, they are the people who live, play, and work there. In our Astrology Charts, the Planets are the DOERS. Each one attempts to perform its function as best it can in the life of its person.

RETROGRADE PLANETS

The RETROGRADE PLANETS have the same function as the Direct Planets; they, too, are actors in the Chart. However, their action takes a unique form. Instead of demonstrating themselves in the world, simply and directly, the Retrogrades turn inward and express themselves within us. If you have a Retrograde, you'll understand that Planet's purpose from the inside out. You'll undoubtedly come up with innovative insights and applications for using this Planet's energy. While your perspective on it may be refreshing to others, your own experience, relative to the Retrograde Planet, may be that of the outsider. You could feel that you don't know the rules of the game and have to invent your own.

Figure 3-15 contains key words that describe the nature, purpose, and task of each Planet. I've included some of the functional and dysfunctional applications so that you can note the range of interpretation that's possible. And, in addition to the basic meaning of each Planet, I've included the Retrograde adaptations. Notice that, with minor modifications, the Retrograde and Direct interpretations can be interchanged with each other. This is appropriate because the distinction between them is subtle. As you're reading through each Planet's interpretation, take a moment to compare it to that of the Sign it Rules. You'll find that the Planet represents the action that logically meets the needs of its Natural Sign. Chapter 6 covers the Planets in more detail.

The Points

The NODES OF THE MOON and the PART OF FORTUNE are similar to Planets in that they perform their functions according to the nature of their Signs within the territory of their Houses. However, they aren't quite as active as the Planets. They are the supporting actors in the theater, and the resourceful friends and relatives who come to visit the home.

The MIDHEAVEN and the ASCENDANT, on the other hand, are less active because they are usually Signs on House Cusps, not locations within Houses. Although they don't perform functions, they do symbolize, by Sign and House, something about the environment into which you've been born. In a theatrical production, they would be especially significant props, inanimate objects on the stage that symbolize the most important themes of the play. In a home, the Midheaven and Ascendant would be specific and noticeable pieces of art or furniture that especially reflect the owner's identity.

Through understanding and interpreting all of these five Points, you can round out your basic analysis of your Natal Chart. Figure 3-16 shows the meaning of each of the Points. They are explained further in Chapter 6.

THE NORTH NODE:	POINT OF CHALLENGE, GROWTH, LEARNING, EXCITE-MENT, NEW BEGINNINGS, STIMULATION, ACQUIRING, CLAIMING, THREAT, FEAR, OR INSECURITY
THE SOUTH NODE:	POINT OF REPETITION, MASTERY, SKILL, TEACHING, FAMILIAR PATTERNS, LETTING GO, RELEASING, EXHAUSTION, LOSS, FATIGUE, OR BOREDOM
THE PART OF FORTUNE:	POINT OF PERSONAL INTEGRATION, PERSONAL POWER, SELF-AWARENESS, WHOLENESS, "MAGICAL" BLESSINGS, SELF-SATISFACTION, OR SMUGNESS
THE MIDHEAVEN:	POINT OF UNIVERSAL DESTINY, LIFE PURPOSE, "DIVINE" MISSION, LIFE MEANING, CONTRIBUTION, VOCATION, OR IMPERSONAL PARTICIPATION IN THE GRAND SCHEME OF THINGS
THE ASCENDANT:	POINT OF HUMAN IDENTITY, PERSONALITY, INDIVID-UAL NAMING, ROLE IN EARTHLY CONTEXT, PARTICI-PATION IN EVERYDAY REALITY, OR IMMERSION IN PERSONAL POINT OF VIEW

Figure 3-16
Expanded Key Words for the Points

The Aspects

The ASPECTS between the Planets and Points are another group of important factors that aid in Chart interpretation. Since they represent interactive patterns and processes and are not actually located in the Chart like the Houses, Signs, Planets, and Points, you have to find them before you can interpret them. If you list your Aspects by one of the means described in Chapter 2, you'll find that you can move into interpreting them quite comfortably. Each Aspect has its own style of linking or combining the features that it connects. Figure 3-17 contains the key words that describe the Aspect processes.

CONJUNCTION:	UNITING, WORKING TOGETHER, SHARING A PERSPECTIVE, JOINING, UNIFYING, CONSUMING, SMOTHERING
SEMI-SEXTILE:	FINE-TUNING, SUBTLY ADAPTING, GENTLY REORIENTLING, SLIGHTLY MODIFYING, DISTURBING, IRRITATING, ANNOYING
SEXTILE:	SUPPORTING, FINDING RESOURCES, REINFORCING, HELPING, INTERVENING, MEDDLING, INTRUDING
SQUARE:	MOTIVATING, CHALLENGING, PRESSURING, CONFRONTING, STIMULATING CREATIVE FRICTION, CATALYZING, CLASHING
TRINE:	ENHANCING, FLOWING, COMBINING, MINGLING, POOLING SKILLS, TAKING FOR GRANTED, LAZILY EMPLOYING
QUINCUNX:	REDIRECTING, REROUTING, DETOURING, SURPRISING, STARTLING, DIVERTING, DIVORCING, JERKING AROUND
OPPOSITION:	COUNTERACTING, CONTRADICTING, LENDING PERSPECTIVE, JUGGLING, COLLABORATING, BALANCING, ANTAGONIZING

Figure 3-17
Expanded Key Words for the Aspects

Applying the Interpretations

Using just the key phrases for the Houses, Signs, Planets, Points, and Aspects that are in Figures 3-13 through 3-17, you can move much further into Chart interpretation. You'll do this by combining the meanings of these building blocks in three important ways: You can interpret your Chart by POSITION, RULERSHIP, and ASPECT.

INTERPRETING BY POSITION

One way of interpreting your Chart is to figure out your needs and attitudes with regard to each area of life. You can do this by locating the Position of each House Cusp within its Sign and describing the nature of that Sign in the context of that House. You can also interpret the Planets and Points by analyzing what they mean according to their Sign and House positions. In the following sections, I'll discuss ways to approach these kinds of interpretations.

The Signs on (or in) the Houses

By simply describing the Signs on the House Cusps, using the key words in Figures 3-13 and 3-14, it's possible to begin detailed Chart interpretation. Remember that the Signs reflect attitudes, needs, and reactions with regard to the kinds of events that occur in their Houses. In essence,

THE SIGN SHOWS THE STYLE IN WHICH
THE EVENTS, ISSUES, AND CONCERNS OF ITS HOUSE
ARE APPROACHED.

When interpreting the Signs on House Cusps you can go House by House around the Chart, using the procedure that follows:

Signs On (Or In) Houses Interpretation Sequence

1. Identify the life issues represented by the House

2. Identify the nature of the Sign on the Cusp (or Intercepted in) the House

3. Use one of these formulae to interpret the combination:

"I need [*nature of the Sign*] with regard to
[*concern of the House*]."

OR

"I approach [*concern of the House*] with a
[*nature of the Sign*] attitude."

OR

"When events related to [*concern of the House*] happen,
I tend to react in a [nature of the Sign] way."

As an example, I've done a partial interpretation of Grace's Chart (Fig. 3-18), using the key words for Signs and Houses. I began by theorizing about her possible orientation (Sign) to each area of life (House). In keeping with my choice centered philosophy, I created three different interpretational possibilities for each Sign and House combination. Then, I interviewed her to find out how she actually experiences herself. In some cases, my interpretations matched her life experiences; in others, one or two of them didn't match. Both my theory and the results of her feedback are included in the analysis that follows.

Key Word Analysis of Signs on Cusps

Figure 3-18: Grace's Chart

Libra on the 1st House Cusp:

- cooperative in persona
- diplomatic in presentation of self
- can be vain about personal appearance

Grace commented that she is very conscious of her appearance, wanting to appear attractive at all times. She also thinks that she comes across to others as being quite cooperative and diplomatic although she doesn't always feel that way inside.

Scorpio on the 2nd House Cusp:

- intense about self-worth
- protective of personal possessions
- can be compulsive about money

Grace feels that money-making is her passion. She is intensely involved in figuring out ways to have a little money transform into a lot more – and she's good at it. Actually, she doesn't think it's compulsive, it's just a personal talent. She *is* protective of her possessions and takes especially good care of them.

Sagittarius on the 3rd House Cusp:

- philosophical about community
- expansive about local travel experiences
- can be preachy toward siblings

Grace knows that, as the oldest of four children, she is extremely "preachy" toward her sisters and brother. She has strong philosophical viewpoints and is quite willing to share them within her community. And, she loves to take day-trips around her neighborhood and region. One of her favorite activities is to take off in her car for a few hours or a weekend.

CAPRICORN ON THE 4TH HOUSE CUSP:

- responsible for mother
- organized at home
- can be rigid with regard to family and clan

Grace has always felt somewhat responsible for her mother's emotional stability. Although her mom is perfectly capable of functioning well in the world, Grace has felt like the "adult" in that relationship. She likes her home to be orderly, with cleared surfaces and simple furniture. She's very committed to her family and her clan to the point of protecting them from outside harm.

AQUARIUS ON THE 5TH HOUSE CUSP:

- visionary with regard to plans for children
- nonconforming about romantic preferences
- can be disruptive in leisure activities

Grace laughed about the disruptiveness in leisure activities; she said that she's always been the one to "quit playing" if she got bored or felt inspired to do something else. Most of her life she's worked with children, helping those that are developmentally delayed and those that have been abused or neglected to function more effectively in the world. Romantically speaking, she likes unusual people.

PISCES ON THE 6TH HOUSE CUSP:

- intuitive about co-workers
- compassionate toward pets
- can be addictive in terms of health

Grace has worked hard on changing her addictions. Alcohol was the substance she abused the most. However, after she quit drinking, she's had to face her twin addictions to caffeine and nicotine. When working in an office or business setting, she's always been intuitively aware of her co-workers' feelings and needs. And, she has several pets, all of whom she has rescued from death's door.

ARIES ON THE 7TH HOUSE CUSP:

- risk-taking with emotional partners
- independent with business partners
- can be pushy in negotiations

Grace once stayed at a car dealership until 1:00 A.M. negotiating a deal. She enjoyed every minute of it, and she did get a good deal, although she had to be very assertive (but not pushy). She's so independent with business partners that she's seldom had any. With her life-mate, she supports a balance of cooperation (Libra on the 1st) and personal independence.

TAURUS ON THE 8TH HOUSE CUSP:

- sensuous in sex
- cautious in intimacy
- can be stubborn regarding the use of shared money

Grace loves to manage the money in her relationship. She's extremely cautious and conscientious about how the money is used — yes, even to the point of being stubborn in wanting to approve her partner's spending. She isn't especially proud of that tendency but admits it's there. On the other hand, she and her partner do have a healthy savings account to show for her efforts. Sexually, she says that she is very sensuous and "touch-oriented." She doesn't really feel that she's cautious about becoming intimate, but she is definitely cautious about making long-term intimate commitments.

GEMINI ON THE 9TH HOUSE CUSP:

- curious about philosophy
- versatile regarding long-distance travel
- can be distractible in terms of higher education

Grace majored in five different areas before finishing her B.S. (in five years). Since leaving school, she has studied law and real estate; she has also paid for, but never finished, specialized courses in taxes, stocks, kayaking, etc., etc., etc. She's fascinated by various world philosophies. Although she's never done much long-distance traveling, she plans to begin soon. And, she expects to enjoy it.

CANCER ON THE 10TH HOUSE CUSP:

- nurturing within profession
- emotional regarding father
- can cling to reputation

Grace does worry about what people will think of her, if it will affect her career, her professional reputation, or her money-making potential. At a personal level, she doesn't really care if others find her outrageous (Aquarius Sun). She says that she does have strong feelings about her father.

LEO ON THE 11TH HOUSE CUSP:

- enthusiastic about future visions
- generous about causes
- can be boastful about friends

Grace loves to have famous friends. But, even more, she wants to be special to her friends (also Leo). She doesn't really need to show off for them, but she wants to know that she's a shining star in their lives. She contributes money and energy quite willingly to the causes that are important to her. And, she always has wonderful plans and visions for the future, most of which come true.

VIRGO ON THE 12TH HOUSE CUSP:

- analytical about spirituality
- discriminating about altered-state experiences
- can be critical of support systems

Grace's spirituality is very practical. She utilizes her connection to the "cosmos" as long as it works for her. If spiritual concepts get too vague and confusing, she'll let them go. They must be pretty practical and concrete for her. She was very discriminating about the altered state achieved by drinking: she preferred certain beers and the best quality of Scotch! She's extremely critical of the social service system and the way that it does (or doesn't) support its dependents.

The Planets in Signs and Houses

As each Planet attempts to express its pure self, it actually adapts its expression according to its placement within a Sign and a House. The same actor, saying the same lines, will seem different if her accent, tonality, costume, lighting, and setting are changed. The same homeowner will be perceived in varying ways, depending on which room she's in, what she's saying or what she's wearing. Similarly, the same Planet, demonstrating itself in different Charts, will change HOW, by Sign, and WHERE, by House, it functions. A basic formula for understanding the Planet–Sign–House interplay is:

EACH PLANET ACTS, FULFULLING ITS FUNCTIONS,

IN THE MANNER AND STYLE OF ITS SIGN

REGARDING THE ISSUES AND CONCERNS OF ITS HOUSE.

For example, while Mars, in its essence, represents the force of initiative and the pursuit of personal desire, its expression will change in the following circumstances:

MARS IN LIBRA IN THE 3RD HOUSE: initiates cooperation with siblings

MARS IN LIBRA IN THE 10TH HOUSE: initiates cooperation in career

MARS IN SCORPIO IN THE 12TH HOUSE: desires depth in spirituality

MARS IN SCORPIO IN THE 8TH HOUSE: desires depth in intimacy

By taking the key words of the Planets and combining them with those of the Signs and Houses according to the sequence of steps that follows, you can expand your basic interpretations of a Chart.

Planet–Sign–House Interpretation Sequence

1. Identify the purpose or function of the Planet

2. Identify the nature of the Planet's Sign

3. Identify the concerns of the Planet's House

4. Say something such as:

   "I act on my urge to [*function of the Planet*], in a [*nature of the Sign*] manner or style, with regard to [*concerns of the House*]."

Here is a further analysis of Grace's Chart (Fig. 3-19), using the Planets, Signs, and Houses. Again, I've included several interpretations for each configuration as well as Grace's reactions to my theorizing.

Key Word Analysis of Planets in Signs and Houses

Figure 3-19: Grace's Chart

THE SUN IN AQUARIUS IN THE 5TH HOUSE:

- illuminates visionary themes with regard to children
- maximizes personal potential through nonconforming leisure activities
- can express essential self by disrupting recreational activities

Grace's visions with regard to children are a strong part of her life. She feels that her own identity is well expressed when she's planning the "best" way to care for kids. Her own leisure activities are nonconforming in that she often identifies unusual activities as "play." Instead of going to the theater, she might prefer to clean the gutters or take the trash to the dump. She also enjoys participating in unique activities with others. And, when she gets bored and moves on, it's always for the purpose of expressing and entertaining herself.

THE MOON IN PISCES IN THE 6TH HOUSE:

- creates emotional security through approaching daily tasks intuitively
- establishes belongingness by being compassionate with co-workers
- can have emotional habits relating to victimization that affect health

Grace feels that she is most emotionally stable and secure when she is able to deal with her daily tasks on a moment-by-moment basis. She isn't fond of deadlines or strict schedules. Instead, she likes to do what she feels like doing, when she intuitively feels like it. By following this approach, she does tend to accomplish what needs to be done and still feel good. She is almost always compassionate toward others and does create a sense of belonging for herself by attending to their needs. Unfortunately, she sometimes ignores herself to the point where she feels taken for granted. If she forgets to attend to herself long enough, she ends up feeling martyr-ish or getting sick.

MERCURY IN CAPRICORN IN THE 4TH HOUSE:

- thinks practically about mother
- seeks variety through organizing the home
- can communicate in a rigid way with family

Grace loves to structure her home. She's always thinking of new ways to re-organize it so that it will function more efficiently. Rather than thinking practically about her mother, she thinks her mother is practical. She would characterize her communication with her family as direct and somewhat abrupt (also Capricorn attributes), not really rigid and unbending.

VENUS IN CAPRICORN IN THE 3RD HOUSE:

- magnetically attracts neighbors through organizing
- cooperates by being responsible for women in the community
- can express values by being domineering with siblings

Grace has always been one to value positive interactions with her neighbors. They tend to like her and her sense of responsibility within the neighborhood. She doesn't especially organize her neighbors, but she does work with them on a practical level, trading off the use of tools, truck, and so forth. She is also willing to take responsibility for people, especially women, in the community who might need help getting to the store, mowing their lawns, or taking trash to the dump. And, she definitely tends to present her own values when she's telling her siblings how she thinks they ought to run their lives!

MARS IN SCORPIO IN THE 2ND HOUSE

- pursues passionate personal interest in financial affairs
- initiates protective actions regarding personal possessions
- can assert the self by being compulsive about money

Grace's passionate interest in her own financial affairs is quite phenomenal. She's been known to spend hours figuring and refiguring various financial plans and directions, with total joy and concentration. To others this may seem compulsive, but to Grace, it's fun. She sometimes chooses not to loan out her possessions (even though she wants to support her friends and neighbors) because she worries about getting them back damaged.

JUPITER IN ARIES IN THE 7TH HOUSE:

- expands horizons through independence in business partnerships
- teaches adventurousness to emotional partners
- can get "more" by being pushy in negotiations

Grace senses that she can get much further by being independent of business partnerships. In fact, in the instances where she's come close to forming partnerships, she's avoided them at the last minute because she realized that she could do more on her own. She encourages adventurousness and risk-taking in her partner. She always feels that if she's assertive in negotiations, she'll get a better deal, but she doesn't think she's really obnoxious or pushy.

RETROGRADE SATURN IN LIBRA IN THE 1ST HOUSE:

- disciplines self to be diplomatic in personality
- establishes personal responsibility by presenting the self as one who shares
- can organize the self by being vain about appearance

Grace sometimes has to stop herself from blurting out what she thinks in a way that would be startling or offensive to someone else. Over the years, she's schooled herself to stop and consider the impact of her words and behavior before she acts. She likes the part of her that's willing to share, feeling that it's a part of her responsible self-image. Because she cares about her personal appearance, she's learned how to organize her closet and be responsible about the care of her clothing.

CHIRON IN CAPRICORN IN THE 4TH HOUSE:

- solves problems for mother in a practical manner
- manifests ideal visions into reality by organizing the family
- can "fix" the home in a domineering way

Grace feels that there's no doubt about her role in the family. She's an organizer and a "make-it-happen" person. While she does move in and take charge, sometimes in a domineering way, she is also one who gets things done. Her family relies on her to create order out of chaos. She also helps them take their dreams and visions and bring them into reality.

RETROGRADE URANUS IN CANCER IN THE 10TH HOUSE:

- moves toward personal future through a nurturing profession
- breaks social patterns by being comforting within career
- embodies rebellion by clinging to social status

Grace has definitely had nurturing careers. In taking care of children and adults from "special" populations, she's worked toward creating a better society for them and for all of us. When working in an institutional setting, however, she was unable to totally follow the rules of protocol. She found herself befriending and comforting people she liked whether or not they were her professional peers. She doesn't feel that she really clings to social status even though she does act out her non-conformity within society.

RETROGRADE NEPTUNE IN LIBRA IN THE 11TH HOUSE:

- alters internal awareness through appearing as a diplomatic person
- seeks personal spiritual experience through partnering role
- can stay in inner world by indecisively presenting self to the world

Grace has such a strong urge to present herself diplomatically that she often changes her own internal experience, reevaluating what she thinks and feels, in order to remain cooperative in her interactions with others. If she can't fully change herself so that she feels comfortable cooperating, she sends confused and mixed signals until she decides what she wants. This means that she's still processing her feelings internally. When she's clear about her direction on the inside, she sends clear messages on the outside.

RETROGRADE PLUTO IN LEO IN THE 11TH HOUSE:

- experiences personal transformation through being self-expressive in groups

- experiences cycles of change through enthusiasm about future visions
- can transform self by being attention-getting with friends

Grace doesn't like to intrude on her friends by expressing too much vulnerability to them. On the other hand, when she is willing to put her feelings and experiences into the spotlight, she finds that her friends do pay attention. And, most of the time, the result is positive. She gains personal awareness or transforms a part of herself as a result of their support. When she gets excited about a particular plan or vision for the future, she also becomes willing to change her self and her life in order to accommodate that future.

The Points in Signs and Houses

Like the Planets, the Points express themselves by performing their functions according to their Sign and House positions. As supporting actors and props, they take on varying significance according to their costuming, design, or position on stage. The formula for interpreting the Points is similar to that for the Planets:

EACH POINT DEMONSTRATES ITS PURPOSE
ACCORDING TO THE NATURE OF ITS SIGN
REGARDING THE ISSUES AND CONCERNS OF ITS HOUSE.

By using the key words from Figures 3-13, 3-14, and 3-16 in the following sequence, you can add Point interpretation to your understanding of your Chart.

Point–Sign–House Interpretation Sequence

1. Identify the purpose or function of the Point

2. Identify the nature of the Point's Sign

3. Identify the concerns of the Point's House

4. Say something such as:

   "In my desire to [*nature of the Point*], I behave in a [*nature of the Sign*] manner, with regard to [*concerns of the House*]".

Examples from Grace's Chart (Fig. 3-20) follow.

Key Word Analysis of the Points

Figure 3-20: Grace's Chart

NORTH NODE IN PISCES IN THE 5TH HOUSE:

- feels excitement and challenge when acquiring skills that will allow her to heal children compassionately
- experiences stimulation and growth when being self-expressive psychically
- feels insecure about how truly to express and utilize her intuition in terms of her creativity

Grace says that she had incredible mentors in college who helped her acquire exquisite therapeutic skills. Through these teachers, she discovered how to be truly compassionate and caring toward children; she learned how to help heal them. At this time, she has friends who also encourage her to use her natural psychic talents. She knows that she has intuitive abilities, but she isn't always sure what to do with them. Most of her life, she just didn't tell anyone what she sensed. Now nearing forty, she's finding ways to validate her sixth sense.

SOUTH NODE IN VIRGO IN THE 11TH HOUSE:

- feels skillful at critiquing and problem-solving her friends' problems
- has a familiar pattern of serving "the cause" by sharing her analytical skills
- feels exhausted and bored when having to attend to all the details in a group

Grace's childhood experiences taught her to be critical and analytical with regard to problems. She's extremely familiar with the process of "fixing" things for other people at a very practical level. Many friends come to her for advice and feedback, and she knows what to tell them to do. She sometimes gets impatient with them, wondering why they keep reenacting the same dilemmas. The solutions seem obvious to her. Whenever she's involved with a "cause" that matters, she's able to commit a tremendous amount of time and energy doing whatever needs to be done. She does reach a point of frustration and boredom, however, if her tasks within a group are too routinized.

PART OF FORTUNE IN SCORPIO IN THE 2RD HOUSE:

- feels whole and personally integrated when intensely and deeply aware of self-worth
- is magically blessed when going through financial transformations
- can become compulsively smug and self-satisfied about possessions

Grace says that the most obvious example of this is her talent for making money. Her ideas and plans do seem "magically blessed." She has repeatedly transformed her financial situation, always for the better. She senses that when she feels badly about her worth, she feels less integrated. When she feels fully aware of her personal worth, she does feel more whole. Sometimes, she can be smug about her possessions: she loves them!

THE MIDHEAVEN IN CANCER ON THE 10TH HOUSE CUSP:

- senses that her "destiny" involves comforting others
- feels that she gains meaning in her life through being nurturing of others
- can get wrapped up in grand schemes that smother her

Grace feels somewhat driven to take care of others. She senses at a very deep level that her life purpose involves nurturance. In fact, she can get so involved in supporting the whole world that she loses sight of her own needs. In that case, she can end up overwhelmed by the enormity of the task she's chosen.

THE ASCENDANT IN LIBRA ON THE 1ST HOUSE CUSP:

- identifies herself as a diplomatic person
- feels that her role in life involves cooperation and fairness
- becomes immersed in indecision when she loses sight of the larger picture

Grace says that she has always seen herself as a negotiator and peacemaker. She feels that she interacts with others by trying to exemplify the qualities of cooperation and fairness. On occasion, she can be so invested in being fair to everyone that she has trouble making decisions. In those instances, she has to remind herself of the broader perspective instead of getting lost in her role as diplomat.

INTERPRETING BY RULERSHIP

In terms of interpretation, the Natural Planet-to-Sign associations are especially critical, perhaps the most critical of all Astrological connections. This is because THE PLANETS ARE THE ACTIVATORS OF THEIR NATURAL SIGNS. By extension, they also affect the HOUSES HAVING THOSE SIGNS ON THEIR CUSPS. As the moving forces in the Chart, the Planets actively meet the needs of their Natural Signs. Wherever they are located in the Chart, whatever they do, the Planets function as messengers or emissaries of these home Signs, creating experiences that will fulfill them. Therefore, a Planet's action is not only felt in its House, it's also felt in the House Ruled by its Natural Sign.

For example, anything that Mars does, anywhere in the Chart, will be felt in Mars's Natal House AND in the House that has Aries on the Cusp (or Intercepted within it). Anything that the Moon does will be felt in its Natal House AND in the House that has Cancer on the Cusp (or Intercepted within it). The following formula helps explain how to interpret the Planets as Rulers of Signs.

EACH PLANET ACCOMPLISHES ITS TASKS,

ACTIVATING THE SIGN IT RULES,

AND AFFECTING THE CONCERNS AND ISSUES OF THAT SIGN'S HOUSE.

By using the Rulerships and the key words describing the Planets, Signs, and Houses according to the sequence that follows, you can add to your Chart interpretation.

Planets As Rulers Interpretation Sequence

1. Identify the Sign Ruled by the Planet

2. Identify the location of that Sign in the Chart on (or in) a House

3. Identify the needs and attitudes of that Sign with regard to the concerns of its House

4. Identify how the Planet acts in its own Sign and House

5. Say something such as:

    "As I act on my urge to [*function of the Planet*], in a [*nature of the Planet's own Sign*] manner or style, with regard to [*concerns of the Planet's own House*], I also satisfy my need to [*nature of the Ruled Sign*], with regard to [*concerns of the Ruled Sign's House*]."

When working with these Rulerships, remember that THE POINTS are unlike Planets in that they are not the messengers or activators of particular Signs.

Further interpretation of Grace's Chart (Fig. 3-21) reveals how she uses the Planetary Rulerships to advantage. Many of the correlations emerged in our previous discussions although most of the negative ones did not apply. I checked the rest of the connections with her and found that she agreed. In this analysis, which is a little more complicated than the last two, I've included the abbreviations of the Planets, Signs, and Houses in parentheses to indicate the references for the interpretations.

Key Word Analysis of Planets as Rulers

Figure 3-21: Grace's Chart

1ST HOUSE / LIBRA – RULER IS VENUS, AND VENUS IS IN CAPRICORN IN THE 3RD

As she finds value (VE) in organizing (CP) her siblings (3), she also satisfies her need to present herself (1) as a cooperator (LI). Or, as she is rigid (CP) about how she shares (VE) her car (3), she might present herself (1) as a vain (LI) person.

2ND HOUSE / SCORPIO – RULER IS PLUTO AND PLUTO IS RETROGRADE IN LEO IN THE 11TH

As she is compelled to transform herself (R PL) by becoming enthusiastic (LE) about a future vision (11), she also satisfies her need for a deep sense (SC) of self-worth (2). And, she makes money (2). Or, as she is destructive (PL) of her friendships (11) through her attention-getting (LE) behavior, she also might base her worth (2) on her compulsive patterns (PL). And, she might lose money (2).

3RD HOUSE / SAGITTARIUS – RULER IS JUPITER
AND JUPITER IS IN ARIES IN THE 7TH

As she teaches (JU) others (7) in a pioneering (AR) manner, she also satisfies her need to play a philosophical role (SA) in the community (3). Or, as she disseminates knowledge (JU) to her partner (7) in a pushy (AR) way, she could become preachy (SG) in her communication (3).

4TH HOUSE / CAPRICORN – RULER IS SATURN
AND RETROGRADE SATURN IS IN LIBRA IN THE 1ST

As she diplomatically (LI) presents herself (1) as a self-disciplined (R SA) person, she also satisfies her need to be authoritative (CP) at home (4). Or, as she limits (R SA) her personal tendency toward appearing (1) indecisive (LI), she could become rigid (CP) within her family (4).

5TH HOUSE / AQUARIUS – RULER IS URANUS
AND RETROGRADE URANUS IS IN CANCER IN THE 10TH

As she demonstrates her innovative abilities (R UR) in a nurturing manner (CA) in her career (10), she also satisfies her need to create a better future (AQ) for children (5). Or, as she establishes a reputation (10) for embodying rebellion against social patterns (R UR) in an emotional (CA) way, she could become inappropriate (AQ) in romantic affairs (5).

6TH HOUSE / PISCES – RULER IS NEPTUNE
AND RETROGRADE NEPTUNE IS IN LIBRA IN THE 1ST

As she changes her internal emotional experience (R NE) by beautifying (LI) her appearance (1), she also satisfies her need to be sensitive (PI) to her health needs (6). Or, as she appears (1) indecisive (LI) because she's lost in her inner world (R NE), her addictive nature (PI) could affect her health (6).

7TH HOUSE / ARIES – RULER IS MARS
AND MARS IS IN SCORPIO IN THE 2ND

As she passionately (SC) pursues her drive (MA) to make money (2), she also satisfies her need to be independent (AR) in her relationships (7). Or, as she establishes her self-worth (2) by violently (SC) asserting her self (MA), she could become pretty aggressive (AR) in her relationships (7).

8TH HOUSE / TAURUS – RULER IS VENUS
AND VENUS IS IN CAPRICORN IN THE 3RD

As she cooperates (VE) in a responsible manner (CP) with her neighbors (3), she also satisfies her need to be practical (TA) with using shared resources (8). Or, as she creates harmony (VE) through domineering (CP) her siblings (3), she could become stubborn (TA) with regard to inheritances (8).

9TH HOUSE / GEMINI – RULER IS MERCURY
AND MERCURY IS IN CAPRICORN IN THE 4TH

As she ambitiously (CP) seeks variety and stimulation (ME) at home (4), she also satisfies her need to be curious (GE) about higher learning and philosophy (9). Or, as she feels the need to set boundaries (CP) in her communication (ME) with her mother (4), she could become distracted (GE) from her educational goals (9).

10TH HOUSE / CANCER – RULER IS THE MOON
AND THE MOON IS IN PISCES IN THE 6TH

As she creates belongingness (MO) through being compassionate (PI) with her co-workers (6), she also satisfies her need to be nurturing (CA) in her career (10). Or, as she repeats addictive (PI) emotional habit patterns (MO) which affect her health (6), she could become fearful of abandonment (CA) within her profession (10).

11TH HOUSE / LEO – RULER IS THE SUN
AND THE SUN IS IN AQUARIUS IN THE 5TH

As she expresses her visionary and inventive (AQ) potential (SU) with regard to her creativity (5), she also satisfies her need to shine (LE) in groups (11). Or, as she discovers herself (SU) by being disruptive (AQ) in her recreational activities (5), she could become boastful (LE) with her friends (11).

12TH HOUSE / VIRGO – RULER IS CHIRON
AND CHIRON IS IN CAPRICORN IN THE 4TH

As she responsibly (CP) fixes things (CH) for her family (4), she also satisfies her need to provide healing services (VI) with regard to addictions (12). Or, as she rigidly (CP) attempts to achieve perfection (CH) in her home (4), she could become critical (VI) of those who support her (12).

Interpreting Rulership of Intercepted and Duplicated Signs

In the case of an Intercepted Sign, the Planet Ruling the Sign actually acts as a key to unlock the Interception. In other words, if you have an Interception, you can begin to understand how to access the energy of its Sign if you utilize its Ruler. Of course, if the Ruling Planet is located in an Intercepted Sign itself, that Sign will need to be unlocked, too. If the Ruler of the second Intercepted Sign is also contained in an Interception, you'll need to use an Aspecting Planet to activate the Intercepted Planet (see next section).

The Planet Ruling a Duplicated Sign has a double job to perform. As it takes action, according to its Sign and House, it's impact is felt in *both* of the Houses carrying its Sign. So, if you have a Duplicated Sign, whenever you utilize the Planet Ruling that Sign, you'll feel the effects in two different areas of life.

You can get an idea of what I mean by looking at the following interpretation of Janie's Interceptions and Duplications (Fig. 3-22).

Key Word Analysis of
Planetary Rulers of Intercepted and Duplicated Signs

LEO IS INTERCEPTED IN THE 9TH HOUSE
AND LEO'S RULER, THE SUN, IS IN AQUARIUS IN THE 3RD

If she wants to shine (LE) in terms of her higher education (9), she'll need to have discovered and expressed herself (SU) in unique ways (AQ) within her early educational experiences and her community (3). However, the ways in which she wants to shine (LE) or to be unique and unusual (AQ) may not be modeled by her family (Interceptions).

At this point, we run into a problem. The Ruler of one Intercepted Sign is located in the other Intercepted Sign. (This is not necessarily the case in most Charts.) So, it's difficult for Janie to access her innovative (AQ) potential (SU) and unlock her enthusiastic (LE) philosophy (9) because the Sun is Intercepted in Aquarius. In order to unlock her Intercepted Leo, she actually needs to unlock Intercepted Aquarius as well.

AQUARIUS IS INTERCEPTED IN THE 3RD HOUSE
AND AQUARIUS'S RULER, URANUS, IS IN SAGITTARIUS IN THE 1ST

In order to have innovative and unique experiences (AQ) in her school and community (3), she'll need to express her nonconforming urges (UR) in an expanded manner (SG) in her basic personality and her appearance (1). By doing this, she'll also release the Sun which will unlock Intercepted Leo.

One way for Janie to combine these features of her life would be for her to wear (1) many (SG) unusual or outrageous things (UR). As a result, she'd automatically find the people and experiences at school and in the community (3) with whom she can be her innovative and unique (AQ) self (SU). Through those connections, she'll have opportunities to have enthusiasm (LE) for college (9). Or, by presenting herself (1) as a self-indulgent (SG) rebel (UR), she could be inappropriate (AQ) in grade school (3) and attention-getting or boastful (LE) when traveling overseas (9). She'll probably find nonfamily mentors (Interceptions) who will demonstrate both these behavior patterns for her.

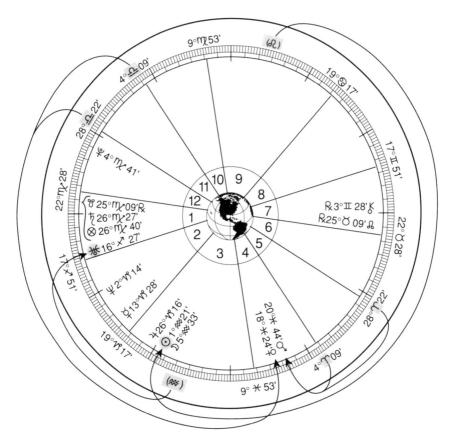

Figure 3-22: Janie's Chart

Since she has two Interceptions, Janie also has two Duplications. Interpretations for them follow:

ARIES IS DUPLICATED ON THE 5TH AND 6TH HOUSE CUSPS
AND ARIES'S RULER, MARS, IS IN PISCES IN THE 4TH

She wants to be independent, pioneering, and adventuresome (AR) with regard to her creativity (5) or her daily routine work (6). She can achieve those goals by pursuing her personal desires (MA) to be psychic (PI) within her family situation (4). She'll actually have these patterns modeled for her within family system. On the other hand, if she asserts herself (MA) in a confused manner (PI) at home, she could become aggressive (AR) with her playmates (5) and pushy (AR) about accomplishing daily tasks (6).

LIBRA IS DUPLICATED ON THE 11TH AND 12TH HOUSE CUSPS
AND LIBRA'S RULER, VENUS, IS IN PISCES IN THE 4TH.

She wants to be cooperative (LI) with regard to her friends (11) and artistic (LI) with regard to her spiritual (12) expression. She can accomplish both of these things by expressing her compassionate and imaginative (PI) values (VE) in her home environment (4). Or, she can become vain (LI) within her friendship circle (11) and indecisive (LI) about her spirituality (12) if she magnetically attracts (VE) addictive (PI) experiences to her home (4). It's quite possible that she'll have role models within her own family system for expressing all of these patterns.

INTERPRETING BY ASPECT

The Aspects among the Planets and Points serve to integrate the various parts of the Chart into a whole. Planets (or Points) interpreted in isolation are certainly meaningful, but when they are interpreted in Aspect to one another, they take on more depth and breadth. In fact, as you interpret the Aspects in your Chart, you'll probably find out how the various parts of your personality work, or don't work, together. The following formula can be used to describe the Aspect relationships.

THIS PLANET (OR POINT)
INTERACTS IN THIS WAY
WITH THIS PLANET (OR POINT).

By using the key words describing the Planets, Points, Signs, Houses and Aspects according to the sequence that follows, you can further develop your Chart interpretation.

Aspect Interpretation Sequence

1. Identify two Planets or Points that are in Aspect to one another

2. Identify how each Planet or Point acts in its own Sign and House

3. Identify the nature of the Aspect between them

4. Say something such as:
"As I act on my urge to [*function of one Planet or Point*], in a [*nature of its Sign*] manner or style, with regard to [*concerns of its House*], this behavior will [*nature of Aspect*] my urge to [*function of other Planet or Point*], in a [*nature of its Sign*] manner or style, with regard to [*concerns of its House*]."

Examples of each type of Aspect, from Grace's Chart, follow:

Key Word Analysis of Aspects

Figure 3-23: Grace's Chart

CONJUNCTION

THE PART OF FORTUNE IS CONJUNCT MARS. BOTH OF THEM ARE IN SCORPIO IN THE 2ND HOUSE (Fig. 3-23).

Grace will feel most intensely (SC) personally integrated (PF), when she is simultaneously (CO) pursuing her desires (MA) in a passionate (SC) manner. When she asserts herself (MA) in an emotionally powerful (SC) way, she'll concurrently (CO) feel deeply (SC) integrated (PF) and worthwhile (2). However, she may become compulsive (SC) about pursuing her sexual drives (MA), feeling that, through them, she can feel whole (PF) and valuable (2). She'll probably feel magically blessed (PF) whenever she's actively going after (MA) money or possessions (2). And, she'll probably have a true knack for taking effective (PF) and immediate (MA) action with regard to investments and financial planning (2).

Grace says that she has had times when she based her wholeness and self-esteem on her attractiveness. Presently, however, she's more aware of the ways in which she actually uses the powerful emotion of anger in a productive way, to create change for herself. And, her ability to assert herself in order to make "magic" with money is well documented.

Figure 3-24: Grace's Chart

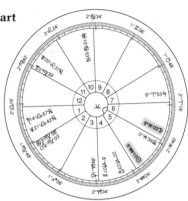

SEMI-SEXTILE

THE MOON, IN PICES IN THE 6TH, IS
SEMI-SEXTILE THE SUN, IN AQUARIUS
IN THE 5TH (Fig. 3-24).

Grace will want to create a true place of belonging (MO) in her work world (6) by rescuing (PI) animals or people (6). On the other hand, she'll also want to be true to her essential self (SU) by expressing her personal creativity and raising her children (5) in a nonconforming (AQ) way. She'll sense that these two parts of her are not fully in conflict but are slightly out of step with each other (SS). In fact, she could frustrate herself by continually worrying (SS) about the part of her that isn't being fully expressed. Ultimately, she'll fine-tune and adapt (SS) her ways of giving compassionate (MO in PI) service (6) to others so that she can raise her children (5) and express her creativity (5) according to her visionary ideas (AQ).

In reality, Grace takes children into her home and is paid well to effect changes in their behavior. With this as her job, she can stay home and raise her children or express her creativity in the inventive ways that she likes.

Figure 3-25: Grace's Chart

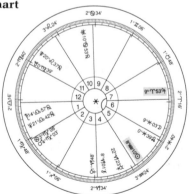

SEXTILE

THE SUN, IN AQUARIUS IN THE 5TH, IS
SEXTILE JUPITER, IN ARIES IN THE 7TH
(Fig. 3-25).

Grace will discover much of her own personal potential (SU) through interacting with unusual or innovative (AQ) playmates (5). She'll be supported (SX) in this by her expansive drive (JU) to take risks and have adventures (AR) with her partner (7). Sometimes, this combination of forces could get her in trouble if she grabs for more (JU) risks (AR) and finds herself inappropriately (AQ) expressing herself (SU). She may also have a drive to express her essence (SU) through interacting with unusual (AQ) children (5). By finding a pioneering (AR) philosopher (JU) for a partner (7), she'll easily be able to raise her unconventional (AQ) children (5) in the utopian way (AQ) that she desires. Over and over, she'll find that her drive for pioneering expansion (JU in AR) and innovative self-expression (SU in AQ) will dovetail and find support in the world (SX).

Grace says that this combination of forces has certainly found support in her life. In her early adulthood, she could always find others who would help her to get in trouble through taking outrageous risks. Other people also stepped forward to show her how to interact with children in pioneering and innovative ways. She took advantage of their support and has worked, with her partner, with children.

Figure 3-26: Grace's Chart

SQUARE

Retrograde Saturn, in Libra in the 1st, Squares Retrograde Uranus, in Cancer in the 10th (Fig. 3.26).

Grace would feel a strong internal conflict (SQ) between the part of her that embodies eccentricity (R UR) and the part of her that is a model of self-control (R SA). Every time she organizes herself (R SA) so that she appears (1) cooperative (LI), she is struck internally with rebellious ideas (R UR) about how the situation could become more truly nurturing and comfortable (CA). The struggle (SQ) between these forces may lead her to jump in and out of career positions (10). She might resolve the tension between these forces by finding a role (1) as a diplomatic (LI) authority figure (R SA) within an emotionally satisfying (CA) career path (10) which allows her to exhibit her radical urges (R UR).

Grace says that she has often found herself to be the voice of dissent or change within organizations. In fact, she pursued a career for years in which she found innovative, but caring, ways to work with developmentally disabled people. Despite her radical urges, she managed to avoid being fired because she also exhibited great diplomacy and self-discipline.

Figure 3-27: Grace's Chart

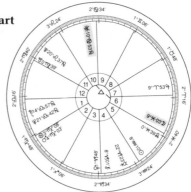

TRINE
THE MOON, IN PISCES IN THE 6TH,
TRINES RETROGRADE URANUS, IN
CANCER IN THE 10TH (Fig. 3-27).

Grace will want to compassionately (PI) serve others (6) by giving them a sense of belonging (MO). Nearly everyday (6), she'll express empathy (MO) for others and want to heal (PI) them. These desires fit in perfectly with her personal visions (R UR) for a nurturing (CA) career (10). Through her professional work (10), she wants to move toward her future vision (R UR) of making the world a more caring and nurturing (CA) place. She might also want to follow her moods (MO) on a daily basis (6), working when she wants to, resting when she intuitively feels like it (PI). In this case, the part of her that's willing to have an erratic, unpredictable (R UR), and self-nurturing (CA) career path (10) supports her in letting go of the "shoulds." She might rely on emotional (MO in PI) or physical health crises (6) as signals of her need for spiritual renewal (PI). Then, her reputation (10) as an eccentric (R UR) but essentially caring person (CA) will prepare others for her healing absences (PI) from work (6).

Grace says that her sensitivity with co-workers, staff, and clients has always merged easily with her vision for creating a better world. She also realizes that she uses ill-health as a signal that reminds her when she needs to take a break from her routine. She's moving toward getting that message intuitively instead of physically.

Figure 3-28: Grace's Chart

QUINCUNX
MERCURY, IN CAPRICORN IN THE 4TH,
IS QUINCUNX RETROGRADE PLUTO, IN
LEO IN THE 11TH (Fig. 3-28).

Grace will want to interact on a communicative basis (ME) in authoritative ways (CP) with her mother. But, she'll also feel a powerful inner calling (R PL) to shine (LE) by participating in causes (11) that will benefit the future of humankind (11). When she tries simply to settle in and enjoy the stimulation (ME) of her organized (CP) home life (4), she'll feel pulled off track (QU) and interrupted (QU). She could find a businesslike (CP) way to network or exchange goods and information (ME) from her home (4). But, it will be truly satisfying only if her products and services are powerful resources (PL) that shine out (LE) and contribute to improving the Earth (11).

Grace says that she is seldom bored at home; she is always stimulated by the variety of tasks and projects that she can accomplish. And, she says it's true that she can't settle into her home life for too long without feeling the urge to contribute to the "cause."

Figure 3-29: Grace's Chart

OPPOSITION
JUPITER, IN ARIES IN THE 7TH, IS OP-
POSED TO RETROGRADE SATURN, IN
LIBRA IN THE 1ST (Fig. 3-29).

Grace will have a need to seek *the* truth (JU) adventurously (AR) with her partner (7). While she'll be tempted to take risks (AR) as she expands her horizons (JU), she'll also want to evaluate her decisions from the perspective (OP) of her drive to be self-disciplining (R SA). She'll want to present herself (1), not as a pushy (AR) preacher (JU), but as an authority figure (R SA) who is willing to cooperate (LI). She may work to harmonize (OP) the part of her that wants to use her philosophy (JU) to lead (AR) her partner (7) with the part of her that limits herself (R SA) so that she can project herself (1) as other-oriented (LI).

Grace feels that she has done a good job of coordinating these two urges. Most of the time, she and her partner jointly consider the practical pros and cons of risk-taking before they act. She finds that she seems to take on the roles of fearless philosopher and cooperative limit-setter in equal measure.

ORGANIZING YOUR INTERPRETATIONAL DATA

If you've applied the concepts from this Chapter to your Chart, you have quite a bit of interpretational data at this point. In fact, you may want a way of organizing some of what you know. You can use a notebook or worksheets, such as those at the end of the chapter, for this purpose. If you fill in the basics now and leave some space, you'll be able to add to your ideas as you read the expanded interpretations in the rest of the book.

SUMMARY

In this Chapter, I've presented the interpretational dynamics of Astrology. These dynamics will hold true no matter how sophisticated you become in terms of your actual definitions of the Houses, Planets, Points, Signs, and Aspects. In fact, if you remember the fundamentals, you'll be able to expand on them as you learn more about Chart interpretation in Chapters 4 through 8. The most important features presented in this Chapter are summarized below.

THE TWELVE HOUSES SET THE STAGE. They represent areas of life, places, situations, issues, and concerns.

THE TWELVE SIGNS SET THE MOOD. They represent needs, attitudes, styles of processing, ways of being, and approaches toward life.

THE SIGNS ON THE HOUSE CUSPS show attitudes and needs with regard to the areas of life associated with those Houses.

INTERCEPTED SIGNS indicate attitudes, needs, and processes that have not been appropriately modeled by the family system.

DUPLICATED SIGNS indicate attitudes, needs, and processes that have been appropriately modeled by the family system.

THE ELEVEN PLANETS ACT. They represent personality functions. They have specific roles to fulfill by accomplishing their tasks.

RETROGRADE PLANETS experience themselves internally before acting outwardly.

EACH PLANET FUNCTIONS by acting in t' e manner of its Sign regarding the concerns and issues of its House.

THE FIVE POINTS also have functions in the Chart. They operate according to their Signs and Houses.

THE PLANETS ARE THE RULERS or activators of their Natural Signs. Their actions in their Natal Houses have an influence on the experiences they'll have in the Houses which have their Natural Signs on the Cusps.

THE ASPECTS symbolize the way in which two Planets or Points interact with one another.

EXERCISES

For Understanding the Fundamentals

3-1   Using the key words, interpret the Signs on the House Cusps for your own Chart. Notice and interpret the Intercepted Signs, too.

3-2   Using the key words, interpret the Planets in their Signs and Houses for your own Chart. Remember to notice and interpret Retrogradation where it's appropriate.

3-3   Using the key words, interpret the Points by Sign and House in your own Chart.

3-4   Using the key words, interpret the Planets as Rulers of the Houses that have their Natural Signs on the Cusps in your own Chart.

3-5   Using the key words, interpret the Aspects in your own Chart.

For Understanding the Details

3-6   Interpret the Signs on the House Cusps for a few friends. Ask them to give you feedback on your accuracy.

3-7   Use the formulae in the Chapter to interpret all the Planets and Points in your Chart, and in several other Charts, by POSITION.

3-8   Use the formula in this Chapter to interpret all the Planets in your Chart, and in several other Charts, by RULERSHIP. (Remember, the Points do not act as Rulers.)

3-9   Use the formula in this Chapter to interpret the Planets and Points, in your Chart and in several others, by ASPECT.

3-10 Tape or write out your interpretations of your Chart thus far. Date it so that you can compare yourself with yourself later.

SIGNS ON CUSPS

HOUSE	SIGN ON CUSP	BASIC INTERPRETATION
1ST		
2ND		
3RD		
4TH		
5TH		
6TH		
7TH		
8TH		
9TH		
10TH		
11TH		
12TH		
HOUSE WITH INTERCEPTION	INTERCEPTED SIGN	
HOUSE WITH INTERCEPTION	INTERCEPTED SIGN	

Worksheet 1
Signs on Cusps

PLANETS AND POINTS IN SIGNS IN HOUSES

PLANETS (RETROGRADE?) AND POINTS   BASIC INTERPRETATION
        by SIGN and HOUSE

THE SUN is in (Sign) in the
_____ House.

THE MOON

MERCURY

VENUS

MARS

JUPITER

SATURN

CHIRON

URANUS

NEPTUNE

PLUTO

NORTH NODE

SOUTH NODE

PART OF FORTUNE

MIDHEAVEN

ASCENDANT

Worksheet 2
Planets and Points in Signs in Houses

PLANETARY RULERS OF SIGNS / HOUSES

HOUSE/SIGN	LOCATION OF NATURAL RULER BY HOUSE/SIGN	BASIC INTERPRETATION
1ST/ (Sign on Cusp)	The Planet (name it) ruling the Sign on the First House Cusp is in (Sign) in the (#) House.	
2ND/_____		
3RD/_____		
4TH/_____		
5TH/_____		
6TH/_____		
7TH/_____		
8TH/_____		
9TH/_____		
10TH/_____		
11TH/_____		
12TH/_____		
INTERCEPTED SIGN (House)/(Sign)		
INTERCEPTED SIGN (House)/(Sign)		

Worksheet 3
Planetary Rulers of Signs / Houses

ASPECTS BETWEEN PAIRS OF PLANETS OR POINTS

MAJOR ASPECTS   BASIC INTERPRETATION

CONJUNCTIONS:

SEMI-SEXTILES:

SEXTILES:

SQUARES:

TRINES:

QUINCUNXES:

OPPOSITIONS:

Worksheet 4
Aspects between Pairs of Planets or Points

FOUR

The Houses

The twelve HOUSES of an Astrological Chart, which symbolize twelve broad compartments of life, can actually represent any issue, thing, or process that might be of interest or concern for anybody. This means that everything from physical appearance to spirituality can be located in a specific House. Of course, the Houses themselves don't do anything about our looks or spiritual persuasions; they don't even dictate how we respond to these concerns. The Houses set the stage; they provide contexts in which we can have feelings and take action. In this Chapter, I'll describe the interpretations of the Houses in detail.

As you learn about the specific topics that are related to each House, remember that you may not have experiences related to every issue in every area of life. In fact, for each House, you'll probably find that some of the people, places, and things are relevant to your life and some are not. So for now, notice the ones that apply to you. Choose the interpretations that make sense, and leave the rest. If you're working with someone else's Chart, be sure to get feedback from him or her about the topics that are relevant at this particular time. Someone may have no interest in your discussion about her attitude toward the 5th House concern of children, but she may be quite fascinated in finding out about her approach to artistic endeavors, another 5th House subject. So, while you're learning about the Houses, remember to ask yourself, and others, which of the many issues related to a given House are currently important. Focus on these topics for your initial exploration into the Houses. Later, when different concerns arise, you can always come back to this Chapter for more details.

THE INTERPRETATIONAL STRUCTURE OF THE HOUSES

Before I get into the specifics for each House, I want you to have a way of organizing them conceptually so that the House-topic associations make sense. Therefore, in the following pages I've included two ways of categorizing and interpreting the Houses: SECTIONS and PAIRS. I find that these systems are most useful in Chart analysis. Traditionally, the Houses have also been broken down in two other ways. These are described briefly in Appendix E.

The Sections

The SECTIONS of an Astrological Chart emerge if you divide the Chart on the basis of the Horizon and Meridian lines. As you can see in Figure 4-1, these lines initially halve the Chart in two different ways, forming four possible HEMISPHERES. Each of the Hemispheres contains six Houses: the Eastern includes Houses 10-12 and 1-3, the Western contains Houses 4-9, the Northern holds Houses 1-6, and the Southern consists of Houses 7-12.

By their overlapping patterns, the Hemispheres divide the Chart into four smaller Sections called QUADRANTS (Fig. 4-1). Each Quadrant contains three Houses: the First begins with the 1st House and goes through the 3rd, the Second goes from the 4th through the 6th, the Third is from the 7th through the 9th, and the Fourth Quadrant starts with the 10th and continues through the 12th.

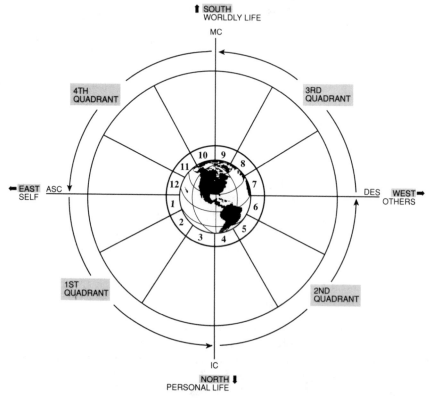

Figure 4-1
The Houses According to Their Sections

Each of the Hemispheres has its own meaning. As they overlap into the Quadrants, the meanings also overlap, forming the Quadrant interpretations. Explanations for the Hemispheres and the Quadrants follow:

The NORTHERN HEMISPHERE Houses (1–6), those below the Horizon, are the PRIVATE Houses. They deal with issues related to basic foundations and personal concerns.

The SOUTHERN HEMISPHERE Houses (7–12), those above the Horizon, are the PUBLIC Houses. They deal with issues related to expanded experiences and worldly concerns.

The EASTERN HEMISPHERE Houses (10–12, 1–3), to the left of the Meridian, are the SELF-ORIENTED Houses. They deal with issues related to explorations of the self and individual interests.

The WESTERN HEMISPHERE Houses (4–9), to the right of the Meridian, are the OTHER-ORIENTED Houses. They deal with issues related to interactions with others and shared interests.

The FIRST QUADRANT Houses (1–3) emerge from the overlap of the Eastern and Northern Hemispheres. Therefore, they contain people, objects, and issues that are associated with basic foundations, personal concerns, explorations of the self, and individual interests.

The SECOND QUADRANT Houses (4–6) come from the overlap of the Western and Northern Hemispheres. Therefore, they contain people, objects, and issues that are associated with basic foundations, personal concerns, interactions with others, and shared interests.

The THIRD QUADRANT Houses (7–9), the result of the overlapping of the Western and Southern Hemispheres, contain people, objects, and issues that are associated with expanded experiences, worldly concerns, interactions with others, and shared interests.

The FOURTH QUADRANT Houses (10–12), created by overlapping the Eastern and Southern Hemispheres, contain people, objects, and issues that are associated with expanded experiences, worldly concerns, explorations of the self, and individual interests.

The Pairs

Since the Houses that are opposite one another mirror each other by size and by concept, it's also useful to look at the Houses as six opposing PAIRS (Fig. 4-2).

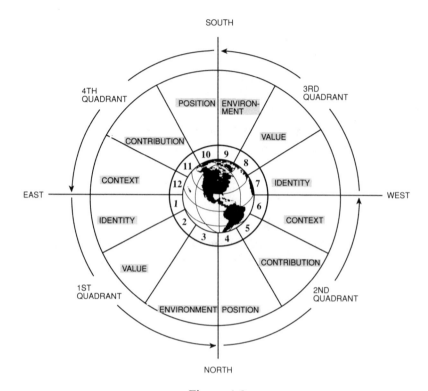

Figure 4-2
The Houses According to Their Pairs

Each Pair is described by a key word that can be expanded into all the concerns and issues of its two Houses. Relative to these concepts, the Houses are associated with the following areas of life:

IDENTITY

1: personality, mask, image, name, title, role, identity, physical appearance

7: identification of a partner, formal involvement with another, "significant other"

VALUE

2: personal skills, resources, self-worth, individual value, money and possessions

8: joint or collective skills and talents, sex, shared money or emotional resources

ENVIRONMENT

3: immediate environment, local travel, communication and dialogue, data, facts, companions in learning, students, siblings, early education

9: far-reaching environment, long-distance travel, ethics, philosophy, beliefs, theories, lectures, mentors, knowledge, teachers, higher education

POSITION

4: position in the home or family, place of belonging, roots, clan, position in ethnic/racial/ cultural environment, security

10: position in the societal structure, reputation in the world, status, basis for worldly recognition, career, vocation, life path

CONTRIBUTION

5: creative contribution, all forms of art and hobbies, romance, fun, recreation, children, childlike behavior

11: visionary contribution, goals, plans, visions, interaction with "causes," future direction and focus

CONTEXT

6: usual daily work and service to others, maintenance of physical health, everyday responsibilities and tasks, mainstream environments

12: non-usual situations; emotional, psychic, or spiritual surrender to a "Higher Power"; secluded or isolated environments

In the rest of this Chapter, the meanings that emerge from these categories are combined and expanded into more detailed explanations of the issues related to the Houses.

The First House: *Self*

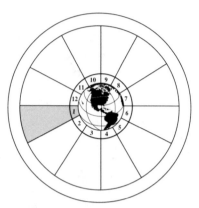

<small>THE 1ST HOUSE IS ASSOCIATED WITH:</small>

SECTION: FIRST QUADRANT:
basic foundations and personal
concerns, explorations of the self
and individual interests

PAIR: IDENTITY: the self

The 1ST HOUSE is the place in which you discover, explore, and express your personal identity. It's the location in which you claim your names, titles, and roles. Generally, the identity you express in your 1st House is your overall personality, not your deepest soul. In fact, this House can even represent the mask you've learned to wear, the persona that's worked best for you over time, the identity that your family and friends reinforce or reward. The 1st House is where you've developed your favorite coping strategy for avoiding or ignoring pain. It's where you've learned to face the world. Since the Ascendant (1st House Cusp) is the boundary between the personal and worldly parts of the Chart on the self-oriented side of the Chart, the 1st House symbolizes the persona that you use in order to move from your vulnerable inner world into the outer world. It also reflects your physical appearance and general vitality. All in all, the 1st House symbolizes the face you present to the world, the first impression that you make on others.

THE SIGN ON YOUR 1ST HOUSE CUSP, your RISING SIGN, indicates something about your personal style and many things about your persona. It will show your needs with regard to self-presentation, your attitudes toward your appearance, and your overall approach to life. This Sign symbolizes your general personality to the extent that many who meet you might think that qualities represented by your Rising Sign fully describe you. It's for you to reveal the rest of yourself, if and when you choose.

1st House Applications

PSYCHOLOGICAL: identity, temperament, self-discovery, persona, mask; part of the self that's been reinforced since childhood; primary coping strategy; instincts; experiences during infancy

PRACTICAL: physical appearance and body structure; general physical condition; personal action; name and name changes, formal role or title

The Second House: *Resources*

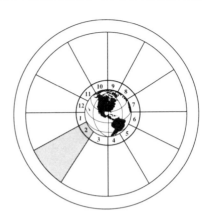

THE 2ND HOUSE IS ASSOCIATED WITH:

SECTION: FIRST QUADRANT: basic foundations and personal concerns, explorations of the self and individual interests

PAIR: VALUE: personal worth, skills, and resources

The 2ND HOUSE is where you concentrate on your self-worth. It's the place in which you focus on ongoing productivity so that your foundations will be solid. This House contains the physical symbols of your worth including money, in all its forms, and movable possessions (*not* immovable property and real estate). As a result, your debts, credits, personal earning power, income level, and expenses are all important concerns of the 2nd House. The meaning of the House goes beyond this, however, to reflect anything that is a personal resource. This could include your talents, skills, and emotional attributes as well as physical items. At a more subtle level, the 2nd House represents your intrinsic value as a human being.

THE SIGN ON YOUR 2ND HOUSE CUSP demonstrates what you need in order to feel personally worthwhile, your attitudes with regard to money, and your approach to collecting or caring for possessions. It symbolizes the specific nature of your skills, talents, and resources. It also shows how you'll react if your financial security, self-esteem, or possessions are threatened or if your skills and talents are not recognized.

2nd House Applications

PSYCHOLOGICAL: self-esteem, evaluation of personal worth; sense of "deserving to be alive"; personal talents, skills and personality attributes; experiences as a toddler

PRACTICAL: money, stocks, bonds, credit cards, jewelry, checkbooks, pleasures, three-dimensional art, banks and banking, all movable possessions, assets

The Third House:
Immediate Environment

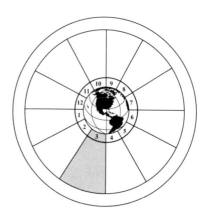

THE 3RD HOUSE IS ASSOCIATED WITH:

SECTION: FIRST QUADRANT:
basic foundations and personal concerns, explorations of the self and individual interests

PAIR: ENVIRONMENT: the immediate environment

The 3RD HOUSE is the location in which you explore your potential for communicating in the immediate environment. Here, you disperse your ideas into the community. At a tangible level, the 3rd House environment includes your personally defined neighborhood and the people in it. This could mean your actual neighborhood and neighbors or the people that you consider to be part of your chosen community. Your siblings, cousins, and schoolmates, those who are theoretically closest to you, also belong here, whether or not you live near them. This House contains the methods you utilize for moving around your community, both literally and figuratively. Therefore, it holds all forms of transportation, communication, and networking. It's also associated with the exchanges of products and information that will help you pursue your interests. As a result, commerce and education are 3rd House matters. Generally speaking, the 3rd House contains your personal environment and your methods of interacting in it.

THE SIGN ON YOUR 3RD HOUSE CUSP describes your needs with regard to neighborhood and community, your attitudes toward your siblings, cousins, and classmates, and your approach to communication. It signifies the type of transportation you prefer and describes your attitude toward vehicles and driving. It's also representative of your general response to community activities and to your early education. And, it shows how you'll react if problems arise with your neighbors or siblings.

3rd House Applications

PSYCHOLOGICAL: representing the self through speech and communication; emotional ties to classmates, siblings, or cousins; exploration of personal needs that can be met-at a local level; experiences as an older toddler; learning style

PRACTICAL: all forms of communication including letters, memos, speech, sign language, debates, arguments, gossip, discussions, dialogue, storytelling; all writing implements; communication tools and equipment including telephone, telegram, fax, copy machines, tape- recorders, typewriters; books, magazines, journals, bookstores, libraries; schools (up through community college); siblings, cousins, and classmates; personal transportation system including cars, bicycles, airplanes, boats, walking or running, trains; commuting; local vacations and travel; neighborhood, community, immediate physical and mental environment; all mechanical things; physical, informational, and social networks

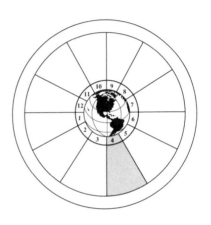

The Fourth House: *Home*

THE 4TH HOUSE IS ASSOCIATED WITH:

SECTION: SECOND QUADRANT: basic foundations and personal concerns, interactions with others and shared interests

PAIR: POSITION: place in the home or family

The 4TH HOUSE is the location in which you sink roots and establish belongingness in your *own* place. Here, you construct a spot for yourself with the others who are important to you. The 4th House contains your dwelling, your land, and your territory. If you're so inclined, it's where you unpack your suitcase, plant flowers, hang pictures, and say "I'm home." Since this includes your childhood home as well as your living situation as an adult, this home base changes as you grow older. The 4th House symbolizes your emotional attachment to a group or culture. It also represents the traditions and history of your original family, your clan, or your race. If you are not involved with your birth family, the 4th House can represent your "chosen" family, culture, or subculture. In any case, it's where you know you belong. It's where you create conditions in which you can feel deeply nurtured, accepted, and secure. Since this House symbolizes your initial secure location, the womb, this is where you establish and develop your relationship to your mother (or other caretakers). And, because the 4th House represents all the private "places" in which you belong, it includes your last location, your "final resting place."

THE SIGN ON YOUR 4TH HOUSE CUSP symbolizes your needs with regard to belonging and nurturance, your attitudes toward your family system, clan, and culture, and your approach to creating solid foundations for yourself. At a tangible level, it shows the kind of home you want and the style in which you decorate it. This Sign also reflects your approach to moving, remodeling, or redecorating your home. The 4th House Sign indicates how you'll react if your home is damaged or if family problems arise. And, it symbolizes the conditions at the end of your life.

4th House Applications

PSYCHOLOGICAL: nurturance, emotional security, belonging, safety; relationship with mother or other key caretaker; locating and accepting self within personal heritage; the family of origin; establishment of own home and family; conclusions, completions; experiences as a young child

PRACTICAL: home, residence, immovable structures, gardens, orchards, yard, grounds, land, territory, sheds, private property, investment property, recreation property; homes away from home, including hotels, motels, inns; rental units; apartments and condos; birthplace; mother, family home, caretaker, genealogy, racial and ethnic origins; conditions at death, burial; conclusions to any undertaking

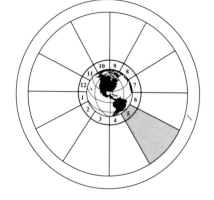

The Fifth House: *Creations*

THE 5TH HOUSE IS ASSOCIATED WITH:

SECTION: SECOND QUADRANT: basic foundations and personal concerns, interactions with others and shared interests

PAIR: CONTRIBUTION: creations

The 5TH HOUSE is the place in which you focus on sharing your creations with others. From one perspective, this House represents your most obvious and tangible creations: your own children. From an expanded point of view, however, everything about your interaction with children, blood-related or not, can be included. And, the children don't have to be people; artistic endeavors of all kinds qualify as the "fruits of your labor." In fact, the 5th House holds your concentrated inspiration. This is the House of creative imagination, playfulness, hobbies, and recreational activities. In fact, your "internal child self" and its desire to involve others in "games" is demonstrated here. These games include sports, gambling, speculation, and love affairs. Everything that lights a spark of fun and excitement in your life is Ruled by the 5th House.

THE SIGN ON YOUR 5TH HOUSE CUSP describes your needs with regard to playfulness and celebration, your attitudes toward your own children and your other creations, and your approach to gambling and games. It's an indicator of how you express your inner child and your ability to play, romance, or have fun. The 5th House Sign shows the nature of your special creative talents and the types of gifts that you'll share with others. It also symbolizes how you'll react if your creativity is blocked, your fun is curtailed, or your children are harmed.

5th House Applications

PSYCHOLOGICAL: children and relating to them; relating to self's own inner child; playfulness; quest for romance; childlikeness; experiences as an older child

PRACTICAL: creations, art of any form; hobbies, leisure activities; spectator or participant sports; children; playmates, play, joy, celebration, entertainment; romance, love affairs of any sort, dating; risks, gambling, speculation, adventure

The Sixth House: *Daily Life*

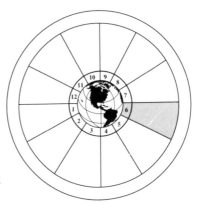

THE 6TH HOUSE IS ASSOCIATED WITH:

SECTION: SECOND QUADRANT: basic foundations and personal concerns, interactions with others and shared interests

PAIR: CONTEXT: ordinary daily work and routine

The 6TH HOUSE is where you physically engage in your personal daily routine. Here, you disperse your productive energy in order to maintain your basic foundations. This is the House of protection, health, and physical survival, the place of nutrition and food plans, exercise routines and medical checkups. Since it involves others, the 6th House includes the services you provide to people such as co-workers, tenants, and the needy, to machines and equipment, and to your pets. These services may be volunteer or job-related. Repair, maintenance, and trouble-shooting all belong here, along with research and problem-solving. In terms of your daily routine, everything about decision-making, schedules, deadlines, and time management is held in the 6th. Generally, the 6th House is associated with the processes you utilize to adapt or "fix" things so that they approach their ideal condition.

THE SIGN ON YOUR 6TH HOUSE CUSP reflects your needs with regard to personal health and maintenance, your attitudes toward the others you serve and support, and your approach to daily tasks and schedules. It will describe the kinds of doctors or healers you prefer. It identifies the mood you want in your normal lifestyle and your style of decision-making and problem-solving. This Sign also shows how you'll respond if your routine is interrupted, your health is challenged, or someone else is in crisis.

6th House Applications

PSYCHOLOGICAL: emotional and physical health and correlations between them; task organization and accomplishment; practical self-care and care of others; joining the work force; ability to problem-solve or find solutions; experiences as an adolescent

PRACTICAL: work, job, daily routine, schedule, time management; task organization and accomplishment; decision-making; nutrition, food plans, stress level, health and health maintenance, healing the body in any way; responsibility for pets, small animals, tenants, employees; coworkers, colleagues; responsibility for protecting the city, state, or country; service and volunteer activities; support staff; research

The Seventh House: *Others*

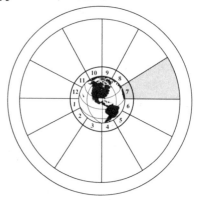

THE 7TH HOUSE IS ASSOCIATED WITH:

SECTION: THIRD QUADRANT:
expanded experiences and worldly concerns; interactions with others and shared interests

PAIR: IDENTITY: others

The 7TH HOUSE Cusp marks the transition from full responsibility at the personal level, represented by the 6th House, into worldly involvement. So, this is where you establish grown-up relationships including both marital and business partnerships. Significant relationships that have not been legally formalized but have been acknowledged in some other way also belong here. Interactions with clients, customers, therapists, and consultants are 7th House concerns. The value of all these important relationships is that they serve as mirrors to you. These people trigger you to examine yourself. They demonstrate qualities of your personality that can be seen only through interactions with others. In another sense, the 7th House represents those "others" who are most removed from your 1st House personality and could include enemies. In that case, your enemies can symbolize the parts of you that have become "others"; they are the lost or alienated parts that you need to reintegrate into your identity. In general, your 7th House contains opportunities for cooperation. Extensions of that include litigation, negotiation, arbitration, and mediation.

THE SIGN ON YOUR 7TH HOUSE CUSP symbolizes the needs that you have in terms of business and emotional partners, the attitudes you have toward clients and customers, and the approach you take in negotiations. It doesn't necessarily indicate the Sun or Rising Sign of your potential mates; it does show that you would want a mate who might exhibit some of the qualities of that Sign. It also reflects the qualities of your own personality that you may not discover independently, attributes that others bring out in you. And, this Sign signifies how you'll react if problems arise in your important relationships.

7th House Applications

PSYCHOLOGICAL: partner, companion, significant other; the process of forming and ending important relationships; the part of the self that seems most distant or removed from the conscious identity; people who act as mirrors to the self; cooperative inclinations and patterns

PRACTICAL: business or affectional partner; marriage and divorce; clients, customers; enemies or opponents; competition

The Eighth House:
Shared Resources

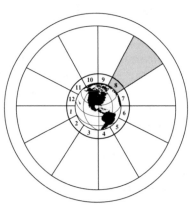

THE 8TH HOUSE IS ASSOCIATED WITH:

SECTION: THIRD QUADRANT:
expanded experience and worldly
concerns; interactions with others
and shared interests

PAIR: VALUE: collective worth, skills,
and resources

The 8TH HOUSE is a place in which you deepen and intensify your relationships with others. Here, you combine or blend feelings, skills, and resources with someone else in order to be more effective. So, this is the House of intimacy, emotional bonding, and psychic or sexual joining. It's the place of shared physical resources, including jointly held money and possessions. In fact, any financial matters in which others are involved, including combined bank accounts, shared ownership of possessions, taxes or debts owed to others, and trust funds or inheritances, are 8th House concerns. At a more symbolic level, this is the House of deep and meaningful interactions with all other beings, of union with collective consciousness. Birth, death, and rebirth processes belong here. Graphically speaking, this is the location of conception, the place where the resources of an egg and a sperm are combined in the creation of a new being. On many levels, the 8th House is the place of concentrated sharing and focused commitment to others.

THE SIGN ON YOUR 8TH HOUSE CUSP indicates your needs with regard to intimacy, your attitudes toward combining money and resources with others, and your approach to personal and interpersonal transformation. It certainly shows your sexual preferences and the ways in which you can be emotionally vulnerable to others. This Sign describes how you'll react if joint resources are threatened or your partner goes bankrupt. And, the 8th House Sign signifies your approach to commitment, separation, birth, and death.

8th House Applications

PSYCHOLOGICAL: intimacy, bonding, sexuality, vulnerability, commitment; emotional issues related to partnering; partner's money, skills, or lack of skills; conception; death, loss, grieving; transformation of self through interaction with others; adult experiences

PRACTICAL: taxes, partner's money, shared resources, inheritance, loans, grants, trust funds, investments; joint financial planning; death and birth

The Ninth House: *Expanded Horizons*

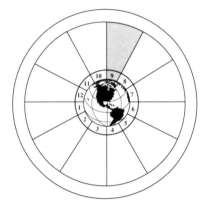

THE 9TH HOUSE IS ASSOCIATED WITH:

SECTION: THIRD QUADRANT: expanded experiences and worldly concerns; interactions with others and shared interests

PAIR: ENVIRONMENT: far-reaching environments

The 9TH HOUSE is the location in which you expand, with others, out into the world. Here, you move out into far-reaching environs in order to find inspiration. This is the House of philosophical and scientific knowledge. So, it's associated with the teachers, mentors, and other sources of wisdom in your life. It contains your religious, philosophical, or scientific "truths," your ethics, and your morals. It includes what you learn from reading or studying, especially from the more advanced levels of professional training, college, or post-graduate work. Traveling is a 9th House concern, since new insights could come through exposure to other people, their lives and belief systems. In addition to all the processes involving learning, the 9th House is associated with your own dissemination of knowledge through teaching, preaching, and publishing. And, it concerns itself with advertising, promotion, journalism, or broadcasting. Every imaginable form of seeking and sharing *the* truth as you know it, is held in the 9th House.

THE SIGN ON YOUR 9TH HOUSE CUSP symbolizes your needs with regard to long-distance travel, your attitudes toward religious and philosophical beliefs, and your approach to higher education and learning. It also indicates how you share your knowledge with others. And, the 9th House Sign shows how you would react if you were challenged about your beliefs or your knowledge.

9th House Applications

PSYCHOLOGICAL: deeply held beliefs, religious orientation, truths about life, self, the Universe; questing for knowing; sharing what's known; adapting self through others' knowledge and input

PRACTICAL: scientific or philosophical questing; international or long-distance travel; long-distance communication; teaching, preaching, promoting, broadcasting, publishing; colleges, universities, advanced training, post-graduate programs; legal proceedings and trials; religion, code of ethics

The Tenth House: *Vocation*

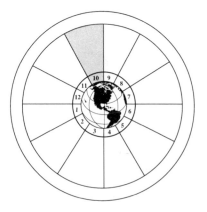

THE 10TH HOUSE IS ASSOCIATED WITH:

SECTION: FOURTH QUADRANT: expanded experiences and worldly concerns, explorations of the self and individual interests

PAIR: POSITION: place in the social structure

In the 10TH HOUSE, you construct your personal position in the world. Here, you commence your exploration of vocational paths and map out a productive plan that will take you where you want to go. Since it usually starts with the Midheaven, the 10th House contains your Universal "destiny," the tasks you want to accomplish in the world, in this life. In fact, all of your accomplishments, your ambitions, and your avenues to personal advancement, are 10th House concerns. Your executive and organizational abilities reside here. And, this House holds your career as well as other activities by which you gain recognition and authority in the world. All the authorities in your life, including but not limited to your father, belong here. And, your own status and reputation as well as your position in the social structure are reflected in this House. The 10th House is at the top of the Chart so it symbolizes the pinnacles that you can reach within the reality of the world.

THE SIGN ON YOUR 10TH HOUSE CUSP shows your needs with regard to status and reputation, your attitudes toward your career and vocation, and your approach to dealing with your father or other authority figures. It defines your professional manner and indicates what kind of boss you would be. It also indicates what you'll become "known for" in the world. And, the 10th House Sign symbolizes how you'll react to changes within your career and challenges to your reputation.

10th House Applications

PSYCHOLOGICAL: concerns related to power, status, position, ambition; ability to be own authority, set boundaries, organize or structure one's life; issues related to father or another childhood authority figure

PRACTICAL: career, vocation, life-path, life-work, destiny; ambition, accomplishments; status, reputation, societal position

The Eleventh House: *Future Visions*

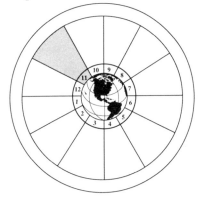

THE 11TH HOUSE IS ASSOCIATED WITH:

SECTION: FOURTH QUADRANT: expanded experiences and worldly concerns, explorations of the self and individual interests

PAIR: CONTRIBUTION: visionary possibilities

In the 11TH HOUSE, you set up situations in which you can focus on your own ideas and contributions. Here, your highest hopes, ideals, and dreams are identified, and your most concentrated mental effort is utilized in making them come true. So, in the 11th House are the others who share your goals. They may be organized into groups, clubs, labor unions, and other idealistic or purposeful organizations. Traditionally, the 11th House has also been seen as the location of friends, but it's not really the house of intimates. Instead, 11th House companions are those who happen to be on your path at any given moment. Your communications with them, and with the world in general, about your conceptual and intellectual plans for humanity are here. As a result, humanitarian, environmental, intellectual, and political causes are found in this House. Your tendencies toward rebellion and disruption are also here, since this is the place in which you can be most motivated by your ideals. This House holds your own future and it is the location of your personal visions for the future of humanity.

THE SIGN ON YOUR 11TH HOUSE CUSP describes your needs with regard to friends and associations, your attitude with regard to joining groups, and your approach to humanity in general. It's an indicator of the kinds of plans and visions you have for your own future and for the future of humankind. This Sign shows how you would go about changing the world, if you could. And, it signifies how you'll respond if your personal future becomes vague, unpleasant, or destroyed.

11th House Applications

PSYCHOLOGICAL: dreams, visions, hopes, and plans for the future; challenges to the status quo, reform, nonconforming ideas and concepts, rebellion; groups of people of like mind; participation in associations or social groups with common interests and goals

PRACTICAL: goals, plans, future directions; clubs, groups, and organizations; unusual, nonconforming, foreign, or rebellious elements; acquaintances of like mind; participation in a cause; politics

The Twelfth House: *Spiritual Life*

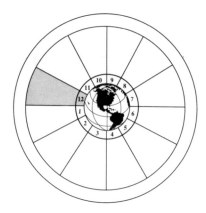

THE 12TH HOUSE IS ASSOCIATED WITH:

SECTION: FOURTH QUADRANT: expanded experiences and worldly concerns, explorations of the self and individual interests

PAIR: CONTEXT: non-ordinary, isolated circumstances

In the 12TH HOUSE, you discover how to adapt and change yourself, through non-ordinary circumstances. You disperse your energy out into the Universe, beyond the physical world. You can do this in 12th House environments such as healing, recovery, and treatment centers. Or, you can enter a spiritual community, convent, or monastery. The 12th House contains all of these "retreats from the world" as well as institutions such as prisons, rehabilitation centers, mental hospitals, and regular hospitals. Psychic and intuitive activities such as meditation, dreams, and hypnosis belong here because they also take you "out of this world" and into deeper levels of experience. Of course, other mind-altering experiences such as psychotic rages, emotional binges, and drunkenness are also contained in the 12th House. In fact, all addictions, including alcohol, food, drugs, sex, or even TV, are in this House. And, because the 12th House is beyond the normal world, it involves secrets, hidden things, and behind-the-scenes activities. In general, this House is concerned with experiences and substances that take you into "other" realities.

THE SIGN ON YOUR 12TH HOUSE CUSP denotes your needs with regard to non-usual mental and emotional experiences, your attitudes toward addictive substances, and your approach to spirituality. It shows the manner in which you most easily pursue psychic experiences and the nature of your intuition. The 12th House Sign reflects your response to experiences that might put you, or someone else, in a hospital or institution.

12th House Applications

PSYCHOLOGICAL: spirituality, psychic and intuitive awareness; the unconscious; experience of a "Higher Power"; substance abuse, dependency on any kind of "fix" to create a high or altered state; escape or retreat from consensus reality; dissolution of self, merger into something larger than the self

PRACTICAL: places of retreat, meditation, relaxation, renewal; prisons, jails, hospitals, mental institutions; alcohol and other drugs; addictions and dependencies; psychic and intuitive activities

SUMMARY

In this Chapter, I've discussed the Houses in detail. They can be seen as a sequence of issues and concerns related to the affairs of our daily lives. Briefly, the Houses contain people, places, and things associated with the following topics:

FIRST QUADRANT

These three Houses symbolize the personality (1), the establishment of its worth (2), and its adaptation to the surrounding environment (3).

SECOND QUADRANT

These three Houses symbolize foundations (4), creations that insure the ongoing existence of those foundations (5), and routines that adjust or improve them (6).

THIRD QUADRANT

These three Houses symbolize relationships (7), intimate interactions that deepen the relationships (8), and growth experiences that occur as we teach and learn from others (9).

FOURTH QUADRANT

These three Houses symbolize vocation (10), future visions that solidify the focus of the vocation (11), and spiritual understandings that give it meaning (12).

EXERCISES

4-1   Expand your interpretations of the Houses in your Chart by using the material in this Chapter.

4-2   Write down five practical, emotional, or philosophical issues that concern you at this time in your life. Now, locate the Houses that are associated with each of these issues. Save this list for use in later Exercises.

4-3   Ask a friend about the issues that are prominent in his or her life at the moment. Locate the Houses related to these concerns. Save this list, too.

FIVE

The Signs

The twelve SIGNS OF THE ZODIAC, representing segments of sky around the Earth, symbolize your attitudes and needs with regard to the areas of life symbolized by the Houses in your Chart. Since the Signs are naturally associated with specific Houses, the Sign concepts, by nature, are analogous to the House concepts. The distinction between them is that the Houses represent locations, things, or ideas about which attitudes can be formed. The Signs are those attitudes. In themselves, the Signs are not actors, although they might suggest modes of action. They do, however, describe the explicit ways in which you'll approach the concerns of a House, including your personal style and response patterns. The Signs on the House Cusps, and those Intercepted within the Houses, also indicate the needs that must be met within each House for you.

Since the Signs represent processes, not things, they can each be experienced in a variety of ways. If you don't find healthy opportunities for expressing and satisfying the needs of a Sign, you'll tend to manifest that Sign's energy in less-than-healthy attitudes and feelings. So, while the Houses can be only neutral, the Signs can be used both positively and negatively. To cover these possibilities in this Chapter, I've included a range of interpretations for each Sign.

As you study them, remember that it's up to you to choose the facet of each Sign that makes the most sense for a given person at a given time. One, many, or none of my interpretational phrases may "fit" you or your friends. If none of mine work, you can make up your own phrases after you've gotten a sense of the basic meanings. Just remember to test your ideas, as well as mine, through feedback.

For your review the Signs and their symbols are shown in Figure 5-1.

THE INTERPRETATIONAL STRUCTURE
OF THE SIGNS

The many meanings of the Signs can be understood best through building the interpretations out of core concepts in a manner similar to that of constructing the House interpretations. There are three primary components of the Signs: the QUALITIES, the ELEMENTS, and the THEMES. Two additional ways of categorizing the Signs are described briefly in Appendix F.

SIGNS	ABBREVIATION	GLYPH
NAME	AB.	SYMBOL
ARIES	AR	♈
TAURUS	TA	♉
GEMINI	GE	♊
CANCER	CA	♋
LEO	LE	♌
VIRGO	VI	♍
LIBRA	LI	♎
SCORPIO	SC	♏
SAGITTARIUS	SG	♐
CAPRICORN	CP	♑
AQUARIUS	AQ	♒
PISCES	PI	♓

Figure 5-1
The Signs, Their Abbreviations, and Their Glyphs

The Qualities

The QUALITIES (or MODALITIES) are CARDINAL, FIXED, and MUTABLE (Fig. 5-2). The three groups of Signs that result from dividing the Zodiac by Quality are also called the QUADRUPLICITIES because there are four Signs in each group.

The CARDINAL SIGNS (ARIES, CANCER, LIBRA, and CAPRICORN) symbolize the energies of assertiveness and initiative. They need to create what they want, motivate action, and trigger the next phase. Their attitudes are generative and directive. They respond to events by PROVOKING and by ORIGINATING new possibilities for what could exist.

The FIXED SIGNS (TAURUS, LEO, SCORPIO, and AQUARIUS) represent the forces of stabilization and intensification. They need to hold onto the status quo, appreciate the current reality, and preserve what's valued. Their attitudes are focused and determined. They respond to events by PERSISTING and by SUSTAINING what already exists.

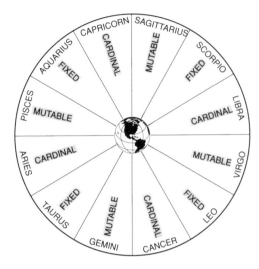

Figure 5-2
The Qualities

The MUTABLE SIGNS (GEMINI, VIRGO, SAGITTARIUS, and PISCES) reflect the processes of adaptation and dispersal. They need to move beyond what currently exists, adjust plans, and redesign patterns. Their attitudes are flexible and exploratory. They respond to events by DIVERSIFYING and by EVOLVING beyond what exists.

The Elements

The ELEMENTS are FIRE, EARTH, AIR, and WATER (Fig. 5-3). The four groups of Signs that emerge when the Zodiac is divided by Element are also called the TRIPLICITIES because there are three Signs in each group.

The FIRE SIGNS (ARIES, LEO, and SAGITTARIUS) exude stimulation and spontaneity. They need to be thrilled, inspired, and free. Their attitudes are catalytic and excitable. In response to events, they are ENTHUSIASTIC and EXPRESSIVE.

The EARTH SIGNS (TAURUS, VIRGO, and CAPRICORN) embody pragmatism and physical survival. They need to concretize plans, get tangible results, and build solid structures. Their attitudes are cautious and reliable. In response to events, they are PRODUCTIVE and PRACTICAL.

Figure 5-3
The Elements

The AIR SIGNS (GEMINI, LIBRA, and AQUARIUS) exemplify logic and relatedness. They need to gather information, explore intellectual ideas, and share concepts. Their attitudes are objective and curious. In response to events, they are COMMUNICATIVE and INTERACTIVE.

The WATER SIGNS (CANCER, SCORPIO, and PISCES) demonstrate sensitivity and intuition. They need to feel deeply, sense psychic connections, and subtly merge with others. Their attitudes are receptive and compassionate. In response to events, they are EMPATHIC and EMOTIONAL.

The Themes

The THEMES (Fig. 5-4) which represent the challenge to integrate opposing Signs, are analogous to the Pairs of Houses. In the case of the Signs, however, the Themes do not denote related areas of life; they do symbolize six sets of needs and attitudes that work toward integration within you. They represent the issues or processes that most commonly need to be addressed, healed, or realigned in the Houses Ruled by the paired Signs. Normally, the Theme will simply denote a psychological pattern that you'll encounter periodically as you mature. However, if a Theme is operating dysfunctionally, it could provide the impetus for you to seek professional support or feedback.

Figure 5-4
The Themes

Each Chart contains all the Themes, but each Theme is not emphasized in every Chart. In fact, it's useful to imagine that the paired Signs represent the two ends of a teeter-totter. The Planets in each Sign weight the ends. A big imbalance between the number of Planets in one Sign, compared with the number in its opposite Sign, may emphasize that pairs' Theme in your Chart. On the other hand, the presence of many Planets or Points in both Signs of a Theme will highlight it as well. And, the locations of the Sun, Moon, Nodes of the Moon, or Ascendant may underline a particular Theme. If a particular Theme seems difficult to integrate into your life, remember that the expressions of the two Signs involved are not necessarily mutually exclusive. These pairs of needs can be combined creatively. In fact, you'll probably discover a variety of ways to balance them throughout your life.

The opposing Signs that make up the Themes always consist of a Fire-Air or Earth-Water combination. As a result, these two basic combinations have some concepts in common. Generally speaking, if Fire and Air are involved, the Theme will revolve around the balancing act between the need for enthusiastic personal expression (Fire) and the need for communicative interaction with others (Air). If the pair of opposing Signs represent the Earth and Water Elements, the Theme will involve the process of establishing equilibrium between the need for practical productivity (Earth) and the need for emotional sensitivity (Water). The expression of the balancing act changes by Sign and by Theme, as follows:

THE THEME OF INTERDEPENDENCE
ARIES: : need to pursue independence and freedom

LIBRA: need to experience partnerships and cooperation

THE THEME OF PARTICIPATION
LEO: need to express individual creativity

AQUARIUS: need to consider the highest good of the group

THE THEME OF KNOWLEDGE
SAGITTARIUS: need to energetically seek and teach *the* truth

GEMINI: need to curiously explore diversity and variety

THE THEME OF GROWTH
TAURUS: need to produce tangible and reliable results

SCORPIO: need to transform through intense experiences

THE THEME OF IMPROVEMENT
VIRGO: need to fix things at a physical level

PISCES: need to heal at an emotional or psychic level

THE THEME OF SECURITY
CAPRICORN: need to establish practical position in the world

CANCER: need to create emotionally nurturing nests

Figures 5-2 through 5-4 show the progression of factors that create the basic meanings of the twelve Signs. These are integrated and explained in more detail in the remainder of the Chapter. Of course, your ways of acting out the needs of the Signs will be unique to you. For this reason, I've included the emotional, mental, spiritual, and physical expressions in the applications for each Sign. I've also created some sample interpretations that describe the Signs on (or in) all of the Houses. The key word in the last sentence is, of course, *sample*. These phrases will give you some ideas; expand on them for yourself.

Aries:
Independence

THE NEEDS AND ATTITUDES OF ARIES ARE:

QUALITY: CARDINAL: assertive, initiatory, motivated, generative, provocative, and originative

ELEMENT: FIRE: catalytic, excited, spontaneous, thrilled, enthusiastic, and expressive

THEME: pursuing independence and freedom

The glyph for ARIES, THE SIGN OF THE RAM, represents the ram's curved horns, which symbolize its aggressiveness.

ARIES is the Sign that most signifies the need for independence, assertiveness, and spontaneous expression. It wants to get up and get going *now*. It has a need for being left alone, for pursuing pioneering adventures, and for taking risks. It tends not to evaluate the consequences of its actions – for itself or for others. It needs to act, in the moment, according to its own desires. Aries's attitudes are reflected when its says, "I can do it, why can't you?" or "Just get out of my way and let me do it!" The typical Aries response to events is "Well, that's over, so what's the next thing to move on to?" or "I don't know what you're going to do now, but I'm getting out of here." All in all, Aries is best at initiating and inspiring action even to the point of acting prematurely.

In a HOUSE WITH ARIES ON THE CUSP, you'll want to be as pioneering as possible, to live on the edge. While you may have a reputation for being competitive here, it's not really that you want to "beat" others. You aren't that interested in others. You do, however, want to get places quickly, with no distractions or limitations. As a result, in Aries's House, you'll gracefully, or ungracefully, move blocking forces out of the way. This certainly helps you to get past any and all obstacles and to arrive directly at your chosen destination. In this House, it's easy for you to operate from your own point of view, sometimes forgetting that others have needs, wants, and opinions. You usually assume that what you know and want is true for everyone. On the other hand, in this department of life, you do encourage and inspire others to be independent and self-directed.

If ARIES IS INTERCEPTED in your Chart, your family's way of being assertive and independent is probably not your way. They may have been perfectly healthy in expressing their pioneering and spontaneous urges – just different from you. They may have been actually unhealthy: bullying and insensitive. Or, they may have been entirely lacking in adventurousness. Whatever they did, you've had to learn how to take risks and pursue what you want, consciously and gracefully.

Your ESSENTIAL THEMATIC CHALLENGES IN AN ARIES HOUSE are:

• to discover how to seek independence and freedom without isolating yourself, and

• to determine how to express assertiveness while being considerate of others.

APPLICATIONS FOR ARIES

EMOTIONAL: spontaneous, naive, childlike, premoral, excited, stimulated, energized, inspired, freedom-loving, unreliable, inconsiderate, insensitive, bullying

MENTAL: motivated, generative, inspired, creative, catalytic, assertive, interruptive, opinionated, self-centered

PHYSICAL: brave, courageous, risk-taking, active, moving, athletic, pioneering, aggressive, pushy

> STRENGTH OR WEAKNESS: head, face, brain, upper teeth, fevers, inflammations, skin eruptions, cuts, burns, headaches, colds, anemia, or surgical procedures

> FEATURES: PEOPLE: red hair, harelips, acne, arched or big nose

> FEATURES: PLACES & THINGS: fairly high up, hilly, hot, sandy; associated with fire, danger, risk, unmapped territory

SPIRITUAL: pursues independent, active spiritual path; eager to manifest personal potential, aware of its separate, individuated purpose; talented at martial arts, running for a high, and fire rituals

SAMPLE INTERPRETATIONS FOR ARIES ON (OR IN) HOUSES

In addition to interpreting ARIES on (or in) the Houses, LOOK FOR MARS. Its location by Sign and House will tell you more about how the Aries needs and attitudes are expressed in the Chart.

1st: red hair, prominent nose; assertive or independent personality

2nd: spontaneous or childlike regarding money; bases self-worth on independence and freedom

3rd: inspired or interruptive in communication; unreliable with siblings; catalytic or active in neighborhood or community

4th: pioneering regarding home; independent of family and clan

5th: generative in creative endeavors; spontaneous in play or romance; active with children

6th: surgery, cuts, burns, damage to face, or headaches as health concerns; independently motivated or unreliable in terms of daily routine

7th: risk-taking in relationships; independent or self-centered with partner

8th: sexually creative or aggressive; spontaneous regarding shared resources

9th: independent or pioneering in travel; courageous or stimulated in terms of higher education

10th: energized or motivated regarding career; aggressive or childlike in reputation

11th: pioneering or courageous with regard to future plans; bullying or self-centered with friends or in groups

12th: martial arts or running as spiritual paths; time-out alone for spiritual renewal; intense physical activity as an addiction

Taurus:
Persistence

THE NEEDS AND ATTITUDES OF TAURUS ARE:

QUALITY: FIXED: maintained, stabilized, focused, determined, persistent, and sustaining

ELEMENT: EARTH: pragmatic, grounded, tangible, concrete, reliable, productive, and practical

THEME: GROWTH: producing tangible and reliable results

The glyph for TAURUS, THE SIGN OF THE BULL, represents the bull's face and horns, which symbolize its immovability.

TAURUS represents the urge and desire for stability, predictability, and cautious progress. It values what it has already created and is loathe to part with it. In fact, in wanting to literally hold onto things, Taurus is quite sensual. It's aware of physical stimuli in its environment and wants to maximize opportunities for pleasant tastes, textures, or touch. It wants to get tangible results for its efforts but is willing to be patient in waiting for the payoff. Taurus tends to maintain the status quo, needing concrete evidence before it will reevaluate the current state of affairs. It needs to test the value of any change, sometimes taking months or years before taking action. Taurus's attitudes are reflected when it says, "If it's really a good idea, it'll still be there tomorrow." and "How useful or productive is it?" In response to an event, Taurus might say, "Let's just keep working along and see what happens," or "This has always worked before, I'm sure it will work out eventually." Taurus has steadfast loyalty and an incredible ability to keep things going indefinitely.

In a HOUSE WITH TAURUS ON THE CUSP, you'll want to be practical, useful, and reliable. You'll also want to be valued and compensated for your contribution, usually at a material level. While you may have a reputation for being stubborn in this area of life, you actually just need time to make changes. The length of time is correlated in some way, to the importance of the decision and to the respect that is its due. So, in the Taurean House, you could take up to two years to make a significant change. If you feel rushed or pressured, you might simply dig in your heels and refuse to cooperate until you've had enough time to think about it. Unfortunately, by refusing to change, you could get stuck in a negative cycle or repetitive pattern. Unwilling to let go, you could hang on while waiting for a payoff. If you can define the payoff as a learned lesson, you might be able to move on even if you haven't achieved what you wanted. Otherwise, you'll just have to wait and make your move when you feel that the time is right.

If TAURUS IS INTERCEPTED, your role models for persistence don't match your personal style. Your family may have been perfectly healthy in demonstrating their consistency and reliability – just different from you. They may have been actually unhealthy: stubborn and immovable. Or, they may have been entirely lacking in dependability. So, you've had to learn from others how to be loyal and consistent in an appropriate way.

Your ESSENTIAL THEMATIC CHALLENGES IN A TAURUS HOUSE are:

• to discover how to build tangible and reliable structures while remaining open to total change and transformation and

• to determine how to hold onto things of value without hoarding.

APPLICATIONS FOR TAURUS

EMOTIONAL: holding, supporting, reliable, dependable, loyal, committed, comfortable, placid, traditional, valuing, persistent, stubborn, stingy, hoarding, possessive

MENTAL: practical, concrete, realistic, conscious of results, deliberate, determined, obdurate

PHYSICAL: value-conscious, sensual, strong, powerful, solid, coordinated, musical, rhythmic, immovable, seeking of pleasure, lazy, hedonistic

> STRENGTH OR WEAKNESS: neck, throat, voice, ears, lower teeth, brow, thyroid, sugar metabolism, lymph, or tongue

> FEATURES: PEOPLE: thick neck, "football player" shoulders, husky build, or graceful, lithe build

> FEATURES: PLACES & THINGS: low, warm, solid, cultivated, associated with stone, brick, dirt, security, resources

SPIRITUAL: values stable spiritual path with some tradition or ritual; grounded, comfortable in the material plane; talented at yoga, bodywork and massage, Tai-Chi, psychometry, telekinesis

SAMPLE INTERPRETATIONS FOR TAURUS ON (OR IN) HOUSES

In addition to interpreting TAURUS on (or in) the Houses, LOOK FOR VENUS. Its location by Sign and House will tell you more about how the Taurus needs and attitudes are expressed in the Chart.

1st: husky shoulders or thick neck; reliable, loyal personality

2nd: practical and realistic regarding money; bases self-worth on persistence or dependability

3rd: realistic or result-conscious in communication; committed to siblings; supportive of community or neighborhood

4th: practical or determined with regard to home; loyal to traditions of family and clan

5th: rhythmic, musical in creative endeavors; coordinated in sports; pleasure-seeking in romantic affairs

6th: neck, throat, thyroid, or lymph problems as health concerns; determined, reliable, or persistent in daily routine

7th: loyal or committed in relationships; immovable or stubborn with partner

8th: sexually sensuous or hedonistic; conscious of results or traditional in the use of shared resources

9th: stingy or practical in travel; persistent in higher education

10th: realistic or result-conscious regarding career; powerful or stubborn in reputation

11th: practical or concrete with regard to future plans; reliable or dependable with friends or in groups

12th: bodywork and yoga as spiritual paths; sensuous or rhythmic activities for spiritual renewal; laziness or hedonism as addictions

Gemini:
Versatility

THE NEEDS AND ATTITUDES OF GEMINI ARE:

QUALITY: MUTABLE: expansive, disseminating, changeable, adaptable, diversified, and evolving

ELEMENT: AIR: conceptual, intellectual, informative, objective; communicative and interactive

THEME: KNOWLEDGE: exploring diversity and variety

The glyph for GEMINI, THE SIGN OF THE TWINS, represents duality or two-ness and symbolizes multiplicity.

GEMINI is the Sign that wants to examine everything in its environment. It is unendingly curious and, fascinated by the multiple options available in any situation, and loves to juggle them all. It has a need for mental stimulation, amusing activities, and varying frames of reference. Gemini needs constant entertainment and desires never to be bored. Its attitudes are reflected when it says, "What else could we do?" and "Let's explore all the possibilities." If events occur in the Gemini House, its response is usually "Well, that's interesting; I wonder how it connects to this other situation?" or "This is getting boring; what could we do that's fun?" Gemini tends to be a networking force, finding the connections among ideas, people, and events, and happily bopping from one to the next without pausing for too long anywhere.

In a HOUSE WITH GEMINI ON THE CUSP, you'll tend to experience either duality or multiplicity. You may have a reputation in that area of life for being somewhat flaky or undependable, but the reality is that you are multi-dimensional. You don't want to be limited to one narrow experience, so you are constantly seeking out new opportunities for diversion. In fact, it is here that you are most easily distractible. You often pursue what seems stimulating in the moment rather than what you've previously planned. This spontaneity and flexibility provides for fun and amusement, but it can sometimes be frustrating to others. In Gemini's House, you'll gather interesting facts and curious experiences while thinking that, someday, they might all correlate with one another. But, in this area of life, someday may never come. With Gemini, you can easily move on to the next fascinating tidbit without ever integrating all the ideas into a whole or caring whether you understand their broader meaning.

If GEMINI IS INTERCEPTED in your Chart, your childhood environment didn't support you in being investigative and communicative in the ways that you wanted. Your family may have been perfectly healthy in their manner of discussion and community exploration – just different from you. They may have been actually unhealthy: argumentative and flighty. Or, they may have been entirely lacking in curiosity about the world. In any event, you've had to figure out, from others, how to communicate effectively and pursue your explorations appropriately.

Your ESSENTIAL THEMATIC CHALLENGES IN A GEMINI HOUSE are:

• to discover how to explore all the immediate options while staying aware of the larger picture and

• to determine how to communicate without being scattered or argumentative.

APPLICATIONS FOR GEMINI

EMOTIONAL: multi-dimensional, versatile, amusing, humorous, quickly bored, flaky, unreliable, superficial, nervous, gossipy

MENTAL: quick, curious, investigative, communicative, fluent, logical, clever, associative, fact-finding, networking, exploratory, facile, scattered, undirected

PHYSICAL: multi-faceted, agile, nimble, quick, up-tempo, hyper; ambidextrous, having more-than-one, twinned

> STRENGTH OR WEAKNESS: shoulders, arms, lungs, respiration, circulation, nervous system, upper body fractures

> FEATURES: PEOPLE: somewhat nondescript features that can mobilize into a myriad of creative facial expressions; youthful

> FEATURES: PLACES & THINGS: high up, airy, dry; associated with words, signals, transportation, or communication

SPIRITUAL: explores various spiritual options; curious, uses the mind to understand other dimensions of reality; talented at automatic writing or drawing, Ouija boarding, palmistry, or handwriting analysis

SAMPLE INTERPRETATIONS FOR GEMINI ON (OR IN) HOUSES

In addition to interpreting GEMINI on (or in) the Houses, LOOK FOR MERCURY. Its location by Sign and House will tell you more about how the Gemini needs and attitudes are expressed in the Chart.

1st: youthful, mobile features; maybe ambidextrous or a twin; curious, versatile personality

2nd: multi-faceted in ways of earning money; bases self-worth on logic or fact-finding abilities

3rd: facile or humorous in communication; gossipy with siblings; oriented to networking in community and neighborhood

4th: more than one home; curious or communicative with family and clan

5th: verbal in creative endeavors; versatile or amusing in play or romance; tendency to have twins

6th: respiratory, nervous, or circulation systems as health concerns; quickly bored or scattered and undirected in terms of daily routine

7th: communicative in relationships; versatile or unreliable with partner; more than one primary partner during lifetime

8th: sexually multi-faceted or bisexual; undirected regarding shared resources

9th: curious or investigative in travel; exploratory about higher education; maybe more than one degree

10th: more than one career; multi-faceted or versatile in terms of reputation

11th: exploratory or undirected with regard to future plans; humorous or gossipy with friends and in groups

12th: community-oriented spiritual path; automatic writing or palmistry as psychic activities; communication and discussion for spiritual renewal; busyness as an addiction

Cancer
Nurturance

THE NEEDS AND ATTITUDES OF CANCER ARE:

QUALITY: CARDINAL: generative, motivated, creative, initiatory, provocative, and originative

ELEMENT: WATER: receptive, intuitive, sensitive, psychic, merged, empathic, and emotional

THEME: SECURITY: creating emotionally nurturing nests

The glyph for CANCER, THE SIGN OF THE CRAB, represents the crab with its soft underbelly, symbolizing vulnerability. It also represents the breasts, sources of nurturance.

The Sign of CANCER is the ultimate symbol of nurturance and caretaking. It needs to feel that it belongs, that it's safe, and that it will be protected. It evaluates things in terms of past, present, and future security. And, security is symbolized by having *enough* of such things as food, love, care, money, or comfort. In fact, Cancer will collect memorabilia, objects, cans of food, money, loved ones – anything that symbolizes abundance for it. And, in order to establish this enough-ness, it will be quite assertive about asking for what it wants. Cancer's attitudes are reflected when it says, "Is there enough?" and "There, there, it'll be okay." In response to events, Cancer will ask "How is everyone feeling?" and "What do we need to feel better?" So, in addition to seeking out nurturance, Cancer takes care of others in a parental way. It surrounds the people and things it loves with care and protection.

In a HOUSE WITH CANCER ON THE CUSP, you'll want to feel secure. You may have a reputation here for being overly sensitive or emotional, but the reality is that you are probably experiencing and expressing everyone's feelings (not just your own) in this area of life. In addition to creating "enough" for you, you want to make sure that others have enough, too. And, you're willing to be the giver or caretaker in Cancer's House. Because you're aware of others' feelings, you intuitively seem to know what they need. However, you might sometimes forget to find out if they want your attention. While ignoring their boundaries, you might smother or suffocate people. On occasion, this could provoke them into abandoning or disappointing you. Then, feeling used, you could demonstrate clingy, dependent, and even addictive behaviors in Cancer's House. Nevertheless, in one form or another, you've worked on building emotional security and long-term foundations here. You've learned some things about how to put limits on your own giving and how to evaluate your expectations of others.

If CANCER IS INTERCEPTED in your Chart, your birth family didn't give you an appropriate experience of nurturance. They may have been perfectly healthy in taking care of themselves and others—just different from you. They may have been actually unhealthy: needy and smothering. Or, they may have been entirely lacking in nurturing qualities. If they focused on their own neediness, they might have demanded that you become the "mother" when you were too young to play that role. So, as you've matured, you've had to relearn parenting patterns. You've had to discover, through others' role-modeling, how to be positively and healthily caring.

Your ESSENTIAL THEMATIC CHALLENGES IN A CANCER HOUSE are:

• to discover how to remain safe and nurtured while still organizing your life in a practical, realistic manner and

• to determine how to find belongingness without draining yourself or others.

APPLICATIONS FOR CANCER

EMOTIONAL: nurturing, belonging, caring, warm, comforting, fluctuating, protective, "mothering," psychic, nostalgic, sentimental, security-oriented, moody, needy, dependent, fearful, addictive, clingy

MENTAL: insightful, instinctive, protective of past patterns, vague, unclear

PHYSICAL: warm, soft, cuddly, round, comforting, easy-going

STRENGTH OR WEAKNESS: breasts, stomach, chest cavity, armpits, eating patterns and disorders, digestion

FEATURES: PEOPLE: rounded body or round face, childlike looks

FEATURES: PLACES & THINGS: deep, wet; associated with homes, food, water, or children

SPIRITUAL: drawn to comforting, loving path with a feeling of belonging; aware of nurturing Universal force; talented at psychic or spiritual counseling, caring for the needy, rituals related to food or home, experiencing other lifetimes, and candle work

SAMPLE INTERPRETATIONS FOR CANCER ON (OR IN) HOUSES

In addition to interpreting CANCER on (or in) the Houses, LOOK FOR THE MOON. Its location by Sign and House will tell you more about how the Cancer needs and attitudes are expressed in the Chart.

1st: rounded body or round face; nurturing or comforting personality

2nd: needy or clingy regarding money; bases self-worth on caretaking or "mothering" skills

3rd: sentimental or insightful in communication; protective of siblings; caring or warm in neighborhood and community

4th: belonging at home; "mothering" or nurturing of family and clan

5th: soft, sentimental in creative endeavors; comforting or dependent in play or romance; nurturing or protective with children

6th: breasts, chest, stomach, or eating patterns as health concerns; protective of past patterns or moody in terms of daily routine

7th: caring or warm in relationships; "belonged," maybe clingy with partner

8th: sexually sentimental or needy; protective or fearful regarding shared resources

9th: nostalgic or instinctive in travel; insightful or fearful in terms of higher education

10th: fluctuating or sentimental regarding career; caring or protective in reputation

11th: fearful or protective of past patterns with regard to future plans; psychic or "mothering" with friends and in groups

12th: food or candle rituals as spiritual activities; self-nurturing for spiritual renewal; food as an addiction .

Leo:
Expressiveness

THE NEEDS AND ATTITUDES OF LEO ARE:

QUALITY: FIXED: appreciative, intense, determined, focused, persistent, and sustaining

ELEMENT: FIRE: catalytic, thrilled, spontaneous, excited, stimulated, enthusiastic, and expressive

THEME: PARTICIPATION: expressing individual creativity

The glyph for LEO, THE SIGN OF THE LION, represents the lion's flowing mane and symbolizes its royal pride and attitude.

The Sign of LEO is a magnanimous, generous, heart-centered force. It wants to experience the full exuberance of life, the richness of it. Out of this desire come Leo's needs for drama, courage, adventure, and nobility. It needs to burst with assuredness, confidence, and pride. Its attitudes are reflected when it says, "Look at me, see what I'm doing," and "Isn't this all exciting!" Leo will typically respond to events by wondering "How could I leap into the spotlight in this situation?" or "How is this a chance for celebration?" Generally, Leo wants to play and entertain others. It can sustain an incredibly high degree of energy and enthusiasm for a long period of time, even after others are ready to quit.

In a HOUSE WITH LEO ON THE CUSP, you'll want to shine and to receive applause, appreciation, attention, and praise. You may even have a reputation in this part of life for being a show-off, but the truth is that you're willing to celebrate others as well as yourself. In Leo's House, you give generous support to anyone's personal expression. You just want to know that you've contributed, directly or indirectly, to joyful, playful living. You also want to play at living here, seeking opportunities to dramatize yourself creatively. In fact, if the House is the stage set, Leo is the spotlight on the star of the show: you. Sometimes, in this House, you can get so caught up in your drama that you forget that "it's only a show." By then, you're into melodrama, and everything becomes a matter of life and death. If no one pays attention, you could experience injured pride and resort to arrogance. But, if people do pay attention, you're charming, magnanimous, and ultimately entertaining in this House.

If LEO IS INTERCEPTED in your Chart, your family's method of applauding and praising you wasn't what you wanted or needed. They may have been perfectly healthy in expressing themselves and encouraging your performance—just different from you. They may have been actually unhealthy: embarrassing and pressuring. Or, they may have been entirely lacking in spontaneity. They may have totally ignored your "show," so that you didn't feel supported and appreciated. If they overdramatized themselves and their experiences too much, you could have become afraid of exuberance or playfulness. In any case, in Intercepted Leo's House you've had to develop an ability to celebrate life without taking yourself too seriously. You've had to learn through someone else's example, how to ask appropriately for applause and how to appreciate yourself even if no one else notices you.

Your ESSENTIAL THEMATIC CHALLENGES IN A LEO HOUSE are:

• to discover how to express yourself in the present in personally satisfying ways, while still considering the impact of your behavior on the future of the group as a whole and

• to seek applause and attention from others without becoming overbearing and boastful.

APPLICATIONS FOR LEO

EMOTIONAL: projecting, expressive, dramatic, generous, magnanimous, romantic, goodhearted, inclusive of others, proud, confident, charismatic, egotistical, overbearing, attention-getting, broken-hearted

MENTAL: self-assured, storytelling, creative, show-off, arrogant, boastful

PHYSICAL: heroic, forceful, strong, energetic, enthusiastic, able to sustain energy, flamboyant, procreative, ruthless, competitive

> STRENGTH OR WEAKNESS: heart, spine, spinal column, upper back, fainting or heat exhaustion

> FEATURES: PEOPLE: flowing, bushy, or manelike hair; "heroic" looks; noticeable jewelry

> FEATURES: PLACES & THINGS: hot, bright, steep, or high; associated with recreation, drama, or glamour

SPIRITUAL: leaps into dramatic spiritual activities that involve some pageantry; aware of self as an expression of "the Force"; talented at channeling, psychic-drama, and fire rituals

SAMPLE INTERPRETATIONS FOR LEO ON (OR IN) HOUSES

In addition to interpreting LEO on (or in) the Houses, LOOK FOR THE SUN. Its location by Sign and House will tell you more about how the Leo needs and attitudes are expressed in the Chart.

1st: manelike hair, noticeable jewelry; dramatic or confident personality

2nd: enthusiastic or competitive regarding money; bases self-worth on heroism or magnanimity

3rd: forceful or storytelling in communication; generous or self-assured with siblings; proud or arrogant in neighborhood and community

4th: flamboyant or attention-getting regarding home; romantic about family and clan

5th: dramatic in creative endeavors; able to sustain energy in play or romance; procreative or competitive with regard to children

6th: heart, spine, or heat exhaustion as health concerns; energetic or overbearing in terms of daily routine

7th: magnanimous in relationships; romantic or enthusiastic with partner

8th: sexually dramatic or boastful; competitive or generous regarding shared resources

9th: heroic or flamboyant in travel; proud or confident in terms of higher education

10th: attention-getting or self-assured regarding career; egotistical or creative in reputation

11th: able to sustain energy with regard to future plans; generous or storytelling with friends and in groups

12th: channeling as a spiritual path; ritual or pageantry for spiritual renewal; melodrama or trauma as an addiction

Virgo
Analysis

THE NEEDS AND ATTITUDES OF VIRGO ARE:

QUALITY: MUTABLE: disseminating, adjustable, adaptable, redesigning, diversified, and evolving

ELEMENT: EARTH: pragmatic, concrete, physical, reliable, solid, productive, and practical

THEME: IMPROVEMENT: fixing things at a physical level

The glyph for VIRGO, THE SIGN OF THE VIRGIN, represents the closed hymen of a female virgin, which traditionally symbolized purity. It's also a symbol for a sheaf of perfectly ripe grain.

The Sign of VIRGO represents the drive to manifest the ideal within the real. Virgo can imagine perfection and is always attempting to reproduce that perfection in physical reality. This leads to its tendency to watch for errors and omissions. Its needs involve analyzing, trouble-shooting, and problem-solving. Virgo also needs to be meticulous, detail-oriented, and precise in its approach to any activity. Its attitudes are reflected when it says, "If you're going to do it, do it right" and "Let's make a list of things to do." If an event occurs, Virgo will respond with, "Okay, what went wrong and how can we fix it?" or "Next time, we'll do this instead."

In a HOUSE WITH VIRGO ON THE CUSP, you'll want to analyze and repair in a detailed way. You may have a reputation, in this area of life for being overly critical or analytical, but actually, you're just focusing on the smallest issues with an eye toward finding the best solution for yourself *and* for others. You may even engage in research and testing before you find the final answer. Practicality and viability are your watchwords here, and ideas have no value until they're proven in reality. While you can be extremely critical of others in the House of Virgo, you're actually hardest on yourself. You tend to run negative self-talk inside your head, constantly commenting on what you "should" be doing. Sometimes, you can become so overwhelmed by your need to do it all and do it right that you collapse inward. At that point, instead of being in charge of life's details, the details are in charge. From there, it's a short step to workaholic patterns. Ideally, though, you can take care of business in a realistic way in this House.

If VIRGO IS INTERCEPTED in your Chart, analysis wasn't well-demonstrated in your early environment. Your family may have been perfectly healthy in its style of critiquing – just different from you. They may have been actually unhealthy: picky and overly critical. Or, they may have been entirely lacking in analytical skills. In any case, you've had to learn from others how to supply constructive criticism and solutions in a graceful manner.

Your ESSENTIAL THEMATIC CHALLENGES IN A VIRGO HOUSE are:

• to discover how to analyze and repair imperfections while having compassion and respect for emotions and

• to determine how to work toward the ideal without losing sight of what's possible in our world.

APPLICATIONS FOR VIRGO

EMOTIONAL: discriminating, problem-solving, methodical, willing to serve others, discreet, self-analytical, critical, self-critical, picky, worrisome, fussy, nervous

MENTAL: analytical, detail-oriented, perfectionistic, editorial, correcting, scheduling, organizing, reminding, nagging

PHYSICAL: health-conscious, scheduled, systemized, mending, repairing, painstaking, efficient, task-oriented, fixing, compulsive, workaholic

STRENGTH OR WEAKNESS: intestines, appendix, abdomen, nutrition, or digestion

FEATURES: PEOPLE: cleft in nose or chin, "worried" brow, noticeable bone structure

FEATURES: PLACES & THINGS: level areas, wet, warm; associated with work, productivity, health, agriculture, or repair

SPIRITUAL: seeks a systemized spiritual practice, especially those including physical disciplines; has a desire to serve at a practical level; talented at yoga, Tai Chi, bodywork, herbs, nutrition, handwriting analysis

SAMPLE INTERPRETATIONS FOR VIRGO ON (OR IN) HOUSES

In addition to interpreting VIRGO on (or in) the Houses, LOOK FOR CHIRON. Its location by Sign and House will tell you more about how the Virgo needs and attitudes are expressed in the Chart.

1st: cleft in nose or chin; analytical or health-conscious personality

2nd: detail-oriented or systemized regarding money; bases self-worth on perfection or repair skills

3rd: correcting or nagging in communication; problem-solving with siblings; serving or organizing in neighborhood and community

4th: methodical or fussy regarding home; analytical of family and clan

5th: detail-oriented in creative endeavors; health-conscious in play or romance; problem-solving or systemized with children

6th: intestines, appendix, nutrition, or digestion as health concerns; routinized or workaholic in terms of daily routine

7th: methodical in relationships; serving or critical with partner

8th: sexually health-conscious or routinized; detail-oriented or analytical regarding shared resources

9th: discriminating or fussy in travel; systemized or self-critical in terms of higher education

10th: serving or perfectionistic regarding career; problem-solving or methodical in terms of reputation

11th: detail-oriented or discriminating with regard to future plans; serving or nagging with friends and in groups

12th: yoga, herbs, or nutrition as spiritual paths; systemized practice for spiritual renewal; health concerns or work as addictions.

Libra:
Cooperation

THE NEEDS AND ATTITUDES OF LIBRA ARE:

QUALITY: CARDINAL: initiatory, motivated, directive, creative, provocative, and originative

ELEMENT: AIR: conceptual, logical, objective, evaluative, communicative, and interactive

THEME: INTERDEPENDENCE: experiencing partnerships and cooperation

The glyph for LIBRA, THE SIGN OF THE SCALES, represents a set of old-fashioned weighing scales, which symbolize balance and equality.

LIBRA represents the desire for peace, truth, light, justice, and fairness. Ideally, it wants everyone to be nice to everyone else and to find perfect harmony and balance within. Libra needs equal-based, respectful relationships that honor all involved. It needs emotional and esthetic beauty, serenity, and calm. Its attitudes are reflected when it says, "How can we all get along?" and "Tell me about you." In reaction to an event, Libra would say "I can understand both sides of it," and "What can we do to patch things up?" At every level, Libra initiates cooperation.

In a HOUSE WITH LIBRA ON THE CUSP, you want to be the agent of beautiful connections. You could have a reputation of being indecisive or of sending mixed signals here, but you're actually just trying to see all sides of an issue before you make a decision. Because you can understand many points of view, you could serve as the mediator in negotiations among people. You could be the artistic director who combines and coordinates creative efforts. And, you could be the insightful consultant who helps others integrate their internal experiences. When you do accomplish your magic in the Libran House, you could become vain about it. You're so good in this area of life – at getting others to cooperate and collaborate with you, even to the point of giving you things and opportunities – that you could ignore or deny that *you* might need to compromise. On the other hand, it's so important for you to have cooperative relationships in this House that you may also do more than your share just to get along with everyone.

If LIBRA IS INTERCEPTED in your Chart, it's unlikely that your family showed you how to be appropriately diplomatic and cooperative. They may have been perfectly healthy in their negotiations – just different from you. They may have been actually unhealthy: self-denying and other-obsessed. Or, they may have been totally lacking in collaborative skills. As a result, you've had to learn how to share and participate.

Your ESSENTIAL THEMATIC CHALLENGES IN A LIBRA HOUSE are:

• to discover how to cooperate fully without ignoring your personal needs or losing your own independence and

• to determine how to create beauty and harmony without being superficial.

APPLICATIONS FOR LIBRA

EMOTIONAL: relationship-conscious, interactive, charming, graceful, social, sharing, other-oriented, fair, egalitarian, coordinating, cooperating, compromising, refined, appearance-conscious, dependent, self- deprecating, manipulative, vain

MENTAL: balanced, mathematical, option-oriented, conscious of alternatives, respectful of feedback, negotiative, arbitrative, mediative, exchanging or sharing of information, uncommitted, indecisive

PHYSICAL: coordinated, balanced, esthetically appealing, beautiful, attractive, oriented to teamwork, cooperative, decorative, observant or nonparticipatory

> STRENGTH OR WEAKNESS: kidneys, adrenals, urinary system, internal reproductive system, sugar metabolism, or the veins

> FEATURES: PEOPLE: fine or balanced features, esthetic bone structure, classical looks

> FEATURES: PLACES & THINGS: hilly, airy, clean, dry; associated with beauty, charm, art, creativity, diplomacy, partners

SPIRITUAL: attracts artistic and esthetically pleasing spiritual experiences; likes social acceptability; aware of cooperating with divine will; talented at automatic or psychic art, consulting or counseling, relationship work, yoga, and Tai Chi

SAMPLE INTERPRETATIONS FOR LIBRA ON (OR IN) HOUSES

In addition to interpreting LIBRA on (or in) the Houses, LOOK FOR VENUS. Its location by Sign and House will tell you more about how the Libra needs and attitudes are expressed in the Chart.

1st: fine features, classical looks; charming or social personality

2nd: respectful of feedback regarding money; bases self-worth on co-operation or negotiation skills

3rd: conscious of alternatives or fair in communication; compromising with siblings; interactive or relationship-conscious in neighborhood and community

4th: decorative regarding home; manipulative of family and clan

5th: creative in the fine arts; cooperative in play or romance; negotiative or fair with children

6th: kidneys, urinary system, or sugar metabolism as health concerns; cooperative or indecisive in terms of daily routine

7th: dependent in relationships; compromising or uncommitted with partner

8th: sexually fair or manipulative; egalitarian regarding shared resources

9th: conscious of alternatives or other-oriented in travel; respectful of feedback or self-deprecating in terms of higher education

10th: collaborative or other-oriented in career; arbitrative or indecisive in reputation

11th: option-oriented or cooperative with regard to future plans; social or interactive with friends and in groups

12th: counseling or art as spiritual paths; cooperative or shared activities for spiritual renewal; love or dependence on people as addictions

Scorpio:
Transformation

THE NEEDS AND ATTITUDES OF SCORPIO ARE:

QUALITY: FIXED: focused, intense, determined, preserving, persistent, and sustaining

ELEMENT: WATER: sensitive, psychic, merged, transformative, empathic, and emotional

THEME: GROWTH: transforming through intense experiences

The glyph for SCORPIO, THE SIGN OF THE SCORPION, represents the scorpion's stinging tail, which symbolizes its laser-like ability to get to the heart of things. Other symbols for this Sign are the PHOENIX and the SNAKE which symbolize the processes of transformation, death, and rebirth.

SCORPIO is the most emotionally intense Sign of the Zodiac. It holds and sustains its own and others' feelings, experiencing them all. It also experiences life as a metaphor, sensing that everything that happens in the world is a symbol of something happening inside itself. Scorpio needs to feel powerful, transforming emotions and psychic events. It needs to know that it has affected others and been changed by them. Its attitudes are reflected when it says, "I can see into your soul," and "Give me some privacy so that I can dig deeper into my experience." When things happen, Scorpio's response tends to be "Let's hold tight until we're forced to change." or "Let's get rid of it all and start over." Generally, Scorpio represents the force of cyclic transformation: gathering energy and releasing it, gathering energy again.

In a HOUSE WITH SCORPIO ON THE CUSP you'll want deep, meaningful, transformational changes to occur. You might even have the reputation in this House of being too intense and passionate, but it's just that everything matters so much. Here, you preserve and condense emotion until it becomes a force that destroys old forms and rebirths new ones. During the period of intensification, you can seem secretive, mysterious, protective, and even defensive. But, if left alone long enough, you'll eventually burst forth with the next cycle of movement. If you focus inward too long, it can become a habit in Scorpio's House, resulting in pent-up emotion, controlling behavior, and repressed anger. In that case, the explosion may be truly destructive, sexually inappropriate, or violent. In most situations, however, the internal pressure finds a natural release.

If SCORPIO IS INTERCEPTED in your Chart, your family didn't demonstrate intensity and passion in a way that felt comfortable for you. They may have been perfectly healthy in their demonstrations of intimacy or focus – just different from you. They may have been actually unhealthy, showing you through abuse and violence that it was unsafe to have strong emotions. Or, they may have been entirely lacking in emotional expression, so repressed that you felt you were bad for having feelings at all. As you've grown up, you've had to find others who could teach you how to be productively powerful and how to express intense emotions appropriately.

Your ESSENTIAL THEMATIC CHALLENGES IN A SCORPIO HOUSE are:

• to discover how to transform yourself and others through intense emotional and psychic experiences while still holding onto some caution and predictability and

• to determine how to preserve intimacy and privacy in your life without hiding behind defensive walls.

APPLICATIONS FOR SCORPIO

EMOTIONAL: releasing, renewing, changing, transforming, seeking depth, hot/cold, passionate, defending, protecting, birthing, destroying, power-oriented, suspicious, jealous, vengeful, compulsive

MENTAL: conscious of life mission, aware of higher purpose, perceptive, penetrative, secretive, incisive, investigative, psychic, focused, defensive, attacking, power-tripping

PHYSICAL: intense, seductive, sexual, birth-oriented, death-oriented, compelled, driven, compulsive

> STRENGTH OR WEAKNESS: genitals, the elimination system, sexual functioning or habits, and surgical procedures

> FEATURES: PEOPLE: intense, brooding, or shuttered look, deep or smoldering eyes

> FEATURES: PLACES & THINGS: extremely deep, wet; associated with water, plumbing, sex, birth, death, shared resources

SPIRITUAL: delves into ritual and trance experiences; enjoys symbols and their interpretation; aware of self as extension of Universal power; fascinated by death or birth experiences; talented at channeling, lifetimes, Tarot, I Ching, Runes, rebirthing, dreams

SAMPLE INTERPRETATIONS FOR SCORPIO ON (OR IN) HOUSES

In addition to interpreting SCORPIO on (or in) the Houses, LOOK FOR PLUTO. Its location by Sign and House will tell you more about how the Scorpio needs and attitudes are expressed in the Chart.

1st: smoldering eyes, intense looking; passionate or defensive personality

2nd: compulsive or psychic regarding money; bases self-worth on sexuality or perceptivity

3rd: incisive or focused in communication; power-tripping with siblings; suspicious or transformative in neighborhood and community

4th: protective regarding home; defensive of family and clan

15th: compulsive in creative endeavors; passionate in play or romance; protective or psychic with children

6th: genitals, sexual functioning, or surgery as health concerns; focused or compulsive in terms of daily routine

7th: renewing in relationships; transforming or jealous with partner

8th: sexually seductive or power-oriented; power-tripping regarding shared resources

9th: investigative or focused in travel; compelled or passionate in terms of higher education

10th: conscious of life mission in career; secretive or driven in terms of reputation

11th: transformative or powerful with regard to future plans; desirous of depth with friends and in groups

12th: Tarot, I Ching, or channeling as spiritual paths; rituals or trances for spiritual renewal; death, sex or psychic activities as addictions

Sagittarius:
Expansion

THE NEEDS AND ATTITUDES OF SAGITTARIUS ARE:

QUALITY: MUTABLE: disseminating, expansive, flexible, exploratory, diversified, and evolving

ELEMENT: FIRE: stimulated, unfettered, inspired, spontaneous, enthusiastic, and expressive

THEME: KNOWLEDGE: seeking and teaching *the* truth

The glyph for SAGITTARIUS, THE SIGN OF THE ARCHER, represents the archer's arrow, which symbolizes the flight into expanded experiences. Another symbol for this Sign is the wise CENTAUR.

With SAGITTARIUS comes the move into wider horizons. It wants to expand beyond the childhood limits and experience the wide world. It finds joy in seeking, questing, discovering, and growing. It needs to be educated at the highest levels, yet it needs to feel free and unfettered, unlimited by anything or anyone. It needs a strong philosophical or ethical foundation out of which it can zealously preach and teach. Its attitudes are reflected when it says, "Don't fence me in," and "This is *the* truth." In response to events, it will say "Oh well, it's not my fault," and "I knew it all along." Sagittarius is most concerned with questing for knowledge and expressing it.

In a HOUSE WITH SAGITTARIUS ON THE CUSP, you'll want to have a sense of limitlessness, abundance, and infinite possibilities. You could have the reputation of being a "moreness" junkie here because you pursue mental growth, physical expansion, or travel in such an avid manner. You might also spend or consume "more" through binges. This is the House where your desire for expansion can lead to over-expansion, self-indulgence, and gluttony. You're more likely to get into that self-indulgent side of Sagittarius if you're feeling especially trapped or restricted. That's because you don't want to be tied to anyone else's principles or limits in this area of life. On the other hand, you are fascinated by your own ethics, beliefs, and truths here, and enjoy passing on your knowledge. In fact, you may be so sure of *the* truth that you totally ignore any contradicting facts. Your Sagittarian knowledge may be of a religious, spiritual, scientific, or political nature, but whatever it is, you'll teach, preach, advertise, promote, and publish it.

If SAGITTARIUS IS INTERCEPTED in your Chart, your family probably didn't demonstrate philosophical and ethical beliefs that match yours. They may have been perfectly healthy in their expansive exploration of *the* truth—just different from you. They may have been actually unhealthy: preachy or self-indulgent. Or, they may have been totally lacking in any urge to seek wider horizons. In fact, they may have restricted their conscious growth so much that they binged in order to get "more." You've had to find others who could help you grow and develop a personal philosophy.

Your ESSENTIAL THEMATIC CHALLENGES IN A SAGITTARIUS HOUSE are:

• to discover how to believe completely in what's "true" for you while remaining open to new data that might change your beliefs, and

• to determine how to grow and expand without being self-indulgent.

APPLICATIONS FOR SAGITTARIUS

EMOTIONAL: expansive, questing, eager, ethical, moral, limitless, free, wanting "more," easygoing, optimistic, benevolent, extravagant, exaggerated, gluttonous, self-indulgent, greedy, scattered

MENTAL: wise, scientific, principled, religious, philosophical, sage, promotional, teacherly, open-ended, oriented to the biggest picture or international world view, globally conscious, know-it-all, pontifical, preachy

PHYSICAL: athletic-especially individual sports involving a feeling of freedom; big, abundant, or fat; inclined to travel or move around

> STRENGTH OR WEAKNESS: hips, thighs, arteries, fat metabolism, over-indulgence
>
> FEATURES: PEOPLE: long-limbed, tall, or lanky; big or fat
>
> FEATURES: PLACES & THINGS: high, open, dry; associated with books, media, religion, education, travel

SPIRITUAL: desires philosophical path with strong moral and ethical principles; quests for a truth that covers all contingencies; talented at studying theories, teaching, automatic writing, and precognition

SAMPLE INTERPRETATIONS FOR SAGITTARIUS
ON (OR IN) HOUSES

In addition to interpreting SAGITTARIUS on (or in) the Houses, LOOK FOR JUPITER. Its location by Sign and House will tell you more about how the Sagittarius needs and attitudes are expressed in the Chart.

1st: tall or fat; questing or philosophical in personality

2nd: abundantly prosperous or self-indulgent with regard to money; bases self-worth on knowledge or ethics

3rd: ethical or know-it-all in communication; teacherly with siblings; principled or preachy in neighborhood and community

4th: expansive at home; philosophical or optimistic regarding family and clan

5th: oriented to writing or preachy in creative endeavors; athletic or eager in play or romance; principled or teacherly with children

6th: hips, thighs, arteries, fat metabolism, or over-indulgence as health concerns; easygoing or scattered in terms of daily routine

7th: oriented to freedom in relationships; optimistic or pontifical with partner

8th: sexually eager or greedy; ethical or principled regarding shared resources

9th: expansive or international in travel; questing or wanting "more" in terms of higher education

10th: promotional in career; religious, philosophical, or pontifical in terms of reputation

11th: open-minded or optimistic with regard to future plans; wise or oriented to considering the biggest picture with friends and in groups

12th: philosophical questing or precognitive processing as spiritual paths; mentors or gurus as inspirations; reading or teaching for spiritual renewal; any kind of self-indulgence as an addiction

Capricorn:
Structure

THE NEEDS AND ATTITUDES OF CAPRICORN ARE:

QUALITY: CARDINAL: creative, assertive, generative, directive, provocative, and originative

ELEMENT: EARTH: pragmatic, building, concrete, reliable, productive, and practical

THEME: SECURITY: establishing practical position in the world

The glyph for CAPRICORN, THE SIGN OF THE MOUNTAIN GOAT, represents the mountain goat's curly horns and symbolizes its sure-footed ascent to the top of the mountain.

The Sign of CAPRICORN is the empire-building Sign. It organizes all of the concrete elements in any situation into a functioning whole. It constructs a basic structure by utilizing the available resources, conserving them so that a little bit will go a long way. In fact, it wants to conserve everything that already exists, valuing anything that has lasted through time. Its attitudes are reflected when it says, "Let's map out a pragmatic strategy," and "I'll be the executive." In response to events, Capricorn will ask "What's the appropriate protocol," and "That's the way the system works." In most cases, Capricorn is cautious about innovations and unstoppable in terms of ambition.

In a HOUSE WITH CAPRICORN ON THE CUSP, you'll want to be in charge of things. Although you might have the reputation of being controlling here, it's really just that you understand how to be organized and constructive. In this House, you tend to conserve historical precedents, past patterns, and proven systems as well as human and ecological resources. You conform to the system and work within it to make it better. As a result, you'll probably move into executive or managerial positions. However, your respect for practical structures can lead you to see people, including yourself, as puzzle pieces instead of living, feeling beings. As a result, you can appear rigid, aloof, or cold in this House. On the other hand, you have the choice of managing and directing your internal reponses to the uncontrollable world instead of trying to squeeze the world into your structure. When you can do this, you'll feel more secure about your position in Capricorn's House.

If CAPRICORN IS INTERCEPTED in your Chart, your family's way of being orderly and authoritative is not suitable for you. They may have been perfectly healthy in their approach to organization and limit-setting—just different from you. They may have been actually unhealthy: repressive and rigid. Or, they may have been entirely lacking in any form of structure. If they didn't provide you with appropriate boundaries and responsible parental back-up, you may have had to learn how to "parent" yourself and others at any early age. Whatever their patterns, you've had to learn from others how to set clear limits and become responsible.

Your ESSENTIAL THEMATIC CHALLENGES IN A CAPRICORN HOUSE are:

• to discover how to structure your worldly ambitions while maintaining healthy sensitivity and

• to determine how to utilize strong structures without crystallizing them into traps.

APPLICATIONS FOR CAPRICORN

EMOTIONAL: disciplining, organizing, industrious, committed, attached to old people/things/processes, willing to wait until later in life, responsible, "fathering," prestige-seeking, parental, formal, managerial, authoritative, ambitious, rigid, dictatorial, bossy, cold, aloof, depressed, gloomy, limited

MENTAL: structured, practical, grounded, respectful, business-oriented, conscious of age or tradition, professional, executive, conservative, constructive, parental, demanding, restrictive

PHYSICAL: constructive, structure-building, strong, brittle, using "less"

STRENGTH OR WEAKNESS: bones, knees, joints, teeth, skeleton, skin, arthritis, or chronic conditions

FEATURES: PEOPLE: noticeable bone structure; missing tooth or body part; "less" body weight or height; timeless appearance; look of maturity

FEATURES: PLACES & THINGS: high, cold, sparse, dark, inaccessible; associated with agedness, professionalism, stone, dirt

SPIRITUAL: constructs pragmatic path, measuring the usefulness of spiritual or psychic tools; stays with established systems or religious structures; talented at Earth-rituals, stone, or mountain rituals, psychometry, bodywork, Runes

SAMPLE INTERPRETATIONS FOR CAPRICORN
ON (OR IN) HOUSES

In addition to interpreting CAPRICORN on (or in) the Houses, LOOK FOR SATURN. Its location by Sign and House will tell you more about how the Capricorn needs and attitudes are expressed in the Chart.

1st: short, bony, or thin; practical or authoritative in personality; early maturity or grown-up-ness

2nd: authoritarian or industrious regarding money; bases self-worth on discipline or respect

3rd: parental or constructive in communication; bossy with siblings; ambitious or prestige-seeking in neighborhood and community

4th: practical regarding home; organizing of family and clan

5th: three-dimensional or concrete in creative endeavors; organizing in play or romance; responsible for children; willing to wait until later in life to have children

6th: bones, knees, joints, teeth, or chronic conditions as health concerns; business-oriented or dictatorial in terms of daily routine

7th: respectful in relationships; committed or parental with partner

8th: sexually traditional or restrictive; authoritative regarding shared resources

9th: business-oriented or practical in travel; professional or ambitious in terms of higher education

10th: executive in career; depressed or prestige-seeking in terms of reputation

11th: professional or ambitious with regard to future plans; dictatorial or organizing with friends and in groups

12th: Earth or stone rituals as spiritual paths; respects spiritual authorities; traditional religious rites for spiritual renewal; work or depression as addictions

Aquarius:
Reform

THE NEEDS AND ATTITUDES OF AQUARIUS ARE:

QUALITY: FIXED: intense, appreciative, focused, determined, persistent, and sustaining

ELEMENT: AIR: logical, informational, conceptual, intellectual, communicative, and interactive

THEME: PARTICIPATION: considering the highest good of the group

The glyph for AQUARIUS, THE SIGN OF THE ENERGY BEARER, represents the flow of pure energy, which symbolizes the movement of visionary concepts and ideas. Aquarius is also often called the Water Bearer, but this is somewhat misleading because it's not a Water Sign.

The Sign of AQUARIUS is the Sign of focused concepts. It concentrates intently on developing its ideas and then applies them to the betterment of humankind. It has a talent for rapidly correlating all the information available into a political, ethical, spiritual, or technological system. Aquarius creates optional futures for individuals and for humanity because it needs alternatives, possibilities, and something to move toward. Its attitudes are reflected when it says, "There must be a better way," and "I'm more interested in what will be than in what has been." In response to events, Aquarius asks "How will this have an impact on where we're headed?" and says "We don't have to stay stuck in this, we can imagine an alternative." Overall, Aquarius is a reformer and visionary, working to create its utopia.

In a HOUSE WITH AQUARIUS ON THE CUSP, you'll want to break away from restrictive systems as you imagine and implement new, more visionary, ones. You may even have a reputation, in this House, for being a rebel and a troublemaker. It's really just that you want to play around with alternatives. You'll be fascinated with anything that's foreign, nontraditional, radical, or unusual here. As a result, you could become involved with groups who are actively working toward reform, revolution, or change. In this area of life, however, group memberships may be brief since the Aquarian energy will press you to move beyond the limitations of any group. In Aquarius's House, your behavior can tend to be somewhat erratic and unpredictable. You may have trouble following directions and sticking to strategies. To others, you may seem uncooperative, eccentric, and individualistic. But, in Aquarius's House you never lose sight of your high goals and the belief that your plans will provide the best future for the highest number of people.

If AQUARIUS IS INTERCEPTED in your Chart, your family didn't support or value nonconformity in a way that works for you. They may have been perfectly healthy in their futuristic thinking – just different from you. They may have been actually unhealthy: unreliable and disruptive. Or, they may have been entirely lacking in any spark of eccentricity or uniqueness. So, you've had to find others to teach you how to be futuristic and nonconforming in a sane and creative manner.

Your ESSENTIAL THEMATIC CHALLENGES IN AN AQUARIUS HOUSE are:

• to discover how to hold fast to your goals and visions for the group without ignoring the very real needs and opinions of the individuals involved and

• to determine how to pursue your radical visions without losing sight of the value of present structures.

APPLICATIONS FOR AQUARIUS

EMOTIONAL: eccentric, visionary, detached, nonconforming, reforming, wishing, unusual, surprising, startling, hoping, unpredictable, unreliable, rebellious, disruptive

MENTAL: visionary, innovative, quick-thinking, computer-minded, conceptual, objective, theoretical, nontraditional, futuristic, oriented to global thinking, open to "foreign" concepts, reforming, erratic, interruptive

PHYSICAL: inventive, acting in intense spurts of energy, erratically capable; technological

> STRENGTH OR WEAKNESS: ankles, calves, or shins, sudden accidents, broken bones, nervous system, circulation, or diseases that come and go unpredictably

> FEATURES: PEOPLE: high foreheads, startling eyes, thick ankles

> FEATURES: PLACES & THINGS: unusual, changeable territory, airy; associated with modern technology, electricity, reform activities, or politics

SPIRITUAL: interested in anything nontraditional or bizarre; fascinated by esoteric systems; talented in Astrology, I Ching, Numerology, precognition, and future lifetimes

SAMPLE INTERPRETATIONS FOR AQUARIUS
ON (OR IN) HOUSES

In addition to interpreting AQUARIUS on (or in) the Houses, LOOK FOR URANUS. Its location by Sign and House will tell you more about how the Aquarius needs and attitudes are expressed in the Chart.

1st: high foreheads, startling eyes, or thick ankles; unpredictable or innovative in personality

2nd: visionary or unreliable regarding money; bases self-worth on nontraditional or eccentric traits

3rd: computer-minded or conceptual in communication; reforming with siblings; rebellious or disruptive in neighborhood and community

4th: open to technological concepts regarding home; detached or nonconforming regarding family and clan

5th: technological or futuristic in creative endeavors; eccentric in play or romance; theoretical regarding children

6th: ankles, accidents, or unpredictable diseases as health concerns; erratic or disruptive in terms of daily routine

7th: innovative in relationships; reforming or unreliable with partner

8th: sexually open to "foreign" concepts or gay; visionary regarding shared resources

9th: internationally oriented or surprising in travel; nontraditional or technological in terms of higher education

10th: reforming or futuristic in career; rebellious or innovative in terms of reputation

11th: internationally oriented or theoretical with regard to future plans; quick-thinking or interruptive with friends and in groups

12th: Astrology, lifetimes, or precognition as psychic or spiritual paths; "foreign" spiritual activities; future visions or eccentric actions for spiritual renewal; rebellion or disruption as addictions

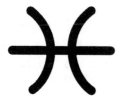

Pisces:
Faith

THE NEEDS AND ATTITUDES OF PISCES ARE:

QUALITY: MUTABLE: disseminating, adjustable, flexible, adaptable, diversified, and evolving

ELEMENT: WATER: sensitive, psychic, compassionate, receptive, empathic, and emotional

THEME: IMPROVEMENT: healing the being at an emotional or psychic level

The glyph for PISCES, THE SIGN OF THE FISH, represents two fish who are connected to each other but swimming in opposite directions. It symbolizes our connectedness to one another in the vast sea of the Universe.

The Sign of PISCES is associated with mysticism, spirituality, and altered states. It is the doorway to imagination and fantasy. It symbolizes emotional adaptability and a willingness to merge completely with other people or forces. Pisces is boundaryless, unaware of where it ends and everything else begins. It needs to lose itself in a greater whole as it finds unity with "all that is." It needs to feel compassion and healing. And, it wants to sustain its faith, trusting that everything is unfolding as it should. Its attitudes are reflected when it says, "Imagine yourself as part of the bigger plan," and "I'll rescue and heal you." In response to events, Pisces will say, "This must have been meant to be," and "I hope the powers-that-be have a reason for this." Pisces tends to dissolve and melt anything that is divisive and blocking.

In a HOUSE WITH PISCES ON THE CUSP, you'll have the urge to merge with others, with nature, or with spiritual forces. You may have a reputation in this area of life for being unaware of the real world because you're sensing things rather than understanding them rationally. In this House, you have faith that the Universe is guiding your every step, but you can also be so trusting as to be naive. As a result, you can set yourself up as a victim here. To avoid or escape confusion in this area of life, you can focus on rescuing other people, using addictive substances, or getting stuck in "crazy" psychological patterns. You can even go underground, into illegal or behind-the-scenes activities. On the other hand, you can also choose to find solace through psychic, imaginative, healing, or spiritual resources. In all cases, you are using Pisces to alter your physical, mental, or emotional state so that you can enhance or cope with reality.

If PISCES IS INTERCEPTED in your Chart, your family's way of altering reality is not the one you want to choose. They may have been perfectly healthy in the ways they expressed sensitivity – just different from you. They may have been actually unhealthy: self-sacrificing, emotionally unstable, or addictive. On the other hand, they may have been entirely lacking in compassion or spiritual awareness. As a result, you've had to find mentors or teachers who could show you how to be intuitive and compassionate in a healthy way.

Your ESSENTIAL THEMATIC CHALLENGES IN A PISCES HOUSE are:

• to discover how to care compassionately and emotionally about yourself and others while staying aware of the practical tasks that must be accomplished and

• to determine how to find spiritual wholeness or a positive "high" without losing track of your body or health.

APPLICATIONS FOR PISCES

EMOTIONAL: sensitive, caring, compassionate, spiritual, intuitive, dreamy, psychic, serene, merged, rescuing, barrierless, disintegrated, isolated, manipulative, disturbed, "crazy," hallucinatory, deluded, fearful, sneaky, confused, dependent, martyred, victimized, paranoid

MENTAL: poetic, imaginative, fantasy-oriented, dreamlike, intuitive, psychic, vague, manipulative, conning

PHYSICAL: rhythmic, mobile, flexible, fluid, creative, wobbly, weak, adaptable

> STRENGTH OR WEAKNESS: feet, mucous membranes, tissues, anesthetics, drugs of all kinds, addictions, allergies, misdiagnosed illnesses, poisons, or toxic reactions

> FEATURES: PEOPLE: dreamy eyes, vague or unfocused gaze

> FEATURES: PLACES & THINGS: low, mushy, flooded, foggy; associated with water, illegal activities, confinement, retreat, or spirituality

SPIRITUAL: interested in all forms of spiritual and psychic activity; tends to slip in and out of various levels of reality easily; talented at reading auras, emotional impressions, being "saved," healing, counseling, dreamwork, other lifetimes, channeling

SAMPLE INTERPRETATIONS FOR PISCES ON (OR IN) HOUSES

In addition to interpreting PISCES on (or in) the Houses, LOOK FOR NEPTUNE. Its location by Sign and House will tell you more about how the Pisces needs and attitudes are expressed in the Chart.

1st: dreamy or unfocused eyes; sensitive or imaginative in personality

2nd: fantasy-oriented or intuitive regarding money; bases self-worth on compassion or psychic ability

3rd: fluid or vague in communication; rescuing with siblings; isolated or mobile in neighborhood and community

4th: spiritual or serene at home; victimized by family and clan

5th: poetic in creative endeavors; imaginative in play or romance; compassionate or merged with children

6th: addictions, allergies, or misdiagnosed illnesses as health concerns; adaptable or confused in terms of daily routine

7th: caring in relationships; compassionate or martyred with partner

8th: sexually imaginative or confused; manipulative regarding shared resources

9th: flexible or dependent in travel; psychic or creative in terms of higher education

10th: conscious of spiritual purpose in career; imaginative or deluded in terms of reputation

11th: flexible or fearful with regard to future plans; isolated or compassionate with friends and in groups

12th: channeling, dreamwork or aura reading as spiritual paths; trances or meditations for spiritual renewal; alcohol, drugs, TV, or movies as addictions

SUMMARY

In this Chapter, I've discussed the twelve Signs in detail. I've reminded you that they represent our needs and attitudes with regard to the twelve areas represented by the Houses. They also reflect the many approaches we can take toward the issues and concerns that arise in each department of life. All of the Signs have positive and negative applications. Briefly, the Signs represent the following modes or styles:

> ARIES: assertive and independent; pushy
> TAURUS: stable and persevering; stubborn
> GEMINI: curious and flexible; distractible
> CANCER: nurturing and security-conscious; clingy
> LEO: self-expressive and spontaneous; boastful
> VIRGO: analytical and problem-solving; critical
> LIBRA: cooperative and other-oriented; indecisive
> SCORPIO: intense and passionate; destructive
> SAGITTARIUS: expansive and wise; self-indulgent
> CAPRICORN: organized and responsible; domineering
> AQUARIUS: eccentric and innovative; shattering
> PISCES: spiritual and compassionate; confused

EXERCISES

5-1　Practice using the key words to make up phrases that describe the meanings of Signs on (or in) Houses.

5-2　Interpret several Charts by talking about the Signs on the House Cusps. Use the expanded meanings in this Chapter to give a full description of the needs and attitudes that must be expressed in each area of each person's life.

5-3　Take the list of issues that you outlined in Exercise 4-2. For each one:

  a. Note the House related to the concern.
  b. Locate the Sign on (or in) this House.
  c. Delineate your current attitude toward the issue and notice how it's related to one or more of the interpretations of the Sign.
  d. Think of three other ways that you could approach this issue, based on other uses of the Sign.
  e. Save your ideas and insights for later use.

5-4　Using the list from Exercise 4-3, go through the process outlined in Exercise 5-3 with your friend.

SIX

The Planets and the Points

The PLANETS are the subpersonalities of your Chart, each with its own role and function. Like purposeful little beings, these parts of your personality are eager to perform their tasks in the best ways they can. The POINTS are similar to the Planets in that they have functions, but they are not as independently active as the Planets. The Nodes of the Moon and the Part of Fortune are aides and resources that can be used by the Planets; the Midheaven and the Ascendant are representations of your birth environment. It's as if, within you, all of the Planets are constantly meeting with each other, discussing possibilities for your growth and choosing options for your thoughts, feelings, and actions. As they decide what they're going to do, they call in the various Points to assist them in acting out their choices. In combination, all of the Planets and Points contribute to your Chart and to your personal expression. In this Chapter, I'll be discussing the nature of these Planets and Points in depth.

NAME	ABBREVIATION	GLYPH	ALTERNATE GLYPH
THE SUN	SU	☉	
THE MOON	MO	☽	
MERCURY	ME	☿	
VENUS	VE	♀	
MARS	MA	♂	
JUPITER	JU	♃	
SATURN	SA	♄	
CHIRON	CH	⚷	⚷
URANUS	UR	♅	
NEPTUNE	NE	♆	
PLUTO	PL	♇	♇

Figure 6-1
The Planets, their Abbreviations, and their Glyphs

164

As you deepen your understanding of the Planets and the Points, bear in mind that my interpretations are only some of the possible choices. You may use your Planets and Points in some, all, or none of the ways that I describe. You may discover other options that I haven't mentioned. Don't limit yourself to my ideas. Do take the ones that fit and expand on them for yourself. As you choose and create definitions for the Planets and Points, remember that your life experiences will give you feedback. The processes and events of your real life will tell you whether your interpretations are appropriate.

THE PLANETS

The specific tasks and functions of the Planets are actually suggested by the patterns of their orbits in the solar system. So, I'll begin this by discussing four broad interpretive categories, based on these orbits, into which we can group the Planets. Then, I'll talk about some of the ways in which we tend to use, and abuse, the personality parts that the Planets represent. And, finally, I'll present their in-depth interpretations. For your review, Figure 6-1 contains the names and symbols of the Planets.

Interpreting the Planets by Their Orbits

The true Planets orbit the Sun, the Moon orbits the Earth, and the Sun's Astrological path is actually determined by the Earth's orbit around the Sun. But, seen from the Earth, all of the galactic bodies appear to be going through the Signs in sequence, taking differing amounts of time in each Sign depending on the lengths and patterns of their orbits. Based on these galactic pathways, we divide the Planets into four interpretational groups: PERSONAL, SOCIAL, BRIDGE, and UNIVERSAL.

The PERSONAL PLANETS, which are the SUN, the MOON, MERCURY, VENUS, and MARS, move through the Signs in relatively short periods of time, creating daily and monthly variations in the general planetary patterns. The Moon with its 28-day cycle moves especially rapidly, and is the planetary body that most strongly symbolizes the individuality of a Chart. If someone was born in the same town as you at about the same time of day, but one or two days before or after you, her Chart would probably be similar to yours – except for the Moon's position. And that one change would make a dramatic difference in how you each expressed and experienced yourselves and the world. The other Personal Planets also move quickly through the Signs: the Sun takes a year, Mercury and Venus take about a year when their Retrograde periods are included, and Mars takes about two years. THE PERSONAL PLANETS EN-SURE THAT YOUR NATAL CHART IS UNIQUE BY ACTIVELY DEFINING AND SUPPORTING YOUR INDIVIDUALIZATION.

The SOCIAL PLANETS, JUPITER and SATURN, with their slightly longer orbits, affect the galactic planetary patterns in another way. Because Jupiter takes nearly twelve years to move through all the Signs, it stays in each Sign for approximately one year. Since Saturn take twenty-nine and a half years to move through the Zodiac, it spends about two and a half years in each Sign. As a result, people born within one or two years of you will probably have these Planets in the same Signs as you. Jupiter and Saturn, acting in these Signs, actually set up the social issues and concerns of your age-group. They do the same thing for every other age-defined peer-group as well. These two Planets and their interactions also symbolize the economic, societal, and political trends that fluctuate year by year. THE SOCIAL PLANETS, SYMBOLS OF YOUR INVOLVEMENT IN THE SURROUNDING CULTURE, CHARACTERIZE AND ENCOURAGE YOUR ACTIVE PARTICIPATION IN THE WORLD.

The BRIDGE PLANET, CHIRON, was discovered in 1977. It has a 51-year fluctuating orbit. Instead of holding to a steady distance from the Sun, Chiron moves back and forth between the paths of Saturn and Uranus, spending irregular amounts of time in each Sign. In fact, it spends approximately ten years in half the Zodiac and the remaining 40-odd years in the other half. In a thousand years or more, it may change its orbit, possibly moving closer to the Sun. For now, Chiron's orbit is reliably predictable, and its inclusion in Charts provides for fascinating interpretational concepts. In connecting Saturn (Earthly structures) to Uranus (Universal consciousness), it does symbolize a bridge. CHIRON WEAVES YOUR HIGHEST IDEALS INTO THE FABRIC OF YOUR PERSONAL AND SOCIAL LIFE.

The UNIVERSAL (or TRANSPERSONAL) PLANETS, URANUS, NEPTUNE, AND PLUTO, have significantly longer orbits. Uranus spends seven years in each Sign and, therefore, takes 84 years to move through the whole Zodiac. Neptune makes the circuit in 165 years, or just under 14 years per Sign. Pluto, with its unique orbit, takes 248 years to move through the Signs. When it's moving inside of Neptune's orbit, it can spend as little as 12 years in a Sign, but when it moves outside of Neptune's path, it takes up to 31 years to move through a Sign. As a result of the long periods of time they spend in each Sign, these Universal Planets represent huge intergenerational growth patterns and interdimensional developments in awareness. You might experience these three energies in terms of pervasive global trends or you might feel them internally as subtle evolutionary themes. AS A GROUP, THE UNIVERSAL PLANETS IN-

SPIRE YOU TO MOVE BEYOND THE LIMITATIONS OF YOUR IDEN-
TITY, CLAN, AND SOCIAL GROUP INTO A LARGER CONTEXT.

Interpreting the Planets by Their Psychological Processes

Although you may wish that you always used all of your Planets in an
ideal manner, in reality you probably work with some of them more comfortably and easily than you do with others. Your skill at utilizing the resources they represent depends on many things, including your genetic
and cultural heritage, your childhood environment and training, and your
personal interests. As you identify the personality parts represented by
the Planets, you'll probably find the ones that you've learned to use FUNC-
TIONALLY, or well, and the ones that you tend to use DYSFUNCTION-
ALLY, or poorly.

You will utilize the Planets in different ways at various times in your
life, and at any particular time, you may use one of them in several of the
ways I've described in this book. However, it's unlikely that you'll you use
all of them in all of the ways I've described and you'll undoubtedly discover possibilities that I haven't mentioned. So, to explore the ways that
you're currently activating your Planets, choose the interpretations that
seem to be most immediately relevant to your life and leave the rest. As
you do that, bear in mind that it's always your choice to change or enhance
how you use your Planets.

USING THE PLANETS FUNCTIONALLY

If you're using a Planet functionally, you're making the most of it. You've
discovered and chosen healthy ways to express its purposes according to
the positive traits of its Sign within the context of its House. If you feel
ethically comfortable and emotionally secure with the force a particular
Planet represents, you're probably using this one functionally.

To understand their functions more fully, imagine that each Planet has a
primary task and a voice. The task is what it's ideally supposed to *do* in
your life. The voice is what it *says* to you and to others, in order to proclaim
its purpose. The more you can fully claim the tasks and the voices, the
more you'll find that your life feels integrated. Of course, the tasks and
voices that I've identified in this Chapter may not exactly be fitting for you.
If so, redefine the tasks and voices for yourself as you come to understand
the function of each Planet. When you feel comfortable with your understanding of how you use a specific Planet, you'll probably be OWNING it.

Owning the Planets

In Owning a particular Planet, you accept that it's a part of you, a part that you can respect and nurture. You may recognize that you haven't always expressed its function in a graceful or ideal manner, but you also recognize that you're making progress. In fact, Ownership of a Planet doesn't imply perfection; it does imply the ability to make the best possible conscious choices, given the circumstances. Owning means that you're able to evaluate yourself honestly and consider changes when you get feedback about your attitudes or behavior. Owning your Planets means improving your choices day by day. In general, I know that I'm Owning my Planets when I feel honestly accepting and loving of them and when I'm making progress toward improving my use of them.

USING THE PLANETS DYSFUNCTIONALLY

If you're having trouble Owning a particular Planet, you're probably using it dysfunctionally in one or more ways. You could be DENOUNCING it as a terrible or undesirable part of you. Conversely, you could by GLORIFYING it as a grand and virtuous part. Or, you could be BLAMING or PROJECTING its actions on someone else. And finally, you could be DENYING that it even exists. In the following sections, I'll explain more about the nature of each of these psychological processes as they relate to the Planets.

Denouncing the Planets

If you're not happy with one of your parts, you may be DENOUNCING it by criticizing or judging it harshly. You could believe that it's an undesirable, non-valuable, and unworthy personality trait. As a result, you can actually criticize yourself and the behavior that reflects that Planet too harshly. If you undervalue it too much, it may "act out" in a negative manner just to get attention. Many of our negative thoughts or inappropriate behavior are based on internal Denouncing. I can tell when I'm Denouncing a part of myself if I find myself listing my faults. I get myself out of Denouncing by using that list as a catalyst for change instead of accepting it as a final estimation of my worth.

Glorifying the Planets

If you're overly enamored of one of your Planets, you could be GLORIFYING it. You could believe that it's so important and valuable that everything else fades by comparison. In fact, by Glorifying this part of you, you could be placing a great deal of pressure on yourself. You could be expecting yourself to live up to unreasonably high standards and expectations. Or, by emphasizing this one, you might be ignoring or smothering other parts of you that are equally valuable. I know that I'm Glorifying a part of myself when I feel righteous, virtuous, and smugly proud of it. I get myself out of Glorifying by reminding myself that, although I use this ability well, it's only one part of me. I try to remember that my skills, however wonderful they may be, don't indicate that I'm intrinsically a better person than anyone else.

Blaming the Planets

Another "great" tactic to use with undesirable personality parts is BLAMING. You can conveniently dodge responsibility for your behavior by Blaming it on someone or something else. You could begin by Blaming your family, your partner, your child, your co-workers, your neighbors, or your friends. If that's not enough, you can Blame your gender, your race, your poverty, or your wealth. Finally, you can move on to Blaming your broken car, the weather, the government, a political system, your God/dess, or even your Astrological Chart. They can all serve the purpose of getting you off the hook. While it's true that we do react to the people, things, and situations in the environment, we also have a choice about *how* we react. I know that I'm Blaming when I find myself feeling uncomfortable about my behavior and then thinking "It's not my fault." I get myself out of Blaming by asking myself how I want to *choose* to act or react.

Projecting the Planets

PROJECTING is another way of taking care of unwelcome personality parts. If this is your preferred mode, you will unconsciously get someone else to act out one of your Planets. Instead of exhibiting its force yourself, you'll attract others who can exemplify that energy into your life. This can be a big relief because you still have the part in your life, you just don't have to claim it as your own.

This doesn't mean that if you have someone else fix your car or help you understand your feelings that you're necessarily Projecting. You may not always want or choose to do everything for yourself. The difference between Projecting and an exchange of services is the level of responsibility involved. It's possible to deliberately make arrangements for particular kinds of feedback or services with someone who has specific practical or emotional skills. When that's done at a conscious level, you are simply taking responsibility for your needs.

You're Projecting if you're unwittingly allowing, or expecting, someone else to act out an un-Owned personality trait for you. Although this may work for a while, a Projected Planet will feel frustrated if it's not functioning more directly in your life. This Planet might even attract someone who uses its energy negatively just to remind you to learn to use it responsibly. I know that I'm Projecting when I find myself feeling extremely annoyed with, or clinging to, a person who demonstrates a specific character trait. I can get myself out of Projecting by asking myself which of *my* personality parts that person is expressing.

Denying the Planets

By DENYING that the force of a particular Planet exists in your life, you don't even have to think about it. You can simply ignore it. Unfortunately, the Denied Planet will undoubtedly become annoyed by your rejection of it. Most likely, it will find a way of expressing its function uncomfortably so that you can no longer avoid recognizing it. You may even become emotionally or physically ill as a result of the bottled up energy. I know that I'm Denying certain parts of myself when I feel sick or crabby. I get myself out of Denying by asking myself how I want to feel instead. Usually the feeling that I want to have is associated with the need or desire that I'm ignoring.

Most of the time, you won't resort to these psychological strategies; most of the time, you'll use most of your Planets creatively and productively. But, on occasion, even if you *Own* them all, life circumstances may make it difficult for you to use them functionally. When this is the case for you, remember that, at every moment in time, you're using these forces in the best ways that you can. Go easy on yourself. Notice the coping strategies that you're using, and gently free yourself to choose to behave in ways that more closely match your conscious preferences.

In the next section of this Chapter, I'll describe ways to Own each of the Planets so that you can use them functionally. I'll also discuss their dysfunctional manifestations, which include the psychological processes just mentioned. It's my intention that, by becoming familiar with many possibilities, you'll have more choices about your own thoughts, feelings, and behavior. At the end of each section, you'll find some sample interpretations of the Planets in the Signs and Houses.

THE SUN:
The Illuminator

ITS ORBIT: PERSONAL: actively define and support individualization

ITS TASK: to express personal potential; to illuminate

ITS VOICE: "I shine. I demonstrate the essential self."

THE SUN represents your core self. Its glyph can be seen as a symbol of the soul (the dot) existing within this physical reality (the circle).

The SUN'S FUNCTION is to express that soul by shining with aliveness. It's a bright light, illuminating itself and its environment, filling up shadowy corners with purpose and meaning. It is conscious of itself, knowing that it exists for a reason, wanting to find that reason and express it. On a daily basis, the Sun discovers itself, respects itself, and enacts itself in the world. It creates direction, choosing paths that will most allow it to manifest its full potential. It's the point of power, the focus of personal dignity, and the embodiment of individualization. The Sun is conscious of its position in the world, constantly aware of its impact on others, continually creating opportunities for others to appreciate and notice it. In fact, it seeks feedback and attention from others as a way of getting perspective on itself. It seeks celebratory experiences with others as a way of renewing its life force and reigniting its spirit. It's aware that it is the ultimate source of energy in any Birth Chart.

THE SUN IS NEVER RETROGRADE so there are no interpretations for a Retrograde Sun.

When you're fully OWNING your Sun, you'll feel alive, conscious, centered in your self, and sure that your life is more or less on track. You may be aware that you're going through changes and adjustments, not all of them pleasant, but you'll feel internally confident that you can survive the changes and make the most of your life.

When the SUN OPERATES DYSFUNCTIONALLY, it may "act out," trying to get attention and remind itself or others that it exists. It creates furor and drama out of nothing simply to get some recognition. The Sun can go overboard in terms of celebration, indulging in orgiastic physical or emotional experiences, forgetting its dignity and its source. It might also search for direction by wandering aimlessly in many directions, feeling purposeless and unfocused. If it doesn't discover a reason for aliveness, the dysfunctional Sun may even resort to suicide. It's lost its purpose.

If you're DENOUNCING your Sun, you may think that personal potential is not valuable. You may be so concerned with others or with a "cause" that you undervalue your need to express yourself. On the other hand, if you're GLORIFYING your Sun, you could think that your own self-expression is the only thing that matters. By expecting so much of yourself all the time, you could set yourself up for failure and disappointment. If you're BLAMING your Sun-related behavior on other people or circumstances, you're probably resentful that you're alive. You may be thinking that the nature of your ego or life purpose is not your fault; after all, "they" made you express yourself like this. If you're PROJECTING your Sun, you could be making something or someone else into your "reason for living." And, if you're DENYING your Sun, you may think that your life is all "used up," that you have nothing left to live for, nothing left to contribute. You might also be ignoring the fact that you have a sense of identity and purpose already. If you're using your Sun in one or more of these dysfunctional ways, remember that deep within is your own source of aliveness. You do have a reason for being here although you're not the only one here.

In the SUN'S HOUSE, you can discover and express your essential identity. You choose companions, experiences, and objects that reflect you. In this area of life, you actively create opportunities for feeling alive, special, and purposeful. If you've used the Sun dysfunctionally, it might help to place yourself in new situations that are governed by its House.

The SUN'S SIGN shows the manner in which you'll act purposeful in your life. The qualities of your Sun Sign provide the reason for being alive. Its nature describes your style of celebration and your approach to joy. The Sign's needs, attitudes, and response patterns show how you'll gain attention, dignity, and applause. Of course, if you're using the Sun dysfunctionally, it's more likely that you're using the negative traits of its Sign. In that case, choosing to use the other characteristics of the Sun's Sign can re-energize its purpose.

As LEO'S NATURAL RULING PLANET, the Sun's actions have a direct bearing on any House with Leo on the Cusp. As you create glory or trauma, through using your Sun, the result will reverberate in any area of life Ruled by Leo. In addition, if Leo is intercepted in your Chart, you can unlock it through using your Sun.

APPLICATIONS FOR THE SUN

PSYCHOLOGICAL: the urge to find and express self, identity, name, essence; the urge to shine, illuminate, demonstrate, glow; actions designed to gain applause, approval, attention; actions that encourage self and others to feel alive

PRACTICAL: vitality, energy level, life force, aliveness; activities related to fire, heart, spine, upper back, children, recreation, gambling, fun, toys, entertainment, jewelry, jewels, gold, royalty, rulers, creativity, art, drama, entertainment, glamour, fame, glory, pride, self-expression, magnanimity, generosity

SAMPLE INTERPRETATIONS FOR THE SUN IN THE HOUSES

1st: express personal potential through title or role; illuminate issues related to identity; shine through personality; celebrate aliveness through physical appearance; demonstrate essential self through persona; gain attention through personal style

2nd: express personal potential through skills and talents; illuminate issues related to self-worth; shine through individual values; celebrate aliveness through material world; demonstrate essential self through actions involving money; gain attention through possessions

3rd: express personal potential through communication; illuminate issues related to community; shine through dialogue; celebrate aliveness with siblings; demonstrate essential self through finding facts; gain attention through short trips and vacations

4th: express personal potential through home and family; illuminate issues related to ethnic or racial origins; shine regarding mother; celebrate aliveness through family and cultural roots; demonstrate essential self through creating belongingness; gain attention through position in home or family

5th: express personal potential through art and creativity; illuminate issues related to play; shine through recreation; celebrate aliveness through romance; demonstrate essential self through children; gain attention through hobbies and leisure activities

6th: express personal potential through daily work and routine; illuminate issues related to everyday tasks; shine through maintenance activities; celebrate aliveness with co-workers; demonstrate essential self through service to others; gain attention through health concerns; deal with health issues involving spine, heart

7th: express personal potential through relating; illuminate issues related to cooperation; shine through arbitration; celebrate aliveness with partner; demonstrate essential self through relationships; gain attention through "significant other"

8th: express personal potential through deep emotional interactions; illuminate issues related to intimacy; shine through utilization of collective money, talents, and resources; celebrate aliveness through sexuality; demonstrate essential self through transformation; gain attention through sex

9th: express personal potential through teaching or preaching; illuminate issues related to philosophy; shine through knowledge; celebrate aliveness with travel or learning; demonstrate essential self through ethics; gain attention through selling or advertising

10th: express personal potential through career; illuminate issues related to profession; shine regarding father; celebrate aliveness with vocation; demonstrate essential self through position in societal structure; gain attention through reputation

11th: express personal potential through future visions; illuminate issues related to the "cause"; shine through goals and plans; celebrate aliveness with friends; demonstrate essential self through theoretical systems; gain attention through schemes

12th: express personal potential through intuition; illuminate issues related to spirituality; shine through psychic ability; celebrate aliveness with addictions or meditation; demonstrate essential self through altered states; gain attention through position in institution

SAMPLE INTERPRETATIONS FOR THE SUN IN THE SIGNS

ARIES: express personal potential assertively; illuminate in a spontaneous, childlike way; shine by taking risks; celebrate aliveness in a stimulated and energized manner; demonstrate essential self by being freedom-loving; gain attention through aggressive or inconsiderate behavior

TAURUS: express personal potential reliably; illuminate in a loyal way; shine through getting results; celebrate aliveness in a sensual, physical manner; demonstrate essential self by being persistent; gain attention through stubborn or stingy behavior

GEMINI: express personal potential versatilely; illuminate in a humorous way; shine through dialogue; celebrate aliveness in a curious, amusing manner; demonstrate essential self by being communicative and investigative; gain attention through gossipy or unreliable behavior

CANCER: express personal potential nurturingly; illuminate in a comforting, caring way; shine by "mothering"; celebrate aliveness in a sentimental way; demonstrate essential self by being protective of past patterns; gain attention through fearful or clingy behavior

LEO: express personal potential dramatically; illuminate in a magnanimous, confident way; shine by storytelling; celebrate aliveness in a flamboyant, flashy manner; demonstrate essential self by being good-hearted; gain attention through egotistical or arrogant behavior

VIRGO: express personal potential analytically; illuminate in a practical, problem-solving way; shine by figuring out the solution; celebrate aliveness in a discriminating, idealized manner; demonstrate essential self by being detail-oriented; gain attention through critical or fussy behavior

LIBRA: express personal potential diplomatically; illuminate in a graceful, charming way; shine by creating beauty; celebrate aliveness in a cooperative, interactive manner; demonstrate essential self by compromising; gain attention through indecisive or vain behavior

SCORPIO: express personal potential passionately; illuminate in a penetrating, transforming way; shine when protecting self or others; celebrate aliveness in a powerful, seductive manner; demonstrate essential self through intensity; gain attention through defensive or vengeful behavior

SAGITTARIUS: express personal potential expansively; illuminate in a philosophical, ethical way; shine by presenting wisdom; celebrate aliveness in an optimistic and easygoing manner; demonstrate essential self by reaching for "more"; gain attention through preachy or self-indulgent behavior

CAPRICORN: express personal potential responsibly; illuminate in a pragmatic, organized way; shine by "fathering"; celebrate aliveness in a prestige-seeking, ambitious manner; demonstrate essential self through professionalism; gain attention through domineering or depressed behavior

AQUARIUS: express personal potential innovatively; illuminate in an eccentric, visionary way; shine by having visions for the future; celebrate aliveness in a nonconforming and inventive manner; demonstrate essential self through unpredictability; gain attention through rebellious or disruptive behavior

PISCES: express personal potential intuitively; illuminate in a spiritual, psychic way; shine by creating fantasies and dreams; celebrate aliveness in an imaginative, serene manner; demonstrate essential self through compassion; gain attention through paranoid or victim-oriented behavior

THE MOON:
The Caretaker

ITS ORBIT: PERSONAL: actively define and support individualization

ITS TASK: to establish belongingness; to nurture

ITS VOICE: "I comfort. I create security."

THE MOON bathes the Earth in reflected light, supporting us even when the Sun itself is absent. Its glyph, the crescent Moon, looks like a cradle – a symbol of supportive parenting.

The MOON'S FUNCTION is to provide emotional and physical support – to make sure that the Sun has "enough" so that it can survive. By being sensitive to its own needs and to the needs of others, the Moon creates environments and circumstances in which nurturance might occur. It reflects early and ongoing experiences of parenting, the "mothering" that it received in childhood and the caretaking it receives from others in adulthood. It also acts out its care and concern for others through nurturing behavior. The Moon is instinctive, psychic, and empathic, aware of fluctuations in the emotional environment and responsive to them. It goes through mood changes itself as it demonstrates its own feelings. The Moon adapts and adjusts its behavior until everyone feels stable and secure.

THE MOON IS NEVER RETROGRADE, so there are no interpretations for a Retrograde Moon.

If you're fully OWNING your Moon, you'll feel that you have the ability to secure nourishment and belongingness for yourself. Although you know that at any given moment you may feel insecure or abandoned, you also know what to do to change the situation. You're aware of your emotional needs and are able to choose appropriate times and methods for meeting them.

When the MOON OPERATES DYSFUNCTIONALLY, it grabs for security without regard for healthiness or consequences. It sets up hopeless, helpless, or needy situations in which it is desperate for love and support. It is so intuitively attuned to nuances that it overreacts to psychic and emotional input, feeling that anything could be a threat to its safety. As a result, its daily mood shifts can be dramatic and uncomfortable for everyone concerned. In its drive to create belongingness, the dysfunctional Moon can cling to inappropriate people or situations. It feels that belonging to a negative situation is better than not belonging at all! Ultimately, the Moon can smother itself or others in trying to be protective.

If you're DENOUNCING your Moon, you might feel that it's bad or silly to have emotional needs or to want to belong. You'll tend to squash your "childish" feelings. On the other hand, if you're GLORIFYING your Moon, you might value your ability to be sensitive and nurturing so much that you expect yourself to be feeling and giving all the time. If you're BLAMING your Moon-related behavior on other people or circumstances, you've probably felt abandoned by your caretakers. Since others gave you such a rotten deal, you now feel that you can irresponsibly grab for nurturance. After all, the way you were treated was not your fault! If you're PROJECTING your Moon, you're probably enlisting others to act out the roles of caregiving and emotional sensitivity for you. This keeps you from having to admit your needs or become too vulnerable. And, if you're DENYING your Moon, you don't think you have emotional needs. You think you're uninterested in belonging and feeling secure. You might also be ignoring the fact that you have a way to express and meet your emotional needs already. If you're using your Moon in one or more of these dysfunctional ways, remember that you *do* deserve to feel emotionally secure and to belong. And, you can find positive, healthy ways to insure that you're safe without becoming overly emotional.

In the MOON'S HOUSE, you experience the legacy of your childhood emotional patterns. If your early nurturance was reliable and steady or if you've learned how to nurture yourself as an adult, you can give yourself a solid base of emotional, spiritual, or financial support in this area of life. Here, as long as you feel nurtured, you'll give out your strongest "mother-love." You'll find people, animals, or things that need your loving attention and give – unconditionally. If your original family was physically neglectful or emotionally unavailable, you might struggle, in the Moon's House, to recreate a womb for yourself. You'll search for experiences of "enoughness." Whatever the quality or quantity of nurturance in your life, the Moon's House is always the place where you'll respond to your daily life in an instinctive, intuitive, and adaptable manner. It's also the area of life in which you'll deal with your mother's role model; you'll sort out which of her methods to accept or reject in the Moon's House.

The MOON'S SIGN shows the ways in which you've been nurtured and the way in which you nurture others. Most of the time, it shows how you experience your mother, whether or not her Chart includes Planets in that Sign. In fact, all of the children in one family usually have different Moon Signs, demonstrating their unique experiences with the same mother. Sometimes, the Moon's Sign will symbolize the general kind of caretaking you received in childhood, not specifically those related to your mother. In either case, this Sign shows how, as a result of these experiences, you prefer to take care of others. It also shows the way in which you meet your emotional and security needs most instinctively and comfortably. If your use of the Moon demonstrates some of the negative characteristics of its Sign, your conscious use of the Sign's healthy traits will increase your feeling of safety and belongingess.

As CANCER'S NATURAL RULING PLANET, the Moon's actions have immediate impact in any House with Cancer on the Cusp. As you create safety and security through your Moon, you'll provide a basis for your sense of belonging in any House that Cancer Rules. If your Cancer is intercepted, you can open it up through using the Moon.

APPLICATIONS FOR THE MOON

PSYCHOLOGICAL: the urge to create belongingness and unconditional support; the urge to act instinctively and protectively; actions designed to attract nurturance or give support; actions that support the self and others to discover and reflect "mothering" qualities

PRACTICAL: physical, financial, spiritual, or emotional support and belonging; activities related to water, breasts, stomach, sinuses, mood fluctuations, mother, parenting, caretaking, babies, homemaking, home, ambiance, food, food service, food production, property, real estate, hotels, motels, inns, pockets, bowls, containers, boats

SAMPLE INTERPRETATIONS FOR THE MOON IN THE HOUSES

1st: establish belongingess through title or role; nurture identity; comfort through personality; "mother" through physical appearance; create security through persona; meet emotional needs through personal style

2nd: establish belongingess through skills and talents; nurture self-worth; comfort through material world; "mother" through individual values; create security through actions involving money; meet emotional needs through possessions

3rd: establish belongingess through communication; nurture community; comfort through dialogue; "mother" siblings; create security through finding facts; meet emotional needs through short trips and vacations

4th: establish belongingness through home and family; nurture ethnic or racial origins; comfort mother; "mother" family and cultural roots; create security through creating belongingness for self and others; meet emotional needs through position in home or family

5th: establish belongingness through art and creativity; nurture play; comfort through recreation; "mother" through romance; create security through children; meet emotional needs through hobbies and leisure activities

6th: establish belongingness through daily work and routine; nurture everyday tasks; comfort through maintenance activities; "mother" co-workers; create security through service to others; meet emotional needs through health concerns; deal with health issues involving breasts, stomach, or sinuses

7th: establish belongingness through relating; nurture cooperation; comfort through arbitration; "mother" partner; create security through relationships; meet emotional needs through "significant other"

8th: establish belongingness through deep emotional interactions; nurture intimacy; comfort through utilization of collective money, talents, and resources; "mother" through sexuality; create security through transformation; meet emotional needs through sex

9th: establish belongingness through teaching or preaching; nurture philosophy; comfort through knowledge; "mother" with travel or learning; create security through ethics; meet emotional needs through selling or advertising

10th: establish belongingness through career; nurture profession; comfort father; "mother" through vocation; create security through position in societal structure; meet emotional needs through reputation

11th: establish belongingness through future visions; nurture the "cause"; comfort through goals and plans; "mother" friends; create security through theoretical systems; meet emotional needs through schemes

12th: establish belongingness through intuition; nurture spirituality; comfort through psychic ability; "mother" with addictions or meditation; create security through altered states; meet emotional needs through position in institution

SAMPLE INTERPRETATIONS FOR THE MOON IN THE SIGNS

ARIES: establish belongingness assertively; nurture in a spontaneous, childlike way; comfort by taking risks; "mother" in a stimulated and energized manner; create security by being freedom-loving; meet emotional needs through aggressive or inconsiderate behavior

TAURUS: establish belongingness reliably; nurture in a loyal way; comfort through getting results; "mother" in a sensual, physical manner; create security by being persistent; meet emotional needs through stubborn or stingy behavior

GEMINI: establish belongingness versatilely; nurture in a humorous way; comfort through dialogue; "mother" in a curious, amusing manner; create security by being communicative and investigative; meet emotional needs through gossipy or unreliable behavior

CANCER: establish belongingness nurturingly; nurture in an intuitive, caring way; comfort by "mothering"; "mother" in a sentimental way; create security by being protective of past patterns; meet emotional needs through fearful or clingy behavior

LEO: establish belongingness dramatically; nurture in a magnanimous, confident way; comfort by storytelling; "mother" in a flamboyant, flashy manner; create security by being good-hearted; meet emotional needs through egotistical or arrogant behavior

VIRGO: establish belongingness analytically; nurture in a practical, problem-solving way; comfort by figuring out the solution; "mother" in a discriminating, idealized manner; create security by being detail-oriented; meet emotional needs through critical or fussy behavior

LIBRA: establish belongingness diplomatically; nurture in a graceful, charming way; comfort by creating beauty; "mother" in a cooperative, interactive manner; create security by compromising; meet emotional needs through indecisive or vain behavior

SCORPIO: establish belongingness passionately; nurture in a penetrating, transforming way; comfort when protecting self or others; "mother" in a powerful, seductive manner; create security through intensity; meet emotional needs through defensive or vengeful behavior

SAGITTARIUS: establish belongingness expansively; nurture in a philosophical, ethical way; comfort by presenting wisdom; "mother" in an optimistic and easygoing manner; create security by reaching for "more"; meet emotional needs through preachy or self-indulgent behavior

CAPRICORN: establish belongingness responsibly; nurture in a pragmatic, organized way; comfort by "fathering"; "mother" in a prestige-seeking, ambitious manner; create security through professionalism; meet emotional needs through domineering or depressed behavior

AQUARIUS: establish belongingness innovatively; nurture in an eccentric, visionary way; comfort by having visions for the future; "mother" in a nonconforming and inventive manner; create security by being unpredictable; meet emotional needs through rebellious or disruptive behavior

PISCES: establish belongingness intuitively; nurture in a spiritual, psychic way; comfort by creating fantasies and dreams; "mother" in an imaginative, serene manner; create security by being compassionate; meet emotional needs through paranoid or victim-oriented behavior

MERCURY:
The Communicator

ITS ORBIT: PERSONAL: actively define and support individualization

ITS TASK: to form networks; to communicate

ITS VOICE: "I speak. I am curious."

MERCURY is the messenger, the communicator, and the connector. Its winged cap symbolizes the speed with which ideas are shared and transferred.

MERCURY'S FUNCTION is to think and communicate in logical, linear ways. It takes thoughts and ideas, lines them up in order, and shares its conclusions. Then it listens, taking in feedback, comments, and new directions, only to begin its process over again. Because it involves both speaking and listening, Mercury really is the Planet of dialogue – two way communication. But, it's not only interested in the interchange of ideas, it's fascinated by any kind of connectedness. In fact, Mercury seeks and creates opportunities for discovering how people, places, and things are related to one another. It gathers and shares data with regard to all these interconnections, and enjoys journeying, literally or figuratively, down many roads.

When MERCURY IS RETROGRADE, its thinking style is extremely personalized. Its neurological "wiring" may actually be unusual. This can result in learning disabilities, such as dyslexia, or in creative but unusual thought patterns. Oftentimes, Mercury Retrograde finds its early school experiences to be either frustrating or irrelevant. Its academic performance may not show it, but it frequently feels either misunderstood or bored in school. In adulthood, it discovers that the reason for its dissatisfaction with education is that it does, indeed, operate mentally in strange or innovative ways. At this point, its biggest challenge is to learn how to translate its internal processing into a "language" that others can understand. Once this occurs, dialogue and feedback ensue, and Retrograde Mercury perceives itself to be less isolated and odd.

When you're fully OWNING your Mercury, you'll find that you can communicate quite clearly in your own way most of the time. You actually want to communicate with others, realizing that through the process of discussion, you get feedback about yourself and your world. If communication breaks down, you know that you can find internal or external resources that will help you to resume the dialogue.

When MERCURY OPERATES DYSFUNCTIONALLY, it scatters energy and ideas indiscriminately, short-circuiting itself and burning out. Mercury can pile up facts and trivia compulsively without cataloging or organizing them, unaware of how they interconnect. It can become mentally hyper, jumping from thought to thought without listening for feedback. Or, it can become dull and uninspired, spinning round and round in one network of people or ideas, avoiding the risk of new environments. When Mercury is badly used, true communication ceases and a babbling imitation takes over.

If you're DENOUNCING your Mercury, you may think that your intellect is a ridiculous or unnecessary part of you. You may think it's more important to isolate yourself than to communicate or network with others. On the other hand, if you're GLORIFYING your Mercury, you could be overvaluing your communication skills, expecting yourself to always be the perfect listener and conversationalist. If you're BLAMING your Mercurial behavior on other people or circumstances, you'll find excuses for why you've said what you've said. You may claim that you're "just like your father," or that you're always rude at this time of month. If you're PROJECTING your Mercury, you'll unconsciously allow someone else to talk for you. Or, instead of thinking for yourself, you'll just go along with what others think. And if you're DENYING your Mercury, you could think that you're incapable of clear communication or effective networking. You'll believe that conversation is just not your skill. You might also be ignoring the fact that you have a unique and workable way of communicating already. If you're using your Mercury in one or more of these dysfunctional ways, remember that your mind is worth something. You may not communicate or connect in ways that others do, but what you think and say is worth hearing. Remember, too, that you'll want to stay conscious of feedback from others and from your internal sensations about the effectiveness of your style of interaction.

MERCURY'S HOUSE is the location in which you seek and create stimulating, interactive experiences. Here, you communicate and dialogue with others, exchanging ideas and thoughts as often as possible. You follow your curiosity in unearthing quantities of data and detail with regard to the concerns of this life area. In Mercury's House, you'll also participate in using or establishing networks of information, people, and places.

MERCURY'S SIGN symbolizes your communication style. It shows how your mind operates internally and how you express what you think. It also indicates the kinds of communication that you'll be most receptive to hearing. This Sign will show the type of stimulation that you want and the manner in which your curiosity will be aroused. If you're having difficulty in communicating with others, a conscious use of Mercury's Sign's positive characteristics will probably enhance your chances of being clearly understood.

As GEMINI'S NATURAL RULING PLANET, Mercury's behavior has consequences in any House with Gemini on the Cusp. As you learn to use its style of cognitive processing more and more effectively, conditions in Gemini's House will be enhanced. And, if your Gemini is intercepted, your use of Mercury will free it up.

APPLICATIONS FOR MERCURY

PSYCHOLOGICAL: the urge to think in left-brain, logical terms; the urge to be communicative and cognitive; actions designed to foster interaction and dialogue; actions that keep the self and others mentally stimulated and curious

PRACTICAL: logical, cognitive thought processes, speech, physical ability to talk or communicate; activities related to air, the mind, nervous system, arms, lungs, shoulders, youths, communication, printing, messages, data, trivia, books, stories, journals, diaries, writing utensils, photographs, transportation, vehicles, paperwork, information, networking, data-processing, commerce, education, exchange of ideas/people/goods, gossip, humor, slang, whispers, news reports, broadcasting, duality, twins, ambidexterity, manual dexterity, vacations, short trips, visits, electrical appliances, networks

SAMPLE INTERPRETATIONS FOR MERCURY IN THE HOUSES

1st: form networks through title or role; communicate about identity; express logic through personality; satisfy curiosity through physical appearance; foster dialogue through persona; stay mentally stimulated through personal style

2nd: form networks through skills and talents; communicate about self-worth; express logic through individual values; satisfy curiosity through material world; foster dialogue through actions involving money; stay mentally stimulated through possessions

3rd: form networks through communication; communicate about community; express logic through dialogue; satisfy curiosity with siblings; foster dialogue through finding facts; stay mentally stimulated through short trips and vacations

4th: form networks through home and family; communicate about ethnic or racial origins; express logic about mother; act on curiosity about family and cultural roots; foster dialogue through creating belongingness; stay mentally stimulated through position in home or family

5th: form networks through art and creativity; communicate about play; express logic through recreation; act on curiosity through romance; foster dialogue through children; stay mentally stimulated through hobbies and leisure activities

6th: form networks through daily work and routine; communicate about everyday tasks; express logic through maintenance activities; act on curiosity with co-workers; foster dialogue through service to others; stay mentally stimulated through health concerns; deal with health issues involving lungs, arms, nervous system

7th: form networks through relating; communicate about cooperation; express logic through arbitration; act on curiosity with partner; foster dialogue through relationships; stay mentally stimulated through "significant others"

8th: form networks through deep emotional interactions; communicate about intimacy; express logic through utilization of collective money, talents, and resources; act on curiosity through sexuality; foster dialogue through transformation; stay mentally stimulated through sex

9TH: form networks through teaching or preaching; communicate about philosophy; express logic through knowledge; act on curiosity with travel or learning; foster dialogue through ethics; stay mentally stimulated through selling or advertising

10th: form networks through career; communicate about profession; express logic regarding father; act on curiosity with vocation; foster dialogue through position in societal structure; stay mentally stimulated through reputation

11th: form networks through future visions; communicate about the "cause"; express logic through goals and plans; act on curiosity with friends; foster dialogue regarding theoretical systems; stay mentally stimulated through schemes

12th: form networks through intuition; communicate about spirituality; express logic through psychic ability; act on curiosity through addictions or meditation; foster dialogue through altered states; stay mentally stimulated through position in institution

SAMPLE INTERPRETATIONS FOR MERCURY IN THE SIGNS

ARIES: form networks assertively; communicate in a spontaneous, child-like way; express logic by taking risks; act on curiosity in a stimulated and energized manner; foster dialogue by being freedom-loving; stay mentally stimulated through aggressive or inconsiderate behavior

TAURUS: form networks reliably; communicate in a loyal way; express logic through getting results; act on curiosity in a sensual, physical manner; foster dialogue by being persistent; stay mentally stimulated through stubborn or stingy behavior

GEMINI: form networks versatilely; communicate in a humorous way; express logic through dialogue; act on curiosity in a curious, amusing manner; foster dialogue by being communicative and investigative; stay mentally stimulated through gossipy or unreliable behavior

CANCER: form networks nurturingly; communicate in a comforting, caring way; express logic by "mothering"; act on curiosity in a sentimental way; foster dialogue by being protective of past patterns; stay mentally stimulated through fearful or clingy behavior

LEO: form networks dramatically; communicate in a magnanimous, confident way; express logic by storytelling; act on curiosity in a flamboyant, flashy manner; foster dialogue by being good-hearted; stay mentally stimulated through egotistical or arrogant behavior

VIRGO: form networks analytically; communicate in a practical, problem-solving way; express logic by figuring out the solution; act on curiosity in a discriminating, idealized manner; foster dialogue by being detail-oriented; stay mentally stimulated through critical or fussy behavior

LIBRA: form networks diplomatically; communicate in a graceful, charming way; express logic by creating beauty; act on curiosity in a cooperative, interactive manner; foster dialogue compromising; stay mentally stimulated through indecisive or vain behavior

SCORPIO: form networks passionately; communicate in a penetrating, transforming way; express logic when protecting self or others; act on curiosity in a powerful, seductive manner; foster dialogue through intensity; stay mentally stimulated through defensive or vengeful behavior

SAGITTARIUS: form networks expansively; communicate in a philosophical, ethical way; express logic by presenting wisdom; act on curiosity in an optimistic and easygoing manner; foster dialogue by reaching for "more"; stay mentally stimulated through preachy or self-indulgent behavior

CAPRICORN: form networks responsibly; communicate in a pragmatic, organized way; express logic by "fathering"; act on curiosity in a prestige-seeking, ambitious manner; foster dialogue through professionalism; stay mentally stimulated through domineering or depressed behavior

AQUARIUS: form networks innovatively; communicate in an eccentric, visionary way; express logic by having visions for the future; act on curiosity in a nonconforming and inventive manner; foster dialogue by being unpredictable; stay mentally stimulated through rebellious or disruptive behavior

PISCES: form networks intuitively; communicate in a spiritual, psychic way; express logic by creating fantasies and dreams; act on curiosity in an imaginative, serene manner; foster dialogue by being compassionate; stay mentally stimulated through paranoid or victim-oriented behavior

VENUS:
The Charmer

ITS ORBIT: PERSONAL: actively define and support individualization

ITS TASK: to establish value; to beautify

ITS VOICE: "I glow. I magnetically attract people, things, and experiences of value."

The symbol for VENUS is also used as the symbol for woman. This is appropriate since Venus does reflect a person's consciousness about women in the culture. For both men and women, Venus's glyph symbolizes the power of receptivity and attraction.

VENUS'S FUNCTION is to be the magnetic force of attraction in a Birth Chart. It is the power that draws any chosen person, experience, or object to itself. Venus isn't blatant or obvious, but in its own subtle way it has the ability to imbue something with value or to withhold approval. Venus evaluates all aspects of a person's life and finds those that are attractive and worthwhile. Then, it finds ways to emphasize, enhance, or artistically express those special attributes. As a result, Venus is the musician or visual artist, creator of beauty and esthetic experience. Its romantic glow surrounds and permeates all the mystique surrounding dating and courtship. As a valuer of diplomatic interactions among people, Venus is also the consultant who aids in personal or political conflict resolution and arbitration.

When VENUS IS RETROGRADE, its values are often mismatched to those of the culture. Specifically, its experience of women may be quite different from that of its peers. Venus Retrograde turns inward and deeply examines its criteria for evaluating worthiness. It has to learn to value itself before it can value anything else in the world. Venus finds that its reasons for treasuring someone or something are distinctly personal and unlike those of the mainstream. As a result, its values will be tested and even challenged until it learns how to stand by them. In adulthood, the qualities and experiences that Venus has appreciated and creatively expressed may find wider acceptance. Ideally, Venus Retrograde finds a way to be true to itself *and* to work within the broader societal context.

When you're fully OWNING your Venus, you'll sense that your values are right for you. You'll know what you like, and don't like, esthetically. And, you'll generally attract experiences that make you feel worthwhile. Although you may not always agree with others, you'll feel comfortable with making space for creative disagreement. Most of the time, you'll feel that, in your own way, you are creating beauty and harmony in the world. Additionally, you'll have found a productive way to integrate "female" qualities into your life.

When VENUS OPERATES DYSFUNCTIONALLY, it becomes gluttonous and greedy, attracting a quantity of people or things to itself while disregarding their quality. It's as though a special magnet has gone haywire, drawing plastic and garbage to itself instead of just fine metal filings. It forgets to evaluate its experiences, feeling that, because an item has arrived—whatever it is—it must have value. It can create romance for its own sake, falling in love with love, regardless of who's involved. As a creator, dysfunctional Venus switches to mass production without regard for quality control. And, as a counselor, Venus can be inappropriate in pushing for surface harmony at the expense of unresolved conflicts. It can actually wage war for the sake of leveling controversy and achieving peace.

If you're DENOUNCING your Venus, you could feel that your values or artistic sensibilities are poor compared with those of others. You might even feel that all "female" qualities are negative. On the other hand, if you're GLORIFYING your Venus, you could have such high expectations of romance that you're under constant pressure to live up to the Cinderella fantasy. If you're BLAMING your Venusian behavior on other people or circumstances, you'll refuse to take responsibility for your own values. You'll say that others caused you to operate according to these rules or criteria. You may even Blame women or the female cultural stereotypes for your situation. If you're PROJECTING your Venus, you'll unconsciously get someone else to act out some "female" qualities for you. Instead of expressing your own "womanly" attributes, you'll find them demonstrated in others. And, if you're DENYING your Venus, you may not think you have any "female" characteristics. You'll simply ignore your artistic ability and your personal values. You might also be ignoring the fact that you have a sense of esthetics and a good grasp of your "female" qualities already. If you're using your Venus in one or more of these dysfunctional ways, remember that you are worthwhile and that your values are important to you. Also remember that, whether you're male or female, you can integrate the supposed "female" qualities into your life to whatever degree you want. It's also up to you to create beauty and value without becoming vain.

In VENUS'S HOUSE, you magnetically attract people and objects that help you to establish and express your values. Here your self-esteem is immediately apparent through the quality of experiences that you create. As you enhance your general self-worth, your interactions in this House improve rapidly. This is an area of life in which you can express your talents for artistic expression or interpersonal mediation. Venus's House is also where you'll react to the training you've received about women's roles in your culture.

VENUS'S SIGN shows the way in which you bestow harmony, beauty, and peace on the world. It shows the style in which you attract people and possessions to yourself. The nature of this Sign can be an indicator of the style of artistic or esthetic expression that you can most easily express. It also reflects your approach to romance, to courtship, to cooperating, and to partnering in general. And, Venus's Sign will describe your attitude toward women. If you find yourself using Venus dysfunctionally, you're probably expressing the negative characteristics of its Sign. By switching to the positive traits of the same Sign, you might be happier with the values that Venus is expressing.

As the NATURAL RULING PLANET OF BOTH TAURUS AND LIBRA, Venus has impact on at least two other areas of life. As you create experiences of value, beauty, or cooperation with Venus, the quality of the result is felt in any Houses with Taurus or Libra on the Cusps. If either Taurus or Libra is intercepted, Venus's harmonizing efforts will bring its needs into the open.

APPLICATIONS FOR VENUS

PSYCHOLOGICAL: the urge to evaluate, harmonize, negotiate, and arbitrate; the urge to create beauty, balance, art, and peace; actions designed to imbue people, objects, and events with value; actions that encourage self and others to test and refine basic values

PRACTICAL: objects, experiences, and people of value or beauty; activities related to balance, lower back, kidneys, urinary system, internal reproductive system, throat, neck, voice, chin, ears, money, bodywork, massage, physical therapy, sensuousness, self-worth, possessions, women, visual and tactile art, pottery, weaving, texture, music, acting, dance, courtship, marriage, partnering, partners, popularity, romance, love objects, lovers, affairs, social occasions, hosts/hostesses, sugar and sweetness, beauty, hair, cosmetics, grooming, vanity, gifts, plants, esthetics, peace, war, values, negotiation, arbitration

SAMPLE INTERPRETATIONS FOR VENUS IN THE HOUSES

1st: create beauty and harmony through title or role; establish the value of identity; glow through personality; magnetically attract people and things through physical appearance; balance conflicting forces through persona; express values through personal style

2nd: create beauty and harmony through skills and talents; establish the value of self-esteem; glow through individual values; magnetically attract people and things through involvement in material world; balance conflicting forces through actions involving money; express values through possessions

3rd: create beauty and harmony through communication; establish the value of community; glow through dialogue; magnetically attract siblings; balance conflicting forces through finding facts; express values through short trips and vacations

4th: create beauty and harmony through home and family; establish the value of ethnic or racial origins; glow about mother; magnetically attract people and things through family and cultural roots; balance conflicting forces through creating belongingness; express values through position in home or family

5th: create beauty and harmony through art and creativity; establish the value of play; glow through recreation; magnetically attract people and things through romance; balance conflicting forces among or about children; express values through hobbies and leisure activities

6th: create beauty and harmony through daily work and routine; establish the value of everyday tasks; glow through maintenance activities; magnetically attract co-workers; balance conflicting forces through service to others; express values through health concerns; deal with health issues involving kidneys, lower back, internal reproductive organs, sugar metabolism

7th: create beauty and harmony through relating; establish the value of cooperation; glow through arbitration; magnetically attract partners; balance conflicting forces through relationships; express values through choice of "significant others"

8th: create beauty and harmony through deep emotional interactions; establish the value of intimacy; glow through utilization of collective money, talents, and resources; magnetically attract people and things through sexuality; balance conflicting forces through transformation; express values through sex

9th: create beauty and harmony through teaching or preaching; establish the value of philosophy; glow through knowledge; magnetically attract people and things with travel or learning; balance conflicting forces through ethics; express values through selling or advertising

10th: create beauty and harmony through career; establish the value of profession; glow about father; magnetically attract people and things through vocation; balance conflicting forces through position in societal structure; express values through reputation

11th: create beauty and harmony through future visions; establish the value of the "cause"; glow regarding goals and plans; magnetically attract groups and friends; balance conflicting forces through theoretical systems; express values through schemes

12th: create beauty and harmony through intuition; establish the value of spirituality; glow regarding psychic ability; magnetically attract people and things through addictions or meditation; balance conflicting forces through altered states; express values through position in institution

SAMPLE INTERPRETATIONS FOR VENUS IN THE SIGNS

ARIES: create beauty and harmony assertively; establish values in a spontaneous, childlike way; glow by taking risks; magnetically attract people and things in a stimulated and energized manner; balance conflicting forces by being freedom-loving; express values through aggressive or inconsiderate behavior

TAURUS: create beauty and harmony reliably; establish values in a loyal way; glow through getting results; magnetically attract people and things in a sensual, physical manner; balance conflicting forces by being persistent; express values through stubborn or stingy behavior

GEMINI: create beauty and harmony versatilely; establish values in a humorous way; glow through dialogue; magnetically attract people and things in a curious, amusing manner; balance conflicting forces by being communicative and investigative; express values through gossipy or unreliable behavior

CANCER: create beauty and harmony nurturingly; establish values in a comforting, caring way; glow by "mothering"; magnetically attract people and things in a sentimental way; balance conflicting forces by being protective of past patterns; express values through fearful or clingy behavior

LEO: create beauty and harmony dramatically; establish values in a magnanimous, confident way; glow by storytelling; magnetically attract people and things in a flamboyant, flashy manner; balance conflicting forces by being good-hearted; express values through egotistical or arrogant behavior

VIRGO: create beauty and harmony analytically; establish values in a practical, problem-solving way; glow by figuring out the solution; magnetically attract people and things in a discriminating, idealized manner; balance conflicting forces by being detail-oriented; express values through critical or fussy behavior

LIBRA: create beauty and harmony diplomatically; establish values in a graceful, charming way; glow by creating beauty; magnetically attract people and things in a cooperative, interactive manner; balance conflicting forces by compromising; express values through indecisive or vain behavior

SCORPIO: create beauty and harmony passionately; establish values in a penetrating, transforming way; glow when protecting self or others; magnetically attract people and things in a powerful, seductive manner; balance conflicting forces through intensity; express values through defensive or vengeful behavior

SAGITTARIUS: create beauty and harmony expansively; establish values in a philosophical, ethical way; glow by presenting wisdom; magnetically attract people and things in an optimistic and easygoing manner; balance conflicting forces by reaching for "more"; express values through preachy or self-indulgent behavior

CAPRICORN: create beauty and harmony responsibly; establish values in a pragmatic, organized way; glow by "fathering"; magnetically attract people and things in a prestige-seeking, ambitious manner; balance conflicting forces through professionalism; express values through domineering or depressed behavior

AQUARIUS: create beauty and harmony innovatively; establish values in an eccentric, visionary way; glow by having visions for the future; magnetically attract people and things in a nonconforming and inventive manner; balance conflicting forces through unpredictability; express values through rebellious or disruptive behavior

PISCES: create beauty and harmony intuitively; establish values in a spiritual, psychic way; glow by creating fantasies and dreams; magnetically attract people and things in an imaginative, serene manner; balance conflicting forces through compassion; express values through paranoid or victim-oriented behavior

MARS:
The Pursuer

ITS ORBIT: PERSONAL: actively define and support individualization

ITS TASK: to pursue desires; to initiate movement

ITS VOICE: "I act. I get what I want when I want it."

MARS is the symbol for man and, as such, does represent each person's experience of male cultural roles and patterns. Whatever a person's gender, Mars's glyph represents the force of personal action.

MARS'S FUNCTION is to identify its desires and pursue them. Its motivation usually comes from strong internal drives, the most common being sexual attraction, desire, and anger. Whatever the source, once Mars's energy is triggered, it initiates action and dares to take risks as it moves as quickly as possible toward satisfaction. It also asserts itself independently and optimistically, never doubting that through its own force of will, it can have whatever it wants. Mars won't take others by the hand, but it may find itself in a leadership position as it inspires others to be more pioneering and daring.

When MARS IS RETROGRADE, it directs its anger or passion at itself before it focuses on others. Instead of moving others out of the way, Retrograde Mars can move itself out of the way, taking quick action to make personal change when any conflict arises. It can even be self-destructive. Normally, however, it needs to clarify its desires and focus its passion internally before it acts. It needs to know that it's truly acting out of its own motivations, not anyone else's. Retrograde Mars may take a little longer to be impulsive than regular Mars, but it is still fast-moving and assertive.

When you're fully OWNING your Mars, you'll know what you want, and you'll have appropriate ways of going after it. You can assert yourself and even take risks without harming yourself. You can also act on your sexual drives in ways that are positive and satisfying. And, although you sometimes feel angry or even furious, you'll have healthy ways of expressing your frustration.

When MARS OPERATES DYSFUNCTIONALLY, it's a steamroller, pushing everything and anything out of the way in its drive toward success or satisfaction. It is so unconscious of others that it may actually hurt them as it zooms forward. Eruptions of anger frequently lead to violence with a dysfunctional Mars, violence that could be physical, emotional, or verbal. Mars is so independent that it not only ignores others, it can ignore aspects of its own personality. It can ride roughshod over the other personality parts, putting its desires for immediate gratification ahead of all other considerations. And, since it's conscious only of short-term results, dysfunctional Mars is usually surprised at the negative long-term consequences of its actions.

If you're DENOUNCING your Mars, you probably think that it's wrong to have desires and angry feelings. You might even think that all "male" energy is bad. On the other hand, if you're GLORIFYING your Mars, you could have such high expectations for how you'll handle these feelings, or for how "masculine" you'll be, that you can't possibly be that perfect all the time. If you're BLAMING your Mars-related behavior on other people or circumstances, you'll think it's not your fault that you're feeling what you feel. You'll believe that others can "force" you to have angry or desirous reactions. If you're PROJECTING your Mars, you'll unconsciously get others to act out your strong feelings, or "male" qualities, for you. And, if you're DENYING your Mars, you'll believe that you never are angry, you never have desires, and you don't want anything. You might also be ignoring the fact that you have an appropriate way of experiencing and expressing your anger and desires already. If you're using your Mars in one or more of these dysfunctional ways, remember that everyone has emotions and desires. It's normal. Our challenge as human beings is to learn how to channel and direct those feelings appropriately. Additionally, remember that, whatever your gender, you can integrate "male" qualities into your own personality to whatever degree you want. It's your choice to be assertive without being a bully.

In MARS'S HOUSE, you go directly after your goals. You usually know what you want, and you move quickly past all obstacles as you move toward your destination. You may be impulsive in this area of life, forgetting to consider the consequences of your behavior. On the other hand, you'll also be motivated to seek out the thrill of risk and adventure. And, in Mars's House you'll respond to your experience of men in your culture.

MARS'S SIGN shows the emotional, verbal, or physical style of assertiveness that you prefer. It indicates how blatant or subtle you'll be in getting what you want. Mars's Sign will not remove Mars's aggressiveness, but it will soften or intensify it. And, if you use your Mars dysfunctionally, you're more likely to use the destructive aspects of its Sign. If you want to change how you're using your Mars, you can examine the positive characteristics of Mars's Sign and choose those that will allow you to be assertive in the ways you prefer.

As ARIES'S NATURAL RULING PLANET, all of Mars's drive has a direct effect on any House with Aries on the Cusp. The more positively assertive you can be in pursuing your desires, the more independence and initiative you'll experience in Aries's House. And, if Aries is intercepted, you'll be able better to express its qualities by utilizing your Mars effectively.

APPLICATIONS FOR MARS

PSYCHOLOGICAL: the urge to act, initiate, drive forward, begin; the urge to pursue own desires, impulsively and immediately; actions designed to clear the path for personal satisfaction; actions that motivate self and others to express anger, frustration, or passion

PRACTICAL: physical energy and aggressiveness; sexual drives; activities related to fire, firefighting, fireplaces, matches, knives, surgery, needles, sharp or pointed objects, poison, head, skin eruptions, scratching, nose, brain, fever, inflammations, injuries, smoking, red, anger, violence, bullies, temper, shoplifting, sex, guns, combat, speed, armed forces, emergencies, heroism

SAMPLE INTERPRETATIONS FOR MARS IN THE HOUSES

1st: pursue personal desires through title or role; initiate action through identity; assert self through personality; follow impulses regarding physical appearance; demonstrate sexual energy through persona; express anger through personal style

2nd: pursue personal desires through skills and talents; initiate action to show worthiness; assert self regarding individual values; follow impulses regarding material world; demonstrate sexual energy through actions involving money; express anger through possessions

3rd: pursue personal desires through communication; initiate action in community; assert self through dialogue; follow impulses with siblings; demonstrate sexual energy when finding facts; express anger through taking short trips and vacations

4th: pursue personal desires through home and family; initiate action regarding ethnic or racial origins; assert self regarding mother; follow impulses regarding family and cultural roots; demonstrate sexual energy when creating belongingness; express anger through utilizing position in home or family

5th: pursue personal desires through art and creativity; initiate action regarding play; assert self through recreation; follow impulses regarding romance; demonstrate sexual energy with children or from own "inner child"; express anger through hobbies and leisure activities

6th: pursue personal desires through daily work and routine; initiate action in everyday tasks; assert self through maintenance activities; follow impulses with co-workers; demonstrate sexual energy through service to others; express anger through health concerns; deal with health issues involving head, nose, surgery

7th: pursue personal desires through relating; initiate action through cooperation; assert self through arbitration; follow impulses with partner; demonstrate sexual energy in relationships; express anger through "significant others"

8th: pursue personal desires through deep emotional interactions; initiate action through intimacy; assert self through utilization of collective money, talents, and resources; follow impulses regarding sexuality; demonstrate sexual energy as transformation; express anger through sex

9th: pursue personal desires through teaching or preaching; initiate action through philosophy; assert self through knowledge; follow impulses regarding travel or learning; demonstrate sexual energy regarding ethics; express anger through selling or advertising

10th: pursue personal desires through career; initiate action through profession; assert self regarding father; follow impulses in vocation; demonstrate sexual energy through position in societal structure; express anger through utilizing reputation

11th: pursue personal desires in future visions; initiate action regarding the "cause"; assert self through goals and plans; follow impulses with friends; demonstrate sexual energy using theoretical systems; express anger through schemes

12th: pursue personal desires with intuition; initiate action through spirituality; assert self through psychic ability; follow impulses with addictions or meditation; demonstrate sexual energy in altered states; express anger through position in institution

SAMPLE INTERPRETATIONS FOR MARS IN THE SIGNS

ARIES: pursue personal desires assertively; initiate action in a spontaneous, childlike way; assert self by taking risks; follow impulses in a stimulated and energized manner; demonstrate sexual energy by being freedom-loving; express anger through aggressive or inconsiderate behavior

TAURUS: pursue personal desires reliably; initiate action in a loyal way; assert self through getting results; follow impulses in a sensual, physical manner; demonstrate sexual energy by being persistent; express anger through stubborn or stingy behavior

GEMINI: pursue personal desires versatilely; initiate action in a humorous way; assert self through dialogue; follow impulses in a curious, amusing manner; demonstrate sexual energy by being communicative and investigative; express anger through gossipy or unreliable behavior

CANCER: pursue personal desires nurturingly; initiate action in a comforting, caring way; assert self by "mothering"; follow impulses in a sentimental way; demonstrate sexual energy by being protective of past patterns; express anger through fearful or clingy behavior

LEO: pursue personal desires dramatically; initiate action in a magnanimous, confident way; assert self by storytelling; follow impulses in a flamboyant, flashy manner; demonstrate sexual energy by being good-hearted; express anger through egotistical or arrogant behavior

VIRGO: pursue personal desires analytically; initiate action in a practical, problem-solving way; assert self by figuring out the solution; follow impulses in a discriminating, idealized manner; demonstrate sexual energy by being detail-oriented; express anger through critical or fussy behavior

LIBRA: pursue personal desires diplomatically; initiate action in a graceful, charming way; assert self by creating beauty; follow impulses in a cooperative, interactive manner; demonstrate sexual energy by compromising; express anger through indecisive or vain behavior

SCORPIO: pursue personal desires passionately; initiate action in a penetrating, transforming way; assert self when protecting self or others; follow impulses in a powerful, seductive manner; demonstrate sexual energy intensely; express anger through defensive or vengeful behavior

SAGITTARIUS: pursue personal desires expansively; initiate action in a philosophical, ethical way; assert self by presenting wisdom; follow impulses in an optimistic and easygoing manner; demonstrate sexual energy by reaching for "more"; express anger through preachy or self-indulgent behavior

CAPRICORN: pursue personal desires responsibly; initiate action in a pragmatic, organized way; assert self by "fathering"; follow impulses in a prestige-seeking, ambitious manner; demonstrate sexual energy professionally; express anger through domineering or depressed behavior

AQUARIUS: pursue personal desires innovatively; initiate action in an eccentric, visionary way; assert self by having visions for the future; follow impulses in a nonconforming and inventive manner; demonstrate sexual energy unpredictably; express anger through rebellious or disruptive behavior

PISCES: pursue personal desires intuitively; initiate action in a spiritual, psychic way; assert self by creating fantasies and dreams; follow impulses in an imaginative, serene manner; demonstrate sexual energy compassionately; express anger through paranoid or victim-oriented behavior

JUPITER:
The Seeker

ITS ORBIT: SOCIAL: actively characterize and encourage participation in the World

ITS TASK: to seek *the* truth; to philosophize

ITS VOICE: "I teach. I expand the possibilities for growth."

JUPITER is the largest Planet in the solar system, and its meaning reflects its size. Its symbol signifies the expansive mind, questing outward for broader knowledge and experience.

JUPITER'S FUNCTION is to create "moreness." It takes what's available and expands it in ever-increasing spirals outward, constantly seeking more freedom and limitlessness. Jupiter searches for the absolute truth, the ultimate peak experience, or the adventure that's beyond the farthest horizon. If one door closes, Jupiter simply quests in new directions until new doors open. It takes the optimistic attitude that a closed door is merely a signal indicating that better doors are opening. In effect, Jupiter accepts that whatever happens is "meant to be" and ultimately for the good. It knows that a new perspective may be required and is sure that a theory can be found somewhere in the world that will explain all the dilemmas. As a result, Jupiter has the ability to turn most situations into opportunities for further growth and expansion. Along the way, as Jupiter discovers new vistas and truths, it willingly shares its insights, usually in a lecturing format. It may teach in person or disseminate its knowledge through media or the written word. In either case, Jupiter presents its information as irrefutable truth, sure that others will hear and understand, confident that it can handle any opposition or argument.

When you're fully OWNING your Jupiter, you'll know that you've tested and established your ethics for yourself. Whether you agree or disagree with others, you'll sense that you're living by your own philosophy. Although you may not have *the* truth yet, you'll be aware that you're seeking it in the ways that are best for you. And that, as you discover what you know, you'll be able to pass it on to others appropriately.

When JUPITER OPERATES DYSFUNCTIONALLY, it overextends itself. It goes too far out on the small limb, reaches for that one extra apple, and falls down. It's self-indulgent, thinking that because it wants "more," it can have more without having to pay the price. Dysfunctional Jupiter tends to binge and to con itself about the binge behavior. It believes that everything will work out; it thinks it can play or indulge now and pay later. But, when Jupiter is dysfunctional, it has no realistic means of paying later. Time, energy, and money get shuffled around in an attempt to keep up with the ever-expanding demands until the whole shaky structure collapses. Even then, dysfunctional Jupiter may not realize the seriousness of the situation, still thinking it can simply walk away from the mess into new opportunities. It believes that the next high or the next theory will erase all the problems and is shocked at having to accept the consequences of its actions. Dysfunctional Jupiter will become preachy, lecturing long and loudly at others, trying to convince them of its point of view even if they don't want to listen. It's sure that its own argument has no flaws, it's just that others are unwilling to be flexible!

If you're DENOUNCING your Jupiter, you might think that seeking expansion and knowledge is wrong or self-indulgent. You might believe that it's bad to outgrow your family or friends. On the other hand, if you're GLORIFYING your Jupiter, you might be so enamored of your questing process that you elevate it above normal status. You expect yourself always to be searching for *the* truth in every situation. If you're BLAMING your Jupiterian behavior on other people or circumstances, you'll think that your beliefs and philosophy are not your fault. You'll feel that if only "they" hadn't taught you this, you'd be fine. If you're PROJECTING your Jupiter, you'll unconsciously get others to act out your beliefs and ethics for you. Or, you might trust others' viewpoints more than your own. If you're DENYING your Jupiter, you'll think that you don't even have any morals or any drive to search for *the* truth. You'll be convinced that you have no urge to expand, travel, or learn. You might also be ignoring the fact that you have a sense of *your* truth and opportunities for expansion already. If you're using your Jupiter in one or more of these dysfunctional ways, remember that everyone has some need to move beyond childhood horizons. You may do it mentally, physically, emotionally, or spiritually, but in some way, you'll need to honor the urge to grow. Additionally, remember that whatever your family background or educational level, you have the ability to develop your own ethics and your own version of *the* truth without becoming pontifical about it.

When JUPITER IS RETROGRADE, it needs to expand inward at a psychological level before it can move out into the world. It quests for its own truth and personal knowing, whether or not its theories agree with those of others. When philosophical or theoretical conflicts arise, Retrograde Jupiter finds its own answers, confident that it has enough perspective and knowledge to explain contradictions and resolve any confusion. It may create elaborate, internally developed systems to explain the nature of things. Whether or not the world listens, Retrograde Jupiter understands and teaches.

In JUPITER'S HOUSE, you consciously and unconsciously provide yourself with opportunities for growth. The growth can occur at the practical level and be symbolized by physical or financial increase. It also can be more scientific, theoretical, or philosophical, demonstrated by the quest for *the* truth. While you may experience periodic setbacks, you'll find that experiences of "moreness" continue to occur in this area of life. It is also in Jupiter's House that you confidently teach, preach, and share what you know or own. In this area of life, you can be generous with your knowledge and possessions because there's always plenty more to be had. JUPITER'S SIGN shows the distinct manner in which you tend to enlarge your experience. It will show whether your expansion occurs in intellectual, physical, or emotional dimensions. This Sign will indicate the healthy and unhealthy possibilities for your experience of "moreness." And, Jupiter's Sign will indicate how you disseminate your store of knowledge to others; it will describe your style of teaching or preaching. If you discover yourself using Jupiter in a dysfunctional manner, a switch into its Sign's positive qualities might help you expand yourself more appropriately.

As SAGITTARIUS'S NATURAL RULING PLANET, Jupiter's expanding horizons bring fulfillment to any House with Sagittarius on the Cusp. Whenever you discover a new dimension of *the* truth or have a peak experience of expansion, Sagittarius's need for growth is satisfied. And, if Sagittarius is intercepted, pursuing Jupiter's quest for growth will allow it to expand outward.

APPLICATIONS FOR JUPITER

PSYCHOLOGICAL: the urge to expand, grow, increase, improve, have "more"; the urge to teach, preach, disseminate, share; actions designed to foster hope and optimism; actions that encourage the self and others to develop a meaningful philosophy of life

PRACTICAL: increased or expanded size, more of it, generosity; activities related to fire, hot air, thighs, hips, weight gain, fatness, harvest, horses, overindulgence, bingeing, exercise that involves large motor skills or an outdoorsy sense of freedom, philosophical or scientific truths, religion, preaching, advice-giving, wisdom, teaching, publishing, writing, broadcasting, promoting, advertising, marketing, travel, international concerns, universities and higher education, legal concerns and documents, judicial system and theory, loans, inheritances, gambling, wealth

SAMPLE INTERPRETATIONS FOR JUPITER IN THE HOUSES

1st:　expand the possibilities for growth through title or role; teach about or through identity; express philosophy through personality; foster hope and optimism through physical appearance; seek *the* truth through persona; over-indulge as a personal style

2nd:　expand the possibilities for growth through skills and talents; teach about self-worth; express philosophy through individual values; foster hope and optimism through activities in the material world; seek *the* truth through actions involving money; over-indulge regarding possessions

3rd:　expand the possibilities for growth through communication; teach in or about community; express philosophy through dialogue; foster hope and optimism with siblings; seek *the* truth through finding facts; over-indulge through short trips and vacations

4th:　expand the possibilities for growth through home and family; teach about ethnic or racial origins; express philosophy to mother; foster hope and optimism regarding family and cultural roots; seek *the* truth through creating belongingness; over-indulge through position in home or family

5th: expand the possibilities for growth through art and creativity; teach about or through play; express philosophy through recreation; foster hope and optimism through romance; seek *the* truth through children; over-indulge through hobbies and leisure activities

6th: expand the possibilities for growth through daily work and routine; teach about or through everyday tasks; express philosophy through maintenance activities; foster hope and optimism with co- workers; seek *the* truth through service to others; over-indulge through health concerns; deal with health issues involving thighs, hips, weight

7th: expand the possibilities for growth through relating; teach about or through cooperation; express philosophy through arbitration; foster hope and optimism with partner; seek *the* truth through relationships; over-indulge regarding "significant others"

8th: expand the possibilities for growth through deep emotional interactions; teach about or through intimacy; express philosophy through utilization of collective money, talents, and resources; foster hope and optimism through sexuality; seek *the* truth through transformation; over-indulge through sex

9th: expand the possibilities for growth through teaching or preaching; teach about or through philosophy; express philosophy through knowledge; foster hope and optimism with travel or learning; seek *the* truth through ethics; over-indulge through selling or advertising

10th: expand the possibilities for growth through career; teach about or through profession; express philosophy to father; foster hope and optimism with vocation; seek *the* truth through position in societal structure; over-indulge as a result of reputation

11th: expand the possibilities for growth through future visions; teach about the "cause"; express philosophy through goals and plans; foster hope and optimism with friends; seek *the* truth through theoretical systems; over-indulge when setting goals

12th: expand the possibilities for growth through intuition; teach about or through spirituality; express philosophy through psychic ability; foster hope and optimism with addictions or meditation; seek *the* truth through altered states; over-indulge through position in institution

SAMPLE INTERPRETATIONS FOR JUPITER IN THE SIGNS

ARIES: expand the possibilities assertively; teach in a spontaneous, child-like way; express philosophy by taking risks; foster hope and optimism in a stimulated and energized manner; seek *the* truth by being freedom-loving; over-indulge in aggressive or inconsiderate behavior

TAURUS: expand the possibilities reliably; teach in a loyal way; express philosophy through getting results; foster hope and optimism in a sensual, physical manner; seek *the* truth by being persistent; over-indulge in stubborn or stingy behavior

GEMINI: expand the possibilities versatilely; teach in a humorous way; express philosophy through dialogue; foster hope and optimism in a curious, amusing manner; seek *the* truth by being communicative and investigative; over-indulge in gossipy or unreliable behavior

CANCER: expand the possibilities nurturingly; teach in a comforting, caring way; express philosophy by "mothering"; foster hope and optimism in a sentimental way; seek *the* truth by being protective of past patterns; over-indulge in fearful or clingy behavior

LEO: expand the possibilities dramatically; teach in a magnanimous, confident way; express philosophy by storytelling; foster hope and optimism in a flamboyant, flashy manner; seek *the* truth by being good-hearted; over-indulge in egotistical or arrogant behavior

VIRGO: expand the possibilities analytically; teach in a practical, problem-solving way; express philosophy by figuring out the solution; foster hope and optimism in a discriminating, idealized manner; seek *the* truth by being detail-oriented; over-indulge in critical or fussy behavior

LIBRA: expand the possibilities diplomatically; teach in a graceful, charming way; express philosophy by creating beauty; foster hope and optimism in a cooperative, interactive manner; seek *the* truth by compromising; over-indulge in indecisive or vain behavior

SCORPIO: expand the possibilities passionately; teach in a penetrating, transforming way; express philosophy when protecting self or others; foster hope and optimism in a powerful, seductive manner; seek *the* truth through intensity; over-indulge in defensive or vengeful behavior

SAGITTARIUS: expand the possibilities open-endedly; teach in a philosophical, ethical way; express philosophy by presenting wisdom; foster hope and optimism in an easygoing manner; seek *the* truth by reaching for "more"; over-indulge in preachy or self-indulgent behavior

CAPRICORN: expand the possibilities responsibly; teach in a pragmatic, organized way; express philosophy by "fathering"; foster hope and optimism in a prestige-seeking, ambitious manner; seek *the* truth through professionalism; over-indulge in domineering or depressed behavior

AQUARIUS: expand the possibilities innovatively; teach in an eccentric, visionary way; express philosophy by having visions for the future; foster hope and optimism in a nonconforming and inventive manner; seek *the* truth through unpredictability; over-indulge in rebellious or disruptive behavior

PISCES: expand the possibilities intuitively; teach in a spiritual, psychic way; express philosophy by creating fantasies and dreams; foster hope and optimism in an imaginative, serene manner; seek *the* truth through compassion; over-indulge in paranoid or victim-oriented behavior

SATURN:
The Organizer

ITS ORBIT: SOCIAL: actively characterize and encourage participation in the World

ITS TASK: to build structure; to limit

ITS VOICE: "I conserve. I represent authority."

SATURN, the Planet that was the outer boundary of the ancient solar system, symbolizes boundaries, limits, and containment.

SATURN'S FUNCTION is to build structures and organize systems. It establishes basic foundations and outlines for development. Its solid plans can be used to construct theories, buildings, and businesses. Saturn always looks to the consequences of its action, takes calculated risks, and makes decisions based on the long-term outcome. It values anything that has lasted or will last for a long time. It reduces things to their fundamentals, wanting to accomplish a lot with a little, conserve resources, and operate with a narrow margin for error. Saturn sets limits and boundaries thinking that it's more important to have a true, reliable security than grandiose, unrealistic schemes. It earns and demands respect for its abilities, often presenting itself as the law enforcer or authority. In fact, Saturn symbolizes childhood authority figures and the "fathering" force of rule-setting. Saturn is the executive, earning its position of prestige through hard work and commitment to the continuance of the system.

When you're fully OWNING your Saturn, you are your own authority figure. Initially, you may have learned how to be "grown up" from others, but now you can claim your own maturity. You can set limits and boundaries with yourself and with others in ways that are appropriate for you. Although you may sometimes act irresponsibly, you know how to get back on track and take responsibility for yourself.

When SATURN OPERATES DYSFUNCTIONALLY, it becomes rigid, brittle, and unbending. It sets so many limits that it's literally entrapping. Instead of foundations for future growth and security, it creates cocoons that later become cages. Dysfunctional Saturn becomes so enamored of its own authority and position that it cannot allow others to make decisions for themselves. It becomes a control freak, bossy and domineering. In its need to conserve resources, it can become stingy and limited in its ability to grow. In its desire to continue the system, Saturn can become hidebound and stuck in traditions.

If you're DENOUNCING your Saturn, you probably think it's stuffy and boring to be responsible and mature. You may even think that all forms of authority are bad or irrelevant. On the other hand, if you're GLORIFYING your Saturn, you may think that your ability to be responsible is your claim to fame. You might demand such a high level of maturity from yourself that it's stressful to try to reach it. If you're BLAMING your Saturnian behavior on other people or circumstances, you'll claim that your drive to set limits and create structure is not your fault. You'll believe that, through their behavior, they're actually "making" you control yourself or the situation. If you're PROJECTING your Saturn, you'll unconsciously get someone to act as your authority figure. You'll let the other person set all the limits in your life so that you don't have to be bothered with those responsibilities. (Incidentally, Saturn is a force that is commonly Projected!) If you're DENYING your Saturn, you'll believe that you're not capable of being mature, responsible, or limit-setting. You'll think that it's just not in your nature to be grown-up. You might also be ignoring the fact that you are adult and organized in your own way already. If you're using your Saturn in one or more of these dysfunctional ways, remember that there is a part of you that wants to manage your life in a mature and reasonable manner. The challenge is to do it appropriately so that you avoid being overly rigid or irresponsible.

When SATURN IS RETROGRADE, it needs to develop internal structures before it can organize the world. It feels compelled to become its own boss before responding to external authorities. It also needs to learn to respect itself before it demands respect from others. Self-control and personal discipline are important to Retrograde Saturn; it will tend to set boundaries for itself before it limits others. It values structures that last through time but tests their validity on its own, not trusting others' discoveries. Retrograde Saturn is often an indicator of emotional or physical distance from the father. It also represents the drive to independently seek out personally satisfying authority figures and role models.

In SATURN'S HOUSE, you'll utilize your resources to create solid organizational structures. The forms may be physical, financial, political, or psychological, but the orderliness is always apparent. In this area of life, you can function as an executive or authority figure, exuding a sense of control and respectability that others find impressive. This is the area where a little goes a long way, where "less than" is the key phrase. You may even be proud of your ability to make do with what you have here. Saturn's House is the place in which you deal with your father's influence in your life by copying or rejecting his rules and behavior.

SATURN'S SIGN symbolizes the style in which you organize your life. Whether you create order around ethical, financial, or physical principles, the Sign will indicate its nature. It also shows how you define your territory and set limits and boundaries for others. Saturn's Sign determines your executive style, and it specifies the approach you'll take in giving and gaining respect. It also signifies the way in which you experienced your father, whether or not his Chart contains Planets in this Sign and whether or not your siblings experienced him in the same way. If Saturn is acting in a dysfunctional manner in your life, you can probably improve its manner of being structured and authoritative by using the positive traits of its Sign.

As CAPRICORN'S NATURAL RULING PLANET, Saturn's behavior triggers responses in any House with Capricorn on the Cusp. As you create structures, gain respect, and establish yourself as an authority through Saturn, you'll satisfy Capricorn's need for a secure position in society. If your Capricorn is intercepted, your Saturn behavior will help it to emerge.

APPLICATIONS FOR SATURN

PSYCHOLOGICAL: the urge to construct, build, organize, solidify, conserve; the urge to set boundaries and establish authority; actions designed to secure a position in society and gain respect; actions that support the self and others in creating solid security and reliable organization

PRACTICAL: the actual form or structure of things; the physical foundations; activities related to stone, earth, minerals, cold, bones, joints, skin, teeth, weight loss, thinness, boniness, depression, chronic conditions, old age, old things, decay, time and time measurement, boundaries, limits, definitions, compactness, less-ness, the boss, organization, executive-ness, authority, control, law-enforcement, ambition, professionalism, construction, architecture, engineering, woodworking, carpentry, sculpture, antiques, posterity, poverty, oppression, status quo

SAMPLE INTERPRETATIONS FOR SATURN IN THE HOUSES

1st: build structures through title or role; set limits through identity; conserve resources and energy through personality; define boundaries through physical appearance; act as an authority through persona; take control through personal style

2nd: build structures through skills and talents; set limits regarding self-worth; conserve resources and energy through individual values; define boundaries in material world; act as an authority about money; take control through possessions

3rd: build structures through communication; set limits in the community; conserve resources and energy in dialogue; define boundaries with siblings; act as an authority about finding facts; take control on short trips and vacations

4th: build structures through home and family; set limits regarding ethnic or racial origins; conserve resources and energy regarding mother; define boundaries through family and cultural roots; act as an authority about creating belongingness; take control through position in home or family

5th: build structures through art and creativity; set limits regarding play; conserve resources and energy through recreation; define boundaries through romance; act as an authority regarding children; take control through hobbies and leisure activities

6th: build structures through daily work and routine; set limits regarding everyday tasks; conserve resources and energy through maintenance activities; define boundaries with co-workers; act as an authority about service to others; take control through health concerns; deal with health issues involving bones, joints, skin, chronic diseases

7th: build structures through relating; set limits through cooperation; conserve resources and energy through arbitration; define boundaries with partner; act as an authority about relationships; take control through "significant others"

8th: build structures through deep emotional interactions; set limits regarding intimacy; conserve resources and energy through utilization of collective money, talents, and resources; define boundaries through sexuality; act as an authority about transformation; take control through sex

9th: build structures through teaching or preaching; set limits through philosophy; conserve resources and energy through knowledge; define boundaries with travel or learning; act as an authority about ethics; take control through selling or advertising

10th: build structures through career; set limits through profession; conserve resources and energy in interactions with father; define boundaries with vocation; act as an authority about societal structure; take control through reputation

11th: build structures through future visions; set limits regarding the "cause"; conserve resources and energy through goals and plans; define boundaries with friends; act as an authority about theoretical systems; take control through schemes

12th: build structures through intuition; set limits through spirituality; conserve resources and energy through psychic ability; define boundaries with addictions or meditation; act as an authority about altered states; take control through position in institution

SAMPLE INTERPRETATIONS FOR SATURN IN THE SIGNS

ARIES: build structures assertively; set limits in a spontaneous, childlike way; conserve resources and energy by taking risks; define boundaries in a stimulated and energized manner; act as an authority by being freedom-loving; take control through aggressive or inconsiderate behavior

TAURUS: build structures reliably; set limits in a loyal way; conserve resources and energy by getting results; define boundaries in a sensual, physical manner; act as an authority by being persistent; take control through stubborn or stingy behavior

GEMINI: build structures versatilely; set limits in a humorous way; conserve resources and energy through dialogue; define boundaries in a curious, amusing manner; act as an authority by being communicative and investigative; take control through gossipy or unreliable behavior

CANCER: build structures nurturingly; set limits in a comforting, caring way; conserve resources and energy by "mothering"; define boundaries in a sentimental way; act as an authority by being protective of past patterns; take control through fearful or clingy behavior

LEO: build structures dramatically; set limits in a magnanimous, confident way; conserve resources and energy by storytelling; define boundaries in a flamboyant, flashy manner; act as an authority by being good-hearted; take control through egotistical or arrogant behavior

VIRGO: build structures analytically; set limits in a practical, problem-solving way; conserve resources and energy by figuring out the solution; define boundaries in a discriminating, idealized manner; act as an authority by being detail-oriented; take control through critical or fussy behavior

LIBRA: build structures diplomatically; set limits in a graceful, charming way; conserve resources and energy by creating beauty; define boundaries in a cooperative, interactive manner; act as an authority by compromising; take control through indecisive or vain behavior

SCORPIO: build structures passionately; set limits in a penetrating, transforming way; conserve resources and energy when protecting self or others; define boundaries in a powerful, seductive manner; act as an authority through intensity; take control through defensive or vengeful behavior

SAGITTARIUS: build structures expansively; set limits in a philosophical, ethical way; conserve resources and energy by presenting wisdom; define boundaries in an optimistic and easygoing manner; act as an authority by reaching for "more"; take control through preachy or self-indulgent behavior

CAPRICORN: build structures responsibly; set limits in a pragmatic, organized way; conserve resources and energy by "fathering"; define boundaries in a prestige-seeking, ambitious manner; act as an authority through professionalism; take control through domineering or depressed behavior

AQUARIUS: build structures innovatively; set limits in an eccentric, visionary way; conserve resources and energy by having visions for the future; define boundaries in a nonconforming and inventive manner; act as an authority about unpredictability; take control through rebellious or disruptive behavior

PISCES: build structures intuitively; set limits in a spiritual, psychic way; conserve resources and energy by creating fantasies and dreams; define boundaries in an imaginative, serene manner; act as an authority about compassion; take control through paranoid or victim-oriented behavior

CHIRON:
The Problem-Solver

ITS ORBIT: BRIDGE: actively weave Universal ideals into personal and social life

ITS TASK: to manifest ideals within reality; to mend

ITS VOICE: "I analyze. I fix whatever's wrong."

CHIRON, the bridge to the Universal Planets, symbolizes the key to integration, both in its orbit and its glyph.

CHIRON'S FUNCTION is to define the highest of ideals and to manifest them in reality. It is able to imagine perfection and to envision the practical applications of its imaginings. Chiron tries to adapt, adjust, restructure, and redefine the existing forms so that they will more closely approximate what's ideally possible. It focuses on the details, believing that if each part is utilizing its potential, the whole will be enhanced. It enjoys problem-solving, working with the pieces until they fall into alignment within the whole puzzle. Since Chiron is constantly searching for ways to improve the system, it tends to notice what's wrong and what's missing. As a result, it's a terrific editor and repair technician. It's unequaled in its ability to compare options and contrast solutions. Oftentimes, Chiron will be concerned with achieving optimum "health" within a physical organism, emotional system, or organization. In fact, Chiron grounds mental, physical, and spiritual absolutes, working to integrate them into daily reality.

When you're fully OWNING your Chiron, you'll appropriately utilize the part of you that solves problems. You'll be aware of imperfections and able to use your own special talents to improve the situation. Although you may sometimes feel critical and annoyed with yourself or others, you'll know how to present your feedback in a constructive manner.

When CHIRON OPERATES DYSFUNCTIONALLY, it becomes nitpicky and critical, finding problems where none exist. It can even be hypochondriacal. It forgets to praise and value the strengths of a situation in its eagerness to announce what's wrong. Dysfunctional Chiron can get bored when things are operating smoothly, sometimes unconsciously stirring up trouble in order to have problems to solve. It tries to "fix" things that are already fine or are better left broken or destroyed. Chiron's most difficult manifestation is its self-criticism. It can produce self-destructive inner dialogues that emphasize regrets and failures; Chiron is its own worst critic and barrier to success.

If you're DENOUNCING your Chiron, you'll tend to think that your ability to analyze and focus on correcting the details is bad. You'll wish to always be accepting of everything, without ever being discriminating. On the other hand, if you're GLORIFYING your Chiron, you could be valuing your discriminatory talents so much that you expect perfection from yourself (and others) all the time. If you're BLAMING your Chiron-related behavior on other people or circumstances, you think that your way of fixing things and finding solutions is not your fault. You'll think that if only "they" had taught you differently, or if only the setup were different, you'd now be able to figure things out more effectively. If you're PROJECTING your Chiron, you'll find others to act out the problem-solving, analytical drives for you. Instead of taking responsibility for being discriminating and solution-oriented in your own way, you'll simply let others find all the answers for you. And, if you're DENYING your Chiron, you'll believe that you don't have any analytical abilities, anyway. You'll think that when critiquing talents were passed out, you were overlooked. You might also be ignoring the fact that you have a personally developed style of problem-solving already. If you're using your Chiron in one or more of these dysfunctional ways, remember that you, too, can be effectively analytical in a way that's appropriate for you. Whether you use your mind, hands, or intuition to solve problems, you have within you a way to effectively and gracefully fix whatever's wrong without obsessing on it.

When CHIRON IS RETROGRADE, it is especially focused on fixing itself before it fixes others. With its high personal ideals and expectations, it is constantly seeking to improve itself and move toward perfection. When in doubt, it tends to reevaluate itself and find ways to adapt rather than trying to change the external situation. Self-healing becomes a focus. Retrograde Chiron believes that, after it has perfected itself, it can move on to improving the world.

In CHIRON'S HOUSE, you have an instinct for ferreting out the missing pieces and putting them back together. If problems arise, this is the area in which you excel at finding solutions. Whether the dilemmas are technical or emotional in nature, you can unravel them here. In this department of life, you might be comparing your real situation to the ideal that you would prefer. Because you are always aware of this desire for perfection, you work especially hard at improving conditions. This is also the area of the Chart in which you may be righting a wrong that was done to you in childhood. You may feel compelled to fix things for others in Chiron's House, because they never worked for you.

CHIRON'S SIGN describes the manner in which you fix or mend people and things in your environment. Whether you operate at a physical, psychological, or psychic level, this Sign will be an indicator of Chiron's style of making things whole. It also delineates the way in which you act on your ideals within your daily reality. And, this Sign's negative traits show the nature of the difficulties that you might have experienced as a child, the kind of pain you're trying now to heal. If you're using Chiron dysfunctionally, you can probably change your patterns and begin to fix things more satisfactorily if you emphasize the positive characteristics of its Sign.

As VIRGO'S NATURAL RULING PLANET, Chiron's ability to find solutions and move toward the ideal satisfies the needs of any House with Virgo on the Cusp. The more you heal the psychological or physical system in Chiron's natal House, the closer Virgo comes to its ideals. If Virgo is intercepted, you can use Chiron to unlock it.

APPLICATIONS FOR CHIRON

PSYCHOLOGICAL: the urge to solve problems, fix things, attend to details; the urge to integrate, heal, mend, and figure it out; actions designed to find what's wrong and repair it; actions that encourage the self and others to manifest the ideal within the real

PRACTICAL: integration, perfection, idealism, functionality, manifestation; activities related to earth, intestines, elimination, removal of toxins, all health professions, symptoms and cures, sanitation, hygiene, productivity, agriculture, farming, repair, maintenance, protection, prevention, security systems, paperwork, filing systems, office management, technical skills, workers, service personnel, details, editing, critiquing, military, mechanical toys, appliances, equipment

SAMPLE INTERPRETATIONS FOR CHIRON IN THE HOUSES

1st: manifest ideals through establishing title or role; heal through identity; repair and mend the personality; solve problems regarding physical appearance; find realistic solutions through persona; criticize through personal style

2nd: manifest ideals through skills and talents; heal regarding self-worth; repair and mend through individual values; solve problems through material world; find realistic solutions through actions involving money; criticize through possessions

3rd: manifest ideals through communication; heal in community; repair and mend through dialogue; solve problems with siblings; find realistic solutions through finding facts; criticize on short trips and vacations

4th: manifest ideals through home and family; heal within ethnic or racial origins; repair and mend regarding mother; solve problems through family and cultural roots; find realistic solutions through creating belongingness; criticize through position in home or family

5th: manifest ideals through art and creativity; heal through play; repair and mend through recreation; solve problems through romance; find realistic solutions through children; criticize through hobbies and leisure activities

6th: manifest ideals through daily work and routine; heal through everyday tasks; repair and mend through maintenance activities; solve problems with co-workers; find realistic solutions through service to others; criticize through health concerns; deal with health issues involving digestion and nutrition

7th: manifest ideals through relating; heal through cooperation; repair and mend through arbitration; solve problems with partner; find realistic solutions through relationships; criticize through "significant others"

8th: manifest ideals through deep emotional interactions; heal through intimacy; repair and mend through utilization of collective money, talents, and resources; solve problems through sexuality; find realistic solutions through transformation; criticize through sex

9th: manifest ideals through teaching or preaching; heal through philosophy; repair and mend through knowledge; solve problems with travel or learning; find realistic solutions through ethics; criticize through selling or advertising

10th: manifest ideals through career; heal through profession; repair and mend regarding father; solve problems with vocation; find realistic solutions through position in societal structure; criticize through reputation

11th: manifest ideals through future visions; heal through the "cause"; repair and mend through goals and plans; solve problems with friends; find realistic solutions through theoretical systems; criticize through schemes

12th: manifest ideals through intuition; heal through spirituality; repair and mend through psychic ability; solve problems with addictions or meditation; find realistic solutions through altered states; criticize through position in institution

SAMPLE INTERPRETATIONS FOR CHIRON IN THE SIGNS

ARIES: manifest ideals assertively; heal in a spontaneous, childlike way; repair and mend by taking risks; solve problems in a stimulated and energized manner; find realistic solutions by being freedom- loving; criticize through aggressive or inconsiderate behavior

TAURUS: manifest ideals reliably; heal in a loyal way; repair and mend through getting results; solve problems in a sensual, physical manner; find realistic solutions by being persistent; criticize through stubborn or stingy behavior

GEMINI: manifest ideals versatilely; heal in a humorous way; repair and mend through dialogue; solve problems in a curious, amusing manner; find realistic solutions by being communicative and investigative; criticize through gossipy or unreliable behavior

CANCER: manifest ideals nurturingly; heal in a comforting, caring way; repair and mend by "mothering"; solve problems in a sentimental way; find realistic solutions by being protective of past patterns; criticize through fearful or clingy behavior

LEO: manifest ideals dramatically; heal in a magnanimous, confident way; repair and mend by storytelling; solve problems in a flamboyant, flashy manner; find realistic solutions by being good-hearted; criticize through egotistical or arrogant behavior

VIRGO: manifest ideals analytically; heal in a practical, problem-solving way; repair and mend by figuring out the solution; solve problems in a discriminating, idealized manner; find realistic solutions by being detail-oriented; criticize through critical or fussy behavior

LIBRA: manifest ideals diplomatically; heal in a graceful, charming way; repair and mend by creating beauty; solve problems in a cooperative, interactive manner; find realistic solutions by compromising; criticize through indecisive or vain behavior

SCORPIO: manifest ideals passionately; heal in a penetrating, transforming way; repair and mend when protecting self or others; solve problems in a powerful, seductive manner; find realistic solutions through intensity; criticize through defensive or vengeful behavior

SAGITTARIUS: manifest ideals expansively; heal in a philosophical, ethical way; repair and mend by presenting wisdom; solve problems in an optimistic and easygoing manner; find realistic solutions by reaching for "more"; criticize through preachy or self-indulgent behavior

CAPRICORN: manifest ideals responsibly; heal in a pragmatic, organized way; repair and mend by "fathering"; solve problems in a prestige-seeking, ambitious manner; find realistic solutions through professionalism; criticize through domineering or depressed behavior

AQUARIUS: manifest ideals innovatively; heal in an eccentric, visionary way; repair and mend by having visions for the future; solve problems in a nonconforming and inventive manner; find realistic solutions through un-predictability; criticize through rebellious or disruptive behavior

PISCES: manifest ideals intuitively; heal in a spiritual, psychic way; repair and mend by creating fantasies and dreams; solve problems in an im-aginative, serene manner; find realistic solutions through compassion; criticize through paranoid or victim-oriented behavior

URANUS:
The Innovator

ITS ORBIT: UNIVERSAL: actively inspire movement into Universal awareness

ITS TASK: to break out of old patterns; to in-novate

ITS VOICE: "I shatter the limits. I move be-yond the status quo."

URANUS, the first Planet beyond the ancient solar system, was discov-ered in 1781 during an era of revolutionary activity. It symbolizes up-heaval and demonstrates its eccentric nature by being the only Planet that lies on its side in its orbit around the Sun.

URANUS'S FUNCTION is to burst past old limitations and obsolete structures and to create alternatives. It is well aware of accepted social or scientific conventions and chooses to ignore them or move past them. As a result, it's the most inventive and innovative of the Planets, using its own behavior as a catalyst for societal change. In going beyond what is known, Uranus can shatter the existing system – for the sake of improving it. It dares to experiment with unusual thoughts and behavior, finding that the unconventional often leads to a creative and stimulating option. Uranus ventures into "foreign" territory through ideas or travel, fascinated by how others think and operate. Once it has a novel idea, Uranus is will-ing to hold onto its unique perspective long enough to discover whether it is a Universal principle or an eccentric whim. Of course, even if it's a whim, Uranus may still decide to stick with it. It enjoys discovering vi-sionary theoretical systems that could improve and enhance life on Earth – for everyone. Usually, Uranus's vision is oriented toward the future; it's not as concerned with present experience as with future possibilities. Because of that perspective, Uranus has a special ability to be detached and observant.

If you're fully OWNING your Uranus, you know that there is a part of you that wants to change things. You trust that the ways in which you challenge the existing system are truly visionary. You feel that you consider the highest good when making innovative suggestions. Although you know that sometimes you can be rebellious, uncooperative, or erratic, you have ways of evaluating whether your actions are appropriate in a given situation.

When URANUS OPERATES DYSFUNCTIONALLY, it is rebellious and disruptive without consciousness. It tears down the system without regard to its functional attributes. It uses weird or bizarre behavior to shock or hurt others, not to enlighten them. Dysfunctional Uranus can explode secure structures, leaving itself or others shattered. In its insistence on the unconventional, it can stubbornly refuse to find a common meeting ground, preferring its own radical position. With its fixation on the future, it can ignore the very real needs of the present, waving them aside with a grand gesture. In fact, Uranus can be so detached that it becomes uncaring and unsympathetic to individual human needs. It can become so obsessed with where it's going that it forgets who and what it needs in order to get there. In its worst expression, Uranus can be truly deviant and sociopathic.

If you're DENOUNCING your Uranus, you probably think that your nonconforming nature is bad. You might feel that the part of you that wants to break free of old restrictions is naughty and deserves to be squashed. On the other hand, if you're GLORIFYING your Uranus, you could be so enamored of your own eccentricity and radicalism that you force yourself to act erratically or rebelliously even when you don't want or need to do so. If you're BLAMING your Uranian behavior on other people or circumstances, you'll imagine that your unique, unpredictable, or unusual characteristics are not your fault. You'll believe that you were "taught" or forced to be a rebel and that you have no choice. If you're PROJECTING your Uranus, you'll unconsciously allow others to act out your own nonconformity or instability. That way, you can be the stable, responsible one, while someone else brings the quality of rebellion and innovation into your life. And, if you're DENYING your Uranus, you'll be convinced that you have no rebellion in you. You'll feel that you are not a reformer, a visionary, or a challenger of the status quo in any way. You might also be ignoring the fact that you have your own unique sense of the future and your own way of changing the system already. If you're using your Uranus in one or more of these dysfunctional ways, remember that you, too, have an innovative contribution to make. Whether it's small or large, it uniquely represents your vision of a better future. Also remember that you will sometimes want to shatter the existing structures. As long as you do it in ways that are appropriate for you, you'll be moving toward improving your circumstances without becoming a total misfit.

When URANUS IS RETROGRADE, it must break out of its own patterns before it can change the world. It turns inside, to the rules and systems that it already uses, and rebels against its own strictures. It's innovative with itself, within its own life, pursuing personal eccentricity and uniqueness without concern for anything outside itself. Retrograde Uranus is also more interested in its personal future, or in how it personally fits into the global future, than it is concerned with creating new Earth-wide trends.

In URANUS'S HOUSE, you burst free of the limitations of your family system and your culture. You might even experiment with unusual, foreign, or nontraditional experiences. You're willing to break or bend the rules because you're being true to your own loftier principles. But, even after you've established your own system here, you'll eventually move beyond it. This makes Uranus's House the most volatile location in your Chart. Changes happen, sometimes at a dizzying speed, in this area of life. Unpredictability is the norm. You actually come to seek and expect the unexpected with Uranus.

URANUS'S SIGN describes the approach you'll take with regard to your eccentricity. It also describes how all people born within seven years of you act out their rebellion. It specifies how you, individually and as a group, contradict the social system by thought or deed. This Sign symbolizes the way in which you approach your visions of the future. It indicates whether they are realistic plans or imaginative fantasies. If you're using Uranus in a dysfunctional manner, you'll be more likely to act out the negative traits of this Sign. In that case, by shifting gears into the more positive characteristics of Uranus's Sign, you might actually effect the changes that you want.

Since Uranus is AQUARIUS'S NATURAL RULING PLANET, its eccentric behavior stimulates any House with Aquarius on the Cusp. The more you experiment with alternatives and move toward nontraditional visions, the more Aquarius's desire for a strong future is realized. And, if Aquarius is intercepted, your Uranian actions will help it to explode out of confinement.

APPLICATIONS FOR URANUS

PSYCHOLOGICAL: the urge to be detached, observant, nonconforming; the urge to rebel, change, break free, break through, burst out; actions designed to explore alternatives and move past limitations; actions that stimulate the self and others to move toward a more utopian future

PRACTICAL: uniqueness, nonconformity, aberrations, abnormalities; activities related to air, lightning, electricity, shins, ankles, sudden or unexpected health conditions, accidents, bone fractures, disruptions, illegalities, computers, space exploration, genius, high- tech equipment and professions, cutting-edge technology, futurism, utopia, collective action, rebellion, revolutions, explosions, blow-ups, desertion, foreigners, nontraditional alliances and relationships, divorce, break-ups, break-ins, breakthroughs, Astrology

SAMPLE INTERPRETATIONS FOR URANUS IN THE HOUSES

1st: shatter existing structures through title or role; break patterns regarding identity; innovate through personality; express nonconformity through physical appearance; create a vision for the future through persona; demonstrate erratic tendencies through personal style

2nd: shatter existing structures through skills and talents; break patterns regarding self-worth; innovate through individual values; express nonconformity through material world; create a vision for the future through actions involving money; demonstrate erratic tendencies through use of possessions

3rd: shatter existing structures through communication; break patterns within the community; innovate through dialogue; express nonconformity with siblings; create a vision for the future through finding facts; demonstrate erratic tendencies through short trips and vacations

4th: shatter existing structures in home and family; break patterns related to ethnic or racial origins; innovate regarding mother; express nonconformity in family and cultural roots; create a vision for the future through creating belongingness; demonstrate erratic tendencies through utilizing position in home or family

5th: shatter existing structures through art and creativity; break patterns regarding play; innovate through recreation; express nonconformity through romance; create a vision for the future through children; demonstrate erratic tendencies in approach to hobbies and leisure activities

6th: shatter existing structures through daily work and routine; break patterns regarding everyday tasks; innovate through maintenance activities; express nonconformity with co-workers; create a vision for the future through service to others; demonstrate erratic tendencies through health concerns; deal with health issues involving ankles, calves, shins, accidents, unexpected illnesses

7th: shatter existing structures through relating; break patterns in co-operation; innovate through arbitration; express nonconformity with partner; create a vision for the future through relationships; demonstrate erratic tendencies regarding "significant others"

8th: shatter existing structures through deep emotional interactions; break patterns regarding intimacy; innovate through utilization of collective money, talents, and resources; express nonconformity through sexuality; create a vision for the future through transformation; demonstrate erratic tendencies in sex

9th: shatter existing structures through teaching or preaching; break patterns through philosophy; innovate through pursuing knowledge; express nonconformity with travel or learning; create a vision for the future through ethics; demonstrate erratic tendencies in selling or advertising

10th: shatter existing structures through career; break patterns in profession; innovate regarding father; express nonconformity with vocation; create a vision for the future through position in societal structure; demonstrate erratic tendencies through reputation

11th: shatter existing structures through future visions; break patterns regarding the "cause"; innovate through goals and plans; express nonconformity with friends; create a vision for the future through theoretical systems; demonstrate erratic tendencies through schemes

12th: shatter existing structures through intuition; break patterns through spirituality; innovate through psychic ability; express nonconformity with addictions or meditation; create a vision for the future through altered states; demonstrate erratic tendencies in institutions

SAMPLE INTERPRETATIONS FOR URANUS IN THE SIGNS

ARIES: shatter existing structures assertively; break patterns in a spontaneous, childlike way; innovate by taking risks; express nonconformity in a stimulated and energized manner; create a vision for the future by being freedom-loving; demonstrate erratic tendencies through aggressive or inconsiderate behavior

TAURUS: shatter existing structures reliably; break patterns in a loyal way; innovate through getting results; express nonconformity in a sensual, physical manner; create a vision for the future by being persistent; demonstrate erratic tendencies through stubborn or stingy behavior

GEMINI: shatter existing structures versatilely; break patterns in a humorous way; innovate through dialogue; express nonconformity in a curious, amusing manner; create a vision for the future by being communicative and investigative; demonstrate erratic tendencies through gossipy or unreliable behavior

CANCER: shatter existing structures nurturingly; break patterns in a comforting, caring way; innovate by "mothering"; express nonconformity in a sentimental way; create a vision for the future by being protective of past patterns; demonstrate erratic tendencies through fearful or clingy behavior

LEO: shatter existing structures dramatically; break patterns in a magnanimous, confident way; innovate by storytelling; express nonconformity in a flamboyant, flashy manner; create a vision for the future by being good-hearted; demonstrate erratic tendencies through egotistical or arrogant behavior

VIRGO: shatter existing structures analytically; break patterns in a practical, problem-solving way; innovate by figuring out the solution; express nonconformity in a discriminating, idealized manner; create a vision for the future by being detail-oriented; demonstrate erratic tendencies through critical or fussy behavior

LIBRA: shatter existing structures diplomatically; break patterns in a graceful, charming way; innovate by creating beauty; express nonconformity in a cooperative, interactive manner; create a vision for the future by compromising; demonstrate erratic tendencies through indecisive or vain behavior

SCORPIO: shatter existing structures passionately; break patterns in a penetrating, transforming way; innovate when protecting self or others; express nonconformity in a powerful, seductive manner; create a vision for the future through intensity; demonstrate erratic tendencies through defensive or vengeful behavior

SAGITTARIUS: shatter existing structures expansively; break patterns in a philosophical, ethical way; innovate by presenting wisdom; express nonconformity in an optimistic and easygoing manner; create a vision for the future by reaching for "more"; demonstrate erratic tendencies through preachy or self-indulgent behavior

CAPRICORN: shatter existing structures responsibly; break patterns in a pragmatic, organized way; innovate by "fathering"; express nonconformity in a prestige-seeking, ambitious manner; create a vision for the future through professionalism; demonstrate erratic tendencies through domineering or depressed behavior

AQUARIUS: shatter existing structures innovatively; break patterns in an eccentric, visionary way; innovate by having visions for the future; express nonconformity in an inventive manner; create a vision for the future through unpredictability; demonstrate erratic tendencies through rebellious or disruptive behavior

PISCES: shatter existing structures intuitively; break patterns in a spiritual, psychic way; innovate by creating fantasies and dreams; express nonconformity in an imaginative, serene manner; create a vision for the future through compassion; demonstrate erratic tendencies through paranoid or victim-oriented behavior

NEPTUNE:
The Transcender

ITS ORBIT: UNIVERSAL: actively inspire movement into Universal awareness

ITS TASK: to dissolve all barriers; to empathize

ITS VOICE: "I heal. I exhibit faith."

NEPTUNE and its glyph, the trident, symbolize fishing in the vast unknown for spiritual insights and direction. Its discovery in 1846 coincided with a period of spiritual and religious growth and with experimentation involving hypnosis, psychoanalysis, and drug use.

NEPTUNE'S FUNCTION is to dissolve barriers that get in the way of unity. It gradually erodes anything that is divisive or defining, preferring amorphousness to clear distinctions. Neptune unifies "all that is" in one cosmic whole, creating emotional or psychic merger as a result. It is empathic; it feels everyone's emotion and wants to heal everyone's pain. Neptune is also mystical; it pursues meditative or psychic activities that will allow it to transcend the earthly plane. These might include everything from chanting to prayer to daydreaming. Neptune might even remove itself from the daily world to a more peaceful, serene, and contemplative environment. It is blessed with faith, trusting that someone or something will provide. Neptune makes an effort to bring its divinity down to Earth through its imagination. It has an incredible ability to fantasize, finding lyrical sounds, words, images, movements, and textures that it wants to weave into its life.

If you're fully OWNING your Neptune, you know that part of you is spiritual, imaginative, and intuitive. You feel that you have appropriate ways of expressing your compassion and of merging with others. Although you may sometimes ignore your psychic talents, you have a way to reconnect with them if necessary. And, even though you might sometimes become too entangled with someone else's emotions, you're able to set boundaries and disentangle yourself when you want to do so.

When NEPTUNE OPERATES DYSFUNCTIONALLY, it creates fogginess, confusion, and disorientation. Uncertain of its psychic location, Neptune can leave the Earth behind altogether. In its efforts to empathize with others, it loses its own identity. It can even sacrifice itself to care for others. Dysfunctional Neptune can become so overwhelmed by others' feelings and the general pain of the world that it seeks escape. Disillusioned about its ability to really heal anything, Neptune may employ drugs, alcohol, food, or other substances to keep itself in an altered state. It can also be attracted to addictive relationships, love, or sex to get its highs. Dysfunctional emotional cycles can be triggered by Neptune, including anxiety attacks, fears, paranoias, and phobias. It can run away from all its pain into illegal situations, physical prisons, or mental institutions. And, Neptune can just fade into daydreams and fantasies, drifting on the edge of the world without really entering it. Dysfunctional Neptune can actually become self-destructive in its drive to avoid reality.

If you're DENOUNCING your Neptune, you may feel that your intuition and spirituality are hogwash. Every time you have a illogical sensation, you dismiss it as irrelevant. On the other hand, if you're GLORIFYING your Neptune, you might be honoring your psychic talents or your sensitivity too much. You could be putting pressure on yourself by expecting intuitive perfection. If you're BLAMING your Neptunian behavior on other people or circumstances, you might feel that your confusion or paranoia have been externally "caused." Instead of taking responsibility for your reactions to the situation, you allow yourself to become a victim. If you're PROJECTING your Neptune, you'll find that everyone is intuitive or spiritual except you. You may also think that you are the rational one and that others are the confused and addicted ones. And, if you're DENYING your Neptune, you might think that intuition, compassion, and spirituality don't really exist in the world – at least not in your world. You may be ignoring the fact that you have a special way of integrating your "sixth sense" into your life already. You could also be Denying the presence of an addiction in your life. If you're using your Neptune in one or more of these dysfunctional ways, remember that you, too, have an intuitive, compassionate part. There are ways in which you can appropriately merge with others and the Universe without becoming some kind of junkie.

When NEPTUNE IS RETROGRADE, it finds spiritual integration within before it shares it with others. It feels drawn to discover its own spiritual path, whether or not it reflects the cultural patterns. Psychic and intuitive activities are very personalized for Retrograde Neptune, existing as an integral part of daily life. Eventually, if its faith and its altered states of consciousness become familiar and grounded enough, it can reach out to merge with others and extend healing.

In NEPTUNE'S HOUSE, you create experiences of oneness, unity, and merger. You express compassion and sympathy for others in this area of life, often reaching out to rescue the unfortunate or relieve their suffering. In this House you also want serenity, peacefulness, and opportunities to drift or dream. In this area of life, you face the challenge of choosing fear or faith; you have to decide whether to trust the Universe or revert to panic and paranoia.

NEPTUNE'S SIGN will be shared by most of the others in your generation. So, its nature not only indicates how you transcend earthly reality and move into other dimensions but also shows how your whole generation experiments with altered states of awareness. The Sign could indicate that you use psychic tools, physical experiences, or intellectual curiosity as the triggers for mystical merger. It symbolizes how you act out compassion and concern for others; it describes the nature of your healing talents. And, it describes what's needed in order for you to experience deep faith instead of fear. If you're using Neptune's Sign dysfunctionally, you can heal yourself by picking up some of its more positive characteristics.

As PISCES'S NATURAL RULING PLANET, Neptune's ability to dissolve the structures in its environment has a direct effect on any House with Pisces on the Cusp. When you affirm faith and healing through Neptune, you create a sense of peace and serenity in Pisces's House. And, if Pisces is intercepted, your use of Neptune will allow it to emerge.

APPLICATIONS FOR NEPTUNE

PSYCHOLOGICAL: the urge to dissolve, soften, imagine, fantasize; the urge to merge, integrate, heal, sympathize, empathize; actions designed to create faith, wholeness, unity, oneness; actions that gently influence the self and others to experience spiritual awareness

PRACTICAL: softness, amorphousness, formlessness, disintegration, vagueness; activities related to water, fog, mist, damp, clouds, feet, drugs, toxins, alcohol, anesthetics, intravenous feeding, misdiagnosed illnesses, antibiotics, delusions, allergies, drowning, addiction, fears, phobias, paranoia, faith, trust, dreams, the invisible, meditation, mysticism, trances, psychic or intuitive experiences, blind spots, hallucinations, fish, oceans, beverages, extortion, illegal or behind-the-scenes activities, bribery, sneakiness, secret societies, secrets, disguises, impersonation, pseudonyms, imitations, mysteries, film, dance, music, movies, imagination, fantasy, poetry, healing, compassion, rescue missions, quacks, spiritual healers, con artists, manipulators

SAMPLE INTERPRETATIONS FOR NEPTUNE IN THE HOUSES

1st: express psychic abilities through title or role; act on spiritual values as part of identity; show trust through personality; merge or identify with others through physical appearance; demonstrate imagination through persona; act out victimization in personal style

2nd: express psychic abilities through skills and talents; act on spiritual values regarding self-worth; show trust through individual values; merge or identify with others through participation in the material world; demonstrate imagination through actions involving money; act out victimization through possessions

3rd: express psychic abilities in communication; act on spiritual values in community; show trust through dialogue; merge or identify with siblings; demonstrate imagination in finding facts; act out victimization on short trips and vacations

4th: express psychic abilities regarding home and family; act on spiritual values regarding ethnic or racial origins; show trust regarding mother; merge or identify with others through family and cultural roots; demonstrate imagination through creating belongingness; act out victimization through position in home or family

5th: express psychic abilities through art and creativity; act on spiritual values in play; show trust in the context of recreation; merge or identify with others in romance; demonstrate imagination through children; act out victimization in hobbies and leisure activities

6th: express psychic abilities in daily work and routine; act on spiritual values in everyday tasks; show trust through maintenance activities; merge or identify with others with co-workers; demonstrate imagination through service to others; act out victimization through health concerns; deal with health issues involving addictions, allergies, feet

7th: express psychic abilities while relating; act on spiritual values in cooperation; show trust during arbitration; merge or identify with partner; demonstrate imagination through relationships; act out victimization through "significant others"

8th: express psychic abilities in deep emotional interactions; act on spiritual values through intimacy; show trust through utilization of collective money, talents, and resources; merge or identify with others through sexuality; demonstrate imagination through transformation; act out victimization through sex

9th: express psychic abilities through teaching or preaching; act on spiritual values through philosophy; show trust through knowledge; merge or identify with others in terms of travel or learning; demonstrate imagination in ethics; act out victimization through selling or advertising

10th: express psychic abilities through career; act on spiritual values through profession; show trust regarding father; merge or identify with others in vocation; demonstrate imagination through position in societal structure; act out victimization through reputation

11th: express psychic abilities through future visions; act on spiritual values as a "cause"; show trust through goals and plans; merge or identify with friends; demonstrate imagination in theoretical systems; act out victimization through schemes

12th: express psychic abilities through intuition; act on spiritual values when in isolation; show trust in psychic ability; merge or identify with others regarding addictions or meditation; demonstrate imagination through altered states; act out victimization through position in institution

SAMPLE INTERPRETATIONS FOR NEPTUNE IN THE SIGNS

ARIES: express psychic abilities assertively; act on spiritual values in a spontaneous, childlike way; show trust by taking risks; merge or identify with others in a stimulated and energized manner; demonstrate imagination by being freedom-loving; act out victimization through aggressive or inconsiderate behavior

TAURUS: express psychic abilities reliably; act on spiritual values in a loyal way; show trust through getting results; merge or identify with others in a sensual, physical manner; demonstrate imagination by being persistent; act out victimization through stubborn or stingy behavior

GEMINI: express psychic abilities versatilely; act on spiritual values in a humorous way; show trust through dialogue; merge or identify with others in a curious, amusing manner; demonstrate imagination by being communicative and investigative; act out victimization through gossipy or unreliable behavior

CANCER: express psychic abilities nurturingly; act on spiritual values in a comforting, caring way; show trust by "mothering"; merge or identify with others in a sentimental way; demonstrate imagination by being protective of past patterns; act out victimization through fearful or clingy behavior

LEO: express psychic abilities dramatically; act on spiritual values in a magnanimous, confident way; show trust by storytelling; merge or identify with others in a flamboyant, flashy manner; demonstrate imagination by being good-hearted; act out victimization through egotistical or arrogant behavior

VIRGO: express psychic abilities analytically; act on spiritual values in a practical, problem-solving way; show trust by figuring out the solution; merge or identify with others in a discriminating, idealized manner; demonstrate imagination by being detail-oriented; act out victimization through critical or fussy behavior

LIBRA: express psychic abilities diplomatically; act on spiritual values in a graceful, charming way; show trust by creating beauty; merge or identify with others in a cooperative, interactive manner; demonstrate imagination by compromising; act out victimization through indecisive or vain behavior

SCORPIO: express psychic abilities passionately; act on spiritual values in a penetrating, transforming way; show trust when protecting self or others; merge or identify with others in a powerful, seductive manner; demonstrate imagination through intensity; act out victimization through defensive or vengeful behavior

SAGITTARIUS: express psychic abilities expansively; act on spiritual values in a philosophical, ethical way; show trust by presenting wisdom; merge or identify with others in an optimistic and easygoing manner; demonstrate imagination by reaching for "more"; act out victimization through preachy or self-indulgent behavior

CAPRICORN: express psychic abilities responsibly; act on spiritual values in a pragmatic, organized way; show trust by "fathering"; merge or identify with others in a prestige-seeking, ambitious manner; demonstrate imagination through professionalism; act out victimization through domineering or depressed behavior

AQUARIUS: express psychic abilities innovatively; act on spiritual values in an eccentric, visionary way; show trust by having visions for the future;

merge or identify with others in a nonconforming and inventive manner; demonstrate imagination through unpredictability; act out victimization through rebellious or disruptive behavior

PISCES: express psychic abilities intuitively; act on spiritual values in a spiritual, psychic way; show trust by creating fantasies and dreams; merge or identify with others in an imaginative, serene manner; demonstrate imagination through compassion; act out victimization through paranoid behavior

PLUTO:
The Transformer

ITS ORBIT: UNIVERSAL: actively inspire movement into Universal awareness

ITS TASK: to manifest power; to regenerate

ITS VOICE: "I transform. I cycle through death and rebirth."

PLUTO, in the last planetary orbit of this solar system, symbolizes the point of transformation, the leap into the unknown. This Planet was discovered in 1930 and symbolizes the worldwide patterns of chaos and destruction which ultimately exploded in the discovery and use of nuclear power.

PLUTO'S FUNCTION is to catalyze experiences of total transformation. These include anything involving physical, psychological, or mental death and a subsequent rebirth. Pluto knows that a space must be cleared if anything new is to be born. As a result, it sets up cyclical patterns of purging and regenerating, cleansing and restarting. It's an all-or-nothing force, avoiding half measures in its desire to get to the root of an issue. Pluto digs to the very bottom of its interest or concern with a passion unmatched by any other Planet. The intensity of its drive takes it beyond that which can be known with the conscious mind and into the realm of Universal mysteries. Inner space and outer space are fascinating to Pluto. When Pluto's gaze is directed at the everyday world, it is passionate and powerful, fully committed to its own discoveries. It joins forces with others to increase its power and talent, finding that it can accomplish miraculous transformations through using joint resources. In all situations, Pluto is motivated by its awareness of deeper meanings. In fact, Pluto represents promises that were made before birth about commitments to be fulfilled in a particular lifetime. For this reason, some of

Pluto's actions can seem fated or meant to be. Additionally, Pluto motivates participation in massive planet-wide movements or large transformational events. In becoming "one" with the force of creation, Pluto unconsciously becomes a mini-God on Earth.

If you're fully OWNING your Pluto, you know that you have personal power and that you can use it effectively and wisely. You sense that you have a place in the Universal scheme of things, that you have a mission to fulfill in your lifetime, and you're willing to act on it. Although you sometimes feel compulsive, you're also aware of how to slow down and powerfully regenerate your energy.

When PLUTO OPERATES DYSFUNCTIONALLY, it destroys without rebuilding and penetrates without mercy. Its laserlike focus strips people and things bare, leaving them exposed and vulnerable. This is certainly a transformative experience, but it can be too forceful to be humane. Dysfunctional Pluto takes its incredible power and wields it abusively. It aligns itself with all that is passionate and intense in the Universe and uses its godlike force for destruction without re-creation. Pluto can be most repressive, using its power *over* others while being most out-of-control itself.

If you're DENOUNCING your Pluto, you probably think it's bad, or maybe even evil, to be powerful. You may be afraid of what you'll do to yourself or others with your power. On the other hand, if you're GLORIFYING your Pluto, you may be power-hungry. You actually may be obsessed with the kind of impact you can have on yourself and others. If you're BLAMING your Pluto-related behavior on other people or circumstances, you may think that your compulsions and powerful actions are not your fault. You could feel that you were trained to act abusively or that the situation "causes" your destructive attitudes. If you're PROJECTING your Pluto, you'll find that others are acting powerfully in your life. You won't have to demonstrate your own ability to be forceful; someone else is doing it for you. And, if you're DENYING your Pluto force, you'll believe that you aren't powerful, that you have no missions and no obsessions. You could also be ignoring the fact that you have a strong and powerful sense of direction and focus already. If you're using your Pluto in one or more of these dysfunctional ways, remember that you, too, are a powerful piece of the Universe. You have an intrinsic, transformative force within you that can be wielded appropriately. You can be positively powerful without being destructive.

When PLUTO IS RETROGRADE, its mandate is to regenerate itself before it attempts to transform the world. It acts as its own experiment, moving through personal cycles of death and rebirth until it fully understands the process from the inside out. Retrograde Pluto is concerned with being powerfully itself, fully conscious of its force and passion although it may never choose to express its power in the world. If it does participate in Earth-changing events, it will work to affect others at the psychological or psychic level, wanting to transform them internally, too.

In PLUTO'S HOUSE, you'll find yourself going through massive cycles of personal transformation. You'll experience incredible gains and equally profound losses. Events at both ends of the spectrum seem significant and meaningful since, with Pluto, you can sense that everything is part of the cosmic plan. In this House, you'll also discover the extent of your personal power and the ways that other powerful beings can have an effect on you. If you choose to participate in mass movements, your personal motivation can usually be traced to events that occur in Pluto's House.

PLUTO'S SIGN is shared by most others in your generation. As a result, it gives clues about the style of regeneration and transformation that you and your peers will seek out. You may act out your cycles of regeneration in your personality, family, or financial patterns. Additionally, you may be thoughtful, dramatic, meticulous, or emotional in style. Pluto's Sign will determine your approach to powerful growth. If you're using Pluto dysfunctionally, you may want to discover how to utilize some of the more positive traits of its Sign.

As SCORPIO'S NATURAL RULING PLANET, Pluto's cycles of death and rebirth bring meaning and depth to any House with Scorpio on the Cusp. Every time you use Pluto's passion to express power and effect change, Scorpio's House feels the reverberations. If Scorpio is intercepted, it's also blasted open by Pluto.

APPLICATIONS FOR PLUTO

PSYCHOLOGICAL: the urge to transform, regenerate, change; the urge to penetrate, find deep meaning, get to the bottom of it; actions designed to gather up power and use it; actions that involve the self and others in Universally motivated planetary transformation

PRACTICAL: power, control, intensity, force; activities related to water, deep pools, abysses, genitals, sex, birth, death, rebirth, endings and beginnings, rejuvenation, prostitution, rape, elimination systems, garbage, detectives, spies, the occult, psychic mysteries, psychic tools, magic, witchcraft, intuition, annihilation, nuclear power, forcefulness, tyranny, ruthlessness, repression, power-trips, crime, corruption, combined resources, money, taxes, inheritances, bankruptcy

SAMPLE INTERPRETATIONS FOR PLUTO IN THE HOUSES

1st: gather and use power through title or role; transform through identity; rebirth through personality; find deep meaning through physical appearance; express the Universal force through persona; destroy through personal style

2nd: gather and use power through skills and talents; transform self-worth; rebirth through individual values; find deep meaning in material world; express the Universal force through actions involving money; destroy through possessions

3rd: gather and use power through communication; transform community; rebirth through dialogue; find deep meaning with siblings; express the Universal force through finding facts; destroy on short trips and vacations

4th: gather and use power through home and family; transform ethnic or racial origins; rebirth regarding mother; find deep meaning through family and cultural roots; express the Universal force through creating belongingness; destroy through position in home or family

15th: gather and use power through art and creativity; transform play; rebirth through recreation; find deep meaning through romance; express the Universal force through children; destroy in hobbies and leisure activities

6th: gather and use power through daily work and routine; transform everyday tasks; rebirth through maintenance activities; find deep meaning with co-workers; express the Universal force through service to others; destroy through health concerns; deal with health issues involving sexuality, genitals, and elimination system

7th: gather and use power through relating; transform through cooperation; rebirth through arbitration; find deep meaning with partner; express the Universal force through relationships; destroy "significant others"

8th: gather and use power through deep emotional interactions; transform through intimacy; rebirth through utilization of collective money, talents, and resources; find deep meaning through sexuality; express the Universal force through transformation; destroy through sex

9th: gather and use power through teaching or preaching; transform through philosophy; rebirth through knowledge; find deep meaning in travel or learning; express the Universal force through ethics; destroy through selling or advertising

10th: gather and use power through career; transform through profession; rebirth regarding father; find deep meaning with vocation; express the Universal force through position in societal structure; destroy through reputation

11th: gather and use power through future visions; transform the "cause"; rebirth through goals and plans; find deep meaning with friends; express the Universal force through theoretical systems; destroy through schemes

12th: gather and use power through intuition; transform through spirituality; rebirth through psychic ability; find deep meaning through addictions or meditation; express the Universal force through altered states; destroy through position in institution

SAMPLE INTERPRETATIONS FOR PLUTO IN THE SIGNS

ARIES: gather and use power assertively; transform in a spontaneous, childlike way; rebirth by taking risks; find deep meaning in a stimulated and energized manner; express the Universal force by being freedom-loving; destroy through aggressive or inconsiderate behavior

TAURUS: gather and use power reliably; transform in a loyal way; rebirth through getting results; find deep meaning in a sensual, physical manner; express the Universal force by being persistent; destroy through stubborn or stingy behavior

GEMINI: gather and use power versatilely; transform in a humorous way; rebirth through dialogue; find deep meaning in a curious, amusing manner; express the Universal force by being communicative and investigative; destroy through gossipy or unreliable behavior

CANCER: gather and use power nurturingly; transform in a comforting, caring way; rebirth by "mothering"; find deep meaning in a sentimental way; express the Universal force by being protective of past patterns; destroy through fearful or clingy behavior

LEO: gather and use power dramatically; transform in a magnanimous, confident way; rebirth by storytelling; find deep meaning in a flamboyant, flashy manner; express the Universal force by being good- hearted; destroy through egotistical or arrogant behavior

VIRGO: gather and use power analytically; transform in a practical, problem-solving way; rebirth by figuring out the solution; find deep meaning in a discriminating, idealized manner; express the Universal force by being detail-oriented; destroy through critical or fussy behavior

LIBRA: gather and use power diplomatically; transform in a graceful, charming way; rebirth by creating beauty; find deep meaning in a cooperative, interactive manner; express the Universal force by compromising; destroy through indecisive or vain behavior

SCORPIO: gather and use power passionately; transform in a penetrating way; rebirth when protecting self or others; find deep meaning in a powerful, seductive manner; express the Universal force through intensity; destroy through defensive or vengeful behavior

SAGITTARIUS: gather and use power expansively; transform in a philosophical, ethical way; rebirth by presenting wisdom; find deep meaning in an optimistic and easygoing manner; express the Universal force by reaching for "more"; destroy through preachy or self-indulgent behavior

CAPRICORN: gather and use power responsibly; transform in a pragmatic, organized way; rebirth by "fathering"; find deep meaning in a prestige-seeking, ambitious manner; express the Universal force through professionalism; destroy through domineering or depressed behavior

AQUARIUS: gather and use power innovatively; transform in an eccentric, visionary way; rebirth by having visions for the future; find deep meaning in a nonconforming and inventive manner; express the Universal force with unpredictability; destroy with rebellious or disruptive behavior

PISCES: gather and use power intuitively; transform in a spiritual, psychic way; rebirth by creating fantasies and dreams; find deep meaning in an imaginative, serene manner; express the Universal force through compassion; destroy through paranoid or victim-oriented behavior

THE POINTS

The five important Points in the Chart are similar to the Planets in that they have key roles to play in our lives. However, they are not moving bodies in the Universe. For this reason, it's harder to imagine them as subpersonalities. Instead, remember to think of the Points as specific assets or resources which can be utilized, according to their Sign and House positions, in a number of functional and dysfunctional ways. You, of course, can choose which of those ways make sense to you. For your reiew, Figure 6-2 contains the names, abbreviations, and symbols for the Points.

NAME	AB.	SYMBOL
NORTH NODE	NN	☊
SOUTH NODE	SN	☋
PART OF FORTUNE	PF	⊗
MIDHEAVEN	MC	M
ASCENDANT	ASC	A

Figure 6-2
The Points, Their Abbreviations, and Their Glyphs

THE NORTH NODE OF
THE MOON: *The Receiver*

THE SOUTH NODE OF
THE MOON: *The Giver*

THEIR COMBINED PURPOSE: balance inflow and outflow

THEIR TASKS: NORTH NODE: to stimulate inflow
SOUTH NODE: to release outflow

THEIR VOICES: NORTH NODE: "I stretch and learn."
SOUTH NODE: "I share and teach."

Since the NORTH AND SOUTH NODES OF THE MOON are always exactly opposite each other they are usually the *only* two Points (or

Planets) in the Chart that are this precisely Aspected to one another. They actually form a line, called the NODAL AXIS, around which the rest of the Chart revolves. Psychologically, the Nodes represent the balance between the inflow (North) and outflow (South) of your energy. Their Signs and Houses represent how and where you achieve that balance.

The NORTH NODE symbolizes the point of challenge and growth for this lifetime. As a result, the qualities represented by the North Node's Sign may feel new, exciting, stimulating, and a little scary at first. You'll experience yourself as young, awkward, unprepared, or unsure in using the North Node's Sign within its House. In fact, you'll probably feel a need to find mentors and role models that can help you to figure out how to gracefully express the North Node themes. This is truly the point of IN-FLOW in your Chart; it's the place where you can receive. Your North Node draws in ideas, feedback, energy, love, money, and support from others. Its experiences fill you up. Ultimately, as you become more and more comfortable with using the North Node, you'll sense that you're stretching yourself, with the support of others, into using your full potential.

THE SOUTH NODE, on the other hand, represents skills and abilities that are easy for you to master and demonstrate in this life. It's even probable that you've developed your South Node gifts in other lifetimes. Talents that you naturally expressed at an early age are likely to be extensions of your South Node themes. Because you feel totally comfortable with using this Sign's energy in this House, you can be a teacher and role model for others here. You may actually feel old, mature, graceful, and experienced in using the South Node Sign. This is the point of OUTFLOW in your Chart, the place where ideas, feedback, energy, love, money, and support can go out of your life. You'll be asked to share and give here. Sometimes, you can give so much out of your South Node that you feel drained and used up. So although you know that you can perform the South Node tasks well, you may feel bored, frustrated, or exhausted by them. If you feel limited to the South Node, you'll probably come to the point of saying "Is this all there is?"

The NODES ARE GENERALLY RETROGRADE, which reflects the fact that they are used to create internal, psychological balance. They also symbolize the sometimes intangible exchange of concepts, information, emotion, and resources. If your Nodes are Retrograde, you've probably chosen to invent your own system for balancing inflow and outflow. If they happen to be Direct in your Chart, you may balance the Nodes at a more tangible level through the exchange of money or goods. And, you may have found that you can effectively and comfortably use the systems of exchange that have been invented already. Defining the differences between the Retrograde and Direct Nodes is somewhat difficult because although they are different in theory, in reality the distinctions between them are quite subtle and sometimes unnoticeable.

Most of the time, you'll naturally and FUNCTIONALLY COMBINE THE NODES by taking in new ideas, experiences, and sensations at the North Node and sharing skills, resources, and knowledge at the South Node. You can, however, use them DYSFUNCTIONALLY if you overemphasize one end or the other. This can leave you feeling that your life is unbalanced and wobbly. If you choose to focus only on the North Node, you could become over-full. You'll have taken in a great deal of energy and information and found no outlet for it. If, on the other hand, you choose to utilize only the South Node, you could become tired and worn out because you'll have given fully of yourself without taking time for replenishment. When you align the Nodal Axis by allowing the inflow and outflow to move between them, you'll feel most balanced and centered.

When you're fully OWNING your Nodes, you'll be taking in new ideas, experiences, and sensations at the North Node and sharing skills, resources, and knowledge at the South Node. You'll be aware that it's important to keep the Nodal Axis in alignment. You'll know that even if your life isn't always in perfect balance, you can rebalance it when you need to do so.

If you're DENOUNCING your Nodes, you might think that it's unimportant to have balance in your life. You might find one end of the Nodal Axis so exciting (North) or comfortable (South) that you criticize the part of you that wants to explore the other end. If you're GLORIFYING your Nodes, you could think that your ability to balance inflow and outflow perfectly is overly important. Unrealistically, you could expect yourself to always be in ideal alignment. If you're BLAMING your Node-related behavior on other people or circumstances, you probably think that you have no control over the balance of inflow and outflow in your life. You think that "they" force you to give or to receive. If you're PROJECTING your Nodes, you rely on others to symbolize the force of balance in your life. Or, you may get someone else to act out one of your Nodes so that you can focus on the other one. If you're DENYING your Nodes, you probably think that you're a closed system; nothing comes in and nothing goes out. You believe that there is no give and take in your life. You could also be ignoring the fact that your life contains a fair amount of balance already. If you're using your Nodes in one or more of these dysfunctional ways, remember that ebb and flow is a natural part of life. You do live in the World, so you will naturally have opportunities to take from others and to share with others. Your only challenge is to learn how to balance the inflow and outflow in appropriate ways.

In the HOUSES AND SIGNS CONTAINING THE NODAL AXIS, you'll

find that you act out your own individual quest for balance. Generally speaking, you've probably utilized the qualities of the South Node's Sign in the affairs of its House in many lifetimes, or at least in the early phases of this life. It still may be tempting to focus your attention solely in this area of life. However, if you stretch yourself into utilizing the qualities of the North Node's Sign within the context of its House, you'll probably feel the thrill of new adventure. Ultimately, you'll want to challenge yourself by taking action in the manner of the North Node's Sign in terms of the issues of its House. Then you'll want to share the results of that action by expressing yourself according to the South Node's Sign in its House.

APPLICATIONS FOR THE NORTH NODE

THE CONTEXT (HOUSE) in which to take, gain, stretch, grow, acquire, receive, dare to brave the unknown, move toward personal enhancement, increase options, challenge the self, attract inflow of people, ideas, energy, and resources

THE MANNER (SIGN) in which to feel stimulated, excited, thrilled, supported, taught, sponsored, daring, young, inexperienced, new, fresh, awkward, unsure, unprepared, threatened, intimidated, or overwhelmed

APPLICATIONS FOR THE SOUTH NODE

THE CONTEXT (HOUSE) in which to give, lose, release, forgive, let go, share, liberate, relinquish, relieve, support others, repeat the familiar pattern, remain in comfort, stay with what's known; experience outflow of people, ideas, energy, and resources; pass on accumulated feelings or things

THE MANNER (SIGN) in which to feel experienced, gifted, talented, mature, graceful, adult, old, wise, resourceful, supportive, sacrificial, drained, exhausted, grief-stricken, or burned out

SAMPLE INTERPRETATIONS FOR THE NORTH NODE
IN THE HOUSES

1st: grow through title or role; dare to brave the unknown regarding identity; increase options through personality; challenge self through physical appearance; attract inflow through persona; express inexperience through personal style

2nd: grow through skills and talents; dare to brave the unknown regarding self-worth; increase options through individual values; challenge self in the material world; attract inflow through actions involving money; express inexperience through possessions

3rd: grow through communication; dare to brave the unknown within the community; increase options through dialogue; challenge self with siblings; attract inflow through finding facts; express inexperience on short trips and vacations

4th: grow through home and family; dare to brave the unknown regarding ethnic or racial origins; increase options through mother; challenge self regarding family and cultural roots; attract inflow through creating belongingness; express inexperience through position in home or family

5th: grow through art and creativity; dare to brave the unknown in play; increase options through recreation; challenge self through romance; attract inflow through children; express inexperience in hobbies and leisure activities

6th: grow through daily work and routine; dare to brave the unknown in everyday tasks; increase options through maintenance activities; challenge self with co-workers; attract inflow through service to others; express inexperience through health concerns; deal with health issues involving too much inflow without enough outflow

7th: grow through relating; dare to brave the unknown through cooperation; increase options through arbitration; challenge self with partner; attract inflow through relationships; express inexperience regarding "significant others"

8th: grow through deep emotional interactions; dare to brave the unknown through intimacy; increase options through utilization of collective money, talents, and resources; challenge self through sexuality; attract inflow through transformation; express inexperience through sex

9th: grow through teaching or preaching; dare to brave the unknown through philosophy; increase options through knowledge; challenge self with travel or learning; attract inflow through ethics; express inexperience through selling or advertising

10th: grow through career; dare to brave the unknown through profession; increase options through father; challenge self with vocation; attract inflow through position in societal structure; express inexperience through reputation

11th: grow through future visions; dare to brave the unknown regarding the "cause"; increase options through goals and plans; challenge self with friends; attract inflow through theoretical systems; express inexperience through schemes

12th: grow through intuition; dare to brave the unknown through spirituality; increase options through psychic ability; challenge self through addictions or meditation; attract inflow through altered states; express inexperience through position in institution

SAMPLE INTERPRETATIONS FOR THE NORTH NODE IN THE SIGNS

ARIES: grow assertively; dare to brave the unknown in a spontaneous, childlike way; increase options by taking risks; challenge self in a stimulated and energized manner; attract inflow by being freedom-loving; express inexperience through aggressive or inconsiderate behavior

TAURUS: grow reliably; dare to brave the unknown in a loyal way; increase options through getting results; challenge self in a sensual, physical manner; attract inflow by being persistent; express inexperience through stubborn or stingy behavior

GEMINI: grow versatilely; dare to brave the unknown in a humorous way; increase options through dialogue; challenge self in a curious, amusing manner; attract inflow by being communicative and investigative; express inexperience through gossipy or unreliable behavior

CANCER: grow nurturingly; dare to brave the unknown in a comforting, caring way; increase options by "mothering"; challenge self in a sentimental way; attract inflow by being protective of past patterns; express inexperience through fearful or clingy behavior

LEO: grow dramatically; dare to brave the unknown in a magnanimous, confident way; increase options by storytelling; challenge self in a flamboyant, flashy manner; attract inflow by being good-hearted; express inexperience through egotistical or arrogant behavior

VIRGO: grow analytically; dare to brave the unknown in a practical, problem-solving way; increase options by figuring out the solution; challenge self in a discriminating, idealized manner; attract inflow by being detail-oriented; express inexperience through critical or fussy behavior

LIBRA: grow diplomatically; dare to brave the unknown in a graceful, charming way; increase options by creating beauty; challenge self in a cooperative, interactive manner; attract inflow by compromising; express inexperience through indecisive or vain behavior

SCORPIO: grow passionately; dare to brave the unknown in a penetrating, transforming way; increase options when protecting self or others; challenge self in a powerful, seductive manner; attract inflow through intensity; express inexperience through defensive or vengeful behavior

SAGITTARIUS: grow expansively; dare to brave the unknown in a philosophical, ethical way; increase options by presenting wisdom; challenge self in an optimistic and easygoing manner; attract inflow by reaching for "more"; express inexperience through preachy or self-indulgent behavior

CAPRICORN: grow responsibly; dare to brave the unknown in a pragmatic, organized way; increase options by "fathering"; challenge self in a prestige-seeking, ambitious manner; attract inflow through professionalism; express inexperience through domineering or depressed behavior

AQUARIUS: grow innovatively; dare to brave the unknown in an eccentric, visionary way; increase options by having visions for the future; challenge self in a nonconforming and inventive manner; attract inflow through unpredictability; express inexperience through rebellious or disruptive behavior

PISCES: grow intuitively; dare to brave the unknown in a spiritual, psychic way; increase options by creating fantasies and dreams; challenge self in an imaginative, serene manner; attract inflow through compassion; express inexperience through paranoid or victim-oriented behavior

SAMPLE INTERPRETATIONS FOR THE SOUTH NODE IN THE HOUSES

1st: pass on accumulated feelings, ideas, or things through title or role; release through identity; share through personality; repeat familiar patterns through physical appearance; outflow through persona; experience loss through personal style

2nd: pass on accumulated feelings, ideas, or things through skills and talents; release self-worth; share through individual values; repeat familiar patterns through material world; outflow through actions involving money; experience loss through possessions

3rd: pass on accumulated feelings, ideas, or things through communication; release within community; share through dialogue; repeat familiar patterns with siblings; outflow through finding facts; experience loss through short trips and vacations

4th: pass on accumulated feelings, ideas, or things through home and family; release ethnic or racial origins; share with mother; repeat familiar patterns through family and cultural roots; outflow through creating belongingness; experience loss through position in home or family

5th: pass on accumulated feelings, ideas, or things through art and creativity; release play; share through recreation; repeat familiar patterns through romance; outflow through children; experience loss in hobbies and leisure activities

6th: pass on accumulated feelings, ideas, or things through daily work and routine; release everyday tasks; share through maintenance activities; repeat familiar patterns with co-workers; outflow through service to others; experience loss through health concerns; deal with health issues involving too much outflow with not enough inflow

7th: pass on accumulated feelings, ideas, or things through relating; release through cooperation; share through arbitration; repeat familiar patterns with partner; outflow through relationships; experience loss of "significant others"

8th: pass on accumulated feelings, ideas, or things through deep emotional interactions; release through intimacy; share through utilization of collective money, talents, and resources; repeat familiar patterns through sexuality; outflow through transformation; experience loss through sex

9th: pass on accumulated feelings, ideas, or things through teaching or preaching; release philosophy; share knowledge; repeat familiar patterns with travel or learning; outflow regarding ethics; experience loss through selling or advertising

10th: pass on accumulated feelings, ideas, or things through career; release through profession; share with father; repeat familiar patterns with vocation; outflow through position in societal structure; experience loss through reputation

11th: pass on accumulated feelings, ideas, or things in future visions; release through the "cause"; share through goals and plans; repeat familiar patterns with friends; outflow through theoretical systems; experience loss through schemes

12th: pass on accumulated feelings, ideas, or things through intuition; release within spirituality; share through psychic ability; repeat familiar patterns through addictions or meditation; outflow through altered states; experience loss through position in institution

SAMPLE INTERPRETATIONS FOR THE SOUTH NODE IN THE SIGNS

ARIES: pass on accumulated feelings, ideas, or things assertively; release in a spontaneous, childlike way; share by taking risks; repeat familiar patterns in a stimulated and energized manner; outflow by being freedom-loving; experience loss through aggressive or inconsiderate behavior

TAURUS: pass on accumulated feelings, ideas, or things reliably; release in a loyal way; share through getting results; repeat familiar patterns in a sensual, physical manner; outflow by being persistent; experience loss through stubborn or stingy behavior

GEMINI: pass on accumulated feelings, ideas, or things versatilely; release in a humorous way; share through dialogue; repeat familiar patterns in a curious, amusing manner; outflow by being communicative and investigative; experience loss through gossipy or unreliable behavior

CANCER: pass on accumulated feelings, ideas, or things nurturingly; release in a comforting, caring way; share by "mothering"; repeat familiar patterns in a sentimental way; outflow by being protective of past patterns; experience loss through fearful or clingy behavior

LEO: pass on accumulated feelings, ideas, or things dramatically; release in a magnanimous, confident way; share by storytelling; repeat familiar patterns in a flamboyant, flashy manner; outflow by being good-hearted; experience loss through egotistical or arrogant behavior

VIRGO: pass on accumulated feelings, ideas, or things analytically; release in a practical, problem-solving way; share by figuring out the solution; repeat familiar patterns in a discriminating, idealized manner; outflow by being detail-oriented; experience loss through critical or fussy behavior

LIBRA: pass on accumulated feelings, ideas, or things diplomatically; release in a graceful, charming way; share by creating beauty; repeat familiar patterns in a cooperative, interactive manner; outflow by compromising; experience loss through indecisive or vain behavior

SCORPIO: pass on accumulated feelings, ideas, or things passionately; release in a penetrating, transforming way; share when protecting self or others; repeat familiar patterns in a powerful, seductive manner; outflow through intensity; experience loss through defensive or vengeful behavior

SAGITTARIUS: pass on accumulated feelings, ideas, or things expansively; release in a philosophical, ethical way; share by presenting wisdom; repeat familiar patterns in an optimistic and easygoing manner; outflow by reaching for "more"; experience loss through preachy or self-indulgent behavior

CAPRICORN: pass on accumulated feelings, ideas, or things responsibly; release in a pragmatic, organized way; share by "fathering"; repeat familiar patterns in a prestige-seeking, ambitious manner; outflow through professionalism; experience loss through domineering or depressed behavior

AQUARIUS: pass on accumulated feelings, ideas, or things innovatively; release in an eccentric, visionary way; share by having visions for the future; repeat familiar patterns in a nonconforming and inventive manner; outflow unpredictably; experience loss through rebellious or disruptive behavior

PISCES: pass on accumulated feelings, ideas, or things intuitively; release in a spiritual, psychic way; share by creating fantasies and dreams; repeat familiar patterns in an imaginative, serene manner; outflow compassion; experience loss through paranoid or victim-oriented behavior

THE PART OF FORTUNE:
The Integrator

ITS PURPOSE: personal integration

ITS TASK: to create wholeness

ITS VOICE: "I magically bless. I unify."

The PART OF FORTUNE (Pars Fortuna), is also called the POINT OF EXPRESSION and the POINT OF PERSONAL INTEGRATION. In ancient Astrology, the Part of Fortune was actually seen as the primary significator of a person's potential for attracting riches. Perhaps the concept of "seeking your fortune" was related to this Astrological point. It makes sense that, by using the combined Sun (personal potential), Moon (security), and Ascendant (personality) energies in an integrated way, the result could have positive financial implications. But, this is not always the case.

Instead, THE FUNCTION OF THE PART OF FORTUNE is to integrate and make whole. This Point symbolizes the way in which you can most "fortunately" combine your skills and talents to express them in a powerful manner. You can utilize the Part of Fortune to make sure that your life runs smoothly. Even better, you can use it to magically bless your life and the lives of others. You'll know that you're OWNING your Part of Fortune when you feel comfortable with using your combined talents in an integrated way.

It is possible to use the Part of Fortune DYSFUNCTIONALLY by using the negative characteristics of its Sign. Additionally, you could DENOUNCE it by judging that it's unimportant to be combining your skills into an integrated whole. You could easily GLORIFY it by expecting yourself to perform its magic at all times. You could BLAME other people or circumstances for the techniques you use to pull yourself together. You might PROJECT your Part of Fortune by expecting others to "make" you become whole or feeling that someone else is your "other half." And, you might DENY your Part of Fortune by claiming that your identity is too fractured and divided to ever be unified. You could also be ignoring the fact that you are integrated already. If you're using your Part of Fortune in one or more of these dysfunctional ways, remember that you are intrinsically whole whether you consciously know it or not. You do have a way in which you can appropriately and healthily feel integrated and make magic in the world.

In the PART OF FORTUNE'S SIGN AND HOUSE, you'll find that you express your integration skills in a manner that's unique to you. When you utilize the positive qualities of this Sign, you'll tend to feel whole, sane, comfortable with yourself, and sure that you're doing your best. When you express those qualities with regard to the concerns and issues of this House, you'll find that the problems tend to vanish and productive solutions seem to appear. Of course, if you use the negative qualities of the Part of Fortune's Sign, you could find yourself in a well-integrated mess. You may be amazed at how cleverly you can get into trouble when you use the Part of Fortune's Sign dysfunctionally. If this happens, you always have the choice of learning to use its Sign in a healthier manner.

APPLICATIONS FOR THE PART OF FORTUNE

THE CONTEXT (HOUSE) in which to create wholeness, make "magic," come up with brilliant solutions, experience a positive self-image, and find luck

THE MANNER (SIGN) in which to feel brilliant, integrated, unified, talented, charmed, blessed, clever, smug, and self-satisfied

SAMPLE INTERPRETATIONS FOR THE PART OF FORTUNE IN THE HOUSES

1st: create wholeness through title or role; feel "magically blessed" through identity; experience luck through personality; project a positive self-image through physical appearance; express integration through persona; demonstrate smugness through personal style

2nd: create wholeness through skills and talents; feel "magically blessed" regarding self-worth; experience luck through individual values; project a positive self-image through material world; express integration through actions involving money; demonstrate smugness through possessions

3rd: create wholeness through communication; feel "magically blessed" regarding community; experience luck through dialogue; project a positive self-image with siblings; express integration through finding facts; demonstrate smugness regarding short trips and vacations

4th: create wholeness through home and family; feel "magically blessed" regarding ethnic or racial origins; experience luck regarding mother; project a positive self-image regarding family and cultural roots; express integration through creating belongingness; demonstrate smugness through position in home or family

5th: create wholeness through art and creativity; feel "magically blessed" in play; experience luck through recreation; project a positive self-image through romance; express integration with children; demonstrate smugness in hobbies and leisure activities

6th: create wholeness through daily work and routine; feel "magically blessed" in everyday tasks; experience luck through maintenance activities; project a positive self-image with co-workers; express integration through service to others; demonstrate smugness through health concerns; deal with health issues involving integration and unification

7th: create wholeness through relating; feel "magically blessed" through cooperation; experience luck through arbitration; project a positive self-image with partner; express integration through relationships; demonstrate smugness regarding "significant other"

8th: create wholeness through deep emotional interactions; feel "magically blessed" through intimacy; experience luck through utilization of collective money, talents, and resources; project a positive self-image through sexuality; express integration through transformation; demonstrate smugness regarding sex

9th: create wholeness through teaching or preaching; feel "magically blessed" through philosophy; experience luck through knowledge; project a positive self-image with travel or learning; express integration through ethics; demonstrate smugness through selling or advertising

10th: create wholeness through career; feel "magically blessed" through profession; experience luck regarding father; project a positive self-image within vocation; express integration through position in societal structure; demonstrate smugness regarding reputation

11th: create wholeness through future visions; feel "magically blessed" regarding the "cause"; experience luck through goals and plans; project a positive self-image with friends; express integration through theoretical systems; demonstrate smugness through schemes

12th: create wholeness through intuition; feel "magically blessed" through spirituality; experience luck through psychic ability; project a positive self-image through addictions or meditation; express integration through altered states; demonstrate smugness through position in institution

SAMPLE INTERPRETATIONS FOR THE PART OF FORTUNE IN THE SIGNS

ARIES: create wholeness assertively; feel "magically blessed" in a spontaneous, childlike way; experience luck by taking risks; project a positive self-image in a stimulated and energized manner; express integration by being freedom-loving; demonstrate smugness through aggressive or inconsiderate behavior

TAURUS: create wholeness reliably; feel "magically blessed" through being loyal; experience luck through getting results; project a positive self-image in a sensual, physical manner; express integration by being persistent; demonstrate smugness through stubborn or stingy behavior

GEMINI: create wholeness versatilely; feel "magically blessed" in a humorous way; experience luck through dialogue; project a positive self-image in a curious, amusing manner; express integration by being communicative and investigative; demonstrate smugness through gossipy or unreliable behavior

CANCER: create wholeness nurturingly; feel "magically blessed" in a comforting, caring way; experience luck by "mothering"; project a positive self-image in a sentimental way; express integration by being protective of past patterns; demonstrate smugness through fearful or clingy behavior

LEO: create wholeness dramatically; feel "magically blessed" in a magnanimous, confident way; experience luck by storytelling; project a positive self-image in a flamboyant, flashy manner; express integration by being good-hearted; demonstrate smugness through egotistical or arrogant behavior

VIRGO: create wholeness analytically; feel "magically blessed" in a practical, problem-solving way; experience luck by figuring out the solution; project a positive self-image in a discriminating, idealized manner; express integration by being detail-oriented; demonstrate smugness through critical or fussy behavior

LIBRA: create wholeness diplomatically; feel "magically blessed" in a graceful, charming way; experience luck by creating beauty; project a positive self-image in a cooperative, interactive manner; express integration by compromising; demonstrate smugness through indecisive or vain behavior

SCORPIO: create wholeness passionately; feel "magically blessed" in a penetrating, transforming way; experience luck when protecting self or others; project a positive self-image in a powerful, seductive manner; express integration through intensity; demonstrate smugness through defensive or vengeful behavior

SAGITTARIUS: create wholeness expansively; feel "magically blessed" in a philosophical, ethical way; experience luck by presenting wisdom; project a positive self-image in an optimistic and easygoing manner; express integration by reaching for "more"; demonstrate smugness through preachy or self-indulgent behavior

CAPRICORN: create wholeness responsibly; feel "magically blessed" in a pragmatic, organized way; experience luck by "fathering"; project a positive self-image in a prestige-seeking, ambitious manner; express integration through professionalism; demonstrate smugness through domineering or depressed behavior

AQUARIUS: create wholeness innovatively; feel "magically blessed" in an eccentric, visionary way; experience luck by having visions for the future; project a positive self-image in a nonconforming and inventive manner; express integration through unpredictability; demonstrate smugness through rebellious or disruptive behavior

PISCES: create wholeness intuitively; feel "magically blessed" in a spiritual, psychic way; experience luck by creating fantasies and dreams; project a positive self-image in an imaginative, serene manner; express integration through compassion; demonstrate smugness through paranoid or victim-oriented behavior

THE MIDHEAVEN:
Universal Context

THE ASCENDANT:
Earthly Context

THEIR COMBINED PURPOSE:
define birth environment; encourage development

THE MIDHEAVEN'S FUNCTION: represent the Universal environment

THE ASCENDANT'S FUNCTION: represent the Earthly environment

The MIDHEAVEN and the ASCENDANT define and describe the nature of the birth environment. Their interplay actually establishes the ways in which you can fit into the Universal and Earthly processes that are unfolding during your lifetime.

The MIDHEAVEN is theoretically the "highest" point in your Chart, since it is a representation of the point directly above your Birth Place. Symbolically, it represents the Universal environment into which you were born. In fact, it signifies the best way that you fit into the cosmic scheme of things. It's often referred to as the point of personal destiny. In this case, destiny is not related to predestination; it is associated with life purpose.

By fully and positively expressing the MIDHEAVEN'S SIGN, you can be sure that you are fulfilling your potential for making a contribution to the Universe, a contribution that is coordinated with all other forces acting in the Universe at this time. Usually, the Midheaven is the same as the 10th House Cusp, so its Sign shows the attitude that you'd have toward your career or life-work. It also shows the needs that must be met in order for you to express your vocational strengths. No matter what the nature of your life work, by approaching it in the style of the Midheaven, you'll feel attuned and connected with Universal purpose, a part of the cosmic design.

The ASCENDANT, a representation of the Eastern Horizon at your birth, symbolizes the Earthly environment into which you were born. Through it, you've been able to assume a role that assures you of a part to play in the drama of ongoing Earthly events. By approaching life through your Ascendant, you can be sure that you will have a place in your family or community; you can use your Ascendant to "fit in."

At many levels, the SIGN ON THE ASCENDANT represents the qualities that were most reinforced by your whole extended family system. Certainly, by using this Sign, you've been able to develop a most effective range of behavior for coping with daily life. Of course, if you've chosen to develop the negative qualities of your Rising Sign in order to survive in your family, you may want to change your expression of it. In that case, by learning to use the positive qualities of your Ascendant, you can find a new way to fit into your current family system or to create a different "family of choice" for yourself. Usually, the Ascendant is the same as the 1st House Cusp, so its Sign shows the approach you take when presenting yourself to the world. It reflects the personality style that you've utilized to fulfill your Earthly purposes.

Every Chart is the expression of some combination of the Universal and Earthly environments. Therefore, the compatibility of your Midheaven and Ascendant Signs is a key indicator of cohesiveness or tension in the Chart. If the two Signs work well together, you've probably found that you can pretty easily act out your role in the family and community and still fit into the cosmic design. If the two Signs seem incompatible, you might feel that you have to negate one in order to accomplish the other. In that case, a major theme of your life may be that of finding the "middle path," an approach to life that allows you to be yourself on this Earth and still fit into the Universal plan.

By interpreting your Midheaven- and Ascendant-based Equal House Charts, you can discover how the relationship between your Universal and Earthly environments has had an impact on your life. The Midheaven-based Equal House Chart shows, through the Signs on each House Cusp, how you would approach each area of life if you were living only in the Universal context. The Ascendant-based Equal House Chart shows your Earthly environment at birth, so the Signs on these Cusps show how you would react to each area of life if you were living only in the Earthly context. In reality, you're living in both environments. You're part of everyday reality here on Earth, and you're part of the grand pattern of the Universe.

Since the Midheaven and the Ascendant have no active roles, you really can't use them functionally or dysfunctionally. You can, of course, choose to utilize the positive or negative attributes of their Signs and you can definitely use the Planets Ruling those Signs in a functional or dysfunctional manner. Therefore, if you want to discover more about how you're fitting into the Universal and Earthly environments, study the Midheaven and Ascendant Signs and their planetary Rulers.

APPLICATIONS FOR THE MIDHEAVEN AND THE ASCENDANT

Reread the sections on the 10th (Midheaven) and 1st (Ascendant) Houses in Chapter 4.

SAMPLE INTERPRETATIONS FOR THE MIDHEAVEN IN THE SIGNS

ARIES: approach career or life-work assertively; pursue ambitions in a spontaneous, childlike way; attain success by taking risks; establish reputation in a stimulated and energized manner; fulfill Universal destiny by being freedom-loving; seek importance through aggressive or inconsiderate behavior

TAURUS: approach career or life-work reliably; pursue ambitions in a loyal way; attain success through getting results; establish reputation in a sensual, physical manner; fulfill Universal destiny by being persistent; seek importance through stubborn or stingy behavior

GEMINI: approach career or life-work versatilely; pursue ambitions in a humorous way; attain success through dialogue; establish reputation in a curious, amusing manner; fulfill Universal destiny by being communicative and investigative; seek importance through gossipy or unreliable behavior

CANCER: approach career or life-work nurturingly; pursue ambitions in a comforting, caring way; attain success by "mothering"; establish reputation in a sentimental way; fulfill Universal destiny by being protective of past patterns; seek importance through fearful or clingy behavior

LEO: approach career or life-work dramatically; pursue ambitions in a magnanimous, confident way; attain success by storytelling; establish reputation in a flamboyant, flashy manner; fulfill Universal destiny by being good-hearted; seek importance through egotistical or arrogant behavior

VIRGO: approach career or life-work analytically; pursue ambitions in a practical, problem-solving way; attain success by figuring out the solution; establish reputation in a discriminating, idealized manner; fulfill Universal destiny by being detail-oriented; seek importance through critical or fussy behavior

LIBRA: approach career or life-work diplomatically; pursue ambitions in a graceful, charming way; attain success by creating beauty; establish reputation in a cooperative, interactive manner; fulfill Universal destiny by compromising; seek importance through indecisive or vain behavior

SCORPIO: approach career or life-work passionately; pursue ambitions in a penetrating, transforming way; attain success when protecting self or others; establish reputation in a powerful, seductive manner; fulfill Universal destiny through intensity; seek importance through defensive or vengeful behavior

SAGITTARIUS: approach career or life-work expansively; pursue ambitions in a philosophical, ethical way; attain success by presenting wisdom; establish reputation in an optimistic and easygoing manner; fulfill Universal destiny by reaching for "more"; seek importance through preachy or self-indulgent behavior

CAPRICORN: approach career or life-work responsibly; pursue ambitions in a pragmatic, organized way; attain success by "fathering"; establish reputation in a prestige-seeking, ambitious manner; fulfill Universal destiny through professionalism; seek importance through domineering or depressed behavior

AQUARIUS: approach career or life-work innovatively; pursue ambitions in an eccentric, visionary way; attain success by having visions for the future; establish reputation in a nonconforming and inventive manner; fulfill Universal destiny through unpredictability; seek importance through rebellious or disruptive behavior

PISCES: approach career or life-work intuitively; pursue ambitions in a spiritual, psychic way; attain success by creating fantasies and dreams; establish reputation in an imaginative, serene manner; fulfill Universal destiny through compassion; seek importance through paranoid or victim-oriented behavior

SAMPLE INTERPRETATIONS FOR THE ASCENDANT IN THE SIGNS

ARIES: express personality assertively; project self in a spontaneous, childlike way; fit into birth environment by taking risks; dress in a stimulated and energized manner; demonstrate Earthly purposes by being freedom-loving; cope with family expectations through aggressive or inconsiderate behavior

TAURUS: express personality reliably; project self in a loyal way; fit into birth environment through getting results; dress in a sensual, physical manner; demonstrate Earthly purposes by being persistent; cope with family expectations through stubborn or stingy behavior

GEMINI: express personality versatilely; project self in a humorous way; fit into birth environment through dialogue; dress in a curious, amusing manner; demonstrate Earthly purposes by being communicative and investigative; cope with family expectations through gossipy or unreliable behavior

CANCER: express personality nurturingly; project self in a comforting, caring way; fit into birth environment by "mothering"; dress in a sentimental way; demonstrate Earthly purposes by being protective of past patterns; cope with family expectations through fearful or clingy behavior

LEO: express personality dramatically; project self in a magnanimous, confident way; fit into birth environment by storytelling; dress in a flamboyant, flashy manner; demonstrate Earthly purposes by being good-hearted; cope with family expectations through egotistical or arrogant behavior

VIRGO: express personality analytically; project self in a practical, problem-solving way; fit into birth environment by figuring out the solution; dress in a discriminating, idealized manner; demonstrate Earthly purposes by being detail-oriented; cope with family expectations through critical or fussy behavior

LIBRA: express personality diplomatically; project self in a graceful, charming way; fit into birth environment by creating beauty; dress in a cooperative, interactive manner; demonstrate Earthly purposes by compromising; cope with family expectations through indecisive or vain behavior

SCORPIO: express personality passionately; project self in a penetrating, transforming way; fit into birth environment when protecting self or others; dress in a powerful, seductive manner; demonstrate Earthly purposes through intensity; cope with family expectations through defensive or vengeful behavior

SAGITTARIUS: express personality expansively; project self in a philosophical, ethical way; fit into birth environment by presenting wisdom; dress in an optimistic and easygoing manner; demonstrate Earthly purposes by reaching for "more"; cope with family expectations through preachy or self-indulgent behavior

CAPRICORN: express personality responsibly; project self in a pragmatic, organized way; fit into birth environment by "fathering"; dress in a prestige-seeking, ambitious manner; demonstrate Earthly purposes through professionalism; cope with family expectations through domineering or depressed behavior

AQUARIUS: express personality innovatively; project self in an eccentric, visionary way; fit into birth environment by having visions for the future; dress in a nonconforming and inventive manner; demonstrate Earthly purposes through unpredictability; cope with family expectations through rebellious or disruptive behavior

PISCES: express personality intuitively; project self in a spiritual, psychic way; fit into birth environment by creating fantasies and dreams; dress in an imaginative, serene manner; demonstrate Earthly purposes through compassion; cope with family expectations through paranoid or victim-oriented behavior

SUMMARY

In this Chapter, I've presented in-depth interpretations for the Planets and the Points. I've reiterated that the Planets represent the active parts of the Chart; they are like sub-parts of us, each working to accomplish its individual purposes. The Points are the supporters, aides, and resources of the Planets. Each Planet and Point fulfills its task, according to the nature of its Sign, within the context of its House. Briefly, the Planets and Points represent the following functions:

THE SUN: illuminates personal potential
THE MOON: establishes emotional comfort
MERCURY: communicates
VENUS: establishes value and beauty
MARS: pursues personal desires
JUPITER: seeks expansion
SATURN: conserves limits
CHIRON: solves problems
URANUS: shatters limits
NEPTUNE: dissolves boundaries
PLUTO: transforms

THE NORTH NODE: stimulates inflow
THE SOUTH NODE: releases outflow
THE PART OF FORTUNE: integrates
THE MIDHEAVEN: reflects Universal context
THE ASCENDANT: reflects Earthly context

EXERCISES

6-1   Expand your interpretations of the Planets and Points in your Chart by using the information in this Chapter.

6-2   Interpret several other Charts in depth by describing the Planets and Points in the Signs and Houses.

6-3   Take the list of issues and attitudes that you outlined in Exercise 5-3. For each one:

a. Locate any Planets or Points in the House.

b. Delineate the actions that you're currently taking with regard to your concerns; notice how these actions are related to the Planets located in the House.

c. Think of three other actions you could take, while still using the energies of these Planets, with regard to your issues.

d. Locate the Ruling Planets of the Signs on (or in) this House.

e. Notice any of your actions that are related to the use of the Ruling Planets in their Signs and Houses.

f. Think of three other ways to use the Ruling Planets so that you could experience your current concern in a different manner.

g. Save your ideas and insights for later use.

6-4   Using the list from Exercise 5-4, go through the process outlined in Exercise 6-3 with your friend.

SEVEN

The Aspects

The ASPECTS show how the personality parts represented by the Planets and Points interact within us by showing us the degree and nature of our internal conflicts, adjustments, and talents. Therefore, a review of the Aspects in your Chart can show you the various ways in which all of the factors of your personality link up. As with the rest of Astrology, you have choices about how to utilize your Aspects. Since each one can be interpreted in several ways and since each Planet and Point has a number of meanings, you have options for expressing each Aspect relationship. Remember that these *are* options. You won't necessarily experience all your Aspects in exactly the ways I've described. However, chances are good that one or more of the interpretations will make sense for your Chart. For now, choose the concepts that fit and create your own additional meanings as you learn more about Aspects.

In the pages that follow, I'll discuss some of your interpretational choices by going over two GROUPS of Aspects and four different STRATEGIES for describing their meanings. I'll also go over a few OTHER CONSIDERATIONS. Then, I'll combine the Groups and the Strategies in the detailed Aspect interpretations. At the end of the Chapter, you'll find a list of possible meanings for Aspects between specific pairs of Planets or Points.

As you get ready to go further into the Aspects, bear in mind that they are symbols of the distances between various pairs of Planets or Points. Since the distance between any pair rarely matches the exact Aspect distance, remember that we allow for a certain amount of leeway, or ORB, when determining whether two Planets or Points are Aspected to each other. For your review, the Aspects and their Orbs are shown in Figure 7-1.

THE ASPECT GROUPS

The Aspects can be loosely organized into two GROUPS that are based on the nature of the linking processes they describe. The BLENDING Aspects are the Conjunction, the Sextile, and the Trine. Each of these Aspects symbolizes an interactive style that smoothly combines the forces of the two Planets or Points involved. The CHALLENGING Aspects are the Semi-Sextile, the Square, the Quincunx, and the Opposition. Each of them

ASPECT NAME	SYMBOL	ABBREV.	# OF DEGREES BETWEEN TWO PLANETS OR POINTS	ALLOWABLE VARIATION (DEGREES OF ORB)
CONJUNCTION	☌	CO	0 DEGREES APART	-8 TO 8 DEGREES (8) (10 FOR SUN OR MOON)
SEMI-SEXTILE	⊻	SS	30 DEGREES APART	24-36 DEGREES (6) (8 FOR SUN OR MOON)
SEXTILE	✶	SX	60 DEGREES APART	52-68 DEGREES (8) (8 FOR SUN OR MOON)
SQUARE	□	SQ	90 DEGREES APART	82-98 DEGREES (8) (10 FOR SUN OR MOON)
TRINE	△	TR	120 DEGREES APART	112-128 DEGREES (8) (10 FOR SUN OR MOON)
QUINCUNX	⊼	QU	150 DEGREES APART	144-156 DEGREES (6) (8 FOR SUN OR MOON)
OPPOSITION	☍	OP	180 DEGREES APART	172-188 DEGREES (8) (10 FOR SUN OR MOON)

Figure 7-1
The Aspects and Their Orbs

symbolizes Planet or Point interactions that encourage adjustment and change. Whatever its Group, each Aspect can be used in both productive and nonproductive ways. As usual, you have the choice of deciding how you'll turn all of your Aspects into assets.

The Blending Aspects

The CONJUNCTION (0°), the SEXTILE (60°), and the TRINE (120°) symbolize the processes of unification, support, and enhancement. They show that the Planets or Points involved will tend to work together, blend smoothly, and combine and utilize available resources. Traditionally speaking, they are the "easy" Aspects, but this does not mean that we always use them effectively. The Planet or Point pairs join together so effortlessly that we can become unmotivated and even bored in taking advantage of them. It's important to remember that Blended Planets and Points represent gifts and talents that we need to mobilize. If you're having trouble activating a Blended combination, you can choose to employ a Planet or Point that forms a Challenging Aspect to one of the Blended ones. The Challenging one will serve as a stimulator and motivator.

The Challenging Aspects

The SEMI-SEXTILE (30°), the SQUARE (90°), the QUINCUNX (150°), and the OPPOSITION (180°) symbolize the processes of fine-tuning, motivation, redirection, and counteraction. Two of them, the Semi-Sextile and the Quincunx, are sometimes called INCONJUNCT, meaning that they are not conjunct, not cohesive. All four of them indicate that the Planets or Points involved will tend to confront, challenge, and force each other to change. Traditionally, they have been viewed as the "hard" Aspects, but they can be used quite effectively. We can experience them as stimulators of movement and catalysts for growth. It's important to remember that Planets and Points that Challenge each other represent forces and sensations that we need to integrate creatively into our lives. If you're having trouble appreciating one of your Challenging Aspects, you can choose to take advantage of a Planet or Point that Blends with one of the Challenged ones. The Blending one will soften and alleviate the intensity of the Challenge.

STRATEGIES FOR ASPECT INTERPRETATION

There are four main strategies for interpreting Aspects. First of all, you can interpret any of the Aspects according to the BASIC FORMULA introduced in Chapter 3; second, you can expand your sense of them by analyzing how the Planets and Points interact according to their relative SPEEDS; next, you can deepen your understanding of the Aspects between the Planets and some of the Points by using their VOICES (as described in Chapter 7); and finally, you can explore the planetary Aspects as connections between the RULERS of Signs and Houses.

In the following descriptions of these strategies, I'll use the example of a Square between Jupiter (in Aries in the 3rd) and Saturn (in Cancer in the 6th) as an example so that you can see how the strategies refine the interpretations in various ways.

JU in AR in 3   □   SA in CA in 6

Aspect Interpretation by Basic Formula

The first strategy for Aspect interpretation is described by the BASIC FORMULA. By using it, you consider the nature, by Sign and House, of the two Planets or Points and the style of their interaction, according to the Aspect between them. This strategy is summarized below:

THIS PLANET OR POINT, ACCORDING TO ITS HOUSE AND SIGN,
[INTERPRET ONE PLANET OR POINT BY HOUSE AND SIGN]

INTERACTS IN THIS WAY WITH
[INTERPRET THE ASPECT]

THIS PLANET OR POINT, ACCORDING TO ITS HOUSE AND SIGN.
[INTERPRET OTHER PLANET OR POINT BY HOUSE AND SIGN]

EXAMPLE

This person's urge to expand her horizons (JU) in a pioneering and adventurous way (AR), through short trips and excursions (3),

IS IN CONFLICT WITH (SQ)

her drive to demonstrate responsibility (SA) in terms of nurturing (CA) co-workers and pets (6).

Aspect Interpretation by Speed

A second strategy for Aspect interpretation involves noticing the relative SPEEDS of the Planets and Points involved. In each Aspect pair, the speed of one, relative to the speed of the other (Fig. 7-2), determines something about their interaction.

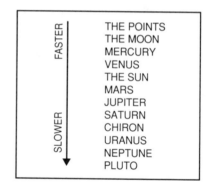

Figure 7-2
Relative Speeds of
Planets and Points

Generally, THE SLOWER PLANET OVERRIDES OR SHAPES THE FASTER PLANET OR POINT. This is because the Planets are decreasingly personal as their orbits move farther from the Sun. As a result, the Planets that represent societal and cosmic forces tend to represent controlling forces until people develop some individuality. If two Points are involved in the Aspect, they are both considered "fast" so they both affect each other. But, in terms of most of the Aspects, it's useful to think first about the faster Planet according to its function. Then, imagine that the slower Planet, according to *its* function, is affecting or molding the fast one. The nature and method of its impact is described by the Aspect itself. The formula for this strategy follows:

THE SLOWER PLANET SHAPES, INFLUENCES, AND AFFECTS
[INTERPRET SLOWER PLANET BY SIGN AND HOUSE]

ACCORDING TO THE NATURE OF THE ASPECT,
[INTERPRET ASPECT]
THE FASTER PLANET OR POINT.
[INTERPRET FASTER PLANET BY SIGN AND HOUSE]

EXAMPLE

Her drive to demonstrate responsibility (SA) in terms of nurturing (CA) co-workers (6) and taking care of (CA) pets (6)

CRITICALLY FRUSTRATES SQ)

her desire to expand her horizons (JU) in a pioneering and adventurous way (AR), through short trips and excursions (3).

Aspect Interpretation by Voice

You can also imagine the Planets and Points "talking to each other." Think of them using their VOICES in the manner of their Signs within the context of their Houses. As each Planet or Point says what it's trying to do, it interacts with the other one according to the nature of the Aspect between them. That interaction might be described as follows:

THIS PLANET OR POINT, WHO SAYS . . .
[INSERT VOICE OF ONE PLANET OR POINT]

INTERACTS IN THIS WAY
[INTERPRET THE ASPECT]

WITH THIS PLANET OR POINT, WHO SAYS . . .
[INSERT VOICE OF THE OTHER PLANET OR POINT]

IN COMBINATION, THEY SAY . . .
[INTERPRET HOW THEIR VOICES WOULD BLEND TOGETHER OR CHALLENGE EACH OTHER]

EXAMPLE

The part of her who says "I represent authority (SA) and I think we should fulfill our responsibilities (SA) with regard to taking care of (CA) our co-workers and pets (6),"

CONFRONTS (SQ)

the part of her who says "well, I expand the possibilities for growth (JU), and I think we should take pioneering and adventurous (AR) short trips and excursions (3)."

In combination, they say "We're challenged and dynamically motivated to find a way in which taking adventurous trips and excursions will actually fulfill our responsibilities with regard to our co-workers and pets."

Aspect Interpretation by Rulership

The RULERSHIP strategy for Aspect interpretation applies only to the Planets, since the Points do not act as Rulers. To interpret Aspects in this way, think of the Aspecting Planets as the representatives of their Signs and the Houses with those Signs on (or in) them. The nature of the Aspect will determine how the affairs and activities of one House are associated with the concerns and issues of the other. The Rulership strategy follows:

THE RULER OF THE (#) HOUSE
[NAME A HOUSE THAT ONE PLANET RULES]

INTERACTS IN THIS WAY WITH
[INTERPRET THE ASPECT]

THE RULER OF THE (#) HOUSE.
[NAME A HOUSE THAT THE OTHER PLANET RULES]

THEREFORE,
ACTIONS IN THE HOUSE RULED BY ONE PLANET
[NAME THE PEOPLE, PLACES, THINGS, OR ISSUES ASSOCIATED
WITH THE HOUSE RULED BY ONE PLANET]

WILL BE INFLUENCED IN THIS WAY BY
[INTERPRET THE ASPECT]

ACTIONS IN THE HOUSE RULED BY THE SECOND PLANET.
[NAME THE PEOPLE, PLACES, THINGS, OR ISSUES ASSOCIATED
WITH THE HOUSE RULED BY THE OTHER PLANET}

EXAMPLE

The Ruler of the 11th House
[Jupiter Rules Sagittarius on the 11th]
STRUGGLES WITH (SQ)
The Ruler of the 12th House.
[Saturn Rules Capricorn on the 12th.]

Therefore, every time this person starts to become involved in a group endeavor (11) she feels a conflicting pressure to isolate herself in spiritual retreat (12).

These four strategies are examples of ways in which you can approach the complex process of Aspect interpretation. You can, of course, combine or adapt them to create your own strategies. It's not important to use the strategies "correctly." It's only important that you get a sense of how the Planets and Points impact one another.

OTHER CONSIDERATIONS IN INTERPRETING ASPECTS

These strategies actually cover Aspect interpretation pretty thoroughly. But, there are a few special cases that bear a little more explanation. In this section, I'll discuss the nature of RETROGRADE and INTERCEPTED Planets and Points in Aspect. I'll also describe the importance of the NUMBER of Aspects that are formed with any one Planet or Point.

Retrograde Planets in Aspect

RETROGRADE PLANETS usually participate in the Aspect relationship at a more subtle level. If one is Retrograde, the other may seem more obvious in its expression, whether or not it is slower moving. When the Retrograde Planet has learned to internalize its energy successfully, it can be more clearly assimilated into the Aspect relationship. If both Planets are Retrograde in one of your Aspects, they will combine themselves inside you according to the nature of the Aspect between them. Later, you may express their joint force at a more public level.

Intercepted Planets in Aspect

If one of the Planets or Points is in an INTERCEPTED SIGN, the other Planet (slow or fast) may actually encourage it to emerge from its closet and express itself. Since the Intercepted Planet may not have positive or productive role-models, the non-Intercepted one can be a trigger for providing possible alternatives. If *both* Planets or Points are Intercepted, they may interact, according to inappropriate family or community models, without benefit of other perspectives. If this is the case in your Chart, other Planets or Points that Aspect both of them will motivate them to interact more effectively. And, the Planets Ruling the Intercepted Signs, as they unlock those Signs, will also unlock the hidden Planets and Points.

Planets with Few or Many Aspects

Planets and Points that are LIGHTLY ASPECTED, or connected, to any other Planets or Points in your Chart probably represent parts of you that haven't always been fully integrated into your identity. They may represent drives and urges that you've tended to Project or Deny. You can, of course, learn to Own them, but it may take conscious effort. Conversely, Planets and Points that are HEAVILY ASPECTED symbolize personality features that you've used frequently and strongly. While you may have coped with their energies by the processes of Denouncing, Glorifying, or Blaming, at least you've known that you're using them. You're probably aware that, whenever you take action with these heavily Aspected Planets or Points, many other facets of your self get triggered, and behavioral or emotional chain reactions occur.

You'll become more familiar with these strategies and considerations as you apply them to specific Aspects. So, I'll discuss the Aspects in more detail in the following pages. In applying the strategies to the Aspects, I'll fill in the blanks with sample Planets or Points that form Aspects in Grace's Chart.

The Conjunction

GROUP: BLENDING: uniting

The CONJUNCTION can be likened to hand-holding. Imagine that two friends are walking along close together, joining forces to leap over any obstacles that appear in their way.

The two Planets or Points that are Conjunct UNITE WITH EACH OTHER BY WORKING TOGETHER FROM A COMMON PERSPECTIVE. They find ways to meld together smoothly and express their synthesized force in unison. If they are in a very tight Conjunction, they can be so integrated that it's difficult to notice that two distinct behavioral forces are operating. If they are more widely Conjunct or in different Signs, they can be separated more easily. But, even then, if one of them is to be utilized independently, it may require some effort to disentangle its actions from that of the other. When you're experiencing one of your Conjunctions, you'll feel that two parts of your life are somewhat inseparable.

If your Chart contains NO CONJUNCTIONS, you may find it difficult to synchronize your actions; your life experiences and issues may seem unrelated to one another. If this is the case, remember that you can choose deliberately and consciously to improve your ability to unify your disconnected parts.

APPLICATIONS FOR CONJUNCTIONS

working together, sharing a perspective, merging, fusing, unifying, coupling, conjoining, joining, assimilating, incorporating, allied to, in league with, melding, inseparable, hand-holding, chorusing, synthesizing, agreeing, synchronizing, simultaneously acting, subsuming, swallowing, smothering, consuming

STRATEGIES FOR INTERPRETING CONJUNCTIONS

For all of the Conjunction Strategies, I'll be using the Aspect between Grace's North Node and her Moon. Her North Node is in Pisces in the 5th; her Moon is in Pisces in the 6th:

NN in PI in 5   ♂   MO in PI in 6

INTERPRETING CONJUNCTIONS BY BASIC FORMULA

Her urge to grow (NN) through intuitive experiences (PI)
with children (5)

UNITES WITH

her urge to create belongingness (MO) through compassionate
experiences (PI) within the day-to-day routine (6).

So, she'll grow psychically if she works compassionately with children
on a day-to-day basis.

INTERPRETING CONJUNCTIONS BY SPEED

Her urge to nurture (MO) co-workers (6) in a compassionate way (PI)

SMOTHERS

her urge to challenge herself (NN) with psychically oriented (PI)
recreational activities (5).

So, she might take care of her co-workers instead of exploring her own
psychic abilities. Or, she could take care of her co-workers by including
them in her psychically oriented activities.

INTERPRETING CONJUNCTIONS BY VOICE

The part of her who says "I stretch and learn (NN) through using my
intuition (PI) in my interactions with children (5) "

SPEAKS IN CHORUS WITH

the part who says "I create security (MO) by expressing compassion (PI) in my daily routine (6)."

In combination, they say

"We interact with children (5) on a daily basis (6) in order that we can challenge ourselves (NN) psychically (PI) and also (CO) nurture others (MO) in an intuitive way (PI)."

So, working with kids helps her to expand her intuitive skills.

INTERPRETING CONJUNCTIONS BY RULERSHIP

Her 10th House Ruler (MO)

WORKS TOGETHER WITH OR SWALLOWS UP

her North Node, which is not a House Ruler.

Therefore,
actions and concerns related to career, reputation, or professional responsibility (10)

WILL BE NATURALLY COMBINED WITH

children or creativity (5).
(Since the North Node is not a Ruler, the Moon's actions will be combined with concerns related to the North Node's Natal placement.)

So, her career will involve children or creativity.

The Semi-Sextile

GROUP: CHALLENGING: fine-tuning

The SEMI-SEXTILE is analogous to the tuner dial on a radio. Imagine that, as the dial is turned, the broadcasts erupt in static or come in loud and clear. Through tiny movements, the dial can be used to bring beautiful music out of seeming discord.

The two Planets or Points that are Semi-Sextile, FINE-TUNE EACH OTHER THROUGH DELICATE ADJUSTMENTS. These refinements are subtle, but their ultimate impact is significant. It's true that the slow Planet may initially rub the fast one the wrong way. The fast one may feel annoyed and irritated, experiencing the slow Planet as a mosquito that needs to be swatted. However, the slow Planet is usually triggering the fast Planet to express its latent abilities. In any case, as they interact over time, they may find that, by gently pushing and shoving, they've realigned themselves so they do work cohesively. When you're experiencing your Semi-Sextiles, you'll feel that two parts of your life are slightly modified by each other.

If your Chart contains NO SEMI-SEXTILES, you may need to ask other people to edit your creative efforts and gently reorient you. If this is the case, remember that you can deliberately and consciously choose to improve your fine-tuning ability.

APPLICATIONS FOR SEMI-SEXTILES

fine-tuning, subtly adapting, delicately adjusting, gently reorienting, refining, altering, slightly modifying, modulating, qualifying, annoying, disturbing, distressing, irritating, rubbing the wrong way

STRATEGIES FOR INTERPRETING SEMI-SEXTILES

For all of the Semi-Sextile Strategies, I'll be using the Aspect between Grace's Sun and her Chiron. Her Sun is in Aquarius in the 5th; her Chiron is in Capricorn in the 4th:

SU in AQ in 5   ⊻   CH in CP in 4

INTERPRETING SEMI-SEXTILES BY BASIC FORMULA

Her urge to express her personal potential (SU) by planning for the future (AQ) of her children (5),

FINE-TUNES

her urge to solve problems (CH) in a responsible way (CP) at home (4).

So, as she gets excited about planning for her children's future, she'll find herself making subtle adaptations in the functioning of her home.

INTERPRETING SEMI-SEXTILES BY SPEED

Her urge to analyze what's wrong (CH) at a structural level (CP) within her family system (4),

DELICATELY ADJUSTS

her urge to express herself (SU) by finding innovative methods (AQ) for raising her children (5).

So, as she figures out what was ineffective in her family system,
she adjusts the way that she raises her own children.

INTERPRETING SEMI-SEXTILES BY VOICE

The part of her who says "I shine (SU) by being nonconforming (AQ)
in my romantic preferences (5) "

MODULATES

the part who says "I fix what's wrong (CH)
in the long-term traditions (CP) of my heritage (4)."

In combination, they say

"By choosing unusual (AQ) romantic partners (5), we can adapt
or modulate (SS) our family traditions (5)."

So, by dating people who are different from her family,
she steps out of her family's patterns.

INTERPRETING SEMI-SEXTILES BY RULERSHIP

Her 12th House Ruler (CH)

REFINES OR IRRITATES

her 11th House Ruler (SU).

Therefore,
actions and concerns related to spirituality or addictions (12)

WILL SLIGHTLY MODIFY

her friendships and future goals (11).

So, as she releases her addictions, she changes some of her friends.
And, as she develops her spirituality she adapts her life goals.

The Sextile

GROUP: BLENDING: supporting

The SEXTILE holds up a sign that says "help is available if only you
reach out for it." Imagine that the fast Planet or Point is sitting at a window

looking out at the world, wanting encouragement and sponsorship. Along comes the slow Planet, walking by outside. The fast Planet has only to ask for help, and the slow one will immediately and favorably respond.

The two Planets or Points that are Sextile SUPPORT EACH OTHER THROUGH FINDING OUTSIDE RESOURCES. The slow Planet can represent counselors, mentors, and friends who support the fast one's growth and expression. Additionally, in the general community, feedback and advice about the association between the two Planets or Points will be readily available. Resources might come to them in the form of money, time, or energy. Ultimately, by tapping into the rich supply of help, the Sextile Planets or Points can function smoothly and easily together. When you're experiencing your Sextiles, you'll feel that two parts of your life are reinforced by each other and by the world.

If you have NO SEXTILES in your Chart, others may have to teach you that the world isn't inhospitable and uncaring. If this is the case, remember that you can choose deliberately and consciously to improve your ability to reach out for help.

APPLICATIONS FOR SEXTILES

helping, supporting, reinforcing, mentoring, aiding, subsidizing, defending, finding external resources, strengthening, assisting, benefiting, fostering, sponsoring, favoring, backing up, encouraging, promoting, facilitating, constructively intervening, intruding, meddling, trespassing

STRATEGIES FOR INTERPRETING SEXTILES

For all of the Sextile Strategies, I'll be using the Aspect between Grace's Mars and her South Node. Her Mars is in Scorpio in the 2nd; her South Node is in Virgo in the 11th:

SN in VI in 11   ✱   MA in SC in 2

INTERPRETING SEXTILES BY BASIC FORMULA

Her urge to assert herself (MA) in a protective way (SC)
with regard to her possessions (2),

IS SUPPORTED BY

her experience of losing (SN) the perfection of her physical things (VI)
when she loans them to friends (11).

So, as some of her possessions are harmed by her friends,
she becomes more assertive about protecting her things.

INTERPRETING SEXTILES BY SPEED

Her urge to experience her self-worth (2)
through the intense interactions (SC) she desires (MA)

ASSISTS

her ability to let go (SN) of her critical standards (VI) with regard to her
friends (11).

So, in order to have the intense kinds of interactive experiences she
wants,
she has learned to be less judgmental of her friends.

INTERPRETING SEXTILES BY VOICE

The part of her who says "I act (MA) in a powerful way (SC)
with regard to financial resources (2)"

PROVIDES BACK-UP FOR

the part who says "I share (SN) my problem-solving abilities (VI)
with my friends (11)."

In combination, they say

"We are encouraged (SX) to initiate opportunities (MA)
to give (SN) focused (SC) financial advice (2)
to our detail-oriented (VI) friends (11)."

So, her friends ask her for specific and detailed financial advice, and
she willingly gives it.

INTERPRETING SEXTILES BY RULERSHIP

Her 7th House Ruler (MA)

STRENGTHENS OR MEDDLES WITH

her South Node, which is not a Ruler.

Therefore,
experiences with her partner (7)

WILL REINFORCE

her natural abilities (SN) for detailed (VI) future planning (11).
(Since the South Node is not a Ruler, Mars's actions
will support concerns related to the South Node's Natal placement.)

So, she experiences her partner's support as she enjoys making plans for their joint future.

The Square

GROUP: CHALLENGING: motivating

The SQUARE is symbolized by two cars on a collision course. Imagine that both cars are traveling rapidly, approaching an intersection at right angles. There is a building between them on the corner so the drivers can't see each other, and there's no traffic light at the intersection. A collision can be avoided but only through concentrated effort.

The two Planets or Points that are Square MOTIVATE EACH OTHER THROUGH DYNAMIC CONFRONTATION. The Square is usually seen as the most difficult of the "hard" Aspects. The actions of the Planets or Points involved seem to be in direct conflict. The slow Planet applies pressure until the fast one reaches a point of critical frustration and is forced to act or change. Actually, through careful and conscious use of the forces, the incipient conflict can become creative friction, a growth-producing force. The Planets can serve as catalysts, challenging each other to be more fully and positively expressive. When you're experiencing your Squares, you'll feel that two parts of you are facing up to each other.

If your Chart contains NO SQUARES, you probably aren't motivated by productive inner tension. Instead, you may have to rely on external resources to be your activators. If this is the case, remember that you can deliberately and consciously choose to improve your ability to be self-mobilizing.

APPLICATIONS FOR SQUARES

catalyzing, encountering, facing up to, challenging, pressuring, dynamically motivating, creating productive tension, stimulating creative friction, critically frustrating, resisting, standing up to, defying, contesting, clashing, confronting, struggling, disputing

STRATEGIES FOR INTERPRETING SQUARES

For all of the Square Strategies, I'll be using the Aspect between Grace's Mercury and her Retrograde Neptune. Her Mercury is in Capricorn in the 4th; her Retrograde Neptune is in Libra in the 1st:

ME in CP in 4   □   R NE in LI in 1

INTERPRETING SQUARES BY BASIC FORMULA

Her urge to embody empathy (R NE) for others (LI)
as a part of her basic personality (1)

MOTIVATES BY CONFRONTING

her urge to communicate (ME) in a domineering manner (CP)
with her family (4).

So, as she tries to be bossy in her family,
her natural empathy for others forces her to change her tactics.

INTERPRETING SQUARES BY SPEED

Her urge to heal herself (R NE) by creating beauty (LI)
in her appearance (1)

CRITICALLY FRUSTRATES

her urge to get her hands (ME) dirty (CP)
through practical projects (CP) at home (4).

So, the part of her that wants to dig right in and make a mess
is overridden by the part that wants to stay clean.
She may have to redefine "dirty" as beautiful!

INTERPRETING SQUARES BY VOICE

The part of her who says "I trust myself (R NE) to be diplomatic (LI)
when I present myself (1) "

CHALLENGES OR CLASHES WITH

the part who says "I speak (ME) in an authoritative (CP) manner as a
result of my upbringing (4)."

In combination, they say

"We're forced (SQ) to find ways in which we can
present ourselves (1) diplomatically (LI), but still communicate (ME)
in an authoritative (CP) manner.

So, she struggles with trying to be gracefully accommodating
and sternly authoritative – simultaneously.

INTERPRETING SQUARES BY RULERSHIP

Her 9th House Ruler (ME)

CONTESTS OR STRUGGLES WITH

her 6th House Ruler (R NE)

Therefore,
activities that expand her horizons through travel
or higher education (9)

WILL BE DYNAMICALLY MOTIVATING

to her health and daily routine (6).

So, as she learns more, she pressures herself
to improve her daily health regime.

The Trine

GROUP: BLENDING: enhancing

The energy of the TRINE is expressed when two different colored, distinctively flavored liquids are poured together in a bowl and briefly stirred. Imagine that the two liquids form a third almost instantly. This new substance has a flavor and color of its own. Since the originals still exist, potent and unique in their own containers, there are now three substances: this one, that one, and the new one.

The two Planets or Points that are Trine ENHANCE EACH OTHER THROUGH COMBINING TALENTS. The force of the Trine is so easy to use that it's almost unthinking. It can even be utilized lazily, taken for granted without being fully employed. The two Planets or Points mingle with each other, pooling their skills and creating new forms without losing their own identities and functions. They instinctively assemble, compound, and exaggerate their collective resources without relying on the outside world for help. The slow Planet will generally set the tone for the interaction of the two, but both Planets or Points are essential to the mix. When you're experiencing your Trines, you'll feel that two parts of you are smoothly interconnected.

If you have NO TRINES in your Chart, others may have to show you how to combine your own talents creatively. If this is the case, remember that you can choose deliberately and consciously to improve your associative ability.

APPLICATIONS FOR TRINES

flowing, combining, mingling, blending, utilizing internal talents, pooling skills with, smoothly interconnecting, assembling, harmonizing, compounding, conglomerating, mixing, smoothly affiliating, easily associating, exaggerating, taking for granted, lazily employing

STRATEGIES FOR INTERPRETING TRINES

For all of the Trine Strategies, I'll be using the Aspect between Grace's Venus and her South Node. Her Venus is in Capricorn in the 3rd; her South Node is in Virgo in the 11th:

SN in VI in 11   △   VE in CP in 3

INTERPRETING TRINES BY BASIC FORMULA

Her urge to create long-lasting (CP) harmony (VE)
in her relationships with her siblings

ENHANCES, THROUGH COMBINING TALENTS WITH

her urge to give (SN) practical (VI) energy to
causes (11) that are important to her.

So, because harmony is an important "cause" to her,
she naturally wants it in her positive interactions with her siblings.

INTERPRETING TRINES BY SPEED

Her urge to establish the value (VE) of traditions (CP)
in the community (3)

TAKES IT FOR GRANTED THAT

she'll share (SN) her practical skills (VI) with her friends (11).

So, she values and contributes to the tradition
of friendly, neighborly support.

INTERPRETING TRINES BY VOICE

The part of her who says "I attract (VE) practical
and realistic (CP) neighbors (3) "

HARMONIZES WITH

the part who says "I teach (SN) by solving problems (VI)
for my friends (11).

In combination, they say

"We easily blend (TR) our abilities by creating (VE)
pragmatic and realistic (CP) relationships
with friendly (11) neighbors (3)."

So, she becomes friends with her neighbors as
she interacts with them at a practical level.

INTERPRETING TRINES BY RULERSHIP

Her 8th House Ruler (VE)

POOLS SKILLS WITH

her South Node, which is not a Ruler.

Therefore,
activities related to intimacy (8)

SMOOTHLY BLEND WITH

activities involving giving energy (SN) to friends (11).
(Since the South Node is not a Ruler, Venus's actions will
support concerns related to the South Node's Natal placement.)

So, she can easily become intimately involved with her friends.

The Quincunx

GROUP: CHALLENGING: redirecting

The QUINCUNX operates as if it's a road sign that says detour. Imagine
that, as a car moves down the road, with its driver minding her own business, someone suddenly and boldly steps out into the road, blocks the
way, and reroutes her car.

The two Planets or Points that are Quincunx REDIRECT EACH OTHER THROUGH PRESENTING ALTERNATIVES. The slow Planet is usually showing the fast one that its route and methods are incompatible with reaching its goal. The fast one is separated from its path and is often surprised at its final destination. Oftentimes, the slow Planet will use a crisis in health or personal transformation as its form of intervention. Of course, despite the interruption, there is always another route; the fast Planet or Point will arrive somewhere, probably wherever it was meant to be all along. When you're experiencing your Quincunxes, you'll feel that two parts of you are strongly and startlingly adjusting each other.

If you have NO QUINCUNXES in your Chart, the element of surprising adjustment may be missing in your life; others will have to show you how to go off on tangents. If this is the case, remember that you can choose deliberately and consciously to improve your ability to search for alternatives.

APPLICATIONS FOR QUINCUNXES

detouring, rerouting, strongly adjusting, surprising, startling, diverting, interrupting, separating, redirecting, presenting alternatives, disbanding, diverging, parting, dividing, diverging, branching, forking, creating off-shoots, going on tangents, finding incompatibilities, interfering, divorcing, taking off-track, jerking around

STRATEGIES FOR INTERPRETING QUINCUNXES

For all of the Quincunx Strategies, I'll be using the Aspect between Grace's Sun and her Retrograde Uranus. Her Sun is in Aquarius in the 5th; her Retrograde Uranus is in Cancer in the 10th:

SU in AQ in 5   ⚹   R UR in CA in 10

INTERPRETING QUINCUNXES BY BASIC FORMULA

Her urge to be her full self (SU) by creating
innovative options (AQ) for children (5)

REDIRECTS AND PRESENTS ALTERNATIVES TO

her urge to embody unreliability (R UR)
because she feels insecure (CA) within her career (10).

So, as she wants to quit her job, she thinks of other ways
to make a creative contribution by working with kids.

INTERPRETING QUINCUNXES BY SPEED

Her urge to demonstrate rebellion (R UR) in a caring manner
(CA) within her profession (10)

INTERFERES WITH

her urge to shine and gain approval (SU) for being
innovatively (AQ) creative (5).

So, as she acts out her nonconformity at work,
she loses some opportunities to be recognized for her creativity.

INTERPRETING QUINCUNXES BY VOICE

The part of her who says
"I shatter my own preconceived limits (R UR)
by sympathizing with (CA) my professional peers (10)

DIVERGES FROM

the part who says "I demonstrate my essential self (SU)
by maintaining some detachment (AQ) from others
because I prefer involvement with my children (5)."

In combination, they say
"We are diverted (QU) from maintaining a detached (AQ) personal life
with our children (5) because we are sensitive (CA)
to our ability to effect change (R UR) out in the world (10)."

So, after she establishes some distance from the world
by focusing on her family life, she feels jerked back
into considering professional activity when she thinks of her ability
to make reformative changes.

INTERPRETING QUINCUNXES BY RULERSHIP

Her 5th House Ruler (R UR)

DETOURS

her 11th House Ruler (SU).

Therefore,
involvement with groups or an important "cause" (11)

WILL BE INTERRUPTED BY

her personal creativity and recreational activities (5).

So, her drive for fun and creativity will tend to pull her away from groups and political causes.

The Opposition

GROUP: CHALLENGING: counteracting

THE OPPOSITION can be likened to two friends holding hands across a chasm. Imagine that they are pulling at each other, each trying to get the other to hop over to its side.

The two Planets or Points that are opposed COUNTERACT EACH OTHER THROUGH PRESENTING OTHER PERSPECTIVES. Usually, the slow Planet encourages the fast one to compromise. But, in all Oppositions, neither can operate without considering the other's point of view; ideally they balance each other. Generally, the Planets or Points involved try to offset and compensate for each other. As a result of juggling the alternatives, decisions involving either of them may take awhile. When you're experiencing your Oppositions, you'll feel that two parts of you are counterbalancing each other.

If you have NO OPPOSITIONS in your Chart, you may have some difficulty in maintaining objectivity or perspective. Others may have to present you with contradictory points of view. If this is the case, remember that you can choose deliberately and consciously to improve your ability to be discriminating.

APPLICATIONS FOR OPPOSITIONS

balancing, lending perspective, alternating, juggling, cooperating, collaborating, equalizing, comparing, creating symmetry, offsetting, compensating, counterbalancing, distinguishing, discriminating, counteracting, contradicting, antagonizing, opposing

STRATEGIES FOR INTERPRETING OPPOSITIONS

For all of the Opposition Strategies, I'll be using the Aspect between Grace's Chiron and her Retrograde Uranus. Her Chiron is in Capricorn in the 4th; her Retrograde Uranus is in Cancer in the 10th:

CH in CP in 4   o–o   R UR in CA in 10

INTERPRETING OPPOSITIONS BY BASIC FORMULA

Her urge to solve problems (CH) in a responsible (CP) manner
within her home and family (4),

COUNTERACTS, BY LENDING PERSPECTIVE TO

her urge to create a better future for herself (R UR)
through nurturing (CA) her career (10).

So, as she sorts out problems at home, she'll naturally
gain perspective on how to better support her career.

INTERPRETING OPPOSITIONS BY SPEED

Her urge to embody future possibilities for
the whole Earth (R UR) in a caring (CA) profession (10)

COUNTERBALANCES OR OPPOSES

her urge to fix what's wrong (CH) at home (4)
in a responsible manner (CP).

So, as she works on those personal issues at home, she'll
balance her energy by also considering her contributions
to the Earth as a whole.

INTERPRETING OPPOSITIONS BY VOICE

The part of her who says "I move beyond my personal limits (R UR)
by fulfilling my reputation (10) as a caretaker (CA)"

OFFSETS OR ANTAGONIZES

the part who says "I heal the pain of the past (CH)
by setting good boundaries (CP) within my personal life (4).

In combination, they say
"We are trying to balance (OP) our desires to go beyond
the limits of endurance (R UR) in taking care of other people (CA)
with our desires to say "no" (CP) in order to maintain
a healthy (CH) home life (4)."

So, one of her challenges is to balance her urge
to take care of others out in the world with her need
to take care of her personal life.

INTERPRETING OPPOSITIONS BY RULERSHIP

Her 5th House Ruler (R UR)

CONTRADICTS

her 12th House Ruler (CH).

Therefore,
activities related to fun and recreation (5)

MUST BALANCE

activities related to spiritual retreat and solitude (12).

So, she tries to find equal time to play and rest.

INTERPRETATIONS FOR
PLANET OR POINT COMBINATIONS

Most pairs of Planets or Points, when combined by Aspect, have consistent forms of expression. However, the nature of the Aspect will determine whether their joint theme is demonstrated in a Blending or Challenging manner. A few of the issues and skills that emerge for each pair of Planets or Points are listed in the following section. Once you get the idea of how to create these interpretations, you might want to come up with your own applications. Remember that these are only examples. You have many choices of ways to use your Aspects.

In the following examples, when you fill in the blanks, you can use these phrases:

CONJUNCTION
    unites with
    incorporated into
    joining or smothering

SQUARE
    motivates
    pressured by
    catalyzing or confronting

SEMI-SEXTILE
    fine-tunes
    subtly adapted by
    gently reorienting or irritating

TRINE
    enhances
    compounded by
    combining with or lazily employing

SEXTILE
    supports
    reinforced by
    sponsoring or meddling with

QUINCUNX
> redirects
> detoured by
> adjusting or interrupting

OPPOSITION
> counteracts
> counterbalanced by
> lending perspective to or
> contradicting

The North Node in Aspect

NORTH NODE IN ASPECT TO ANY PLANET OR POINT:

- Your sense of challenge, growth, excitement, and learning is shaped, affected, and influenced by the force of the other Planet or Point by [*insert phrase for Aspect*] it.

- The personality part represented by that other Planet or Point [*insert phrase for Aspect*] your ability to stretch into new learning.

- The other Planet or Point can also represent the reason for your fear of new beginnings.

SPECIFIC NORTH NODE ASPECTS

NORTH NODE and ANY PLANET OR POINT: talents and issues derived from responding to challenges and growth

NORTH NODE and PART OF FORTUNE: self-integration as an exciting or stimulating, or frightening activity

NORTH NODE and MIDHEAVEN: growth and learning through life work

NORTH NODE and ASCENDANT: growth and learning through expressing personality

NORTH NODE and MOON: learning from nurturers; challenge and stimulation from relationship with mother

NORTH NODE and MERCURY: communication as a stimulating challenge, for this lifetime

NORTH NODE and VENUS: growth through interactions with women or "female" energy

NORTH NODE and SUN: self-expression as a new, exciting, and somewhat fearful experience

NORTH NODE and MARS: growth through interactions with men or "male" energy

NORTH NODE and CHIRON: growth and learning through analytical thinking

NORTH NODE and JUPITER: challenge and stimulation from travel or education

NORTH NODE and SATURN: learning from authority figures; challenge and stimulation from relationship with father

NORTH NODE and URANUS: excitement or fear regarding radical or rebellious energy

NORTH NODE and NEPTUNE: growth and learning from psychic and intuitive experiences

NORTH NODE and PLUTO: challenge and excitement from situations involving power

THE SOUTH NODE IN ASPECT

SOUTH NODE IN ASPECT TO ANY PLANET OR POINT:

- Your sense of utilizing familiar patterns, releasing old things, and recognizing previously mastered skills is shaped, affected, and influenced by the force of the other Planet or Point by [insert phrase for Aspect] it.

- The personality part represented by that other Planet or Point [insert phrase for Aspect] your ability to share your knowledge with others.

- The other Planet or Point can also represent the force that drains or exhausts you.

SPECIFIC SOUTH NODE ASPECTS

SOUTH NODE and ANY PLANET OR POINT: talents and issues derived from responding to loss and letting go

SOUTH NODE and PART OF FORTUNE: self-integration as a familiar, easily mastered activity

SOUTH NODE and MIDHEAVEN: sharing or burn-out through life work

SOUTH NODE and ASCENDANT: boredom and exhaustion through expressing personality

SOUTH NODE and MOON: teaching nurturers; giving to mother or being drained by relationship with mother

SOUTH NODE and MERCURY: communication as a mastered skill for this lifetime

SOUTH NODE and VENUS: drain or fatigue through interactions with women or "female" energy; giving to women

SOUTH NODE and SUN: self-expression as a familiar, mastered, and somewhat boring experience

SOUTH NODE and MARS: drain or fatigue through interactions with men or "male" energy; giving to men

SOUTH NODE and CHIRON: mastery of healing and analytical thinking

SOUTH NODE and JUPITER: sharing of skills through travel or education

SOUTH NODE and SATURN: teaching authority figures; giving to father or being drained by relationship with father

SOUTH NODE and URANUS: boredom or familiarity with radical or rebellious energy

SOUTH NODE and NEPTUNE: sharing through psychic and intuitive experiences; burn-out from addictions

SOUTH NODE and PLUTO: releasing or unleashing power

The Part of Fortune in Aspect

PART OF FORTUNE IN ASPECT TO ANY PLANET OR POINT:

- Your sense of personal integration and individual wholeness is shaped, affected, and influenced by the force of the other Planet or Point by [*insert phrase for Aspect*] it.

- The personality part represented by that Planet or Point [*insert phrase for Aspect*] your ability to feel "magically" blessed and personally powerful.

- The other Planet or Point could also represent the force that makes you feel most smug or self-satisfied.

SPECIFIC PART OF FORTUNE ASPECTS

PART OF FORTUNE and ANY PLANET OR POINT: talents and issues derived from the process of self-integration

PART OF FORTUNE and MIDHEAVEN: magically blessed career; self-integration through life work

PART OF FORTUNE and ASCENDANT: self-integration through expressing personality

PART OF FORTUNE and MOON: magically blessed by mother; self-integration through dealing with mother or nurturance

PART OF FORTUNE and MERCURY: communication as a part of becoming more whole; good communication skills

PART OF FORTUNE and VENUS: creatively talented and "blessed"; self-integration through interactions with women or "female" energy

PART OF FORTUNE and SUN: self-expression as a form of feeling whole and integrated

PART OF FORTUNE and MARS: physically talented and "blessed"; self-integration through interactions with men or "male" energy

PART OF FORTUNE and CHIRON: personal unity through analytical thinking; healing talent

PART OF FORTUNE and JUPITER: magically blessed through travel or education; talented teacher

PART OF FORTUNE and SATURN: self-integration from setting boundaries and limits; magically blessed by father; self-integration through dealing with father

PART OF FORTUNE and URANUS: sense of personal wholeness through radical or rebellious energy

PART OF FORTUNE and NEPTUNE: self-integration through altered-state experiences; psychic talents

PART OF FORTUNE and PLUTO: ability to integrate through the use of personal power

The Midheaven in Aspect

MIDHEAVEN IN ASPECT TO ANY PLANET OR POINT:

M

- Your sense of destiny, vocation, or life mission is shaped, affected, and influenced by the force of the other Planet or Point by [insert phrase for Aspect] it.

- The personality part represented by that other Planet or Point [insert phrase for Aspect] your ability to participate in the Universal scheme of things.

- The other Planet or Point can also represent the ways that you get stuck in the "big" picture and forget to consider the personal applications.

SPECIFIC MIDHEAVEN ASPECTS

MIDHEAVEN and ANY PLANET OR POINT: talents and issues derived from responding to sense of Universal purpose or direction in life

MIDHEAVEN and ASCENDANT: relatedness between Universal purpose and Earthly purpose

MIDHEAVEN and MOON: nurturance as career path; Universal goal related to caregiving; impact of mother on life work

MIDHEAVEN and MERCURY: communication as part of life work; diversity in career

MIDHEAVEN and VENUS: art and creativity related to life work; interactions with women or "female" energy within career

MIDHEAVEN and SUN: self-expression as a part of life work; drive for recognition or fame within career

MIDHEAVEN and MARS: assertiveness or physical activity related to life work; interaction with men or "male" energy within career

MIDHEAVEN and CHIRON: healing related to career; analytical thinking as part of life work

MIDHEAVEN and JUPITER: teaching, advertising, or travel, as part of career; strong ethics as part of Universal purpose

MIDHEAVEN and SATURN: authority or executive positions as part of career path; Universal purpose related to responsibility; impact of father on life work

MIDHEAVEN and URANUS: erratic career path; life work related to technology, the "cause," or futuristic visions

MIDHEAVEN and NEPTUNE: confusion regarding career path; life work involving intuitive or imaginative skills

MIDHEAVEN and PLUTO: strong sense of divine mission in life work; career path involving use of power

The Ascendant in Aspect

ASCENDANT IN ASPECT TO ANY PLANET OR POINT:

- The identity you present to others and your role, title, or persona are shaped, affected, and influenced by the force of the other Planet or Point by [*insert phrase for Aspect*] it.

- The personality part represented by that other Planet or Point [*insert phrase for Aspect*] your ability to express yourself from your own individual point of view.

- The other Planet or Point can also represent the ways in which you get stuck in your own reality and forget to consider broader perspectives.

SPECIFIC ASCENDANT ASPECTS

ASCENDANT and ANY PLANET OR POINT: talents and issues derived from responding to Earthly purpose or personal appearance

ASCENDANT and MOON: personality or appearance influenced by mother; nurturance as part of persona

ASCENDANT and MERCURY: communication as part of personality; manual dexterity

ASCENDANT and VENUS: art and creativity as part of personality; identification with women or "female" energy in persona or appearance

ASCENDANT and SUN: shining self-expression as part of personality; relatedness between inner soul and outer persona

ASCENDANT and MARS: assertiveness and physical activity as part of personality; identification with men or "male" energy in persona or appearance

ASCENDANT and CHIRON: problem-solving qualities in personality; detail-oriented in appearance; health conscious in persona

ASCENDANT and JUPITER: tallness or fatness in appearance; search for knowledge as part of persona; teacher or preacher personality

ASCENDANT and SATURN: shortness or thinness in appearance; urge to control or assume authority as part of persona; appearance or personality influenced by father

ASCENDANT and URANUS: erratic or nonconforming in personality; unusual or "foreign" appearance; futuristic thinking as part of persona

ASCENDANT and NEPTUNE: vague or confused personality; imaginative or "soft" appearance; intuitive or psychic persona

ASCENDANT and PLUTO: powerful persona; charismatic in appearance and impact; compulsive personality

The Moon in Aspect

THE MOON IN ASPECT TO ANY POINT:

- Your urge to create emotional security and belongingness will shape, affect, and influence the personality part represented by that Point by [insert phrase for Aspect] it.

- That part of you will be [insert phrase for Aspect] your Moon's ability to comfort and nurture you and others.

- Your experience of your mother or other nurturers will be [insert phrase for Aspect] your experience of that Point.

- You may sometimes feel that your tendency to be emotional overrides the functions of the Point by [*insert phrase for Aspect*] it.

THE MOON IN ASPECT TO ANY PLANET:

- Your urge to create emotional security and belongingness will be shaped, affected, and influenced by the function of that Planet in a [*insert phrase for Aspect*] manner.
- The personality part represented by that Planet will tend to override your emotional needs by [*insert phrase for Aspect*] them.
- It will, however, consider your feelings and attempt to [*insert phrase for Aspect*] your Moon's emotions as it acts.
- This part also [*insert phrase for Aspect*] your drive to comfort and nurture yourself and others.
- Your experience of your mother or other nurturers will be [*insert phrase for Aspect*] the ways that you use the slower Planet.
- On occasion, you may sense that your emotional sensitivity is being [*insert phrase for Aspect*] the slow Planet's behavior.

SPECIFIC MOON ASPECTS

MOON and ANY PLANET OR POINT: talents and issues derived from responding to mother

MOON and MERCURY: instinctive or emotional communication

MOON and VENUS: intuitive esthetic sense; comfort from women or "female" energy

MOON and SUN: urge to use consciousness to uncover unconscious patterns

MOON and MARS: unconscious desires; comfort from men or "male" energy

MOON and CHIRON: instinctive orientation to healing

MOON and JUPITER: urge to seek more nurturance; binge behavior

MOON and SATURN: talents and issues related to parenting

MOON and URANUS: nonconforming or unusual affectional or nurturing choices; strong intuitive sense; genius-like insights

MOON and NEPTUNE: instinctive psychic ability; lack of emotional boundaries; addictions

MOON and PLUTO: compulsive habits that need to be transformed

Mercury in Aspect

MERCURY IN ASPECT TO FASTER PLANETS
OR ANY POINT:

- Your urge to think logically and communicate will shape, affect, and influence the personality part represented by the faster Planet or Point who is [*insert phrase for Aspect*] it.

- That part of you will be [*insert phrase for Aspect*] your Mercury's curiosity and drive to form networks.

- Your experience of your siblings will be [*insert phrase for Aspect*] experience of that Point.

- You may sometimes feel that your tendency to babble and get distracted overrides the functions of the other Planet or Point by [*insert phrase for Aspect*] it.

MERCURY IN ASPECT TO ANY SLOWER PLANET:

- urge to think logically and communicate will be shaped, affected, and influenced by the function of the slower Planet in a [*insert phrase for Aspect*] manner.

- The personality part represented by that Planet will tend to override your mental processes by [*insert phrase for Aspect*] them.

- It will, however, consider them while it [*insert phrase for Aspect*] your Mercurian ideas.

- This part is usually [*insert phrase for Aspect*] to your desire to pursue variety and stimulation.

- Your experience of your siblings or neighbors will be [*insert phrase for Aspect*] the ways that you use the slower Planet.

- On occasion, you may sense that your ability to think clearly is being [*insert phrase for Aspect*] the slow Planet's behavior.

SPECIFIC MERCURY ASPECTS

MERCURY and VENUS: creativity with words; value placed on communication

MERCURY and SUN: personal expression through words; manual dexterity

MERCURY and MARS: assertiveness in communication

MERCURY and JUPITER: talking about it to figure it out; drive to speak what is known

MERCURY and SATURN: limits or structure related to speech or communication

MERCURY and CHIRON: precision in communication

MERCURY and URANUS: unique mind; quick mental connections

MERCURY and NEPTUNE: poetic talent or interest; propensity toward altered mental states

MERCURY and PLUTO: transformation in communication skills or patterns

Venus in Aspect

VENUS IN ASPECT TO ANY FASTER PLANET OR POINT:

- Your urge to support cooperative efforts and establish beauty and harmony will shape, affect, and influence the personality part represented by the faster Planet or Point who is [*insert phrase for Aspect*] it.

- That part of you will be [*insert phrase for Aspect*] your Venus's ability to magnetically attract things, people, and experiences of value.

- Your experience of women is also [*insert phrase for Aspect*] your use of that Planet or Point.

- You might sometimes feel that your tendency to be vain or indecisive overrides the functions of the other Planet or Point by [*insert phrase for Aspect* it.

VENUS IN ASPECT TO ANY SLOWER PLANET:

- Your urge to support cooperative efforts and establish beauty and harmony will be shaped, affected, and influenced by the function of the slower Planet in a [*insert phrase for Aspect*] manner.

- The personality part represented by that Planet will tend to override your negotiation skills by [*insert phrase for Aspect*] them.

- It will, however, consider your Venusian diplomacy while it [*insert phrase for Aspect*] it.

- This part is usually [*insert phrase for Aspect*] to your desire to create balance and peace.

- Your experience of women will be [*insert phrase for Aspect*] the ways that you use the slower Planet.

- On occasion, you may sense that your ability to express your artistic talents is being [*insert phrase for Aspect*] the slow Planet's behavior.

SPECIFIC VENUS ASPECTS

VENUS and SUN: personal expression through art and creativity; diplomatic orientation; urge to integrate "female" qualities into identity

VENUS and MARS: urge toward physical creativity; drive to combine "male" and "female" cultural roles

VENUS and JUPITER: urge to disseminate and share creativity or resources

VENUS and SATURN: urge to structure creativity or resources

VENUS and CHIRON: detail-oriented art or creativity; analysis of "female" energy

VENUS and URANUS: unusual or nonconforming creativity; urge to break out of "female" cultural roles

VENUS and NEPTUNE: talent or interest in dance or music; merger with "female" energy or women's roles; issues related to sugar metabolism

VENUS and PLUTO: regeneration of art or creativity; transformation of women's cultural roles

The Sun in Aspect

THE SUN IN ASPECT TO ANY FASTER PLANET OR POINT:

- Your urge to express your personal potential and shine will shape, affect, and influence the personality part represented by the faster Planet or Point who is [insert phrase for Aspect] it.

- That part of you will be [insert phrase for Aspect] your Sun's ability to illuminate everything around you.

- Your experience of your essential self also [insert phrase for Aspect] your use of that Planet or Point.

- You may sometimes feel that your tendency to be boastful or proud overrides the functions of the other Planet or Point by [insert phrase for Aspect] it.

THE SUN IN ASPECT TO ANY SLOWER PLANET:

- Your urge to express your personal potential and shine will be shaped, affected, and influenced by the function of the slower Planet in a [insert phrase for Aspect] manner.

- The personality part represented by that Planet will tend to override your energy and vitality by [insert phrase for Aspect] them.

- It will, however, try to consider your Sun's life force while it [*insert phrase for Aspect*] it.

- This part is usually [*insert phrase for Aspect*] to your desire to celebrate your individuality.

- Your experience of your essential self will be [*insert phrase for Aspect*] the ways that you use the slower Planet.

- On occasion, you may sense that your ability to be fully yourself is being [*insert phrase for Aspect*] the slow Planet's behavior.

SPECIFIC SUN ASPECTS

SUN and MARS: identity expressed physically; assertiveness as part of self-expression; identification with "male" energy

SUN and JUPITER: personal identity expressed philosophically; expansion and growth as part of self-discovery

SUN and SATURN: limits or structures around identity; influence of father on self-knowing or self-expression

SUN and CHIRON: urge toward personal perfection; healing as a part of self-expression

SUN and URANUS: identity associated with unusual perspectives; nonconformity as part of self-expression

SUN and NEPTUNE: lyrical self-expression; low physical energy; intuitive talents; confusion about identity

SUN and PLUTO: powerful self-expression; cyclical patterns of rebirthing identity; compulsiveness

Mars in Aspect

MARS IN ASPECT TO ANY FASTER PLANET OR POINT:

- Your urge to pursue your own desires and initiate movement will shape, affect, and influence the personality part represented by the faster Planet or Point who is [*insert phrase for Aspect*] it.

- That part of you will be [*insert phrase for Aspect*] your Mars's ability to go after what you want, when you want it.

- Your experience of men also [*insert phrase for Aspect*] your use of that Planet or Point.

- You may sometimes feel that your tendency to be pushy or inconsiderate overrides the functions of the other Planet or Point by [*insert phrase for Aspect*] it.

MARS IN ASPECT TO ANY SLOWER PLANET:

- Your urge to pursue your own desires and initiate movement will be shaped, affected, and influenced by the function of the slower Planet in a [insert phrase for Aspect] manner.

- The personality part represented by that Planet will tend to override your assertiveness by [insert phrase for Aspect] it.

- It will, however, consider your Mars's drive and energy while it [insert phrase for Aspect] it.

- This part is usually [insert phrase for Aspect] to your desire to take risks and inspire action.

- Your experience of men will also be [insert phrase for Aspect] the ways that you use the slower Planet.

- On occasion, you may sense that your ability to express your independence is being [insert phrase for Aspect] the slow Planet's behavior.

SPECIFIC MARS ASPECTS

MARS and JUPITER: drive for more physical activity; push toward freedom; expansion through "male" energy

MARS and SATURN: limits or structures around physical activity; issues related to use and abuse of control and discipline; limitations through "male" energy

MARS and CHIRON: drive for physical perfection; surgical talents; analysis of "male" energy

MARS and URANUS: assertiveness regarding unusual perspectives; accidents; urge to break out of men's cultural roles

MARS and NEPTUNE: lyrical physical movements; merger with "male" energy or men's roles; inactivity or fatigue

MARS and PLUTO: issues related to use and abuse of power; transformation of men's cultural roles

Jupiter in Aspect

JUPITER IN ASPECT TO ANY FASTER PLANET OR POINT:

- Your urge to seek the truth and expand your horizons will shape, affect, and influence the personality part represented by the faster Planet or Point who is [insert phrase for Aspect] it.

- That part of you will be [insert phrase for Aspect] your ability to teach or sell what you believe.

- Your experience of mentors or religious leaders also [*insert phrase for Aspect*] your use of that Planet or Point.
- You may sometimes feel that your tendency to be preachy or self-indulgent overrides the functions of the other Planet or Point by [*insert phrase for Aspect*] it.

JUPITER IN ASPECT TO ANY SLOWER PLANET:

- Your urge to seek the truth and expand your horizons will be shaped, affected, and influenced by the function of the slower Planet in a [*insert phrase for Aspect*] manner.
- The personality part represented by that Planet will tend to override your beliefs and ethical concerns by [*insert phrase for Aspect*] them.
- It will, however, consider your Jupiter morals while it is [*insert phrase for Aspect*] them.
- It is usually [*insert phrase for Aspect*] to your desire to practice what you preach.
- Your experience of mentors or religious leaders will also be [*insert phrase for Aspect*] the ways that you use the slower Planet.
- On occasion, you may sense that your ability to express your true philosophy is being [*insert phrase for Aspect*] the slow Planet's behavior.

SPECIFIC JUPITER ASPECTS

JUPITER and SATURN: discovery and expansion of social responsibility

JUPITER and CHIRON: urge to analyze *the* truth in detail

JUPITER and URANUS: breakthroughs regarding philosophy or science

JUPITER and NEPTUNE: spiritual or religious calling

JUPITER and PLUTO: philosophical or religious conversion

Saturn in Aspect

SATURN IN ASPECT TO ANY FASTER PLANET OR POINT:

- Your urge to build structures and set limits will shape, affect, and influence the personality part represented by the faster Planet or Point who is [*insert phrase for Aspect*] it.
- That part of you will be [*insert phrase for Aspect*] your ability to establish authority.

- Your experience of your father or other authority figures also [*insert phrase for Aspect*] your use of that Planet or Point.

- You may sometimes feel that your tendency to be rigid or domineering overrides the functions of the other Planet or Point by [*insert phrase for Aspect*] it.

SATURN IN ASPECT TO ANY SLOWER PLANET:

- Your urge to build structures and set limits will be shaped, affected, and influenced by the function of the slower Planet in a [*insert phrase for Aspect*] manner.

- The personality part represented by that Planet will tend to override your conservation skills by [*insert phrase for Aspect*] them.

- It will, however, consider your Saturn's caution while it [*insert phrase for Aspect*] it.

- This part is usually [*insert phrase for Aspect*] to your desire to establish order.

- Your experience of your father or other authority figures will also be [*insert phrase for Aspect*] the ways that you use the slower Planet.

- On occasion, you may sense that your ability to express your authority and responsibility is being [*insert phrase for Aspect*] the other Planet's behavior.

SPECIFIC SATURN ASPECTS

SATURN and ANY PLANET: talents or issues derived from responding to father

SATURN and CHIRON: analysis of structures and systems; urge to be perfectly responsible

SATURN and URANUS: urge to radically change societal patterns and structures

SATURN and NEPTUNE: spiritual application of practical abilities; urge to avoid or ignore the rules and authorities

SATURN and PLUTO: issues related to use and abuse of power and control

Chiron in Aspect

CHIRON IN ASPECT TO ANY FASTER PLANET OR POINT:

- Your urge to heal and create ideal conditions will shape, affect, and influence the personality part represented by the faster Planet or Point who is [*insert phrase for Aspect*] it.
- That part of you will be [*insert phrase for Aspect*] your ability to fix whatever's wrong.
- Your experience of healers also [*insert phrase for Aspect*] your use of that Planet or Point.
- You may sometimes feel that your tendency to be critical or fussy overrides the functions of the other Planet or Point by [*insert phrase for Aspect*] it.

CHIRON IN ASPECT TO ANY SLOWER PLANET:

- Your urge to heal and create ideal conditions will be shaped, affected, and influenced by the function of the slower Planet in a [*insert phrase for Aspect*] manner.
- The personality part represented by that Planet will tend to override your analytical skills by [*insert phrase for Aspect*] them.
- It will, however, consider your Chiron's awareness of details while it [*insert phrase for Aspect*] it.
- This part is usually [*insert phrase for Aspect*] to your desire to solve problems and correct errors.
- Your experience of healers will also be [*insert phrase for Aspect*] the ways that you use the slower Planet.
- On occasion, you may sense that your ability to perform repairs and make amends is being [*insert phrase for Aspect*] the other Planet's behavior.

SPECIFIC CHIRON ASPECTS

CHIRON and URANUS: breakthroughs in all kinds of analysis, including medical

CHIRON and NEPTUNE: specific healing abilities

CHIRON and PLUTO: intense drive to fix the Earth

Uranus in Aspect

URANUS IN ASPECT TO ANY FASTER PLANET OR POINT:

- Your urge to break out of old patterns and rebel will shape, affect, and influence the personality part represented by the faster Planet or Point who is [insert phrase for Aspect] it.

- That part of you will be [insert phrase for Aspect] your Uranus's ability to move you beyond the status quo.

- Your experience of future-oriented visionaries also [insert phrase for Aspect] your use of that Planet or Point.

- You may sometimes feel that your tendency to be erratic or disruptive overrides the functions of the other Planet or Point by [insert phrase for Aspect] it.

URANUS IN ASPECT TO ANY SLOWER PLANET:

- Your urge to break out of old patterns and rebel will be shaped, affected, and influenced by the function of the slower Planet in a [insert phrase for Aspect] manner.

- The personality part represented by that Planet will tend to override your nonconformity and innovative tendencies by [insert phrase for Aspect] them.

- It will, however, consider your Uranus's nontraditional concepts while it [insert phrase for Aspect] it.

- This part is usually [insert phrase for Aspect] to your desire to improve conditions for the entire group.

- Your experience of future-oriented visionaries will be [insert phrase for Aspect] the ways that you use the slower Planet.

- On occasion, you may sense that your ability to be unique and eccentric is being [insert phrase for Aspect] the slow Planet's behavior.

SPECIFIC URANUS ASPECTS

URANUS and NEPTUNE: unusual spirituality

URANUS and PLUTO: explosive transformation

Neptune in Aspect

NEPTUNE IN ASPECT TO ANY FASTER PLANET
OR POINT

- Your urge to imagine, dream and fantasize will shape, affect, and influence the personality part represented by the faster Planet or Point who is [*insert phrase for Aspect*] it.

- That part of you will be [*insert phrase for Aspect*] your Neptune's ability to have faith and to intuitively empathize with everyone around you.

- Your experience of psychics or spiritual leaders also [*insert phrase for Aspect*] your use of that Planet or Point.

- You may sometimes feel that your tendency to be confused or paranoid overrides the functions of the other Planet or Point by [*insert phrase for Aspect*] it.

NEPTUNE IN ASPECT TO THE SLOWER PLANET:

- Your urge to imagine, dream, and fantasize will be shaped, affected, and influenced by the function of the slower Planet in a [*insert phrase for Aspect*] manner.

- The personality part represented by that Planet will tend to override your faith and trust by [*insert phrase for Aspect*] them.

- It will, however, consider your Neptune's spiritual involvement while it [*insert phrase for Aspect*] it.

- This part is usually [*insert phrase for Aspect*] to your desire to merge with others and feel their experiences.

- Your experience of psychics or spiritual leaders will be [*insert phrase for Aspect*] the ways that you use the slower Planet.

- On occasion, you may sense that your ability to be fully intuitive is being [*insert phrase for Aspect*] the slow Planet's behavior.

SPECIFIC NEPTUNE ASPECT

NEPTUNE and PLUTO: spiritual transformation; addictive compulsions

Pluto in Aspect

PLUTO IN ASPECT TO ANY FASTER PLANET
OR POINT:

- Your urge to utilize power and move through large cycles of change will shape, affect, and influence the personality part represented by the faster Planet or Point who is [*insert phrase for Aspect*] it.

- That part of you will be [*insert phrase for Aspect*] your Pluto's ability to transform everything around and within you.

- Your experience of powerful people and forces also [*insert phrase for Aspect*] your use of that Planet or Point.

- You might sometimes feel that your tendency to be destructive and merciless overrides the functions of the other Planet or Point by [*insert phrase for Aspect*] it.

PLUTO IS THE SLOWEST PLANET, SO IT CAN'T ASPECT ANY SLOWER PLANETS.

INTERPRETATIONS FOR
THE RULING PLANETS IN ASPECT

As demonstrated in the Ruling Planet Aspect Interpretation Strategy, the Planets do impact each other as the representatives of their Signs (and Houses). Figure 7-3, at the end of this chapter, is a table that shows some examples of ways to describe these Rulers in Aspect. To use this table, choose a pair of Planets that are in Aspect to analyze. Then, pick a topic from the first column that's related to the House Ruled by one Planet, add a key word for the Aspect, and choose a topic from the third column that's related to the House Ruled by the other Planet.

Once again, remember that these are just ideas and possibilities. *You* choose the ones that make sense; you create new combinations!

SUMMARY

In this Chapter, I've described the Aspects in expanded detail. I've emphasized that they represent the ways in which the Planets and Points interact with each other. I've also shown that no Aspect is "good" or "bad." Each one, whether it's Blending or Challenging by nature, can be used effectively or ineffectively. Briefly, the Aspects link the Planets and Points in the following ways:

CONJUNCTION: uniting and joining
SEMI-SEXTILE: fine-tuning and subtly adapting
SEXTILE: supporting and finding resources
SQUARE: motivating and challenging
TRINE: enhancing and pooling skills
QUINCUNX: redirecting and surprising
OPPOSITION: counteracting and balancing

EXERCISES

7-1 Find and interpret all the Aspects in your Chart. Use the Aspect interpretation strategies.

7-2 Find and interpret the Aspects in someone else's Chart. Ask that person for feedback about your accuracy.

7-3 Take the list of issues and concerns that you've developed in Exercises 4-2, 5-3, and 6-3. For each one:

a. Find any Planets or Points that Aspect the Planets or Points within the House related to this concern.

b. Delineate how you're currently using each of these Planets or Points, according to their nature and according to the Aspects they form, to maintain the status quo.

c. Think of three other ways that you could use these Planets or Points, according to their nature and according to the Aspects they form, to change the status quo.

d. Go through steps a, b, and c with Planets or Points that Aspect the Ruling Planets of the Signs on (or in) this House.

e. Save your ideas and insights for later use.

7-4 Using the lists from Exercises 4-3, 5-4, and 6-4, go through the process outlined in Exercise 7-3 with your friend.

ACTIVITIES RELATED TO THESE ISSUES AS REPRESENTED BY THE (House #) RULER	INTERACT IN THIS WAY WITH	
1: APPEARANCE CONCERNS SELF-AWARENESS ISSUES PERSONALITY FEATURES	CO:	ARE INCORPORATED INTO UNITE WITH SMOTHER
2: MONEY CONCERNS SELF-ESTEEM ISSUES PERSONAL POSSESSIONS		
3: COMMUNITY INTERESTS COMMUNICATION ISSUES SIBLINGS	SS:	FINE-TUNE SUBTLY ADAPT IRRITATE
4: CONCERNS ABOUT FAMILY RESIDENCE ISSUES MOTHER OR NURTURERS	SX:	SUPPORT REINFORCE MEDDLE WITH
5: CONCERNS ABOUT ROMANCE ISSUES ABOUT CREATIVITY CHILDREN		
6: CONCERNS ABOUT WORK HEALTH ISSUES PETS	SQ:	MOTIVATE PRESSURE CONFRONT
7: CONCERNS ABOUT RELATING ISSUES ABOUT COOPERATION PARTNERS		
8: CONCERNS ABOUT JOINT RESOURCES INTIMACY ISSUES SEXUAL PARTNERS	TR:	ENHANCE COMPOUND TAKE FOR GRANTED
9: CONCERNS ABOUT HIGHER EDUCATION ETHICAL ISSUES MENTORS AND TEACHERS		
10: CONCERNS ABOUT CAREER ISSUES REGARDING REPUTATION FATHER OR AUTHORITY FIGURES	QU:	REDIRECT DETOUR INTERRUPT
11: CONCERNS ABOUT THE FUTURE ISSUES REGARDING GOALS FRIENDS AND ACQUAINTANCES		
12: CONCERNS ABOUT SPIRITUALITY ISSUES REGARDING ADDICTIONS PSYCHIC INFLUENCES	OP:	COUNTERACT COUNTERBALANCE CONTRADICT

Figure 7-3
The Ruling Planets in Aspect

**ACTIVITIES RELATED TO THESE
ISSUES AS REPRESENTED BY
THE (House #) RULER**

1: APPEARANCE CONCERNS
SELF-AWARENESS ISSUES
PERSONALITY FEATURES

2: MONEY CONCERNS
SELF-ESTEEM ISSUES
PERSONAL POSSESSIONS

3: COMMUNITY INTERESTS
COMMUNICATION ISSUES
SIBLINGS

4: CONCERNS ABOUT FAMILY
RESIDENCE ISSUES
MOTHER OR NURTURERS

5: CONCERNS ABOUT ROMANCE
ISSUES ABOUT CREATIVITY
CHILDREN

6: CONCERNS ABOUT WORK
HEALTH ISSUES
PETS

7: CONCERNS ABOUT RELATING
ISSUES ABOUT COOPERATION
PARTNERS

8: CONCERNS ABOUT JOINT RESOURCES
INTIMACY ISSUES
SEXUAL PARTNERS

9: CONCERNS ABOUT HIGHER EDUCATION
ETHICAL ISSUES
MENTORS AND TEACHERS

10: CONCERNS ABOUT CAREER
ISSUES REGARDING REPUTATION
FATHER OR AUTHORITY FIGURES

11: CONCERNS ABOUT THE FUTURE
ISSUES REGARDING GOALS
FRIENDS AND ACQUAINTANCES

12: CONCERNS ABOUT SPIRITUALITY
ISSUES REGARDING ADDICTIONS
PSYCHIC INFLUENCES

EIGHT
Reading a Natal Chart

A READING of your Natal Chart will give you a sense of its general themes and patterns. Since it's easy to get immersed in the detailed analysis of the Houses, Signs, Planets, Points, their Positions, their Rulerships, and their Aspects, an overall analysis can give you a broader perspective. In this Chapter, I'll discuss some techniques that will help you approach and organize the data that the Chart reveals. Specifically, I'll give you some ideas for how to structure your Readings and phrase your interpretations. And, at the end of the Chapter, I'll include two Tables that may help you integrate your Readings. One of them uses key words that can be combined to interpret the Planets and Points in the Signs and Houses. The other is a Quick Reference List for finding the Houses, Signs, Planets, and Points associated with specific issues.

As usual, remember that these are just ideas. As you continue to explore the world of Astrology, you'll find that some Astrological configurations seem more important to you than others. As you discover which features you want to emphasize, you may naturally develop a "plan" for doing Readings. If you don't have one yet, the Reading plans I've included in this Chapter can be catalysts for you. Use them as they are for as long as they're useful to you. Then, combine and recombine the steps into sequences that make sense to you. And, finally, create your own approach to Astrology Readings, an approach that reflects your personal philosophy and orientation.

I've organized this Chapter similarly to Chapters 2 and 3, in that I've included both fundamentals and details. So, as you get ready to "read" your Chart and those of your friends and family, you can choose whether to give yourself a basic Reading or a more advanced one.

THE READING FUNDAMENTALS

From reading Chapter 3, you already know most of the factors that are notable in terms of Chart interpretation. In order to do a Reading, you simply take those factors and organize them in a READING SEQUENCE for presentation. Use of a sequence will help you feel confident that you've covered all the significant features when doing a Reading for yourself. If you're working with friends or family members, it'll give you a way to structure what you have to tell them.

The Fundamental Reading Sequence

1. First, present an OVERVIEW of the Chart by discussing one or more of the following factors:

    a. The number of RETROGRADES, excluding the Nodes. This indicates whether you tend to figure things out for yourself (4 or more Retrograde Planets) or utilize other people's examples (0–3 Retrograde Planets).

    b. Houses or Signs that are "LOADED" with three or more Planets or Points. These indicate that you have an emphasis in that part of the Chart. You will probably strongly utilize the energy of the Loaded Sign or seek many experiences related to the concerns of the Loaded House.

    c. The INTERCEPTED AND DUPLICATED SIGNS. These indicate something about the way you were raised. By analyzing them you can discover the qualities that your family reinforced appropriately (Duplicated Signs) and those that your family tended not to support appropriately (Intercepted).

2. Then, interpret the PLANETS BY POSITION AND RULERSHIP. Discuss the ways in which each one fulfills its function according to its Sign and House. Talk about the impact this has on the Sign (and therefore, House) it Rules.

3. Now, interpret the POINTS BY POSITION.

    a. Discuss the balance of inflow and outflow created by the Nodal Axis.

    b. Describe the Part of Fortune as the Point of personal integration.

    c. Analyze the Midheaven and Ascendant as the representatives of the Universal and Earthly environments.

    4. Last, interpret the PLANETS AND POINTS BY ASPECT. Use the four Aspect interpretation strategies to do so.

    If you interpret your Chart according to the four main steps that I've just outlined, you'll find that you have a good fundamental understanding of your natal potential and themes. If you want to understand your Chart or those of others even more thoroughly, you can choose to go into a more detailed Reading.

THE READING DETAILS

For an expanded analysis of your Natal Chart, you can utilize several techniques that will expand Step 1. You can also enhance the approach you take to interpretation in Steps 2, 3, and 4. In the following sections, I'll show you what to look for in a more detailed Reading and I'll also give you some phrases to use when presenting each concept.

Step 1: The Overview

In order to give yourself or someone else a detailed Chart Overview, you'll need to add a few features to the ones listed in the fundamental section. These factors emerge when you analyze a Chart according to overall planetary groupings within it. The groupings, which are quite obvious in an accurate Chart, symbolize certain personality themes. In this part of the Chapter, I'll discuss the groupings by SECTION, CHART PATTERN, and ASPECT PATTERN. I'll also point out some OTHER NOTICEABLE AND NOTABLE FEATURES that help define Chart emphasis.

SECTIONS

An initial scan of the Chart will reveal the positioning of the Planets and other Points with regard to the Chart SECTIONS. These Sections are defined according to the QUADRANTS AND HEMISPHERES that were described in Chapter 4. As a reminder, Figure 8-1 shows the Hemispheres and Quadrants for a generic Chart.

A Quadrant or Hemisphere is emphasized in your Chart if most, or many, of the Planets seem to fall within it. An obvious Hemisphere or Quadrant focus may set the tone for your whole Chart interpretation. On the other hand, if your Chart doesn't have a Sectional focus, don't struggle to make one fit. Not every Chart will have this, or any other, feature. If you have a Quadrant or Hemisphere emphasis, you can interpret it as follows:

Since the SOUTHERN HEMISPHERE represents the PUBLIC portion of life, if you have a planetary focus in the top of the Chart you'll tend to orient yourself to the world at large. Your talents and accomplishments will be noticeable publicly. You'll want to obtain and increase your conscious awareness and knowledge. You'll make an effort to fit in with the greater scheme of things, philosophically or practically. You'll view life objectively. "WHAT'S GOING ON OUT THERE?" is your question.

Since the NORTHERN HEMISPHERE represents the PRIVATE portion of life, if you have many Planets at the bottom of the Chart, you'll be more introspective and focused on your inner reality. Home, roots, and founda-

Figure 8-1
The Sections

tions will play an important role in your life. You'll tend to seek out intuitive insights and to be motivated by your unconscious awareness. Your accomplishments will have personal value, and your talents will be shared privately. You'll be aware of the subjective dimensions of life. "WHAT'S GOING ON INSIDE?" you'll wonder.

Since the EASTERN HEMISPHERE represents the part of the Chart that is oriented to SELF-AWARENESS, self-sufficiency, and personal growth, if you have this focus, you'll usually take a proactive role in life. You'll tend to initiate things, assert yourself, and pursue "it." You may not always know what you want, but you do know that, once you discover your direction, you can count on yourself to go after it. As you lead your life, others follow – whether or not you've invited them. Your guiding question will be "WHAT DO I WANT TO DO OR DISCOVER NEXT?"

Since the WESTERN HEMISPHERE reflects OTHER-AWARENESS, receptivity to feedback, and growth in relationships, if you have a right-side emphasis you'll tend to react to others and respond to their direction. You'll support collective efforts and cooperate with others as much as possible. Being *part* of "it" is more important to you than pursuing it. You know that you can count on others, and they can rely on you. You'll look around for an inspiring leader or group and join up. You'll want to know "WHAT ARE *WE* DOING OR DISCOVERING NEXT?"

The interpretations of the FOUR QUADRANTS follow quite naturally from those of the Hemispheres:

If the FIRST QUADRANT, which is both self-oriented and private, is emphasized in your Chart, you'll focus on personal discovery and self-awareness without too much interest in the involvement of others or in public acclaim. "WHO AM I?" and "WHAT DO I WANT TO EXPERIENCE IN MY PRIVATE LIFE?" you'll ask.

If the SECOND QUADRANT, which is other-oriented and private, is your focus, your home, family, and co-workers will be important to you. You'll want feedback and insight from others about your thoughts, feelings, and creativity. "WHO ARE YOU?" and "WHAT SHALL WE EXPERIENCE PRIVATELY?" are your questions.

If the THIRD QUADRANT, which is other-oriented and public, is strongly inhabited in your Chart, you'll be continually involved with others in an obvious, socially noticeable way. You might be emotionally, legally, or philosophically committed to them or to their teachings. You'll ask "WHO ARE YOU?" and "HOW DO YOU AND THE WORLD HAVE AN IMPACT ON ME?"

If the FOURTH QUADRANT, which is self-oriented and public, is important in your Chart, you'll want to express yourself in public. You'll become known for your opinions; you'll be willing to act on your beliefs. And, you'll pursue your growth and interests in ways that will affect the world at large. You'll inquire, "WHO AM I?" and "HOW CAN I HAVE AN IMPACT ON THE WORLD?"

In Janie's Chart, the First Quadrant is clearly the emphasized one (Fig. 8-2). So, much of her life will revolve around the question of discovering herself within her personal life.

Figure 8-2:
Janie's Chart

In Grace's Chart, no Quadrant is particularly emphasized, but the Northern Hemisphere (bottom) of the Chart is definitely more inhabited by Planets than the Southern (Fig. 8-3). She'll focus more intently on establishing a strong personal and home life, both independently and with others, than on moving out into the world.

Figure 8-3:
Grace's Chart

Phrases to Use in Interpreting the Sectional Emphasis

"I find it interesting that most of your Planets fall in this [*name Section*] portion of your Chart. That's the part that has the most to do with [*interpret emphasis*]. So, your Chart and your life emphasize these interests."

CHART PATTERNS

In addition to the sectional emphasis, your Chart may reflect an overall planetary pattern that is significant. If so, the Planets will be grouped in a CHART PATTERN that is often easily identifiable. Traditionally, the Nodes of the Moon, and the Part of Fortune are not considered when figuring out Chart Patterns. Therefore, I have left them out when creating the following examples. In my work, if their inclusion completes or changes a Pattern, I sometimes consider them, but I don't give these Points the same weight as the Planets. Because the Midheaven and the Ascendant are always located in certain parts of the Chart, they are never counted when determining Chart Patterns. The most common Patterns and their basic meanings are described here. As you look for them in your Charts, be aware that not every Chart will have one of them. Also, remember that the Patterns can fall in various locations. They are not limited to the placements shown in the examples.

The Locomotive

The LOCOMOTIVE PATTERN looks like a pie with a piece missing. The empty space, or the missing piece, usually covers about 90°–120°, or the equivalent of three or four Signs. That open space can fall in any section of the Chart.

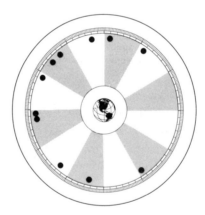

Figure 8-4
The Locomotive Chart Pattern

The Locomotive symbolizes aggressive pursuit, usually of the qualities and experiences symbolized in the empty space. If you have this pattern, you have a tried and true style of pursuing your goals which you use effectively and sometimes relentlessly. Like a locomotive, once you're on track with a full head of steam, you're hard to stop. In fact, you have a natural ability to inspire others to get on your train or join your project. Your enthusiasm and charisma sometimes influence others to overly commit themselves. These companions, fueled by your locomotive energy instead of by their own enthusiasm, may abandon you or your project later. By then, you could be feeling burdened by having to keep everyone going and resentful of their lack of commitment. You will probably have greater success with cooperative projects if you encourage others to take plenty of time to evaluate whether they want to participate. A single hour of true involvement is often worth more than eight unpredictable hours. And, an honest NO is easier to handle than an unreliable YES. Lack of commitment can be a bit difficult for you to understand since you fully commit yourself and are seldom deterred from accomplishing your objectives.

The Wedge

The WEDGE, or BUNDLE, is the opposite of the Locomotive in that all the Planets are grouped within approximately four Signs, a distance of about 120°. The grouping can, of course, fall in any portion of the Chart.

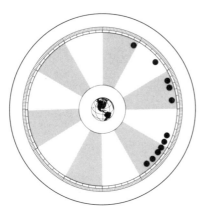

Figure 8-5
The Wedge Chart Pattern

The Wedge is a pattern of extreme focus and intensity. If you have this pattern, you'll be happiest when you're choosing a few goals and concentrating all the force of your personality on them. You're not as concerned with multiple opportunities but rather with fully utilizing a few. In fact, you have a talent for making a little bit of anything go a long way. If others are drawn to your intensity, you'll accept them, though you've done little to actively seek them out. When they *do* appear, you'll effectively utilize every ounce of their talent and ability. Your personal specialty can become an obsession, more important than either yourself or others. But, your ability to concentrate and mobilize resources is truly incredible.

The Tripod

The TRIPOD (SPLAY) PATTERN has three evenly spaced groups of Planets with empty spaces in between them. Each blank space is 60°–90° or the equivalent of two or three Signs. A single Planet might form one of the "groups" though usually there is more than one Planet in each group.

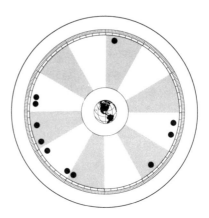

Figure 8-6
The Tripod Chart Pattern

The Tripod represents a sure and solid base. If this is symbolized in your Chart, you know that, whatever happens, you'll land on your feet and balance yourself again. With this surety, you can approach life with confidence, knowing that you can do almost anything you want. Despite that assurance, your interests will probably be fairly narrow in scope. You'll have a creative approach to your chosen field and will probably become an expert in it. Once you're established, you'll tend to stick with your initial brilliant concept. As circumstances change, others may take your ideas and expand or adapt them, but you may not choose to move beyond the initial vision yourself. You may have limited tolerance for those who face struggles and obstacles because you rarely experience frustration. You can provide a role model, however, since you're a shining example of a gifted individual.

The Bowl

The BOWL is an obvious hemispheric pattern, but it does not have to be defined by the horizontal or vertical axis of the Chart. If all of the Planets fall in one half, any half, of the Chart, it's a Bowl.

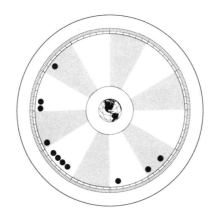

Figure 8-7
The Bowl Chart Pattern

The Bowl Chart emphasizes containment and inclusion. If this is your pattern, your energy is focused in a broad, but defined, direction that incorporates your own talents with those of others. While you want to participate in collective goals and fit into the movements and trends of your group, subculture, or era, you don't want to lose yourself in the process. You want your personal talents to be utilized – for the greater good. You can effectively and independently represent the group because you are committed to everyone else and are also personally reliable. Depending on the Quadrants that are emphasized in your Chart, your "groups" could be personal growth companions (First Quadrant), family and clan (Second Quadrant), partners and intimates (Third Quadrant), or fellow devotees of a "cause" (Fourth Quadrant).

The Bucket and Fanhandle

The BUCKET and the FANHANDLE patterns are so related that it's possible to discuss them together. The Bucket is a Bowl with a single Planet forming a handle while the Fanhandle is a Wedge with a planetary handle. Usually, the handle Planet is opposite the center of the grouped Planets, but sometimes, it will be off-center.

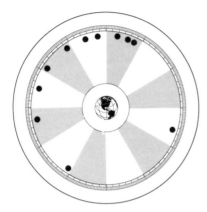 

Figure 8-8
The Bucket Chart Pattern

Figure 8-9
The Fanhandle Chart Pattern

The Bucket and Fanhandle patterns express the concept of personal integration. If this is your kind of Chart, the separated Planet probably symbolizes a significant or problematic issue that has needed resolution in your life. In each phase of your life, as you've figured out how to utilize the functions of your handle Planet positively, you've found that everything has flowed more smoothly. You'll probably need to go through the pattern of integration a number of times because, at each stage in life, the handle Planet comes to signify slightly different things. Nevertheless, each time you resolve another attribute of that Planet, you feel a sense of relief and peace. Understandably, you may be very involved, even obsessed with, using your handle Planet. It's been your challenge to learn to use it positively and productively. The distinction between these two patterns is that the Fanhandle represents a very focused integration process, since the base of its pattern is a Wedge; the Bucket pattern symbolizes a broader selection of integration styles.

The See-Saw

The SEE-SAW (HOUR-GLASS) pattern looks just like its name. It consists of two or more Planets in a fairly tight grouping, opposite the rest of the Planets, which are also grouped together. The two groups can, of course, fall in any Hemispheres and Quadrants as long as they're opposite each other. Ideally, each of the empty spaces between them contain at least 60° (or about two Signs).

Figure 8-10
The See-Saw Chart Pattern

The See-Saw pattern reflects the process of balance. If this is your Chart pattern, you can always see both sides of any issue, whether it involves yourself, others, or a whole group. You are most comfortable when everything is flexible and everyone can be right. In fact, you can be a good negotiator or mediator. You can coordinate opposing points of view and integrate conflicting ideas. Sometimes, you have a hard time making final decisions and coming to conclusions because there's always one more perspective or piece of data to be included. As a result, you may waver about a decision for eons as you gather information and repeatedly adjust your plans. Fortunately, you usually enjoy the balancing act.

The Splash

In the SPLASH pattern, the Planets are scattered over the whole Chart. Ideally, it has Planets dispersed into almost every House and Sign and it contains no empty spaces bigger than 60°.

The Splash Chart symbolizes variety. If you have this pattern, you have a multitude of interests and abilities. You're fascinated by the stimulation available in the world and feel free to express yourself in many ways. This multi-dimensional orientation to life could indicate that you hop around in terms of careers or relationships, but that doesn't have to be the case. You could maintain a single (but not boring) base in these areas and express your other personality facets through hobbies, travel, or community activities. You'll probably feel frustrated if you try to focus or limit your life too much. And, it may be useful for you to remember that the modern,

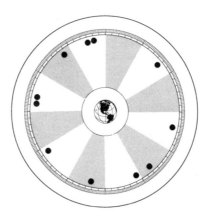

Figure 8-11
The Splash Chart Pattern

Western world is linear, goal-oriented, and directed by nature. You, on the other hand, are more instinctively holistic and spherical in your approach to life. Rest assured that, eventually, all the threads of your life will form a tapestry.

Janie's Chart is a definite FAN-HANDLE (Fig. 8-12). Most of her Planets fall in the First Quadrant with Retrograde Chiron, off by itself, in Gemini in the 7th House. So, she'll get a handle on life by positively utilizing Retrograde Chiron. This means that she'll be curiously looking (GE) for ways to fix, mend, and heal herself (R CH) through a variety (GE) of one-to-one relationships (7).

Figure 8-12: Janie's Chart

As she does this, she'll find that her quest for identity, symbolized by the Wedge in the First Quadrant, will be enhanced. On the other hand, if she gets too caught up in finding many ways (GE) of being overly self-critical (R CH), she could feel that she's not "good enough" for a relationship (7). This would have a negative influence on her sense of identity and self-worth (First Quadrant).

Grace's Chart is a Locomotive with the empty space in the Third Quadrant (Fig. 8-13). This woman will be hard to stop. She'll move forward in life and make "it" happen. Since the Third Quadrant is empty, she'll be seeking relationships with others in the public sphere as she charismatically inspires them to ride into adventure with her.

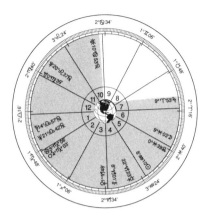

Figure 8-13: Grace's Chart

On the other hand, she could also use her Locomotive energy to ride roughshod over those very relationships she seeks. Out of her fear of not understanding the nature of give and take in relationships (empty Third Quadrant), she could try to control and direct others (Locomotive). In that case, she would still feel that she was missing something and be motivated to seek "it" even harder.

Phrases to Use in Interpreting Chart Patterns

"Notice how these Planets over here form this shape with these other Planets? [*Describe Chart Pattern shape*]. That Pattern is called a [*name Chart Pattern*]. It means that, in your life, you tend to [*interpret Chart Pattern*]."

ASPECT PATTERNS

ASPECT PATTERNS, or combinations of Aspects, are often apparent in an Aspect analysis. These patterns emerge when two or more planetary Aspects interconnect. For example, if several Conjunctions occur in the same location, the result is called a Stellium. If a Square and an Opposition hook up to each other, they form a T-Square. These multiple Aspects are important because they reflect the most primary and recurrent themes in the Chart. Most Charts contain at least one major Aspect Pattern; some contain many.

One strategy for finding Aspect Patterns is to look for combinations of Aspects by Quality and Element. Look at all the Cardinal, then Fixed, and then Mutable Signs, noticing if several Planets or Points fall at similar Degrees within one Quality. Do the same for the Elements; look at the Fire, Earth, Air, and Water Signs. Then, remember to check for out-of-Sign, out-of-Quality, and out-of-Element possibilities.

Five of the most important Aspect Patterns are discussed in the following sections. They are the STELLIUM, T-SQUARE, GRAND CROSS, GRAND TRINE, and the YOD. After you understand them, you can logically combine these five Aspect Patterns with other Aspects and with each other to form even more complicated Aspect Patterns. A few of these other possibilities are named and described briefly in Appendix G.

When looking for Aspect Patterns, it's important to remember that they can pop up in any location of the Chart. They are not limited to the Houses shown in the examples. It's also useful to bear in mind that the tighter the Aspects, the stronger the pattern; the wider the Aspects, the weaker the pattern. Additionally, whenever the Aspects cross Sign or House boundaries, the patterns will be experienced less intensely.

The Stellium

THE STELLIUM is a pattern that combines four or more Planets that are Conjunct. The Planets at the outer edges of the group may not Conjunct each other technically, but they are pulled together by the intermediate Planets. Generally, the whole spread is contained within 16°.

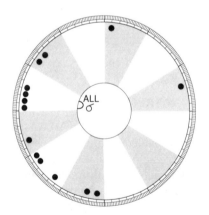

Figure 8-14
The Stellium Aspect Pattern

A STELLIUM focuses attention or drive quite intensely in its location. The Planets work in concert to express their united functions, in the manner of their Signs, with regard to the issues of their Houses. Utilization of their joint energy has far-reaching impact, because any action they take affects the four or more Houses that the Stellium Planets naturally Rule. If you have a Stellium, you may use it to the exclusion of all other planetary forces, since its expression has such a huge influence on many areas of life. On the other hand, you may ignore the themes of your Stellium in the hopes of avoiding massive life changes. Planets that Trine or Square the Stellium Planets can be catalysts that inspire or pressure them to act.

The T-Square

THE T-SQUARE, or T-Cross, is formed when a Planet Squares two Opposing Planets. In other words, it's half-way between them, forming Squares to both of them.

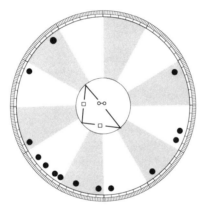

Figure 8-15
The T-Square Aspect Pattern

THE T-SQUARE symbolizes incredible pressure toward movement. It may produce dramatic crises or creative friction to achieve its ends, but in one way or another it will motivate action. If you have a T-Square, the squaring Planet is, in effect, trying to motivate and pressure the two Opposing ones. It will do this regardless of its speed. Through using the squaring Planet's energy, the Opposing Planets are forced to find a way to balance their drives and cooperate. After you've learned to combine the three Planets, you may feel a release of tension or a creative rush in the House opposite the Squaring Planet. You can use Planets that Trine or Sextile any of the T-Square Planets to bring ease and resources into the whole pattern.

The Grand Cross

The GRAND CROSS, or GRAND SQUARE, is a combination of two pairs of Opposing Planets which all Square each other. If lines were drawn to connect the two Opposing pairs, they would intersect each other at right angles.

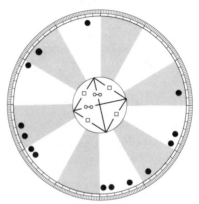

Figure 8-16
The Grand Cross Aspect Pattern

The GRAND CROSS indicates that four different Planets are locked together, confronting each other in various ways, working to find some form of coordinated expression. Every time one of the Planets finds a way to perform its function, the opposing Planet presents an alternative perspective, and the squaring Planets put pressure on it to change. Even when the slowest Planet tries to assume leadership, the same frustrating sequence can result. This can create an incredible feeling of tension and frustration, a sense that there is no "right" direction to be found. Inaction and even paralysis may result. Ultimately, productive movement can occur, but all four Planets have to act, nearly simultaneously, in one giant effort toward change. The presence of a Grand Cross often indicates that long periods of calm or stagnation can occur, followed by a massive upheaval and a total lifestyle reorganization. Planets that Sextile and Trine the Grand Cross Planets help reduce the tension and support the action.

The Grand Trine

The GRAND TRINE consists of three Planets that are all Trine to one another.

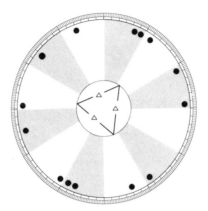

Figure 8-17
The Grand Trine Aspect Pattern

The GRAND TRINE pattern symbolizes three forces that work smoothly or easily together. Since all three Planets are often in the same Element, operating in its realm is natural and comfortable. It's possible for the energy of the Grand Trine to be so familiar and taken for granted that it's not completely appreciated or utilized. If a Planet outside the Grand Trine squares or opposes one of the Grand Trine Planets, it can motivate all of them to manifest their potential more fully.

The Yod

The YOD is a combination of two Quincunxes and a Sextile. Two Planets (B and C) that are Sextile one another are both Quincunx to a third Planet (A).

The YOD is also called the "finger of fate" or the "hand of God," because it brings such strong and surprising twists and turns. Over and over, as decisions are made and directions are established by Planet A, Planets B, and C redirect it. This holds true even if A is the slowest Planet. The other two set up detours and force adjustments, seemingly by whim. In fact, it's usually hard to recognize that the B and C forces really belong to the same person. Because of the Sextile between them, they utilize external resources to influence A, making it appear that "fate" has intervened. If A at-

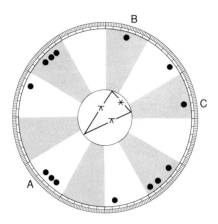

**Figure 8-18
The Yod Aspect Pattern**

tempts to resist the required rerouting, it may find itself in a health crisis. At that point, adaptation becomes nonnegotiable. If A is willing to creatively realign its direction, the final result is usually more satisfying and enlightening than the original goal.

In Janie's Chart, there is a YOD between Retrograde Chiron, Neptune, and Pluto (Fig. 8-19). Chiron is in position A. So, as she attempts to solve her own problems (R CH) through communicating (GE) in her primary relationships (7), she'll find that she's forced to adjust her behavior because of seemingly incompatible drives or insights (QU).

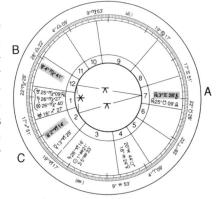

Figure 8-19: Janie's Chart

Her powerful drive (PL) to dig deeply (SC) into her own spirituality (12) may seem to take her away from finding solutions (R CH) through interacting (GE) with others (7). And, her urge to trust (NE) her own practical (CP) resources (2) may seem to remove her from those interactions as well. In actuality, if she uses her YOD well, her focus on spirituality and self-worth can enhance her relationships. On the other hand, if she compulsively (SC) goes through cycles (PL) of addiction (12) and naively trusts

(NE) her own rigidity (CP) regarding money (2), she could find herself becoming a compulsive spender. Then, her partner (7) might feel that she's undependable or superficial (GE) in terms of really examining her own faults (R CH).

In Grace's Chart, there is a GRAND CROSS between Jupiter, Retrograde Saturn, Chiron, and Retrograde Uranus (Fig. 8-20). So, Grace would feel tremendous pressures to coordinate the activities of the 1st (R SA), 4th (CH), 7th (JU), and 10th (R UR) Houses.

Figure 8-20: Grace's Chart

She would want to limit herself (R SA) by appearing (1) cooperative (LI), but also expand her experience (JU) by being risk-taking and independent (AR) in her relationship (7). She would want to actively fix problems (CH) at home (4), in a practical manner (CP), and still pursue a career (10) in which she personally contributes to the future of the Earth (R UR) in a nurturing way (CA). Whenever she acts on one of these four Planets, she's always forced to consider the others, through the conflicts (SQ) or differing perspectives (OP) that arise.

In utilizing Retrograde Saturn, when she sets out to be (1) a team-playing (LI) authority figure (R SA), either her internal rebellion (R UR), her urge to seek freedom (JU), or her perfectionism (CH) will interfere with her desire to take on responsibility (R SA).

In working with Retrograde Uranus, if she finds a career (10) in which she can exhibit her radical (R UR) but nurturing (CA) tendencies, she might find that her internal realism (R SA), philosophy of life (JU), and tendency toward analysis (CH) would actually stop her from taking her innovative ideas too far.

In focusing on Jupiter, if she creates a relationship (7) in which she can develop a pioneering (AR) philosophy (JU), she could find that her internal limits (R SA), her desire to embody eccentricity (R UR), and her drive to fix what's wrong (CH) could get in the way of her ability to freely pursue her expansion.

And, in operating from Chiron's position, by discovering how to contribute realistically to the healing (CH) of her family (4), she could discover that her own internal boundaries (R SA), her desire to make a break with her own past patterns (R UR) and her need to expand her horizons (JU) might actually take her away from solving problems at home.

Grace says that she has had quite a struggle in trying to combine these forces. In the course of her life, she's come up with several solutions that work. Two of them are described below:

At one time, she lived in a child-development center and worked as an authority figure with children and their families. She collaborated with them, teaching them to solve their problems in unique and visionary ways. In an extension of this work, she went on the road, training other professionals and families (in their homes) to use these innovative, problem-solving techniques. Her romantic and professional partners, at the time, were fully and philosophically involved in this work.

At another time she worked out of her own home, as a behavioral consultant, providing analytical services to other professionals who work with disturbed children and their families. At this time, she and her partner worked directly with exceptionally needy children. Through consistent limits and radical interventions, she was able to effect great changes in their behavior.

Phrases to Use in Interpreting Aspect Patterns

"Some of your Planets and other Chart Points have specific angular relationships to each other. These are called Aspects, and they describe *how* the parts of your personality interact with one another. In other words, they indicate whether parts of you blend easily together or challenge each other. Several of the Planets and Points in your Chart are joined together in an Aspect Pattern called a [*name Aspect Pattern*]. The Pattern looks like this [*draw out or outline pattern on Chart, indicating the Planets and Points included and diagramming the Aspect Pattern itself*]. It means that [*interpret Aspect Pattern*]."

OTHER NOTICEABLE AND NOTABLE CHART DATA

Your survey of the overall Chart configurations is almost complete. With the addition of a few more easily identifiable details, you'll have a working overview of most of the significant features in your Chart.

Retrogrades

The NUMBER OF RETROGRADE PLANETS is one of these features. Most Charts have one to three Retrogrades, which can be interpreted individually, Planet by Planet. If a Chart contains no Retrogrades or more than three Retrogrades, their absence or presence, as a group, is notable. (In figuring this out, ignore Retrograde Nodes.)

If you have NO RETROGRADES in your Chart, you'll probably tend to take life at face value, learn from others' experiences, and generally go along with the values of your culture or subculture. You won't waste time reinventing the wheel. Instead, you'll add to others' creations.

On the other hand, if you have FOUR OR MORE RETROGRADES in your Chart, you'll reevaluate most things. You'll want to learn from your own experience, figure everything out for yourself, and reinvent a better wheel. Sometimes, you might feel that you don't exactly "fit in," but you'll also find value in your self-discovered truths and personally tested experiences.

Janie has one Retrograde Planet, Chiron (Fig. 8-21). The North and South Nodes of the Moon are also Retrograde, but we don't count them in this case. She'll mostly learn from others' experiences, except with regard to Chiron. So, she'll have to figure out her own self-healing process. This will be especially important, since Chiron, as part of her Fanhandle pattern and her Yod is her "handle" on life.

Figure 8-21: Janie's Chart

Grace has four Retrograde Planets, so they are significant as a group (Fig. 8-22). Generally speaking, this woman will want to learn from her own experience. She'll test many things out for herself and have to find a way to "fit in" with the group.

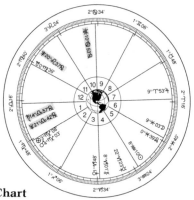

Figure 8-22: Grace's Chart

Grace says that she does tend to learn from her own experiences. She rarely takes anyone's word for anything and likes to test theories on her own. As a result, she feels creative but somewhat isolated from others.

Phrases to Use in Interpreting Retrogrades

MANY RETROGRADES

"Do you see these little Rs after the Planets? You have a lot of them. They indicate that these Planets were RETROGRADE at the time of your birth. This means that, seen from the Earth at that time, the Planets looked as if they were moving backwards. Since you have many of them, it means that you have to figure things out for yourself, without taking someone else's word for it. You may end up reinventing the wheel sometimes, but once you've got yourself sorted out, THEN you can interact more comfortably in the world."

NO RETROGRADES

"Since all the Planets appeared to be moving forward at your Birth Time (yes, sometimes there's an optical illusion that makes it appear that some of them are moving backward!), it looks as though you take life as it comes. You respect what others have figured out, use their insight and wisdom, and don't stop to reinvent the wheel."

"Loaded" Signs and Houses

The presence of THREE OR MORE PLANETS WITHIN A SIGN OR HOUSE is another signal of significance. If you have this kind of emphasis in your Chart, issues related to the Loaded Signs or Houses are probably extremely important to you. This is because all the Planets in the House are also Rulers of other Signs and Houses. Because of the Rulerships, whenever you take action in the Loaded area, you feel the results in several other areas of your life. With this awareness, you may choose to either avidly pursue or deliberately avoid the activities related to the emphasized Sign or House. In either case, you'll be conscious of its potential for changing your life.

The total ABSENCE OF PLANETS IN A PARTICULAR SIGN OR HOUSE is notable but not as significant as their presence. Since the Planets that Rule the Signs activate them, and those Planets are always located and functioning somewhere in the Chart, the needs of empty areas are met by their Ruling Planets. Nothing is "missing" from the Chart. As long as the Ruling Planets are somewhere, all needs will be met.

In Janie's Chart, the 1st House is extremely Loaded (Fig. 8-23). So, she'll be quite focused on her appearance, name, and role in life (1). She'll discover that, by taking action related to her personality (1), she'll passionately share her skills (SN in SC), present a focused, responsible (SA in SC) image, feel deeply integrated (PF in SC), expansively invent new visions (UR in SG), become an authority in the community (SA Rules CP on 3), and change the community (UR Rules AQ in 3).

Figure 8-23: Janie's Chart

In addition to that, Scorpio, which Rules this House, is also Loaded, containing five key Points and Planets. So, passionate intensity will be either her delight or her nemesis.

Janie's 3rd House is also Loaded. Because its two Rulers are in the 1st House, all the powerful activity mentioned above will naturally move things along in the 3rd. She'll use the Planets located here to pragmatically teach (JU in CP), innovatively shine (SU in AQ), and uniquely belong (MO in AQ) in the community (3). As a result of these activities, she'll be able to expand her financial situation (JU Rules SG on 2) and nurture her opportunities for personally fulfilling higher education or travel experiences (SU Rules LE in 9 AND MO Rules CA on 9).

Grace's Chart isn't quite as tangled as Janie's in terms of this feature. It's only Loaded area is the Sign of Capricorn (Fig. 8-24) which includes Planets in two Houses. The Capricorn emphasis implies that Grace will utilize her pragmatic, responsible, and organizational approach to life in numerous areas.

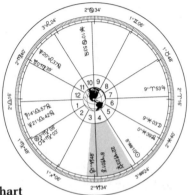

Figure 8-24: Grace's Chart

First of all, she'll demonstrate these Capricorn traits in her home (4) and community (3). Next, through the Rulerships, she'll become an authority figure in her basic personality (VE Rules 1), within her intimate relationships (VE Rules 8), with regard to her spirituality (CH Rules 12) and in the context of travel (ME Rules 9).

As you can tell from this example, even a fairly simply trail can lead from a Loaded Sign into several directions. All in all, noticing and interpreting the emphasized Signs and Houses can be a valuable process.

Phrases to Use in Interpreting Loaded Houses and Signs

"You can see that you have a whole pile of Planets in this House (Sign). That means that you'll be especially concerned with [*describe House or Sign*]."

Interceptions and Duplications

The PRESENCE OF INTERCEPTED AND DUPLICATED SIGNS is another feature that is important to notice. In a House containing an Intercepted Sign, two different sets of needs must be met. Two different sets of attitudes will also be expressed with regard to the issues of that House. If you have Interceptions, you may feel some conflict about which needs and attitudes are truly yours. You may expend a great deal of time and energy in this area of life, trying to doubly satisfy yourself. While you may be pretty familiar with ways to utilize the Sign on the Cusp, you probably have few appropriate role models for how to use the Intercepted Sign productively. The Duplicated Signs show attitudes and needs that you demonstrate in two areas of life. You may feel that you frequently act on the needs and attitudes represented by these Signs.

Janie's Chart has Aquarius and Leo Intercepted in the 3rd and 9th Houses, respectively (Fig. 8-25). Therefore, with regard to the concerns of these Houses, she'll have two sets of needs that must be met. In the 3rd, with regard to her early education, she'll be especially challenged because she'll need to be both responsible (CP) and rebellious (AQ).

Figure 8-25: Janie's Chart

In the 9th, she'll want to be nurtured and safe (CA) but also shining and enthusiastic (LE) in her quest for higher education.

Her Duplications are Aries, on the 5th and 6th Houses, and Libra, on the 11th and 12th. She'll utilize the energies of these two Signs quite a bit, working on balancing her needs for independence (AR) and cooperation (LI). She'll be especially self-motivated and pioneering in terms of her creativity (5) and her daily routine (6), while she'll be other-oriented and diplomatic in the context of her friendships (11) and spiritual activities (12).

Grace's Chart has no Interceptions and, therefore, no Duplications.

Phrases to Use in Interpreting Interceptions and Duplications

"Do you see how these Signs [*name the Signs*] are totally contained within these Houses? [*Point to Houses.*] Well, it's as though they were closeted. This means that, however your family system used these energies, it didn't work for you. It may have been that members of your family were actually dysfunctional or destructive in their use of these processes; it may just mean that you're different from them. But, in any case, you've probably had to find mentors or role models for how to be [*describe Signs*].

"You also have these Signs [*name Signs*] on two separate House Cusps [*name Houses*]. That means that your family showed you how to use these energies in ways that were pretty appropriate for you. As a result you've probably used them quite a bit, and quite effectively. The qualities symbolized by these two Signs are [*describe nature of the Signs*]."

Focus Planets

A FOCUS PLANET can jump out from a Chart, indicating that it has a special place in that Chart's interpretation. Focus Planets can be those that seem to be separated from the other Planets by some empty Signs or Houses. These Planets seem "set off" somehow. They can also be those that are on the cutting edge (going clockwise) of a group of Planets. And, they can be Planets that are Aspected by many other Planets and Points. If you have a Focus Planet, you'll find that by using its energy in a positive way, your life seems to become more integrated and whole. Conversely, if you use your Focus Planet in a destructive manner, you may end up feeling fragmented and torn apart.

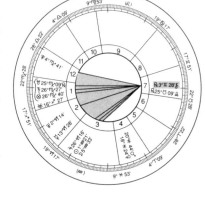

Janie's obvious focus Planet is Retrograde Chiron (Fig. 8-26). It's set off by itself, and it has quite a few Aspects to it. The North Node is also set off from the Chart, but since it's not a Planet, it isn't quite as important in terms of this analysis. Once again, Chiron crops up as a significant force in this one's life. She'll really feel compelled to explore a variety of ways for mending herself within relationships.

Figure 8-26: Janie's Chart

Grace's Retrograde Uranus is on the cutting edge of all the Planets (Fig. 8-27). She'll feel drawn to embody the nonconformity of Uranus personally. She'll find it extremely important to be rebellious or nontraditional, in a caring way, within her vocation.

Figure 8-27: Grace's Chart

We know that this is true because Grace has given us ongoing feedback about her drive to be innovative in her work. As you can see, important themes repeat themselves within any given Chart.

Phrases to Use in Interpreting Focus Planets

"Now, this planet is quite important in your Chart because [*tell why it's a Focus Planet*]. Its job is to [*describe Planet in Sign in House*]. So, when you act that way, your behavior provides a focus for many other parts of your life to either fall apart or come together."

Emphasized or Deemphasized Qualities or Elements

Your Chart may have many PLANETS OR POINTS IN PARTICULAR QUALITIES OR ELEMENTS. To find out if this is the case, simply list them by category and count them up. You can use a little table such as the one in Figure 8-28 to make sure that you've located all of them.

CARDINAL	FIRE
FIXED	EARTH
MUTABLE	AIR
	WATER
TOTAL 16	16

Figure 8-28
The Planets and the Points
in Qualities and Elements

If you have an emphasis in CARDINAL Signs, much of your energy will be given to generating new ideas and experiences and to originating possibilities for what could exist. If the Cardinal Signs are deemphasized, you generally prefer not to be in the position of initiating things. Once something has begun, however, you might enjoy maintaining it or changing it. If your emphasis is in FIXED Signs, you'll be more focused on persisting in your interests and patterns and sustaining what already exists. If Fixed Signs are deemphasized, you'll probably feel bored if you have to stick with the same thing for too long. You'd rather get things started or adapt and adjust them. If your emphasis is in MUTABLE Signs, you'll be most interested in diversifying your activities and interactions and evolving beyond what exists. If Mutable Signs are deemphasized, you'll tend to stick with the status quo or move on to something new rather than adapting what already exists.

If your emphasis is in FIRE Signs, you'll generally approach life with enthusiasm as you seek opportunities for personal expression. If Fire Signs are deemphasized, you'll find it more difficult to be in the spotlight; you'll prefer a supporting role. If your Chart emphasizes EARTH Signs, you'll be productive and practical most of the time. If Earth Signs are deemphasized, physical reality may be a mystery to you; you'd rather think or dream than deal with the material world. If most of your Planets and Points fall in AIR Signs, you'll find yourself communicating and interacting in most situations. If Air Signs are deemphasized, you'll tend to act more than interact and listen more than talk. And, if WATER is your strong Element, you'll sense your way through life with empathy and emotion. If Water Signs are deemphasized, the world of feelings will not be your favorite playground.

Janie's Chart definitely emphasizes the FIXED QUALITY and the WATER ELEMENT (Fig. 8-29). This means that she'll generally persist in feeling empathy with others and be able to sustain her emotions for a long time. This could mean that she'll be a very caring friend or that she'll get "stuck" in her feeling states.

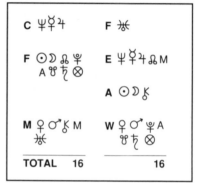

Figure 8-29: Janie's Chart

The CARDINAL Signs and FIRE Signs are deemphasized in her Chart, so she may not enjoy initiating activities that bring her too much attention. Being "first" into the spotlight is not her aim.

Grace's Chart emphasizes the CARDINAL QUALITY and the WATER ELEMENT (Fig. 8-30). This means that she'll tend to generate a great deal of empathy. She'll also originate emotions in that she'll feel and express them herself, without being influenced by others.

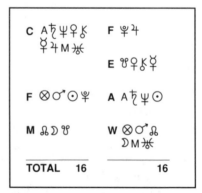

Figure 8-30: Grace's Chart

The MUTABLE and FIRE Signs are deemphasized in her Chart, so she'll be least inclined toward diversifying her modes of self-expression and fairly uninterested in evolving into a center-stage position.

Grace says that she is often quick to experience her feelings, especially those of joy and anger. The moments pass quickly, though, as she rarely holds onto an emotional state for long. She also does have the ability to inspire empathy in others. She sticks with her own tried and true forms of self-expression so it takes quite a bit of feedback before she'll actually adapt her ways of presenting herself to the world. And, she's not too interested in developing a variety of methods for being in the spotlight.

Phrases to Use in Interpreting
Emphasized or Deemphasized Qualities or Elements

"The Signs can be divided into two different kinds of categories called the Qualities and Elements. You may have heard of the Elements. They are Fire, Earth, Air, and Water. Anyway, in looking at your Chart, I notice that you have many of your Planets and Points in the Element of [*name the emphasized Element*]. You also have an emphasis in the [*name the emphasized Quality*] Quality. This means that, generally speaking, you approach life by [*describe emphasized Element and Quality*]."

"On the other hand, you have few [or no] Planets and Points in the Quality of [*name the deemphasized Quality*] and the Element of [*name the deemphasized Element*]. This means that, most of the time, your least favorite approaches to life are [*describe emphasized Element and Quality*]."

Emphasized Pairs or Themes

The grouped locations of the Planets and Points in your Chart may also emphasize a particular PAIR of Houses (see Chapter 4) or a THEMATIC set of Signs (see Chapter 5). A pair or Theme will be important if one of the Houses or Signs is heavily occupied while the other is not. It may also come into focus if two or three Planets or Points fall into each of the opposing Houses or Signs.

Given Janie's Chart configuration (Fig. 8-31), the most important Pair of Houses is that of IDENTITY (1st–7th). Since it also contains her Focus Planet, it's doubly important.

Figure 8-31: Janie's Chart

This indicates that one of Janie's life-long issues will revolve around balancing her sense of self (1) with her experience of others (2). More specifically, she'll need to find ways to fully express her independent personality (1) while still allowing for collaborative interaction with others (7).

In Grace's Chart (Fig. 8-32), the most strongly emphasized THEME is that of SECURITY (Cancer-Capricorn) because she has two Chart features (R UR and M) in Cancer and three features (VE, CH, and ME) in Capricorn.

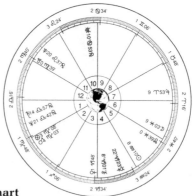

Figure 8-32: Grace's Chart

This means that Grace will be attempting to resolve Security issues throughout her life. She'll focus on balancing her need for establishing a solid, practical position in the world (CP) with her drive to create emotionally nurturing nests (CA). Since Cancer and Capricorn are on the 4th (CA) and 10th (CP) House Cusps, this further emphasizes that the desire to integrate the home-career dichotomy is important for her.

Grace says that she has resolved this issue by making home-like nests at work and by bringing her work into her home. She is still attempting to balance the responsible parts of her that think she "should" be accomplishing things with the nurturant parts of her that want her to relax and find comfort.

Phrases to Use in Interpreting Interceptions and Duplications

"Notice that these two Houses [or Signs] have quite a few Planets and Points located within them [*point out emphasized Pair or Theme*]. Since they are opposite each other, they show two opposing forces that you're trying to balance in your life. Since they are emphasized, it means that the integration of those forces will be important to you. The two energies that you're trying to coordinate are [*describe domains of the two Houses or needs and attitudes of the two Signs*]."

Step 2:
Interpreting the Planets by Position and Rulership

After you've gotten an Overview of your Chart, it's time to get into the individual Planets and their interpretations. Since you already know how to discuss the significance of the Planets and Points from reading Chapters 3 through 7, I'll just remind you of the key factors to consider when interpreting each one:

THE SUN
- how (Sign) and where (House) you demonstrate your core self (or boast)
- impact on Houses with Leo on Cusp
- impact on Intercepted Leo

THE MOON
- how (Sign) and where (House) you establish security (or cling)
- impact on Houses with Cancer on Cusp
- impact on Intercepted Cancer

MERCURY
- how (Sign) and where (House) you communicate (or babble)
- effect of Retrogradation
- impact on Houses with Gemini on Cusp
- impact on Intercepted Gemini

VENUS
- how (Sign) and where (House) you create beauty and value (or preen)
- effect of Retrogradation
- impact on Houses with Taurus on Cusp
- impact on Intercepted Taurus
- impact on Houses with Libra on Cusp
- impact on Intercepted Libra

MARS
- how (Sign) and where (House) you go after what you want (or bully)
- effect of Retrogradation
- impact on Houses with Aries on Cusp
- impact on Intercepted Aries

JUPITER
- how (Sign) and where (House) you expand and teach (or "preach")
- effect of Retrogradation
- impact on Houses with Sagittarius on Cusp
- impact on Intercepted Sagittarius

SATURN
- how (Sign) and where (House) you structure your life (or control)
- effect of Retrogradation
- impact on Houses with Capricorn on Cusp
- impact on Intercepted Capricorn

CHIRON
- how (Sign) and where (House) you fix things (or criticize)
- effect of Retrogradation
- impact on Houses with Virgo on Cusp
- impact on Intercepted Virgo

URANUS
- how (Sign) and where (House) you innovatively change things (or rebel)
- effect of Retrogradation
- impact on Houses with Aquarius on Cusp
- impact on Intercepted Aquarius

NEPTUNE
- how (Sign) and where (House) you have faith (or addict)
- effect of Retrogradation
- impact on Houses with Pisces on Cusp
- impact on Intercepted Pisces

PLUTO
- how (Sign) and where (House) you are transformative (or compulsive)
- effect of Retrogradation
- impact on Houses with Scorpio on Cusp
- impact on Intercepted Scorpio

Phrases to Use in Interpreting the Planets by Position and Rulership

"Now, let's talk about the heart of your Chart, the Planets. I'll point them out and then tell you what they symbolize. Here's the [name the Planet]. It's in [Sign] in the [#] House. That means that you express your self by [describe Planet in its House and Sign]."

"This Planet is also especially associated with the activities of the [name House that the Planet Rules through its Natural Sign]. That means that whenever you [interpret Planet by House and Sign], it affects your [describe some of the topics and concerns of the Ruled House]."

Step 3: Interpreting the Points by Position

You can interpret the Points in the same manner as the Planets, except that there are no Rulerships to consider. Additionally, consider the special relationships between the two Nodes and between the Ascendant and the Midheaven.

NORTH NODE
- how (Sign) and where (House) you challenge yourself and grow

SOUTH NODE
- how (Sign) and where (House) you share your skills and resources

NODAL AXIS
- how (Signs) and where (Houses) you balance the inflow and outflow in your life

PART OF FORTUNE
- how (Sign) and where (House) you feel magically "blessed"

ASCENDANT
- Sign shows general personality
- The Planet Ruling the Rising Sign shows how (Sign) and where (House) you most easily demonstrate this personality.

MIDHEAVEN
- Sign shows life "mission"
- The Planet Ruling the Midheaven Sign shows how (Sign) and where (House) you most easily act out this mission.

ASCENDANT TO MIDHEAVEN RELATIONSHIP
- interaction between the Ascendant and Midheaven Signs shows how you coordinate your place in the Universe (Midheaven) with your position on Earth (Ascendant)

COMBINING THE NODES

Here's an example of how the North and South Node (Fig. 8-33) interpretations could be combined in Grace's Chart.

She works at balancing the urge to
contribute all her practical, problem-
solving energy to the public "cause"
(SN in VI in 11)

WITH

her urge to learn and grow through
her intuitive and compassionate responses in her personal life (NN in PI
in 5).

Figure 8-33: Grace's Chart

Grace is still learning how to balance the part of her that thinks she
"should" be contributing to others with the part of her that wants to be personally creative. Since she has so much personal interest in children, she
finds that by being creative and compassionate toward disturbed children,
she can also serve a "cause." She's reaching a point of burn-out with the
kids, however, and is aware that a new balancing act is ready to emerge.
This time, she thinks it will involve her intuition. She expects she'll find a
way to make a contribution to the world through her psychic skills and interests.

COMBINING THE MIDHEAVEN AND THE ASCENDANT

Here's how the Earthly and Universal forces could interact in Janie's
Chart (Figs. 8-34 and 8-35).

Figure 8-34: Janie's Chart
Universal Environment
Midheaven-Based
Equal House Chart

Figure 8-35: Janie's Chart
Earthly Environment
Ascendant-Based
Equal House Chart

In the case of the UNIVERSAL ENVIRONMENT CHART, the Midheaven Sign would be Virgo and the Sign at the beginning of the First House would be Sagittarius. If she lived out this Chart, she would approach her life work from a practical, problem-solving perspective and express her personality philosophically and optimistically. The Signs on the rest of the House Cusps, as shown, would indicate her needs and attitudes with regard to the remaining areas of life.

The EARTHLY ENVIRONMENT CHART shows that her family system would have encouraged her to be intense, self-protective, and much more focused than her Universally defined Sagittarian personality. And, instead of helping her to approach her life work with a healing or service orientation (Virgo), her family system might encourage her to express herself creatively, gaining recognition and applause (Leo). As in the Midheaven Chart, the Signs on the remaining Cusps would bring in their needs and attitudes.

In combining the Universal and Earthly forces, Janie has Virgo on the 10th and Scorpio Rising. She'll feel compelled to experience life at a deep and meaningful level and to express her personality in a powerful manner. On the other hand, she'll approach her "mission" in life very practically, truly wanting to be of service and solve the problems of the Earth today. Her utilization of her Ascendant and Midheaven energies, combined with her expression of the Signs on the rest of the House Cusps, results in her unique and personal integration of the Universal and Earthly environmental themes.

Phrases to Use in Interpreting the Points

"There are several important Points in the Chart that are not actually Planets so they don't represent objects in the sky. They are *mathematical* Points, but they are quite significant from an interpretational perspective. The [*name the Point*] is over here. It symbolizes [*describe its general function*]. In your Chart, it's in [*name Sign and House*] so that means that you fulfill its function by [*interpret Point in Sign and House*]."

Step 4: Interpreting the Planets and Points by Aspect

The last, but definitely not least, step in a Natal Chart analysis is the interpretation of the Aspects. You can pick out the ones that you find most interesting or the ones that seem most important to you. Generally speaking, Aspects to the Sun, Moon, and Ascendant are a good place to start. After that, you can simply discuss the Aspects, in groups, according to their nature.

CONJUNCTIONS: pairs of Planets or Points that unite and work together

SEMI-SEXTILES: pairs of Planets or Points that fine-tune and subtly adapt each other

SEXTILES: pairs of Planets or Points that support each other by finding outside resources

SQUARES: pairs of Planets or Points that confront and catalyze each other

TRINES: pairs of Planets or Points that enhance each other and pool skills

QUINCUNXES: pairs of Planets or Points that redirect and reroute each other

OPPOSITIONS: pairs of Planets or Points that give each other perspective and balance

For examples of Aspect interpretations, reread Chapter 7.

Phrases to Use in Interpreting the Planets and Points by Aspect

"The Planets and Points that we've been talking about are all related to each other in different ways depending on how far apart they are. Some of the specific distances have been identified as Aspects and given individual names. In your Chart, several of these Planet-Point connections stand out. Over here, you have [name first Planet or Point], which is about [name number of Degrees of the Aspect] away from [name the second Planet]. That distance is called a [name the Aspect]. It means that when you [describe behavior of first Planet], then this other Planet who wants to [describe the behavior of the second Planet], will tend to [describe nature of the Aspect] towards the first one."

Putting It All Together

The following Tables are resources that you can use to help you integrate your interpretations. One includes KEY PHRASE INTERPRETATIONS for each Planet, Point, Sign, and House. The other is a QUICK REFERENCE GUIDE. You can use it to locate the Planets, Points, Signs, or Houses that are associated with particular issues.

To use the KEY PHRASE INTERPRETATIONS, choose a Planet (the R indicates Retrograde) or Point from the first column and find its location by Sign and House in the remaining columns. Choose any of the expressions related to the Planet you've chosen, add any of the descriptors related to its Sign, and combine them with any of the subjects related to their House. The resulting sentence will be a basic interpretation for your Chart. If you have Mars in Gemini in the 6th House, you might come up with one of these two possibilities:

I ASSERT MYSELF (MA) IN MORE THAN ONE WAY (GE)
REGARDING MY HEALTH (6).

I EXPRESS ANGER (MA) COMMUNICATIVELY (GE)
REGARDING MY JOB (6).

Remember, though, that this mixing and matching only gives you *samples;* you can use your expanded understanding of the Planets, Signs, and Houses to invent more possibilities.

KEY PHRASE INTERPRETATIONS FOR
THE PLANETS AND POINTS IN THE SIGNS AND HOUSES

THE PLANET ACTS

THE SUN:
I EXPRESS MY POTENTIAL
I ILLUMINATE ISSUES
I DEMONSTRATE MYSELF
I NAME MYSELF
I GAIN APPLAUSE
I APPROACH JEWELRY AND FAME

THE MOON:
I CREATE BELONGINGNESS
I CREATE SECURITY
I ACT INSTINCTIVELY
I EXPERIENCE MY MOTHER
I ATTRACT NURTURANCE
I APPROACH FOOD AND HOME

MERCURY:
I COMMUNICATE
I FORM NETWORKS
I AM CURIOUS
I EXPERIENCE MY SIBLINGS
I THINK
I APPROACH VEHICLES AND COMMUNITY
(R) MY OWN THOUGHT PROCESSES WORK

VENUS:
I ESTABLISH VALUE
I BEAUTIFY
I NEGOTIATE
I MAGNETICALLY ATTRACT
I HARMONIZE
I APPROACH BEAUTY AND "FEMALE" ENERGY
(R) I ESTABLISH MY OWN VALUES

THE PLANET ACTS

MARS:
I ASSERT MYSELF
I PURSUE MY DESIRES
I TAKE ACTION
I INITIATE
I EXPRESS ANGER AND SEXUALITY
I APPROACH SURGERY AND "MALE" ENERGY
(R) I CLARIFY MY OWN DESIRES

JUPITER:
I SEEK THE TRUTH
I PHILOSOPHIZE AND TEACH
I CREATE "MORE"
I SELL THINGS OR IDEAS
I DEMONSTRATE MY ETHICS
I APPROACH MARKETING AND TRAVEL
(R) I DEVELOP MY OWN ETHICS

SATURN:
I BUILD STRUCTURES
I SET LIMITS AND BOUNDARIES
I EXPERIENCE MY FATHER
I ORGANIZE AND CONTROL
I ESTABLISH AUTHORITY
I APPROACH TIME AND AGEDNESS
(R) I DISCIPLINE MYSELF

THE PLANET ACTS	THE POINT IS EXPRESSED

THE PLANET ACTS

CHIRON:
I CREATE THE IDEAL, IN REALITY
I FIX WHAT'S BROKEN
I ANALYZE
I SOLVE PROBLEMS
I SERVE OTHERS
I APPROACH REPAIR AND DETOXIFICATION
(R) I HEAL MYSELF

URANUS:
I BREAK OUT OF OLD PATTERNS
I INNOVATE
I OBSERVE AND DETACH
I AVOID CONFORMING
I CREATE FUTURE OPTIONS
I APPROACH REBELLION AND TECHNOLOGY
(R) I EMBODY ECCENTRICITY

NEPTUNE:
I DISSOLVE BARRIERS
I EMPATHIZE
I TRUST AND HAVE FAITH
I HEAL
I IMAGINE
I APPROACH SPIRITUALITY AND ADDICTION
(R) I MERGE WITH MY SPIRITUAL SOURCE

PLUTO:
I DEMONSTRATE POWER
I REGENERATE
I TRANSFORM
I MOVE THROUGH BIG CYCLES
I PENETRATE TO THE DEPTHS
I APPROACH THE OCCULT AND RECYCLING
(R) I EXPERIENCE MY PERSONAL POWER

THE POINT IS EXPRESSED

THE NORTH NODE:
I CHALLENGE MYSELF
I STRETCH MYSELF
I MOVE INTO MY POTENTIAL
I EXPERIENCE GAIN

THE SOUTH NODE:
I SHARE MY GIFTS
I TEACH WHAT I KNOW
I USE WHAT I HAVE
I EXPERIENCE LOSS

THE PART OF FORTUNE:
I INTEGRATE MYSELF
I FEEL MOST WHOLE
I AM MAGICALLY BLESSED

THE ASCENDANT:
I EXPRESS MY IDENTITY
I COPE WITH MY FAMILY
I INTERACT WITH LIFE

THE MIDHEAVEN:
I EXPRESS MY "MISSION"
I REACH MY PINNACLE
I CONTRIBUTE TO THE WORLD

ACCORDING TO THE NATURE OF ITS SIGN

ARIES:
SPONTANEOUSLY, NAIVELY
INDEPENDENTLY, ENTHUSIASTICALLY
IN A CHILDLIKE MANNER
COURAGEOUSLY, CATALYTICALLY
ASSERTIVELY, ATHLETICALLY
INCONSIDERATELY, SELF-CENTEREDLY

TAURUS:
SOLIDLY, DEPENDABLY
RELIABLY, COMMITTEDLY
SENSUALLY, REALISTICALLY
PRACTICALLY, PERSISTENTLY
RHYTHMICALLY, MUSICALLY
STUBBORNLY, HOARDINGLY

GEMINI:
AMUSINGLY, LOGICALLY
COMMUNICATIVELY, FACILELY
INVESTIGATIVELY, VERSATILELY
MULTI-DIMENSIONALLY, QUICKLY
IN MORE-THAN-ONE WAY
SUPERFICIALLY, UNRELIABLY

CANCER:
CARINGLY, WARMLY
PROTECTIVELY, MOTHERINGLY
PSYCHICALLY, INTUITIVELY
FLUCTUATINGLY, SENTIMENTALLY
BY USING PAST PATTERNS
CLINGINGLY, DEPENDENTLY

LEO:
DRAMATICALLY, GENEROUSLY
PROUDLY, CONFIDENTLY
FORCEFULLY, CREATIVELY
THROUGH STORYTELLING
FLAMBOYANTLY, ROMANTICALLY
ARROGANTLY, BOASTFULLY

VIRGO:
ANALYTICALLY, DISCRIMINATINGLY
METHODICALLY, SELF-ANALYTICALLY
ROUTINELY, SYSTEMATICALLY
IN A DETAIL-ORIENTED MANNER
IN A HEALTH-CONSCIOUS WAY
NAGGINGLY, CRITICALLY

LIBRA:
COOPERATIVELY, INTERACTIVELY
ESTHETICALLY, CHARMINGLY
WHILE I'M CONSCIOUS OF ALTERNATIVES
DECORATIVELY, GRACEFULLY
WHILE I RESPECT FEEDBACK
MANIPULATIVELY, INDECISIVELY

SCORPIO:
TRANSFORMATIVELY, REGENERATIVELY
PASSIONATELY, INTENSELY
PERCEPTIVELY, PENETRATINGLY
PROTECTIVELY, RENEWINGLY
AS I'M AWARE OF DEEPER PURPOSE
VENGEFULLY, COMPULSIVELY

SAGITTARIUS:
EXPANSIVELY, OPEN-ENDEDLY
WISELY, SCIENTIFICALLY
RELIGIOUSLY, PHILOSOPHICALLY
QUESTINGLY, ETHICALLY
OPTIMISTICALLY, EASY-GOINGLY
SELF-INDULGENTLY, GREEDILY

CAPRICORN:
INDUSTRIOUSLY, RESPONSIBLY
PARENTALLY, AUTHORITATIVELY
AMBITIOUSLY, RESPECTFULLY
PRACTICALLY, STRUCTUREDLY
IN AN ORGANIZED MANNER
CONTROLLINGLY, DICTATORIALLY

AQUARIUS:
ECCENTRICALLY, REFORMINGLY
THEORETICALLY, SURPRISINGLY
INNOVATIVELY, DETACHEDLY
TECHNOLOGICALLY, FUTURISTICALLY
IN A VISIONARY MANNER
ERRATICALLY, UNRELIABLY

PISCES:
SENSITIVELY, COMPASSIONATELY
SPIRITUALLY, INTUITIVELY
BY MERGING WITH THE "WHOLE"
SERENELY, POETICALLY
IMAGINATIVELY, DREAMILY
CONFUSEDLY, AS A VICTIM

REGARDING THE CONCERNS AND ISSUES OF ITS HOUSE

1ST:
REGARDING MY PERSONALITY,
TEMPERAMENT, APPEARANCE,
IDENTITY, NAME, TITLES, ROLES,
FIRST IMPRESSION ON OTHERS,
PERSONA, MASK

2ND:
REGARDING MY MONEY, STOCKS,
BONDS, BANKS, MOVABLE
POSSESSIONS, THINGS,
SELF-ESTEEM, VALUES,
WORTH, TALENTS,
ASSETS, RESOURCES

3RD:
REGARDING MY SPEECH,
COMMUNICATION, NEIGHBORS,
NEIGHBORHOOD, COMMUNITY,
VEHICLES, SHORT TRIPS,
COMMUNICATION METHODS,
SIBLINGS

4TH:
REGARDING MY HOME,
EMOTIONAL SECURITY,
MOTHER, NURTURANCE,
FAMILY, CLAN, ROOTS, CULTURE,
END OF LIFE SITUATION,
RESIDENCE

5TH:
REGARDING MY CHILDREN,
CREATIVITY, DATING, LOVE,
LOVE AFFAIRS, HOBBIES, SPORTS,
GAMES, SPECULATION,
INNER CHILD, PLAY

6TH:
REGARDING MY HEALTH,
NUTRITION, TASKS, SCHEDULES
DAILY WORK, JOB,
STRESS, DECISION-MAKING,
VOLUNTEERISM, SERVICE

7TH:
REGARDING MY PARTNER, MATE,
COMPANION, PEER, BUSINESS,
ASSOCIATE, ENEMIES, CUSTOMERS,
UNCLAIMED PARTS OF SELF

8TH:
REGARDING MY INTIMACY,
BONDING, SEXUALITY, COMMITMENT,
SHARED RESOURCES,
PARTNER'S MONEY,
DEATH, CONCEPTION, BIRTH

9TH:
REGARDING MY BELIEFS, MORALS,
ETHICS, RELIGION, PHILOSOPHY,
FOREIGN TRAVEL, SALES,
HIGHER EDUCATION, TEACHING,
SCIENCE, BROADCASTING

10TH:
REGARDING MY STATUS, REPUTATION,
CAREER, LIFE WORK, VOCATION,
FATHER, AUTHORITIES, DESTINY,
POSITION IN SOCIETY

11TH:
REGARDING MY VISIONS, DREAMS,
FUTURE PLANS, GOALS, REBELLION,
POLITICS, FRIENDS, ACQUAINTANCES,
CAUSES, GROUP ASSOCIATIONS

12TH:
REGARDING MY SPIRITUALITY,
FAITH, PSYCHIC EXPERIENCES,
PHYSICAL AND MENTAL RETREATS,
ADDICTIONS, DEPENDENCIES,
ILLEGAL OR HIDDEN THINGS

Sometimes, it's easier to start with a topic and then find out what the Chart says about it. This is because, even though you may understand the structure of the Houses and Signs and the nature of Rulerships, you might still not remember where embezzlement, advertising, or farming belong. So, the following list is for those times. In the blank spaces at the end of each alphabetical section, you may even want to add in some of the topics that you frequently research. That way you'll end up with a personalized quick reference guide.

THE QUICK REFERENCE GUIDE

ACCIDENTS (URANUS, AQUARIUS, 1st – BODY, 3rd – VEHICLE, 3rd Ruler, Planets in 3rd)
ACQUAINTANCES (URANUS, AQUARIUS, 11th, 11th Ruler, Planets in 11th)
ACUPUNCTURE (CHIRON, VIRGO, 6th, MARS, ARIES, 1st)
ADDICTIONS (NEPTUNE, PISCES, 12th, 12th Ruler, Planets in 12th)
ADVERTISING (JUPITER, SAGITTARIUS, 9th, 9th Ruler, Planets in 9th)
AIR (MERCURY, GEMINI, VENUS, LIBRA, URANUS, AQUARIUS)
ALCOHOL (NEPTUNE, PISCES)
ALLERGIES (MOON, CANCER, NEPTUNE, PISCES)
ANESTHETICS (NEPTUNE, PISCES)
ANIMALS (CHIRON, VIRGO, 6th, SOME – 12th)
ANKLES (URANUS, AQUARIUS)
ANXIETY (MERCURY, GEMINI, 3rd, CHIRON, VIRGO, 6th)
APPEARANCE (1st, 1st Ruler, Planets in 1st)
ARBITRATION (VENUS, 7th, 7th Ruler, Planets in 7th)
ARMS (MERCURY, GEMINI)
ART (VENUS, LIBRA, 7th, SUN, LEO, 5th)
ARTISTIC EXPRESSION (SUN, 5th, 5th Ruler, Planets in 5th)
ASSOCIATIONS (URANUS, AQUARIUS, 11th, 11th Ruler, Planets in 11th)
AUTHORITY (SATURN, CAPRICORN, 10th, 10th Ruler, Planets in 10th)

BACK, LOWER (VENUS, LIBRA)
BACK, UPPER (SUN, LEO)
BANK ACCOUNTS (VENUS, 2nd, 2nd Ruler, Planets in 2nd)
BANK LOANS (PLUTO, SCORPIO, 8th, 8th Ruler, Planets in 8th)
BANKRUPTCY (PLUTO, SCORPIO, 8th, 8th Ruler, Planets in 8th)
BELONGINGNESS (MOON, 4th, 4th Ruler, Planets in 4th)
BINGE BEHAVIOR (JUPITER, SAGITTARIUS)
BIRTH (PLUTO, SCORPIO, 8th, 8th Ruler, Planets in 8th)
BLESSINGS (PART OF FORTUNE)
BOATS (MOON, CANCER, 4th, MERCURY, GEMINI, 3rd)
BONDING (PLUTO, SCORPIO, 8th, 8th Ruler, Planets in 8th)
BONES (SATURN, CAPRICORN)
BOOKS (MERCURY, GEMINI, 3rd)
BOSS (SATURN, CAPRICORN, 10th, 10th Ruler, Planets in 10th)
BUILDING (SATURN, CAPRICORN, 10th, 10th Ruler, Planets in 10th)
BURNS (MARS, ARIES, 1st, 6th)

CALVES (URANUS, AQUARIUS)
CAREER (SATURN, CAPRICORN, 10th, 10th Ruler, Planets in 10th)
CARS (MERCURY, 3rd, 3rd Ruler, Planets in 3rd)
CHALLENGES (NORTH NODE)
CHILDREN (SUN, 5th, 5th Ruler, Planets in 5th)
CHIN (VENUS, TAURUS)
CHIROPRACTORS (CHIRON, VIRGO, 6th, SATURN, CAPRICORN, 10th)
CLEANSING (PLUTO, SCORPIO, 8th, SOUTH NODE, CHIRON, VIRGO, 6th)
CLIENTS (VENUS, 7th, 7th Ruler, Planets in 7th)
CLOUDS (NEPTUNE, PISCES, 12th)
CLUBS (URANUS, AQUARIUS, 11th, 11th Ruler, Planets in 11th)
CO-WORKERS (CHIRON, 6th, 6th Ruler, Planets in 6th)
COCAINE (NEPTUNE, PISCES, MERCURY, GEMINI)
COLD (SATURN, CAPRICORN)
COLLECTIONS (MOON, CANCER, 4th)
COLLEGE (JUPITER, SAGITTARIUS, 9th, 9th Ruler, Planets in 9th)
COMMITMENT (PLUTO, SCORPIO, 8th, 8th Ruler, Planets in 8th)
COMMUNICATION (MERCURY, 3rd, 3rd Ruler, Planets in 3rd)
COMMUNITY (MERCURY, 3rd, 3rd Ruler, Planets in 3rd)
COMMUNITY COLLEGE (MERCURY, GEMINI, 3rd, 3rd Ruler, Planets in 3rd)
COMPETITION (MARS, ARIES, 1st, 1st Ruler, Planets in 1st, PLUTO,
      SCORPIO, 8th)
COMPULSIVE BEHAVIOR (PLUTO, SCORPIO)
COMPUTERS (URANUS, AQUARIUS, 11th, 11th Ruler, Planets in 11th,
      MERCURY, GEMINI, 3rd)
CON ARTISTS (NEPTUNE, PISCES, 12th, 12th Ruler, Planets in 12th)
CONCEPTION (PLUTO, SCORPIO, 8th, 8th Ruler, Planets in 8th)
CONFUSION (NEPTUNE, PISCES, 12th, 12th Ruler, Planets in 12th)
CONSTRUCTION (SATURN, CAPRICORN, 10th, 10th Ruler, Planets in 10th)
CONSULTANTS (VENUS, 7th, 7th Ruler, Planets in 7th)
CONTAINERS (MOON, CANCER, VENUS, TAURUS, 2nd)
CONTRACTION (SATURN, CAPRICORN, 10th, 10th Ruler, Planets in 10th)
CONTRACTS (MERCURY, GEMINI, 3rd, 3rd Ruler, Planets in 3rd, 7th, 7th
      Ruler)
CONVENTS (NEPTUNE, PISCES, 12th, 12th Ruler, Planets in 12th)
COOPERATION (VENUS, 7th, 7th Ruler, Planets in 7th)
COUSINS (MERCURY, 3rd, 3rd Ruler, Planets in 3rd)
CREATIVITY (SUN, 5th, 5th Ruler, Planets in 5th)
CRYSTALS (SATURN, CAPRICORN)
CULTURAL ORIGINS (MOON, 4th, 4th Ruler, Planets in 4th)
CUSTOMERS (VENUS, 7th, 7th Ruler, Planets in 7th)

DAILY ROUTINE (CHIRON, 6th, 6th Ruler, Planets in 6th)
DATING (SUN, 5th, 5th Ruler, Planets in 5th)
DEATH (PLUTO, SCORPIO, 8th, 8th Ruler, Planets in 8th)
DEBTS (PLUTO, SCORPIO, 8th, 8th Ruler, Planets in 8th)
DESERT (SUN, LEO, 4th)
DIAGNOSTIC EQUIPMENT (MERCURY, GEMINI, 3rd, CHIRON, VIRGO,
      6th, PLUTO, SCORPIO, 8th)

DIARY (MERCURY, GEMINI, 3rd)
DIETING (CHIRON, VIRGO, 6th, SATURN, CAPRICORN, 1st, 6th Ruler, Planets in 6th)
DIVORCE (VENUS, LIBRA, 7th, PLUTO, SCORPIO, 8th, URANUS, AQUARIUS)
DOCTORS (CHIRON, VIRGO, 6th)
DREAMS (NEPTUNE, PISCES, 12th, 12th Ruler, Planets in 12th)
DRUGS, ILLEGAL (NEPTUNE, PISCES, 12th, 12th Ruler, Planets in 12th)
DRUGS, PRESCRIPTION (NEPTUNE, PISCES, 12th, 12th Ruler, Planets in 12th)

EARS (VENUS, TAURUS)
EARTH (SATURN, CAPRICORN, VENUS, TAURUS, CHIRON, VIRGO)
EARTHQUAKES (URANUS, AQUARIUS, PLUTO, SCORPIO, 4th)
EATING DISORDERS (MOON, CANCER, 4th, 4th Ruler, PLUTO, SCORPIO, 8th)
ECCENTRICS (URANUS, AQUARIUS, 11th, 11th Ruler, Planets in 11th)
ELBOWS (SATURN, CAPRICORN)
ELECTRICAL THINGS (MERCURY, GEMINI, 3rd)
ELECTRICITY (MERCURY, GEMINI, 3rd, 3rd Ruler, Planets in 3rd)
ELECTRONICS (URANUS, AQUARIUS, 11th, 11th Ruler, Planets in 11th, 3rd)
ELEMENTARY SCHOOL (MERCURY, GEMINI, 3rd, 3rd Ruler, Planets in 3rd)
EMBEZZLEMENT (NEPTUNE, PISCES, 12th, 12th Ruler, Planets in 12th)
EMPLOYEES (CHIRON, 6th, 6th Ruler, Planets in 6th)
EMPLOYER (SATURN, CAPRICORN, 10th, 10th Ruler, Planets in 10th)
ENEMIES (VENUS, 7th, 7th Ruler, Planets in 7th)
ENVIRONMENT (MERCURY, GEMINI, 3rd)
ENVIRONMENTAL CONCERNS (MERCURY, GEMINI, 3rd, PLUTO, SCORPIO, 8th)
ETHICS (JUPITER, SAGITTARIUS, 9th, 9th Ruler, Planets in 9th)
ETHNIC ORIGINS (MOON, 4th, 4th Ruler, Planets in 4th)
EXECUTIVES (SATURN, CAPRICORN, 10th, 10th Ruler, Planets in 10th)
EXHAUSTION (SOUTH NODE)
EXPANSION (JUPITER, SAGITTARIUS, 9th, 9th Ruler, Planets in 9th)
EYES (MOON, CANCER)

FAMILY OF ORIGIN (MOON, 4th, 4th Ruler, Planets in 4th)
FANTASIES (NEPTUNE, PISCES, 12th, 12th Ruler, Planets in 12th)
FARMING (CANCER, VIRGO)
FASTING (CHIRON, VIRGO, 6th, SATURN, CAPRICORN)
FAT AND FAT METABOLISM (JUPITER, SAGITTARIUS)
FATHER (SATURN, CAPRICORN, 10th, 10th Ruler, Planets in 10th)
FEET (NEPTUNE, PISCES)
FILMS (NEPTUNE, PISCES, 12th, 12th Ruler, Planets in 12th)
FINGERS (MERCURY, GEMINI)
FIRE (MARS, ARIES, SUN, LEO, JUPITER, SAGITTARIUS)
FISHING (NEPTUNE, PISCES, MOON, CANCER)
FLOODS (NEPTUNE, PISCES, 4th)
FLUID IN BODY (NEPTUNE, PISCES, MOON, CANCER)

FLUIDS (NEPTUNE, PISCES)
FOREIGN CONCEPTS (URANUS, AQUARIUS, 11th, 11th Ruler, Planets in
    11th)
FOREIGN PEOPLE (URANUS, AQUARIUS, 11th, 11th Ruler, Planets in 11th)
FOREIGN PLACES (URANUS, AQUARIUS, 11th, 11th Ruler, Planets in 11th,
    9th)
FOREIGN THINGS (URANUS, AQUARIUS, 11th, 2nd)
FOREST (JUPITER, SAGITTARIUS, 9th, 4th)
FRIENDS (URANUS, AQUARIUS, 11th, 11th Ruler, Planets in 11th)
FUTURE PLANS (URANUS, AQUARIUS, 11th, 11th Ruler, Planets in 11th)

GAIN (NORTH NODE, JUPITER, SAGITTARIUS, SUN, LEO, 5th)
GAMBLING (SUN, LEO, 5th, JUPITER, SAGITTARIUS, 5th Ruler, Planets in
    5th)
GAMES (SUN, LEO, 5th)
GARBAGE (PLUTO, SCORPIO, 8th)
GARDEN (VENUS, TAURUS, 2nd, 4th)
GENITALS (MARS, PLUTO, SCORPIO)
GOALS (URANUS, AQUARIUS, 11th, 11th Ruler, Planets in 11th)
GOD/DESS (NEPTUNE, PISCES, 12th, 12th Ruler, Planets in 12th)
GOSSIP AND RUMORS (MERCURY, 3rd, 3rd Ruler, Planets in 3rd)
GRADUATE SCHOOL (JUPITER, SAGITTARIUS, 9th, 9th Ruler, Planets in
    9th)
GROUPS (URANUS, AQUARIUS, 11th, 11th Ruler, Planets in 11th)
GROWTH (NORTH NODE, JUPITER, SAGITTARIUS, 9th)

HALLUCINATIONS (NEPTUNE, PISCES, 12th, 12th Ruler, Planets in 12th)
HANDS (MERCURY, GEMINI)
HEAD (MARS, ARIES)
HEALERS (CHIRON, VIRGO, 6th, NEPTUNE, PISCES, 12th)
HEALTH (CHIRON, 6th, 6th Ruler, Planets in 6th)
HEARING (VENUS, TAURUS, 2nd, LIBRA)
HEART (SUN, LEO, 5th, 1st)
HEROIN (NEPTUNE, PISCES)
HIGH SCHOOL (MERCURY, GEMINI, 3rd, 3rd Ruler, Planets in 3rd)
HIGHER POWER (NEPTUNE, PISCES, 12th, 12th Ruler, Planets in 12th)
HIPS (JUPITER, SAGITTARIUS)
HOLIDAYS (VENUS, TAURUS, 2nd, MOON, CANCER, 4th)
HOMEOPATHY (CHIRON, VIRGO, 6th)
HOSPITALS (NEPTUNE, PISCES, 12th, 12th Ruler, Planets in 12th)
HOT (MARS, ARIES)
HOUSE (MOON, 4th, 4th Ruler, Planets in 4th)
HURRICANES (URANUS, AQUARIUS, 4th)

ILLEGAL ACTIVITIES (NEPTUNE, PISCES, 12th, 12th Ruler, Planets in 12th)
IMAGINATION (NEPTUNE, PISCES, 12th, 12th Ruler, Planets in 12th)
INSTITUTIONS (NEPTUNE, PISCES, 12th, SATURN, CAPRICORN, 10th)

INSURANCE (PLUTO, SCORPIO, 8th)
INTEGRATION (PART OF FORTUNE)
INTIMACY (PLUTO, SCORPIO, 8th, 8th Ruler, Planets in 8th)

JAW, LOWER (VENUS, TAURUS)
JAW, UPPER (MARS, ARIES)
JOB (CHIRON, 6th, 6th Ruler, Planets in 6th)
JOINTS (SATURN, CAPRICORN)
JOURNALS (MERCURY, GEMINI, 3rd)
JUDGE, COURT OF LAW (JUPITER, SAGITTARIUS, 9th)
JUDGMENTS, GOSSIP (MERCURY, GEMINI, 3rd)
JUDGMENTS, LEGAL (JUPITER, SAGITTARIUS, 9th)

KNEES (SATURN, CAPRICORN)

LAW (JUPITER, SAGITTARIUS, SATURN, CAPRICORN, VENUS, LIBRA)
LIBRARIES (MERCURY, GEMINI, 3rd)
LIFE PURPOSE (SUN, MIDHEAVEN)
LOSS (SOUTH NODE, PLUTO, SCORPIO, 8th)
LOVE AFFAIRS (SUN, 5th, 5th Ruler, Planets in 5th)
LUCK (NORTH NODE, PART OF FORTUNE, JUPITER, SAGITTARIUS, 9th,
    5th)
LUNGS (MERCURY, GEMINI

MAGAZINES (MERCURY, GEMINI, 3rd)
MARIJUANA (NEPTUNE, PISCES)
MARKETING (JUPITER, SAGITTARIUS, 9th, 9th Ruler, Planets in 9th)
MARRIAGE (VENUS, 7th, 7th Ruler, Planets in 7th)
MECHANICAL THINGS (MERCURY, GEMINI, 3rd, CHIRON, VIRGO, 6th)
MEDIA (JUPITER, SAGITTARIUS, 9th)
MEDITATION (NEPTUNE, PISCES, 12th, 12th Ruler, Planets in 12th)
MEN (MARS)
MENTAL HEALTH CENTERS (NEPTUNE, PISCES, 12th, 12th Ruler, Planets in
    12th)
MENTORS (JUPITER, SAGITTARIUS, 9th, 9th Ruler, Planets in 9th)
MERGERS (NEPTUNE, PISCES, 10th)
MILITARY (CHIRON, VIRGO, 6th, 6th Ruler, Planets in 6th)
MISSION, CAUSE (URANUS, AQUARIUS, 11th)
MISSION, LIFE (MIDHEAVEN, SUN)
MONASTERIES (NEPTUNE, PISCES, 12th, 12th Ruler, Planets in 12th)
MONEY (VENUS, 2nd, 2nd Ruler, Planets in 2nd)
MONEY, JOINT (PLUTO, SCORPIO, 8th, 8th Ruler, Planets in 8th)
MONEY, COMPULSIVE OVERSPENDING (JUPITER, SAGITTARIUS)
MORALS (JUPITER, SAGITTARIUS, 9th, 9th Ruler, Planets in 9th)
MOTHER (MOON, 4th, 4th Ruler, Planets in 4th)
MOUNTAINS (SATURN, CAPRICORN, 10th, 4th)
MUSIC (VENUS, TAURUS, 2nd, LIBRA, 7th, 5th)

NAME AND NAME CHANGES (1st, 1st Ruler, Planets in 1st)
NATUROPATHY (CHIRON, VIRGO, 6th)
NEGOTIATIONS (VENUS, 7th, 7th Ruler, Planets in 7th)
NEIGHBORHOOD (MERCURY, 3rd, 3rd Ruler, Planets in 3rd)
NEIGHBORS (MERCURY, 3rd, 3rd Ruler, Planets in 3rd)
NEWS REPORTS (MERCURY, GEMINI, 3rd)
NEWSPAPERS (MERCURY, GEMINI, 3rd, JUPITER, SAGITTARIUS, 9th)
NONCONFORMITY (URANUS, AQUARIUS, 11th, 11th Ruler, Planets in 11th)
NOSE (MARS, ARIES)
NUCLEAR ENERGY (PLUTO, SCORPIO, 8th)
NURSES (CHIRON, VIRGO, 6th)

OBJECTS (VENUS, 2nd, 2nd Ruler, Planets in 2nd)
OCEAN (NEPTUNE, PISCES, 12th, 4th)
OIL (NEPTUNE, PISCES, 12th)
OIL SPILLS (NEPTUNE, PISCES, 12th, 4th)
OPTIMISM (JUPITER, SAGITTARIUS, 9th, 9th Ruler, Planets in 9th)
ORGANIZATION (SATURN, CAPRICORN, 10th, 10th Ruler, Planets in 10th)
OTHER LIVES (SOUTH NODE, 12th HOUSE, SATURN)
OVEREATING (MOON, CANCER, JUPITER, SAGITTARIUS)

PARTNERS (VENUS, 7th, 7th Ruler, Planets in 7th)
PERSONALITY (1st, 1st Ruler, Planets in 1st, ASCENDANT)
PETS (CHIRON, 6th, 6th Ruler, Planets in 6th)
PHILOSOPHY (JUPITER, SAGITTARIUS, 9th, 9th Ruler, Planets in 9th)
PHOTOGRAPHS (NEPTUNE, PISCES, 12th, MERCURY, GEMINI, 3rd)
PLANS (URANUS, AQUARIUS, 11th, 11th Ruler, Planets in 11th)
PLAY (SUN, 5th, 5th Ruler, Planets in 5th)
PLUMBING (PLUTO, SCORPIO, NEPTUNE, PISCES, 4th)
POCKETS (MOON, CANCER)
POLICE (PLUTO, SCORPIO, 8th, SATURN, CAPRICORN, 10th, CHIRON,
     VIRGO, 6th)
POLITICS (URANUS, AQUARIUS, 11th, 11th Ruler, Planets in 11th)
POLLUTION (PLUTO, SCORPIO, 8th)
POSSESSIONS (VENUS, 2nd, 2nd Ruler, Planets in 2nd)
POST-GRADUATE SCHOOL (JUPITER, SAGITTARIUS, 9th, 9th Ruler, Planets
     in 9th)
PRACTICALITY (SATURN, CAPRICORN, 10th, 10th Ruler, Planets in 10th)
PRAYER (NEPTUNE, PISCES, 12th, 12th Ruler, Planets in 12th)
PRESCRIPTIONS (MERCURY, GEMINI, NEPTUNE, PISCES)
PRESIDENT (SATURN, CAPRICORN, 10th, 10th Ruler, Planets in 10th)
PRISONS (NEPTUNE, PISCES, 12th, 12th Ruler, Planets in 12th)
PROFESSION (SATURN, CAPRICORN, 10th, 10th Ruler, Planets in 10th)
PROFESSIONALISM (SATURN, CAPRICORN, 10th, 10th Ruler, Planets in
     10th)
PROMOTION (JUPITER, SAGITTARIUS, 9th, 9th Ruler, Planets in 9th)
PSYCHIC EXPERIENCES (NEPTUNE, PISCES, 12th, 12th Ruler, Planets in
     12th, PLUTO, SCORPIO, 8th, 8th Ruler, Planets in 8th, URANUS,
     AQUARIUS)

RACIAL ORIGINS (MOON, 4th, 4th Ruler, Planets in 4th)
REAL ESTATE (MOON, 4th, 4th Ruler, Planets in 4th)
REBELLION (URANUS, AQUARIUS, 11th, 11th Ruler, Planets in 11th)
REBIRTH (PLUTO, SCORPIO, 8th, 8th Ruler, Planets in 8th)
RECOVERY, FROM ADDICTIONS (NEPTUNE, PISCES, 12th, CHIRON, VIRGO, 6th)
RECOVERY, FROM MEDICAL PROCEDURES (CHIRON, VIRGO, 6th)
RECREATION (SUN, 5th, 5th Ruler, Planets in 5th)
RELIGION (JUPITER, SAGITTARIUS, 9th, 9th Ruler, Planets in 9th)
RELIGIOUS LEADERS (JUPITER, SAGITTARIUS, 9th, 9th Ruler, Planets in 9th)
RENTAL PROPERTY (MOON, 4th, 4th Ruler, Planets in 4th)
REPUTATION (MIDHEAVEN, SATURN, CAPRICORN, 10th, 10th Ruler, Planets in 10th, 1st, LEO)
RESOURCES, SHARED (PLUTO, SCORPIO, 8th, 8th Ruler, Planets in 8th)
RESPONSIBILITY (SATURN, CAPRICORN, 10th, 10th Ruler, Planets in 10th)
RETREAT CENTERS (NEPTUNE, PISCES, 12th, 12th Ruler, Planets in 12th)
REVOLUTION (URANUS, AQUARIUS, 11th, PLUTO, SCORPIO, 8th)
ROLE OR TITLE (1st, 1st Ruler, Planets in 1st)
ROMANCE (SUN, 5th, 5th Ruler, Planets in 5th)

SALES (JUPITER, SAGITTARIUS, 9th, 9th Ruler, Planets in 9th)
SCHEDULE (CHIRON, 6th, 6th Ruler, Planets in 6th)
SELF-WORTH (VENUS, 2nd, 2nd Ruler, Planets in 2nd)
SEX (MARS, PLUTO, SCORPIO, 8th, 8th Ruler, Planets in 8th)
SHINS (URANUS, AQUARIUS)
SHOULDERS (MERCURY, GEMINI)
SINUSES (MOON, CANCER)
SISTERS AND BROTHERS (MERCURY, 3rd, 3rd Ruler, Planets in 3rd)
SPECULATION (SUN, LEO, 5th, 5th Ruler, Planets in 5th)
SPIES (NEPTUNE, PISCES, 12th, 12th Ruler, Planets in 12th, PLUTO, SCORPIO)
SPINAL CHORD (SUN, LEO)
SPINAL COLUMN (SATURN, CAPRICORN)
SPINE (SUN, LEO)
SPIRITUALITY (NEPTUNE, PISCES, 12th, 12th Ruler, Planets in 12th)
SPORTS (SUN, 5th, 5th Ruler, Planets in 5th)
STAFF (CHIRON, VIRGO, 6th, VENUS, LIBRA, 7th)
STATUS (MIDHEAVEN, SATURN, CAPRICORN, 10th, 10th Ruler, Planets in 10th)
STOCKS AND BONDS (PLUTO, SCORPIO, 8th, 8th Ruler, Planets in 8th)
STOMACH (MOON, CANCER)
STRESS (CHIRON, 6th, 6th Ruler, Planets in 6th)
STRUCTURES (SATURN, CAPRICORN, 10th)
SUGAR AND SUGAR METABOLISM (VENUS, LIBRA)
SURGERY (CHIRON, MARS, 6th, 6th Ruler, Planets in 6th)
SYSTEMS, ORGANIZATIONAL (SATURN, CAPRICORN, 10th)
SYSTEMS, PHYSICAL (CHIRON, VIRGO, 6th)
SYSTEMS, THEORETICAL (URANUS, AQUARIUS, 11th)

TAXES (PLUTO, SCORPIO, 8th, 8th Ruler, Planets in 8th)
TEACHERS (MERCURY, GEMINI, 3rd, 3rd Ruler, Planets in 3rd, JUPITER, SAGITTARIUS, 9th, 9th Ruler, Planets in 9th)
TECHNICIANS (CHIRON, VIRGO, 6th)
TECHNOLOGY (URANUS, AQUARIUS, 11th, 11th Ruler, Planets in 11th)
TEETH (SATURN, CAPRICORN)
TELEPHONE (MERCURY, 3rd, 3rd Ruler, Planets in 3rd)
TENANTS (CHIRON, 6th, 6th Ruler, Planets in 6th)
THIGHS (JUPITER, SAGITTARIUS)
THROAT (VENUS, TAURUS)
TOYS (SUN, LEO, 5th)
TRADITIONS (VENUS, TAURUS, 2nd, MOON, CANCER, 4th, SATURN, CAPRICORN, 10th)
TRANSFORMATION (PLUTO, SCORPIO, 8th, 8th Ruler, Planets in 8th)
TRANSPORTATION (bus, train, etc.) (MERCURY, 3rd, 3rd Ruler, Planets in 3rd)
TRAVEL, INTERNATIONAL (JUPITER, SAGITTARIUS, 9th, 9th Ruler, Planets in 9th)
TRIPS, SHORT (MERCURY, 3rd, 3rd Ruler, Planets in 3rd)

ULCERS (MOON, CANCER)
UNIONS (URANUS, AQUARIUS, 11th)
UNIVERSITY (JUPITER, SAGITTARIUS, 9th, 9th Ruler, Planets in 9th)
UTOPIAN VISIONS (URANUS, AQUARIUS, 11th, 11th Ruler, Planets in 11th)

VACATIONS (MERCURY, 3rd, 3rd Ruler, Planets in 3rd)
VEHICLES (MERCURY, 3rd, 3rd Ruler, Planets in 3rd)
VERTEBRAE (SATURN, CAPRICORN)
VOC-TECH SCHOOLS (MERCURY, GEMINI, 3rd, 3rd Ruler, Planets in 3rd)
VOCATION (SATURN, CAPRICORN, 10th, 10th Ruler, Planets in 10th)
VOLCANOES (PLUTO, SCORPIO, 4th)
VOMITING (PLUTO, SCORPIO, 8th, SOUTH NODE)

WATER (NEPTUNE, PISCES, MOON, CANCER, PLUTO, SCORPIO)
WEATHER (MOON, CANCER, 4th)
WEATHER REPORTS (MERCURY, GEMINI, 3rd)
WEIGHT LOSS (SATURN, CAPRICORN, 1st)
WEIGHT GAIN (JUPITER, SAGITTARIUS, 1st)
WOMEN (VENUS)
WORKERS (CHIRON, VIRGO, 6th)
WRISTS (SATURN, CAPRICORN, MERCURY, GEMINI)

X-RAYS (NEPTUNE, PISCES, 12th)

YOGA (VENUS, TAURUS, CHIRON, VIRGO, 6th)

SUMMARY

In this Chapter, I've given you some ideas about how to actually "read" your Chart and the Charts of others. You can pick and choose from the techniques and categories that I presented and make a combination that best suits your style. You'll be creating your Reading by considering the following elements of the Chart:

THE OVERVIEW
    Sectional Focus
    Chart Pattern
    Aspect Patterns
    Loaded Signs or Houses
    Number of Retrogrades
    Interceptions and Duplications
    Focus Planets
    Emphasized or Deemphasized Qualities and Elements
    Emphasized Pairs or Themes

INTERPRETING THE PLANETS BY POSITION AND RULERSHIP

INTERPRETING THE POINTS BY POSITION

INTERPRETING THE PLANETS AND POINTS BY ASPECT

EXERCISES

For Understanding the Fundamentals

8-1   Do an Overview interpretation of your Chart. Notice the factors that are emphasized by:

    RETROGRADATION
    LOADED SIGNS OR HOUSES
    INTERCEPTIONS AND DUPLICATIONS

For Understanding the Details

8-2   Using several Charts, compare and contrast them according to Hemisphere or Quadrant emphasis and Chart Pattern.

8-3   Using several Charts, figure out and interpret the Aspect Patterns.

8-4   Ask some friends to let you practice giving them Readings. Look over their Charts ahead of time and organize the data according to:

OVERVIEW INFORMATION
> Sectional Emphasis
> Chart Pattern
> Aspect Patterns
> Loaded Signs or Houses
> Number of Retrogrades
> Interceptions and Duplications
> Focus Planets
> Qualities and Elements
> Pairs and Themes

THE PLANETS
> Position by House and Sign
> Influence by Rulership

THE POINTS
> Position by House and Sign

THE ASPECTS
> Those to the Sun, Moon, and Ascendant
> Those to Planets representing current concerns
> The remaining Aspects

8-4   Do the Readings with your friends. Tape them so that they or you can have a record of what you said.

AUTHOR'S AFTERWORD

I hope you've found CHOICE CENTERED ASTROLOGY: THE BASICS to be stimulating, insightful, easy, challenging, engrossing, and *useful*. Whether you were a novice or a professional when you began, you're now more fully launched on your journey into Astrology. The Appendices that follow may expand your understanding of Astrology but they are not necessary to that understanding. Dip into them if and when you want. Meanwhile, enjoy yourself as you proceed on your own!

Appendix A
Using a Pendulum to Divine Your Birth Time

The best way to DIVINE YOUR BIRTH TIME is to use a pendulum. If you don't have one, you can make one by attaching a small, heavy object to the bottom of a string or chain (you can even use a pendant-type necklace or a fishing bob). Then, rest your elbow firmly on a table with your hand up in the air. Holding the end of the string lightly between your thumb and forefinger, allow the pendulum to move of its own accord. It will swing after awhile. If you hold it above the base points of diagrams such as the ones below, you'll be able to determine, by noting the direction of the pendulum's swing, when you were born.

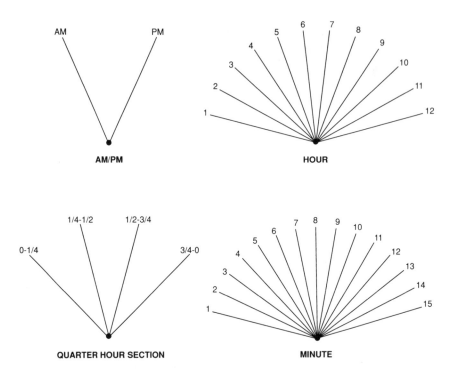

Appendix B
Computer and Other Resources

Name / Address / Phone (*Alphabetical Order*)	Types of Resources
ASTRO-COMPUTING SERVICES P.O. BOX 16430 SAN DIEGO, CA 92116-0430 (800) 888-9983	Charts in many formats software some books and other tools
ASTROLABE P.O. BOX 28 ORLEANS, MA 02653 (508) 896-5081	Charts in many formats software some books and other tools
ASTROLOGY ET AL 4728 UNIVERSITY WAY N.E. SEATTLE, WA 98105 (206) 524-6365	various Charts many books and other tools (this is a bookstore)
MATRIX SOFTWARE 315 MARION BIG RAPIDS, MI 49307 (800) PLANETS	Charts in many formats software some books and other tools (ask for personal sample order form)
RAMP CREEK PUBLISHING, INC. P.O. BOX 3 SMITHVILLE, IN 47458-0003	anything by Gail Fairfield some books and other tools learning tapes
SEARCH P.O. BOX 75362 SEATTLE, WA 98125 (206) 672-8548	some books and other tools correspondence courses

Appendix C
The Asteroids

There are quite a number of ASTEROIDS that have been named and interpreted for Astrological purposes. Four of them are considered Major Asteroids: CERES, PALLAS ATHENE (or PALLAS), VESTA, and JUNO. The remaining eleven or twelve are considered to be Minor. Chiron is sometimes included with these Minor Asteroids, but in this book, I've moved it to Planet status. You can get information (including Ephemerides) about all of the Asteroids from your local Astrology bookstore. Most computer services will also include the Asteroids in your Charts if you so request.

The Asteroids operate like Planets in that they have functions to perform. They are actors; they fulfill their tasks in the manner of their Signs regarding the affairs of their Houses. Although the Asteroids often represent qualities that have been seen as "feminine" in the Western world, they are not limited to women. Every Chart can contain the Asteroids; every person can use them. Brief descriptions of the four Major Asteroids follow.

CERES (Fig. A-1): THE EARTH "MOTHER": to nourish and sustain through the expression of unconditional love; to act as the Universal Nurturer; to love and accept the self and others; to work productively in order to care for the self and others

Figure A-1
Ceres

BY SIGN, CERES will show how you nurture yourself and others, how you experience acceptance and rejection, and how you bond or release dependency.

BY HOUSE, CERES will show the contexts in which you need to feel unconditionally loved and the arenas in which you are willing to work hard to take care of others.

PALLAS ATHENE or PALLAS (Fig. A-2): THE CONSCIOUS CREATRIX: to use current knowledge in a Universally creative way; to perceive the whole pattern; to strategize and plan for concrete success; to create what has been consciously imagined; to balance "male" and "female" energies within

Figure A-2
Pallas Athene

BY SIGN, PALLAS will show you how you use your conscious mind as a trigger for your creativity, how you perceive the world as a whole, and how you integrate the "male" and "female" roles within your own persona.

BY HOUSE, PALLAS will show you the contexts in which you want to succeed by your wits and creativity and the arenas in which you want to create wholeness for yourself and others.

VESTA (Fig. A-3): THE COMMITTED DEVOTEE: to completely commit the self, body and soul, to a spiritual, physical, mental, or emotional path; to sacrifice for the sake of larger goals; to use the sexual or life-force energy in order to fully and intensely demonstrate beliefs

**Figure A-3
Vesta**

BY SIGN, VESTA will show you how you can effectively focus your energy, how you will be able to be self-denying for the sake of your beliefs and values, and how you'll express your sexuality or your life-force.

BY HOUSE, VESTA will show you the contexts in which you are completely dedicated and willing to serve the greater good and the arenas in which you'll unreservedly channel your energies.

JUNO (Fig. A-4): THE PARTNERED MATRIARCH: to create meaningful relationships that allow both partners to remain powerful; to protect and maintain the chosen or biological family or clan; to create intimacy through charm or confrontation; to affirm the balance of power in all situations

**Figure A-4
Juno**

BY SIGN, JUNO will show how you stand up for yourself and others, how you create powerful and intimate relationships, and how you support equality in the world.

BY HOUSE, JUNO will show you the contexts in which you are willing to use all your power to fight for equality and the arenas in which strong relationships are important to you.

Appendix D
Calculating the Part of Fortune

You can calculate the Part of Fortune by following these steps:

1. Translate the positions of the Sun, Moon, and Ascendant into their positions within the 360-Degree zodiac (see Appendix G, Step One of Calculating Aspects, for how).

2. Add and subtract their positions according to this formula:

   ASCENDANT + MOON − SUN

   If the result is greater than 360 Degrees, simply subtract 360 until you get a number that is smaller than 360.

3. Translate the new 360-Degree position back into its appropriate Sign position.

Grace's Part of Fortune would be calculated as follows:

STEP ONE

ASCENDANT at 2° LI 16' = 182° 16'

MOON at 9° PI 03' = 339° 03'

SUN at 8° AQ 10' = 308° 10'

STEP TWO

ASCENDANT	182° 16'	(compute the
PLUS MOON	+ 339° 03'	two columns
MINUS SUN	− 308° 10'	separately)

213° 09'

STEP THREE

213° 09' = 3° SC 09' = GRACE'S PART OF FORTUNE*

---

* The computer, which is more accurate than we are, calculates the Part of Fortune using the Seconds (within the Minutes) as well as the Degrees and Minutes. As a result, it calculated Grace's Part of Fortune as 3 SC 08'. In terms of interpretation, the difference is pretty negligible.

Appendix E
More about the Structure of the Houses

In addition to the categories discussed in Chapter 4, the Houses can be organized by TYPE and by MODE.

THE TYPES

The twelve Houses can be divided into three groups and classified according to their TYPES: ANGULAR, SUCCEDENT, and CADENT. As you can see in Figure A-5, the Types begin in the First House and repeat themselves, in order, around the Chart.

The ANGULAR Houses (1, 4, 7, and 10) are those in which action is motivated, inspired, and begun. These Houses hold processes that are associated with COMMENCING and ORIGINATING.

In SUCCEDENT Houses (2, 5, 8, and 11), the previously initiated actions are intensified, sustained, and supported. These Houses hold processes that are associated with CONCENTRATING and FOCUSING.

In CADENT Houses (3, 6, 9, and 12), the now solidified constructs are enhanced, rearranged, or dissolved. These Houses hold processes that are associated with ADAPTING AND DISPERSING.

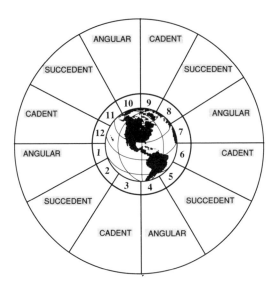

Figure A-5
The Houses According to Their Types

THE MODES

The Houses can also be divided into four groups, identified as the MODES of ENERGY, SUBSTANCE, CONNECTEDNESS, and DEPTH. Like the Types, the Modes are repeated in a regular sequence, starting from the First House and going counterclockwise around the Chart (Fig. A-6).

In the Houses of ENERGY (1, 5, and 9), which can also be named the Houses of Life, enthusiasm is generated. These Houses are support experiences that are associated with EXPRESSION and INSPIRATION.

In the Houses of SUBSTANCE (2, 6, and 10), also called the Vocational Houses, interactions with the material world are activated. These Houses support experiences that are associated with PHYSICALITY and PRODUCTIVITY.

In the Houses of CONNECTEDNESS (3, 7, and 11), sometimes referred to as the Relationship or Social Houses, mental exchanges occur. These Houses support experiences that are associated with COMMUNICATION and RELATEDNESS.

In the Houses of DEPTH (4, 8, and 12), also called the Houses of Endings or the Subjective Houses, intuitive experiences happen. These Houses support experiences that are associated with EMOTIONS and DEEP MEANING.

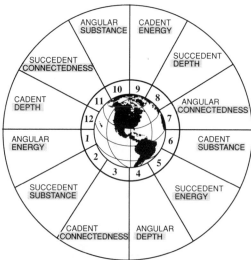

Figure A-6
The Houses According to Their Modes

Appendix F
More about the Structure of the Signs

In addition to the structural elements presented in Chapter 5, the Signs can be organized by POLARITY and by DECANATE.

THE POLARITIES

The POLARITIES (Fig. A-7) are a way of dividing the twelve Signs into two groups which are defined by alternating Signs. One group begins with Aries and includes all the Fire and Air Signs. The other group begins with Taurus and contains the Earth and Water Signs. By organizing the Signs in this way, every other Sign can be characterized, depending on your preference, as yang or yin, masculine or feminine, active or receptive, and positive or negative (magnetic poles). In all of these pairs, the concept of opposites is symbolized and a movement toward unity is implied. No value judgment is placed on either of the poles. Just as speaker and listener are both critical to a conversation, day and night are both necessary to survival, and left and right brain activities are both vital in whole persons, both sides of this polarity are useful. I like to characterize the two sides as LEFT BRAIN (yang, masculine, active, positive) and RIGHT BRAIN (yin, feminine, receptive, negative).

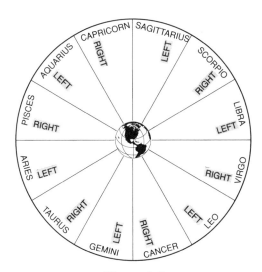

Figure A-7
The Polarities

The LEFT BRAIN Signs (FIRE AND AIR) are generally progressive, assertive, forward-moving, and restless. They have a tremendous desire for activity, doing things, and expressiveness. In most situations, they tend to go for what they want in the future; they ACT FIRST and ASSIMILATE the results LATER.

The RIGHT BRAIN Signs (EARTH AND WATER) are generally resourceful, receptive, stabilizing, and productive. They have a deep desire for security, unity, and supportiveness. In most situations, they tend to ASSIMILATE their experiences FIRST and ACT LATER.

THE DECANATES

The DECANATES (Fig. A-8) are a way of dividing up the Signs internally to give fuller richness to their interpretations. They are found by taking the 30 Degrees contained in each Sign and dividing them into three 10-Degree sections: 0°–9°59'; 10°–19°59'; 20°–29°59'. These parts are called the First, Second, and Third Decanates of the Sign.

Interpretationally, the Decanates add the flavor of the other Signs of the same Element to their sections. In other words, Taurus, by its Decanates, would have hints of Capricorn and Virgo within it. More specifically, the First Decanate emphasizes the Sign itself; the Second Decanate adds a touch of the next Sign in the Zodiac (going in order) of the same Element; the Third Decanate includes a touch of the remaining Sign in the Zodiac of the same Element. Specific applications for the Decanates follow:

ARIES
  First: Aries: extra independence and assertiveness
  Second: Leo: emphasis on celebration and drama
  Third: Sagittarius: emphasis on questing and teaching

TAURUS
  First: Taurus: extra resourcefulness and productivity
  Second: Virgo: emphasis on perfection and analysis
  Third: Capricorn: emphasis on status and structure

GEMINI
  First: Gemini: extra curiosity and communicativeness
  Second: Libra: emphasis on cooperation and balance
  Third: Aquarius: emphasis on futuristic visions

CANCER
  First: Cancer: extra caring and sensitivity
  Second: Scorpio: emphasis on intimacy and passion
  Third: Pisces: emphasis on intuition and spirituality

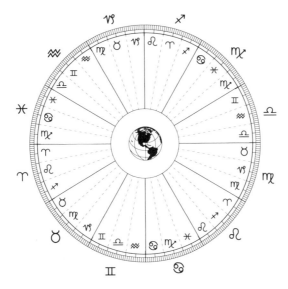

Figure A-8
The Decanates

LEO
   First: Leo: extra confidence and generosity
   Second: Sagittarius: emphasis on growth and optimism
   Third: Aries: emphasis on pioneering and independence

VIRGO
   First: Virgo: extra discrimination and service
   Second: Capricorn: emphasis on order and discipline
   Third: Taurus: emphasis on caution and loyalty

LIBRA
   First: Libra: extra diplomacy and charm
   Second: Aquarius: emphasis on unconventional ideas
   Third: Gemini: emphasis on networking and fact-finding

SCORPIO
   First: Scorpio: extra depth and passion
   Second: Pisces: emphasis on spirituality and intuition
   Third: Cancer: emphasis on nurturance and belonging

SAGITTARIUS
   First: Sagittarius: extra expansiveness and ethics
   Second: Aries: emphasis on independence and pioneering
   Third: Leo: emphasis on performance and playfulness

CAPRICORN
> First: Capricorn: extra organization and control
> Second: Taurus: emphasis on loyalty and predictability
> Third: Virgo: emphasis on solutions and analysis

AQUARIUS
> First: Aquarius: extra future vision and uniqueness
> Second: Gemini: emphasis on communication and diversity
> Third: Libra: emphasis on relatedness and cooperation

PISCES
> First: Pisces: extra intuition and compassion
> Second: Cancer: emphasis on nurturance and caretaking
> Third: Scorpio: emphasis on intensity and passion

Appendix G
More about the Aspects

In this Appendix, I'll give you some hints for finding the Aspects visually and show you how to calculate the Aspects by hand. Then, I'll briefly describe and interpret eight Minor Aspects and five Minor Aspect Patterns.

FINDING THE ASPECTS

In order to find the Aspects visually or to calculate them by hand, it's valuable to keep the 360° of the Zodiac and its Sign divisions in mind (Fig. A-9).

Hints for Finding the Aspects Visually

THE CONJUNCTION ☌ (0°) : Planets that are very close together are considered to be Conjunct. Even if they cross House or Sign boundaries, as long as they are within 8° of each other, they're still in Conjunction. A Planet at 2° of Leo will be conjunct a Planet at 4° Leo. An OUT-OF-SIGN CONJUNCTION would be demonstrated by the Aspect between a Planet located at 29° Scorpio and one that's at 6° Sagittarius.

THE SEMI-SEXTILE ⊻ (30°) : Planets that are about a Sign apart are Semi-Sextile. Most of the time, they'll be at about the same Degree of Signs that are next to each other. A Planet at 17° Gemini will be Semi-Sextile a

Planet at 19° Cancer, the next Sign. It could also be Semi-Sextile a Planet at 15° Taurus, the Sign before it. OUT-OF- SIGN Semi-Sextiles don't honor the "neighboring Sign" rule. A Planet at 2° Aquarius will be Semi-Sextile (about 30° away from) another Planet at 29° Aquarius.

THE SEXTILE ✶ (60°): Planets that are two Signs apart are Sextile. The easily recognized ones will be at the same Degrees of Signs that have one extra Sign between them. A Planet at 8° Virgo will be Sextile one at 4° Scorpio (Libra is between the two Signs). It will also Sextile a Planet at 5° Cancer (Leo is between these two). OUT-OF-SIGN Sextiles are 60°, but not exactly two Signs, apart. A Planet at 29° Sagittarius is Sextile one at 0° Pisces. The one at 0° Pisces would also Sextile another Planet at 27° Aries.

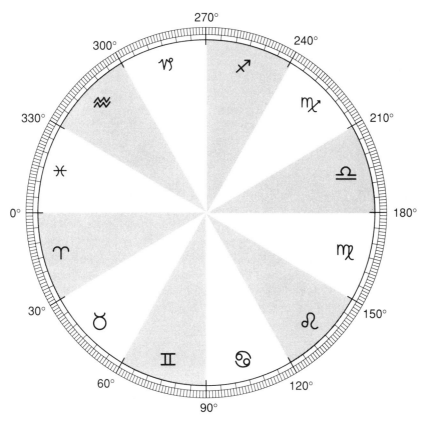

Figure A-9
The 360-Degree Zodiac

THE SQUARE □ (**90°**) : Squared Planets are three Signs, or a fourth of the Zodiac, apart. As a result, they usually fall in Signs that reflect the same Quality. A Planet at some Degree of a Cardinal Sign will Square a Planet at a similar Degree of the adjoining Cardinal Signs. The opposite Sign of the same element would, of course, be farther than 90° away and not considered a Square. The same principle would apply for the other Qualities. A Planet at 3° Gemini would be Square Planets at 3° Virgo or 6° Pisces (all Mutable Signs). AN OUT-OF-QUALITY SQUARE would be one between a Planet at 28° Libra and 2° Aquarius.

THE TRINE △ (**120°**) : Planets that Trine one another are four Signs, or about a third of the Zodiac, apart. They often fall in Signs that reflect the same Element. A Planet in the middle of an Earth Sign would be Trine any Planet in the middle of either of the other Earth Signs. The same would hold true for all the other elements. A Planet located at 20° Pisces would Trine Planets at 15° Scorpio or 22° Cancer. AN OUT-OF-ELEMENT TRINE would be one between a Planet at 26° Libra and another at 2° Pisces.

THE QUINCUNX ⊼ (**150°**) : Quincunx Planets are in Signs that are one away from being opposite each other. In other words, a Planet at 4° Aries would be Quincunx one at 3° Virgo (Virgo is one away from Libra, Aries's opposite). It would also Quincunx a Planet at 1° Scorpio. An OUT-OF-SIGN Quincunx would be one from 2° Leo to 29° Sagittarius. By element (Fire) they would seem to be Trine but by Degree (close to 150), they are actually Quincunx.

THE OPPOSITION ⚭ (**180°**) : Planets that are opposite each other are also opposed by Aspect. They will ordinarily fall in Signs of the same Quality: A Planet at 16° Cancer will form an Opposition with one at 13° Capricorn (both Cardinal Signs). Of course, OUT-OF-QUALITY Oppositions can occur, as well: A Planet located at 4° Leo will Oppose one at 28° Capricorn. Remember that the NODES will always be opposed to one another; therefore, don't count their relationship to each other as a significant Aspect. Do include them in Aspect to the other Points and the Planets.

Calculating the Aspects by Hand

Use the following steps to calculate the Aspects by hand.

STEP ONE

TRANSLATE THE POSITIONS OF THE TWO PLANETS OR POINTS INTO NON-SIGN POSITIONS ON THE 360-DEGREE CIRCLE OF THE ZODIAC.

To do this, use Figure A-9 to help you view the 360° of the zodiac as a whole. Notice that every Degree has its unique number in the 360°, and that every Degree is also assigned to a specific Degree and Minute of Sign. To translate a specific position within the Signs into the 360-Degree wheel, add the Degrees and Minutes of Sign to the number within the 360° that correlates to the beginning of that Sign. For example, 0° Aries corresponds to 0° in the whole Zodiac circle, but 0° Taurus is 30° in the bigger picture, 0° Scorpio is 210°, and 0° Aquarius is 300°. More specifically, 5° Taurus would then be 35°, 17° Scorpio would be 227°, and 23° Aquarius would be 323°.

Figure A-10 shows the translations for the Planets and Points from the Sign positions to the whole circle positions in Grace's Chart.

POINT OR PLANET	DEGREE/MINUTES BY SIGN	DEGREE/MINUTES BY WHOLE CIRCLE	ROUNDED OFF
ASCENDANT	2 LIBRA 16	182 16	182
SATURN	14 LIBRA 57	194 57	195
NEPTUNE	21 LIBRA 42	201 42	202
PART OF FORTUNE	3 SCORPIO 08	213 08	213
MARS	4 SCORPIO 03	214 03	214
VENUS	1 CAPRICORN 48	271 48	272
CHIRON	8 CAPRICORN 10	278 10	278
MERCURY	22 CAPRICORN 23	292 23	292
SUN	8 AQUARIUS 10	308 10	308
NORTH NODE	0 PISCES 39	330 09	330
MOON	9 PISCES 03	339 03	339
JUPITER	9 ARIES 53	9 53	10
MIDHEAVEN	2 CANCER 34	92 34	93
URANUS	10 CANCER 53	100 53	101
PLUTO	20 LEO 37	140 37	141
SOUTH NODE	0 VIRGO 39	150 39	151

Figure A-10: Grace's Chart
Translation of Planets and Points into Positions on the 360-Degree Circle

STEP TWO

SUBTRACT THE POSITIONS OF ANY TWO PLANETS OR POINTS
FROM EACH OTHER IN ORDER TO FIND THE DISTANCE BETWEEN
THEM.

The actual distance between any two Planets can be found by subtracting
their whole Degrees and Minutes from each other. For the purpose of figuring the Aspects, round the Degrees and Minutes off. The rounded-off
Degrees are easy to subtract from each other. Round up if the Minutes are
greater than 30'; round down if they're less than 30'. (The positions for
Grace's Chart have been rounded off in Fig. A-10.) Also, always subtract
the smaller number from the larger.

Some examples from Grace's Chart are:

ASCENDANT TO MIDHEAVEN $= 182° - 93° = 89°$

NEPTUNE TO SATURN $= 202° - 195° = 7°$

SATURN TO JUPITER $= 195° - 10° = 185°$

JUPITER TO URANUS $= 10° - 101°$ *or* $101° - 10° = 91°$

SUN TO PLUTO $= 308° - 141° = 167°$

STEP THREE

DECIDE WHICH, IF ANY, OF THE ASPECTS ARE RELEVANT AS SYM-
BOLS OF THE RESULTING DISTANCES.

If you figure out the distances between all the pairs of Planets or Points,
you'll find that many of them do fall within the allowable Orbs of specific
Aspects. Other distances will not. In the examples from Grace's Chart
given in Step Two, the following Aspects are formed:

ASCENDANT TO MIDHEAVEN $= 89° =$ SQUARE

NEPTUNE TO SATURN $= 7° =$ CONJUNCTION

SATURN TO JUPITER $= 185° =$ OPPOSITION

JUPITER TO URANUS $= 91° =$ SQUARE

SUN TO PLUTO $= 167° =$ NO ASPECT

THE MINOR ASPECTS

The Minor Aspects, their Degrees, and their Orbs are listed in Figure A-11. Brief interpretations of them follow.

NAME	SYMBOL	DEGREES	ORB
SEMI-SEMI-QUINTILE	**SSQ**	18	1
SEMI-QUINTILE (OR DECILE)	⊥	36	1
NONAGEN	**N**	40	1
SEMI-SQUARE	∠	45	3
SEPTILE	**S**	51-1/2	1
QUINTILE	**Q**	72	1
SESQUIQUADRATE (OR SESQUARE)	⊡	135	3
BI-QUINTILE	⊥	144	1

Figure A-11
The Minor Aspects

SEMI-SEMI-QUINTILE: routine activities of the Planets or Points, when they are combined with each other, seem to be filled with enthusiasm or have more than ordinary significance

SEMI-QUINTILE: combination of the Planets or Points represents technical abilities that are skillfully applied

NONAGEN (or NOVILE): combined force of the Planets or Points represents qualities that seem to be in "bondage" for the first 40 years of life; at age 40, the two forces may be freed to act smoothly together

SEMI-SQUARE: the Planets or Points are untrained to work together; the tension that results from feeling unprepared to use their combined force leads you to take action or gain skills

SEPTILE: the Planets or Points work together unconsciously; they create hidden motivations or unseen compulsions which seem to "force" you to act or react; often seen as "karma"

QUINTILE: the combination of the Planets or Points represents special talents and skills, often artistic in nature, which are intrinsically yours

SESQUIQUADRATE: the Planets or Points strive to combine themselves in exceptionally efficient and perfect ways

BI-QUINTILE: the combined force of the Planets or Points can lead to a deep "ah ha!" experience of Universal truth

THE MINOR ASPECT PATTERNS

The Minor Aspect Patterns are diagrammed (Figs. A-12 through A-16) and described briefly below:

The MINI-TRINE (Fig. A-12) symbol-izes easy movement of energy between all three of the Planets involved; inner and outer resources can be combined smoothly.

Figure A-12: The Mini-Trine

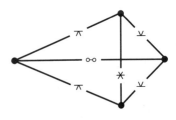

The YOD-KITE (Fig. A-13) symbolizes multiple experiences of adjustment and surprise. Resources represented by the Sextiling Planets may help to create a unique solution for dilemmas that arise as a result of the Yod.

Figure A-13: The Yod-Kite

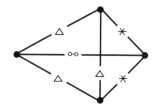

The TRINE-KITE (Fig. A-14) symbolizes internal and external resources that
are combined easily. This Pattern may
work so smoothly that other Aspects
and Aspect Patterns are ignored.

Figure A-14: The Trine-Kite

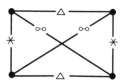

The GRAND RECTANGLE (Fig. A-15)
symbolizes resources that are readily
available to support the balancing acts
between the pairs of opposing Planets
or Points.

Figure A-15: The Grand Rectangle

The STAR (Fig. A-16) symbolizes the
presence of very special gifts and talents which can be used easily and in
alignment with Universal trends.

Figure A-16: The Star

About the Author

Gail attributes her willingness to have her photograph appear in this book and her large collection of earrings to her Leo Rising. She suspects that her 7th House Pisces Sun has something to do with her compassionate interest in her clients. She feels that her three Aquarian Planets and her 11th House Moon–Uranus conjunction symbolize her fascination with Astrology. And, since one of those Aquarian Planets – Venus in the 6th – is her 10th House Ruler, it makes sense that this fascination has become a working career. With the North Node in Aries in the 9th, she is challenged and excited by traveling, writing, and teaching. If you're interested in consulting privately with Gail or in inviting her to travel to your location to teach a seminar, contact her at P.O. Box 8, Smithville, IN 47458-0008 or at (812) 331-0501.

Consultations with Gail Fairfield

You can experience Gail's work first-hand by scheduling a consultation session with her. These can be done by phone or in person (when you're in Indiana or when Gail is lecturing in your area). In either case, Gail will tape the conversation so that you'll have a record of your reading. In a 50-minute session, you can ask questions about your Natal Chart and about current astrological trends that might be affecting you. You can also use your time with Gail in a tutorial fashion as you utilize her expertise to expand your understanding of Astrology in general.

About Gail's readings, others have said:
    "Your reading was the most stimulating, accurate, and supportive one I've had. As I replay it a third time, I continue to find new insights relevant to my present activities."
    "This is the best birthday present I've ever given myself."
    "Your talk with Grandma really helped her put some of the old hurts and bitterness aside. She is having me teach her to swim – and horseback-riding is next on the list!
    "I've rarely run into anybody who rang so many bells – defining my issues in a way I could work with."
    "Your search has greatly facilitated and supported my search. And I am awed when I think of how many others you have probably helped."
    "Your energy level is wonderful, and your ability to pass that along to your clients is refreshing to say the least. The session was not only informational, but fun, and that is very important to me as an individual."

Seminars with Gail Fairfield

If you want to learn more about Astrology, Tarot, or other aspects of choice centered living, you can sponsor or attend a Choice Centered Seminar. Gail's lectures and workshops can be an hour to a week in length and can be located anywhere in the world. They are always insightful, informative, and fun. Participants feel that they learn a great deal about the topic in general and about how it applies to them in particular.

About Gail's seminars, others have said:
    "Your workshop has shown me that I can say yes – to myself! The Tarot stands demystified in my eyes and I feel I can return to the study of it . . . with confidence."

"This is the first time I ever understood anything about my chart and I've had it done twice!!"

"Gail is the best teacher of Tarot and Astrology that I know. Her skills bring the highest quality of clarity and organization to subjects that are difficult to learn."

"Gail Fairfield was outstanding. She practiced 'in the moment' what she presented. She is absolutely excellent in knowledge, warmth, caring, supportiveness, responsiveness, and synthesis. What she outlined, she delivered."

"Gail Fairfield's discussion of therapeutic themes in Astrology was absolutely invaluable to me."

"The seeming simplicity of how Gail spoke of the meaning of the cards and how effortlessly she appeared to work with me (as an example in the workshop) was a joy . . . We began to put order and clarity around a very encompassing issue for me."

YES! *There are other things to order from Ramp Creek Publishing . . .*

ONE FREE NATAL CHART

Just for buying this book, you can get one free Astrological Birth Chart. To order, you'll need to send the revelant data:

- Birth Date (day, month, and year)
- Birth Time (as close to the minute as possible)
- Birth Place (name of actual village, town, city, state, country)

You'll also need to enclose a self-addressed, stamped envelope (SASE). If you're ordering from outside the U.S.A., you may want to attach Air Mail postage. Your Chart will be sent out as soon as possible.

CHOICE CENTERED ASTROLOGY: THE BASICS
by Gail Fairfield $15.95

Do you need extra copies of this book for yourself, your friends, relatives, clients, or students? Think of the people who could benefit from understanding Astrology and themselves from a choice centered perspective. When you order, indicate whether you want the books sent to you or directly to others.

THREE SAMPLE CHOICE CENTERED ASTROLOGY READINGS
by Gail Fairfield $29.95 for set of 3 tapes

Here's your chance to listen in on Gail Fairfield's readings with three different clients. As you examine the accompanying copies of their Charts, you'll hear how Gail applies the principles of CHOICE CENTERED ASTROLOGY in consultations. Each tape is 60 minutes long and each client has unique concerns and issues.

Tape #1 is a reading with a client who has just resettled his life after radically changing careers. His questions involve the future of his new career, his relationships with his parents and siblings, and his personal struggle with the issue of procrastination.

Tape #2 is a consultation with a woman who is recovering from incest and food abuse. She is most concerned with her healing process and with discovering ways to take good care of herself: emotionally, physically, and spiritually.

Tape #3 is a session with a PhD candidate who is just completing her time in graduate school. After many years in school and training, she's deep in the process of deciding how and where to reenter the working world.

CHOICE CENTERED TAROT
by Gail Fairfield $8.95

First published in 1981, CHOICE CENTERED TAROT is a classic in its field. This book was at the forefront of the movement to make Tarot more human, accessible, and choice oriented. It is still an invaluable tool. CHOICE CENTERED TAROT contains insight and information that can help you design individualized card layouts and approach Tarot readings with confidence. It also includes in-depth interpretations that present the psychological and practical meanings of the cards in understandable terms!

About CHOICE CENTERED TAROT, people have said:

"I love its flexibility and the strong sense of empowerment you feel and extend to your readers. . . . Your serious and playful attitude is quite refreshing."

"Every time I pick up CHOICE CENTERED TAROT, I am delighted. I love the clarity and sensitivity of your writing style."

"Just wanted to let you know – after reading many books on the Tarot – yours is still the very best!"

"Thank you, thank for your book. . . . It is totally empowering. My readings are developing as a teaching/counseling tool."

CHOICE CENTERED TAROT: THE LEARNING TAPES
by Gail Fairfield $49.95 for set of 6 tapes

These six 60-minute tapes expand on Gail's book with some of the material and exercises usually included in her beginning Tarot class. Through listening to the tapes, you'll have an oppportunity to deepen your understanding of the principles and applications of CHOICE CENTERED TAROT. The tapes include sample client readings as well as information on Tarot history, sybmolism, interpretation, layout design, and the reading process. They are accompanied by a workbook containing examples of the layouts discussed in the tapes and optional "homework" questions.

About these tapes, noted Tarot author Mary Greer has said:

"Gail does an amazing job of breaking down the process of Tarot reading, and communicates its essential aspects in a straightforward, well-organized manner. While [these tapes are] excellent for the novice, [they] may also benefit those who are proficient in Tarot and wish to expand their approach."

Here's How to Order

Send your name, address, zip or postal code, phone numbers, birth data, and order form with a check or money order (U.S. dollars) to:

RAMP CREEK PUBLISHING, INC.
P.O. BOX 3
SMITHVILLE, IN 47458-0003

- -

MY DATA

NAME _____

ADDRESS _____

_____

ZIP OR POSTAL CODE _____ COUNTRY _____

PHONE(S): Day _____ Evening _____

BIRTH DATA (if ordering Natal Chart): DATE _____

PLACE (town, state, country): _____

TIME (as close to the minute as possible)_____ A.M. or P.M.

_____

MY ORDER

__1__ computerized Natal Chart (include data and SASE) . . . . __FREE__

_____ copies of CHOICE CENTERED TAROT (book) at $8.95 . . . . _____

_____ copies of CHOICE CENTERED ASTROLOGY: THE BASICS
(book) at $15.95 . . . . _____

_____ tape sets of 6 CHOICE CENTERED TAROT LESSONS
at $49.95 . . . . _____

_____ tape sets of 3 NATAL CHART READINGS at $29.95 . . . . _____

SUBTOTAL _____

Postage and handling fee of $1.00/book, $2.50/tape set . . . . _____

Indiana residents add sales tax . . . . _____

TOTAL _____

Here's How to Order

Send your name, address, zip or postal code, phone numbers, birth data, and order form with a check or money order (U.S. dollars) to:

RAMP CREEK PUBLISHING, INC.
P.O. BOX 3
SMITHVILLE, IN 47458-0003

- -

MY DATA

NAME _____

ADDRESS _____

_____

ZIP OR POSTAL CODE _____ COUNTRY _____

PHONE(S): Day _____ Evening _____

BIRTH DATA (if ordering Natal Chart): DATE _____

PLACE (town, state, country): _____

TIME (as close to the minute as possible)_____ A.M. or P.M.

MY ORDER

__1__ computerized Natal Chart (include data and SASE) . . . . __FREE__

____ copies of CHOICE CENTERED TAROT (book) at $8.95 . . . . _____

____ copies of CHOICE CENTERED ASTROLOGY: THE BASICS
(book) at $15.95 . . . . _____

____ tape sets of 6 CHOICE CENTERED TAROT LESSONS
at $49.95 . . . . _____

____ tape sets of 3 NATAL CHART READINGS at $29.95 . . . . _____

SUBTOTAL _____

Postage and handling fee of $1.00/book, $2.50/tape set . . . . _____

Indiana residents add sales tax . . . . _____

TOTAL _____